# THE *Diaries* OF ADAMAS AND THE CONFESSIONS OF HANAVEL, BOOK 2

ENRICO GALLEGOS

THE DIARIES OF ADAMAS AND THE CONFESSIONS OF HANAVEL, BOOK 2
Copyright © 2026 by Enrico Gallegos.

All rights reserved. No part of this publication may be reproduced, distributed, or transmitted in any form or by any electronic or mechanical means, including information storage and retrieval systems, without a prior written permission from the publisher, except by reviewers, who may quote brief passages in a review, and certain other noncommercial uses permitted by the copyright law.

ISBN: 979-8-89228-986-3 (Paperback)
ISBN: 979-8-89228-985-6 (eBook)

Printed in the United States of America

# Contents

1. **ANDRO-GENESIS, ADAMEVA AND THE "UNICELLULAR" AM-EVA CELL…. THE SINGLE CELL THAT BEGAN ALL LIFE NAMED AFTER "EVA" OR "EBA" OR THE MOTHER OF ALL LIFE ON EARTH**

Amoeba is a unicellular organism, and just like bacteria, it reproduces through binary fission. After replicating its genetic material through mitotic division, the cell divides into two equal-sized daughter cells. In this method, two similar individuals are produced from a single parent cell. (BYIUS)

AM NOT SAYING THAT THE AMOEBA IS THE ORI-GENE-ALL CELL BUT THE ORI-GENE-ALL CELL WAS LIKE AN AM-EVA. ISN'T IT INTERESTING THAT THE WORD AMOEBA SOUNDS LIKE…

"AM EVA" or "I AM EVA!" THE MOTHER OF ALL LIVING BEINGS ON EARTH!!!

IN THE DEFINITION ABOVE FROM (BYIUS) YOU WILL FIND THE DESCRIPTION FOR THE MULTIPLICATION OF UNICELLULAR AMOEBAS WHICH FOLLOWS THE SAME COSMIC PATTERN AS IN THE CASE OF "THE FUSION OF YIN-YANG AS ONE UNICELLULAR" BEING DIVIDING ITSELF INTO TWO EQUAL PARTS THAT CORRESPOND TO THE DIVISION OR FRAGMENTATION OF DA-AT OR ADAM KADM-ONNE.

AS BELOW SO IS ABOVE, AND AS ABOVE SO IS BELOW!!!

SINCERELY,
"AM-EVA" THE MOTHER OF ALL LIVING BEINGS

---

2. **EARTHLY ADAM AND EVE: THE FIRST GOLEM (AN INTERPRETATION)**

NOW WE COME TO THE SECOND CREATION STORY OF ADAM AND EVE. THE STORY IN WHICH ADAM AND EVE ARE BORN AT THE SAME TIME OR APPEAR ALIVE SIMULTANEOUSLY.

IN ORDER TO UNDERSTAND HOW IT IS THAT THE EARTHLY ADAM AND EVE CAME ABOUT, WE NEED TO FIRST LEARN ABOUT MORE JEWISH LEGEND OR LORE. IT'S IN THESE LEGENDS AND MYTHOLOGIES THAT BITS AND PIECES OF TRUTH LIE UNDERNEATH. TO UNDERSTAND HOW EARTHLY ADAM AND EVE ARE FORMED, WE NEED TO UNDERSTAND THE LEGEND AND CONCEPT OF THE GOLEM.

THE GOLEM IS A HUMAN-LIKE BEING THAT IS CREATED WITH EARTH AND WHO IS ALMOST HUMAN BUT INCOMPLETE. THE GOLEM IS AN UNFINISHED BEING AND LACKING IN CONSCIOUSNESS. AS A RESULT THE GOL-EM EVENTUALLY GOES BAD AND HAS TO BE DESTROYED.

REMEMBER HOW THE CREATION OF ADAM IN GENESIS WAS FROM THE EARTH? AND THE STORY SAYS ADAM WAS FORMED FROM THE CLAY OF THE GROUND. AND SO THIS SECOND CREATION STORY IS THE STORY OF HOW THE ELOHIM CREATED ADAM AND EVE OR HUMANKIND AND THEIR PHYSICAL BODIES FROM THE GROUND. IN OTHER WORDS, THAT SECOND CREATION STORY IS THE CREATION OF THE FIRST GOLEM WHOM ARE ADAM AND EVE BORN SIMULTANEOUSLY.

AND GOD CREATED THEM MALE AND FEMALE, AFTER THE IMAGE AND LIKENESS OF CHOKMAH AND BINAH AND LESSER HEAVENLY ADAM AND HEAVENLY EVE. IN THE CASE OF EARTHLY ADAM AND EVE, THEY WERE GOLEM IN THE BEGINNING BECAUSE THEY WERE IN AN INCOMPLETE STATE. SOMETHING WAS STILL MISSING IN THEM. THEY WERE STILL NOT TOTALLY AT THE IMAGE AND LIKENESS OF OUR DIVINE PARENTS. THEY WERE LIKE GOLEM AND "INNOCENT." HUMANOIDS AT THIS POINT. MEANING THAT THEY WERE BOTH LIKE LITTLE CHILDREN HAVING TO BE TOLD BY ELOHIM WHAT TO DO, WHERE TO GO, WHAT NOT TO DO, HOW TO SPEAK, ETC. THEY WERE BOTH LIKE CHILDREN. THEY WERE UNABLE TO UNDERSTAND THEMSELVES AND THEIR ENVIRONMENT. THEY WERE NOT YET AFTER THE IMAGE AND LIKENESS OF BOTH CHOCHMA WHO IS WISDOM AND BINNAH WHO IS UNDERSTANDING.

WHY WERE THEY STILL INCOMPLETE? BECAUSE IN ORDER TO ACQUIRE BOTH WISDOM AND UNDERSTANDING HUMANS HAVE TO GO THROUGH A LENGTHY AND ARDUOUS PROCESS CALLED LIFE. AND LIFE AS YOU KNOW IS AN EVOLUTIONARY PROCESS THAT INVOLVES PAIN, HEARTACHE, SUFFERING AS WELL AS JOY. GOING THROUGH THIS IMPERFECT JOURNEY HELPS US GAIN UNDERSTANDING AND WISDOM. OTHERWISE WE REMAIN STAGNANT AND CHILD-LIKE STUCK IN OUR OWN COMFORT ZONE AND IMMATURE WAYS. HAVING A LIMITED AND NARROW-MINDED VIEW OF LIFE AND UNABLE TO REASON FOR OURSELVES.

ELOHIM HAD ANIMATED BOTH ADAM AND EVE AS THE FIRST GOLEM. THEY POSSESSED LIFE BUT THEY WERE STILL INCOMPLETE HAVING NOT YET CONSCIOUSNESS AFTER THE IMAGE AND LIKENESS OF THE ELOHIM.

IF YOU WILL REMEMBER, AT TZIM-TZOOM OR AT THE MOMENT THAT DA-AT BREAKS UP AND SPLITS AND SEPARATES INTO TWIN PRINCIPLES, THESE MULTIPLY AND DIVIDE EXPONENTIALLY AND BRING ABOUT THE CREATIVE PROCESS. THIS CREATIVE PROCESS IS ETERNAL. MEANING

THAT CREATION IS NOT A ONE TIME ONE MOMENT EVENT BUT AN EVENT AND PROCESS THAT IS CONSTANTLY TAKING PLACE AND SUSTAINING ITSELF. IT IS HAPPENING RIGHT NOW AND FOREVER. AND SO, DURING THIS DIVISION AND CREATION OF LIFE THAT BEGAN EONS AGO, AND CONTINUING IN THE PRESENT MOMENT, THE LIFE PRINCIPLES OF ADAM AND EVE IN THEIR SPIRITUAL - ENERGY FORMS ARE CONSTANTLY TAKING RESIDENCE AND INCARNATING ON EARTH THROUGH HUMANITY AND ALL OTHER LIFE FORMS.

AND SO, THE DIVINE FORMED THE GOLEM OR BODIES FORMED OF THE CLAY OF THE EARTH, MALE AND FEMALE S-HE FORMED THEM UNTIL THE LIFE PRINCIPLES WERE CALLED DOWN BY THE DIVINE TO INHABIT THESE BODIES AND SO HUMANITY CAME TO BE. THEY CAME TO LIFE. THEY WERE ACTIVATED.

SINCE IT WAS THE BEGINNING, BOTH EARTHLY ADAM AND EVE WERE STILL IN THEIR INFANCY AND IN AN INCOMPLETE STATE. THEREFORE, THE PROCESS TOWARDS BECOMING AFTER THE IMAGE AND LIKENESS OF THE DIVINE WAS TO BE A PROCESS THAT WOULD TAKE A SPAN OF TIME. FOR BOTH ADAM AND EVE, NOW IN THIS EARTHLY PLANE OF EXISTENCE AND EARTH SCHOOL, THEIR MAIN GOAL WOULD BE TO LEARN AND GAIN UNDERSTANDING FROM LIFE AND THE UNIVERSE AROUND THEM.

IN THE BEGINNING, BOTH ADAM AND EVE WERE ANIMATED BUT CLUELESS AS LITTLE CHILDREN UNABLE TO TELL THE DIFFERENCE BETWEEN GOOD AND EVIL. HAVING ELOHIM TELLING THEM WHAT TO DO AND WHAT TO THINK, THEY STILL DID NOT POSSESS FREE WILL. THEY BOTH WERE STUCK IN A STATE OF BEING CHILDLIKE AND SEMI CONSCIOUS ` UNABLE TO UNDERSTAND THE DIFFERENCE BETWEEN ONE THING FROM THE OTHER. IT WAS UNTIL LATER "WHEN THEY BOTH WOULD PARTAKE OF THE FORBIDDEN FRUIT OF THE TREE OF KNOWLEDGE" THAT "THEIR EYES WOULD OPEN" AND AT LAST THEY WOULD BE ABLE TO TELL THE DIFFERENCE BETWEEN GOOD AND EVIL AND ALL OTHER POLAR OPPOSITES AFTER THE DIVINE. AFTER ALL, THE DIVINE IS A UNION OF OPPOSITES DESCRIBED AND REPRESENTED IN THE SYMBOL OF THE TREE OF KNOWLEDGE OF GOOD AND EVIL.

ADAM AND EVE WERE "INFANTS" IN THEIR EVOLUTIONARY STATE. THEY WERE NOT YET LIKE ELOHIM WHO COULD TELL DIFFERENCES AND ASSESS SITUATIONS AND MAKE CHOICES. THEY WERE AS BABIES AND AS LITTLE CHILDREN. EVERYTHING WAS FLAT AND THE SAME TO THEM. BUT THAT WAS TO CHANGE IF THE DIVINE WILL AND PURPOSE FOR HUMANITY WAS TO HAPPEN ON THIS EARTH PLANE. THAT DIVINE PURPOSE FOR

ADAM AND EVE IS TIGHTLY INTERTWINED WITH THE DIVINE PURPOSE FOR THIS EARTHLY REALM AND THE REASON HUMANKIND IS HERE TODAY.

SINCERELY,
"ADAMEVA"

---

3.   **HEAVENLY ADAM AND HEAVENLY EVE: THE FIRST HEAVENLY COUPLE AND ORIGINS (AN INTERPRETATION)**

THE STORY OF ADAM AND EVE IS ANOTHER ONE OF THOSE STORIES TAKEN LITERALLY AND OUT OF CONTEXT. THE LITERAL STORY IS MUCH MORE COMPLEX THAN ITS USUAL INTERPRETATION. THIS STORY HAS MYSTICAL AND COSMIC MEANINGS THAT ARE MORE AKIN WITH SCIENCE THAN WITH ITS LITERAL INTERPRETATION. ADAM AND EVE ARE THE SURFACE OF A HUGE ICEBERG THAT HIDES MUCH MORE UNDERNEATH. IT IS SIMILAR TO THE MIND IN THAT THE BOOK OF GENESIS IN ITS LITERAL FACE WOULD BE THE NORMAL STATE OF CONSCIOUSNESS AND ITS DEEPER MEANING IS HIDDEN IN THE DEEP UNCONSCIOUS WAITING FOR US TO FIND, DISCOVER, UNCOVER.

AND SO ADAM AND EVE APPEAR IN THE GENESIS ACCOUNT FIRST AS ONE UNIT. EVE EXISTS BUT HIDDEN WITHIN ADAM. IT'S SIMILAR TO ADAM KADMON WHOM IS ONE UNIT MADE UP OF TWIN ASPECTS, ONE MALE AND ANOTHER FEMALE. THE DIVINE ANDROGYNE.

IN THE CASE OF THE EARTHLY ADAM, HE IS "CREATED" AFTER THE IMAGE AND LIKENESS OF THE HEAVENLY ADAM WHOM IS A BINARY UNIT. IN OTHER WORDS, THE POSITIVE ASPECT OF REALITY IS REPRESENTED BY ADAM AND THE NEGATIVE ASPECT IS HIDDEN IN ADAM AS EVE NOT YET DIFFERENTIATED AND SEPARATED FROM ADAM.

AS YOU CAN NOTICE. ADAM AND EVE FOLLOW A PATTERN IN THE TREE OF GOOD AND EVIL WHICH IS ALSO A TREE OF PAIRS THAT ARE SEPARATED BUT UNITED AT THE SAME TIME. THEY ARE IN A COSMIC RELATIONSHIP. ADAM BELONGS TO THE HEAVENLY FATHER CHOKMAH WHILE EVE BELONGS TO THE HEAVENLY MOTHER BINNAH. HOWEVER, BOTH BELONG TO EACH OTHER TOO. BOTH CHOCMAH AND BINNAH ARE LINKED TO KETER WHOM IS THE SOURCE OF LIFE FOR BOTH OF THEM. ADAM AND EVE ARE LINKED TO CHOCHMA AND BINNAH IN DA-AT, THE LATTER WHO REPRESENTS THE SON/ DAUGHTER OF MAN OR THE SPIRITUAL-ENERGETIC TEMPLATE FOR BOTH MAN AND WOMAN ON EARTH. DA-AT IS THE SON/ DAUGHTER OF MAN WHOM IS A UNITED-BINARY BEING AND BOTH MALE AND FEMALE, POSITIVE AND NEGATIVE, ETC.

THERE ARE TWO CREATION STORIES IN GENESIS. ONE IN WHICH WOMAN IS CREATED FROM THE SIDE OF MAN. AND ANOTHER WHERE BOTH MAN AND WOMAN APPEAR AT THE SAME TIME . WHAT IS THIS??? IS THE STORY CONTRADICTING ITSELF??? WELL, REMEMBER THAT THIS GENESIS STORY IS A TEMPLATE FOR SOME DEEPER MEANING. IT IS LIKE THE KEY THAT OPENS THE DOORS TO OTHER INTERPRETATIONS AND MEANINGS WITHIN SUCH A SIMPLE STORY. THE ADAM AND EVE STORY IS DESCRIBING TWO EVENTS THAT ARE LINKED TO EACH OTHER AND THAT ARE A MIRROR OF EACH OTHER. THERE IS THE HEAVENLY ADAM AND EVE WHO ARE CREATED SEPARATELY FROM EACH OTHER AS CHOKMAH THE GOD AND BINAH THE GODDESS. AND, THERE IS ON THE OTHER HAND ADAM KADMON OR DA'AT (IN THE TREE OF LIFE) WHO IS BORN FROM CHOKMAH AND BINAH AFTER THEIR IMAGES AND LIKENESSES BUT AS ONE UNIT MADE UP OF TWO "TWIN" COSMIC PRINCIPLES.

EVENTUALLY, KETER SEPARATES THE TWIN UNITS OF ADAM KADMON. SEPARATING THE SPIRITUAL CHILD EVE FROM THE SIDE OF THE SPIRITUAL CHILD ADAM WHO TOOK THE POSITION OF DA-AT IN THE TREE OF GOOD AND EVIL. DA-AT OCCUPIES THE MIDDLE PILLAR AS IN THE THIRD PRINCIPLE OF CREATION THAT IS BORN OF BOTH THE MOTHER AND THE FATHER AND WHICH IS THE DIVINE CHILD. THIS DIVINE CHILD IS IN A PLACE WHERE S-HE IS ALSO ANDROGYNOUS AND BIPOLAR. THIS UNIT IS REPRESENTED IN TAOISM AS THE TAO AND THE YIN-YANG PRINCIPLES. THESE TWINS ARE THE LESSER HEAVENLY TWINS ADAM AND EVE, CHILDREN OF GREATER HEAVENLY ADAM AND EVE WHO ARE CHOKMAH AND BINAH RESPECTIVELY.

THE DIVINE CHILD DA-AT IS ALSO THE MEETING POINT OR RECONCILER OF BOTH CHOKMAH AND BINAH SINCE IT IS THROUGH THIS THIRD PRINCIPLE OR CHILD THAT BOTH BINAH AND CHOKMAH COMMUNICATE WITH EACH OTHER. BEFORE THE BIRTH OF DA-AT aka ADAM KADMON, BOTH BINAH AND CHOKMAH WERE UNABLE TO UNDERSTAND EACH OTHER SINCE THEY WERE/ARE TOTAL OPPOSITES BORN OF KETER OR THE COSMIC WOMB. IT WAS ONLY THROUGH KETER THAT BOTH CHOKMAH AND BINAH COULD FIND OUT ABOUT EACH OTHER AND TRY TO UNDERSTAND EACH OTHER AS BEST THEY CAN IF THAT WAS EVEN POSSIBLE AT THAT POINT. KETER WOULD EXPLAIN TO BINNAH AND CHOCHMAH WHAT EACH OTHER WAS ABOUT AND REPRESENTED. ITS LIKE BINAH TELLING CHOKMAH THAT SHE IS BLACK, BUT CHOKMAH NOT BEING ABLE TO UNDERSTAND WHAT BLACK IS SINCE HE IS WHITE AND SO THRU KETER BOTH TRY TO FIND MORE INFORMATION OR MORE UNDERSTANDING ABOUT EACH OTHER. THEIR RELATIONSHIP AND COMMUNICATION IS SUPERFICIAL BECAUSE THEY CANNOT TOTALLY UNDERSTAND EACH OTHER AND COMMUNICATE WITH INTIMACY.

ONCE DA-AT IS BORN WITH THE HELP OF KETER THINGS CHANGE. BOTH BINAH AND CHOKMAH COMBINE THEIR ESSENCES WITH THE HELP OF KETER AND CREATE A BOND THAT GIVES BIRTH TO THE DIVINE CHILD DA-AT aka ADAM KADMON. NOW THE RELATIONSHIP IS ONE OF MOTHER, FATHER, DIVINE CHILD AND KETER WHO THE LATTER IS LIKE THE GRANDPARENT AND SOURCE OF EVERYONE. CONSEQUENTLY WITH DA-AT BOTH CHOKMAH AND BINAH ARE ABLE TO UNDERSTAND EACH OTHER PERSONALLY THROUGH DIRECT EXPERIENCE AND COMMUNICATION BECAUSE THE DIVINE CHILD IS A MIRROR OF THEM ENERGETICALLY WHICH CONNECTS BOTH CHOKMAH AND BINAH DIRECTLY TO EACH OTHER. THEY NO LONGER NEED TO COMMUNICATE THRU A THIRD PARTY AS IN KETER. THROUGH DA-AT WHOM IS THE ANDROGYNOUS HEAVENLY ADAM AND EVE, MOTHER AND FATHER CAN SEE AND PERCEIVE EACH OTHER THROUGH THE CHILD THEY HAVE IN COMMON WITH EACH OTHER. THIS DIVINE SON/DAUGHTER IS EQUIVALENT TO THE TAO AND PENTAGRAMMATON AND IT IS THROUGH HIM-HER THAT EVERYTHING IN THE COSMOS AND UNIVERSES IS CREATED AND EXISTS.

THIS IS THE STORY OF EVE BORN OF THE SIDE OF ADAM AND THIS STORY IS POINTING TO THE COSMIC BIRTH AND ORIGINS OF THE UNIVERSE. THESE ARE THE FIRST ADAMS AND EVES. THE HEAVENLY ONES.

SINCERELY,
"MOTHER EVE THRU THE BIPOLAR GATES OF COMMUNICATION"

---

## 4. THE BIPOLAR SON-GOD AND "THE FATHER-GOD" OF UNI-ONNE: THE KAD-UTA OR FALL of ADAM THE ONE I

You know how YIN becomes YANG and YANG becomes YIN. You can see it clearly in the symbol of the YIN-YANG in which the YIN EXISTS WITHIN THE YANG and THE YANG EXISTS WITHIN THE YIN.

If you read the TANAKH, there are many stories about GOD being glad and at other times angry and decimating populations. Many can't believe how a loving GOD could cause such mass extinction as is described in the book of Genesis and the Great Flood. However, as WE explained before, this GOD of the O.T. is the ARCHETYPE of the BI-POLAR CHILD or YIN-YANG or DEITY OF OPPOSITES that created this world or by whom THE HIGHER UPS in the DIVINE HIERARCHY created the universes and material planes. This is WHY the O.T. GOD gets angry and later forgives. Destroys to later rebuilds. etc. etc. etc. You can notice there the POLARITIES ACTIVE and reacting according to the environment and the actions of man. This is WHAT THE STORIES STAND FOR as a treatise for the YIN-YANG energies in relation and in reaction to HUMAN history and activity. In the case of the O.T. deity, this deity or Tetragrammaton is a state of NON-INTEGRATION unlike that of the PENTAGRAMMATON.

The N.T. GOD on the other hand is the HIGHER UP GOD or THE FATHER. In other words, YESHUA represents the "CHILD" incarnate ADAM KAD-MON IN ITS INTEGRATED STATE and MEDIATOR between THE FATHER OF PURE LIGHT or CHOKMAH and EARTH. In other words, the CHRIST PRINCIPLE activates and descends and takes abode in flesh in order to LIVE WITH HUMANKIND and give mankind a new opportunity. THESE ENERGIES activate and begin WALKING AMONGST THE PEOPLE to FEEL the environment and take note of WHERE MANKIND needs help. These energies are ADAM KAD-M-ONNE'S YIN AND YANG TWIN ENERGIES.

KAD is a root word that means TO FALL in LATIN! Therefore, "AN ASPECT" OF ADAM THE FALLEN ONE or ADAM KAD-M-ONNE activates "or falls into this earth" to help people OPEN THEIR EYES BEFORE THEY FALL INTO THE PIT. The FRAGMENTATION on the way down activates the ENERGIES and THEY BEGIN TO LIVE AMONGST HUMANKIND. The italian for TO FALL is KAD-ERE which comes from OLDER LANGUAGES. As in the FIRE or F-"ERE" (from the ancient root word for fire or URI) that FALLS as in the story of PROME-THEUS. That FIRE is KNOWLEDGE that THEUS or THE DIVINE PROMISED on behalf of THE SOURCE to humanity.

KAD means:

Falling under this category of words that derive from the Latin root "cadere," meaning "to fall," are some surprises: "incident," "accident," and a ll of those "-cide" words having to do with killing. (GOOGLE)

As you can see from the meanings above, KAD stands for ADAM KAD-M-ON'S "FALL" or descent which caused ALL UNIVERSES TO BE BORN. But it not only stands for FALLING but also for a FALL that brings about CAUSATION as in the CAUSE AND EFFECT processes in the realm of matter. This FALLING AND FRAGMENTING PROCESSES also bring about the process of DECAY as in MATERIAL PROCESS OF PUTREFACTION AND DEATH. This is exactly WHAT the story of GENESIS refers to which is a COSMIC PROCESS of DEATH AND REBIRTH. And this is the reason HUMANS die because they are part of NATURE WHICH MANIFESTS AS MATTER and matter decays and dies. And just as matter decays and later THIS MATTER is reborn as something else in SPRINGTIME "such as in the EASTER story," so do human-beings die in matter to be reborn over and over again with a new body and so is the cycle of death and rebirth in matter or REINCARNATION.

In other words, THE ACT OF INCARNATING in the material plane is equivalent to FALLING and fragmenting ourselves from our original UNITY because it is inherent in the material plane to BE IN THE WORLD OF OPPOSITES AND POLARITIES. It's just the way it is.

SINCERELY,
ADAM THE FALLEN ONE

---

## 5. THE BIPOLAR SON-GOD AND "THE FATHER-GOD" OF UNI-ONNE: KAD-MON PROME-THEUS "THE FALLEN" VISITS THE EARTH II

THE CHRIST principle is like PROME-THEUS which stands for THE PROMISED SON OF THEOS or GOD who comes down to earth like superman to bring down the SACRED LIGHT, FIRE AND KNOWLEDGE. THIS "SON" of GOD is an ARCHETYPE that also represents the HOLY SHE-QI-INNA as the DAUGHTER OF GOD. BOTH together are THE TWINS or THE DIVINE PRESENCE and these PRINCIPLES are SACRED. THE SOPHIA AND THE LIVING CHRIST.

THE CHRIST PRINCIPLE activates in the person of the SHA-MAN in order to admonish the people and to CHECK OUT the earth just as in the story of SOD-OM AND GOM-ORRAH and in the GOSPEL story. This happens when THE EARTH is at the brink of destruction by human actions and humans are about to TRANSITION into a NEW CYCLE.

"SOD" is ENGLISH SLANG that stands for a CONTEMPTIBLE OR LOW PERSON as in EVIL and MEAN. SOD- HOM as in Castilian HOM-BRE or man is THE SOD or THE "DESPICABLE" type of MAN. As you can see this has nothing to do with SEXUAL POSITIONS but has to do with EVIL - CORRUPT IN THE HEART TYPE OF MEN who TREAT OTHERS LIKE DUNG and never feel any remorse or repentance for their evil path. GOM in Sanskrit, on the other hand, - is to SMEAR or tarnish with COW DUNG. Therefore, GOM-ORA IS THE SMEARING OF THE LIGHT or "ORA- URI", or the SMEARING OF THE DIVINE SPARK WITH DUNG WHICH IS ANOTHER WAY OF SAYING.... "CORRUPTING THE LIGHT" in others!!!!!This is when IGNORANCE IS GREATER THAN THE LIGHT. "THIS IS WHEN THE CHRIST IS SMEARED BY THE WORLD WITH DUNG or EVIL." This is the state of humankind today when VIOLENCE prevails and the value of LIFE in general has been DEVALUED. And so it was written and we are reminding humankind:

John 3:19 And the judgment is based on this fact: GOD'S LIGHT came into this world, but people loved the darkness more than the light, for their actions were EVIL. (GOSPEL OF THE CHRIST)

WHAT both SOD AND GOM teach us is that WHEN humans no longer have any reverence and respect for the SACRED, s-he begins to have no reverence for anything else in his or her environment such as Natural and Divine values and principles of LIFE. At that point everything is for grabs and for destruction and so humanity goes here and there clueless and wandering in the wilderness without any INNER COMPASS TO GUIDE THEM ANYMORE. And so we end up with a world OUT OF BALANCE and without HARMONY and on the brink of SELF ANNIHILATION. This is another teaching about SOD/ GOM as in EVIL MEN WHO SOIL THE SACRED and AS A RESULT THEY NO LONGER FEAR THE HEAVENS AND SO DO AND UNDO AS THEY PLEASE spreading evil everywhere until the earth no longer resembles a SCHOOL but a HELLISH REALM.

UNIVERSAL COSMIC VALUES AND PRINCIPLES ARE SACRED AND WHEN PEOPLE CORRUPT THEM TO SUIT THEIR NEEDS, IT'S LIKE SMEARING THE DIVINE SPARK OR LIGHT WITH DUNG.

Therefore, THE CHRIST PRINCIPLE AND HIS SHE-KI-INNA walk the earth and point to — what needs help. THESE REPRESENT THE "TWO WITNESSES OF DEITY." Unfortunately, NOT MANY RECOGNIZE "THE CHRIST PRINCIPLE" walking within the HEALERS OF THIS WORLD and will ignore THEM AND CLAIM THEY ARE INSANE. Humans HAVE "FREE WILL" and nobody can save this world unless one LISTENS AND ACTS to help lift up what is broken collectively and in a spirit of GOODWILL. You can't expect one person to be able to do that. Just as it's happening now when THE ELOHIM tell people what is faulty and PEOPLE GET ANGRY, some believing that it is all nonsense and or that it is a plot to take away FREE WILL. Others are unable to understand because they cannot reason; meanwhile others who are accustomed to the status quo of the world see nothing wrong with people committing violent acts towards each other and other abominations. Having CHRIST tell you TO NOT MAKE WAR and yet YOU IGNORE AND MAKE WAR. etc. etc. etc. DO NOT COMMIT GENOCIDE AND YET YOU DO. DO NOT HATE AND YET YOU DO until you are on the brink of WWIII. What else do you expect will happen?

Remember that KAD stands for CAUSE AND EFFECT and eventually what you do here reverberates in HEAVEN and returns back down here until man crosses the line and then there is no way back. WILL YOU LISTEN AND DO GOOD OR WILL YOU IGNORE AND LOOK THE OTHER WAY just as in the story of the days of NOAH? WE are willing to meet YOU …HALFWAY.

SINCERELY,
"THE FALLEN GUY, ADAM KAD-MON"

**6.    THE "TREE OF GOOD AND EVIL" IS ..."THE TREE OF LIFE:" SEEING THE TREE OF DUALITY ON REVERSE AS THE TREE OF THE UNION OF POLARITIES INTO COMPLEMENTS**

IF ONE OBSERVES THE TREE OF LIFE ONE WILL NOTICE THAT IT IS ACTUALLY THE TREE OF DUALITY OR FRAGMENTATION WHICH CAUSES THE EXISTENCE OF THIS MATERIAL UNIVERSE. IT IS THE TREE OF "THE FALL OF THE PRIMORDIAL MAN." THE TREE OF COSMIC ENERGIES AND EMANATIONS.

WE CAN SEE THIS FRAGMENTATION IN THE DESCENDING ORDER OF THE SEFIROT FROM ONENESS TO TWINS TO TRIADS AND SO AND SO UNTIL WE GET TO —EARTH OR MALKUT WHICH REPRESENTS THE MATERIAL UNIVERSE AS A WHOLE. THEREFORE, IF THE TREE OF POLARITIES OR DUALITIES MANIFESTS AS A DESCENT AND AS A MULTIPLICATION OF THE SEFIROT AS WE EXPLAINED BEFORE, THE "CONJOINED TWINS AT DA-AT" MULTIPLY AND BECOME MANY BORN FROM THE SEPARATION OF BOTH THE YIN AND YANG PRINCIPLES WHICH CREATES MATTER AND SPIRIT ENERGY SIMULTANEOUSLY. SINCE MATTER IS TEMPORARY AND SPIRIT IS ETERNAL, THE SPIRIT TRAPPED IN MATTER "DIES" BUT ONLY IN REGARDS TO MATTER. IT IS ALL "MAYA" OR ILLUSION BECAUSE "SPIRIT ENERGY" CONTINUES ON AND ON TAKING ON DIFFERENT MATERIAL BODIES AS IT PROGRESSES IN ITS SPIRITUAL -ENERGETIC EVOLUTION AND CONTINUUM.

AND SO IF WE SEE THE TREE AS A DUALITY TRICKLING FROM ABOVE DOWN BELOW UNTIL ALL THESE ENERGIES PRODUCE OR GIVE BIRTH TO THE UNIVERSE, IT MEANS THAT IF WE LOOK AT THE TREE OF DUALITY FROM THE "BOTTOM-UP" THE TREE OF DUALITY BECOMES "THE TREE OF UNION AND OF LIFE." THE TREE IS THE TREE OF THE FALL BUT BECOMES THE TREE OF "YOU RAISE ME UP" WHEN IT MOVES UPWARDS.

SO IF WE LOOK AT THE TREE FROM THE BOTTOM UP WHAT DO WE NOTICE? WE NOTICE THAT THE —OPPOSITE PROCESS—OCCURS. FROM FRAGMENTATION IT MOVES TO UNION AND INTEGRATION. WHAT WE MEAN TO SAY IS THAT FROM MALKUTH WHICH A MATERIAL MIRROR OF DA-AT ABOVE, MALKUTH BECOMES ONE UNIT MADE UP OF TWO PRINCIPLES IN YESOD THEN IT BECOMES TWO AND THEN ONE ONCE AGAIN AND SO UNTIL IT REACHES DA-AT ABOVE IN THE TREE OF LIFE. WHAT WE MEAN TO SAY IS THAT THE OPPOSITES BEGIN TO UNITE ONCE AGAIN RATHER THAN SEPARATING THEMSELVES; THE PRINCIPLES ACHIEVING UNION AND UNTIL THEY ARRIVE "TO THE EDGE OF THE ABYSS" BACK TO —DA-AT— WHO IS THE ENERGY - MENTAL TEMPLATE AND ARCHITECT OF THE

UNIVERSE AFTER WHOM THE WORLDS AND UNIVERSES AND DIMENSIONS ARE BORN.

AND SO AS THE UNION TAKES PLACE AND THE "YIN AND YANG" BECOME —YIN-YANG UNITED AS ONE UNIT MADE UP OF ONE FORCE MANIFESTING AS TWO—- THE TREE OF "GOOD AND EVIL" BECOMES THE "TREE OF LIFE." OR THE TREE OF THE UNION OF DUALITIES AND OPPOSITES. MEANING THAT THERE IS NO MORE OPPOSITION AND NEITHER —MATTER— BUT EVERYTHING GOES BACK TO "MIND AND ENERGY" AND SO BACK TO THE "SOURCE OF EVERYTHING."

AND SO WE HOPE THAT THIS BRIEF METAPHYSICAL TREATISE ON THE TREE OF GOOD AND EVIL AND OF LIFE CLARIFIES BETTER HOW —BOTH— TREES ARE THE SAME TREE BUT SEEN FROM DIFFERENT PERSPECTIVES AND ANGLES.

THE TREE OF GOOD AND EVIL ON REVERSE BECOMES THE TREE OF LIFE OR THE TREE OF THE "REDEMPTION AND RETURN/ RESURRECTION (METAPHORICALLY) OF THE PRIMORDIAL WO-MAN" ADAM KAD-MON.

SINCERELY,
"ADAMEVA KAD-M-ANNIE" THE PRIMORDIAL WO-MAN THRU THE BIPOLAR GATES

---

## 7.  ADAM KADMON AND THE GREAT FALL FROM GRACE

I FEEL AWFUL. AT THIS MOMENT I AM ASSAILED BY FEELINGS OF HELPLESSNESS AND HOPELESSNESS. I FEEL EMPTY AND NUMB. I HAVE BEEN FEELING THIS WAY AND IN DEEP DEPRESSION SINCE MY GREAT FALL. FOR I FEEL THAT I WAS BEING TESTED AND I FAILED. I'M CONSTANTLY OVERTAKEN BY GUILT AND SHAME AND MEMORIES OF WHAT COULD HAVE BEEN AND THAT "I SHOULD HAVE KNOWN BETTER." IT IS THE DEEPEST CREVICE I HAVE FALLEN INTO DURING MY WHOLE LIFE. I HAVE GONE THROUGH VALLEYS BEFORE AS I HAVE BEEN DEALING WITH DEPRESSION SINCE I WAS 21 YEARS OLD, BUT THIS TIME IN THE YEAR 2016-2019 IS "THE ONE," THE ONE THAT MAKES ME WONDER IF I WILL EVER BE ABLE TO GET UP AGAIN.

WHAT HAS BROUGHT ME TO MY KNEES HAVE BEEN DIVERSE FACTORS THAT CAME TOGETHER AT A CERTAIN POINT IN MY LIFE AND GAVE ME A HUGE BLOW. ONE THAT I DIDN'T SEE COMING. PSYCHO-EMOTIONAL DISTRESS, RELATIONSHIP PROBLEMS, HOMELESSNESS, TRUSTING THE WRONG PEOPLE, MAKING BAD DECISIONS, VICES AND OBSESSIONS, ETC. IT WAS AS IF SOMETHING WAS BRINGING ME TO A REALLY BAD PLACE

LITTLE BY LITTLE WITHOUT ME EVEN REALIZING IT. IT WAS UNTIL I FOUND MYSELF AT THE EDGE OF A DEEP ABYSS, AND SADLY, I WAS NOT ABLE TO KEEP MY BALANCE AND FELL INTO IT DEEPER AND DEEPER AS I HAD NEVER BEFORE AND NOW I HAVE TOUCHED BOTTOM. GETTING OUT OF IT IS MOST DIFFICULT AS MY EMOTIONS AND THOUGHTS SEEM TO BE KEEPING ME STUCK IN SHAME AND GUILT. IT FEELS AS IF I HAD FALLEN FROM A STATE OF GRACE AND NOW I'M IN A STATE OF PAIN AND DEEP SUFFERING.

AS I AM GOING THROUGH THIS SEVERE PROCESS OF BREAKING UP INTO PIECES AND TRYING TO FIND MEANING IN THE EXPERIENCE, I CAN'T HELP TO THINK ABOUT THE ARCHETYPE OF THE ORIGINAL MAN WHOM IS CALLED ADAM KADMON IN JEWISH LEGEND AND MYTHOLOGY. HOW THIS ANDROGYNOUS ORIGINAL MAN WHO IS INITIALLY IN A STATE OF HARMONY AND EQUILIBRIUM FINALLY RISKS IT ALL IN ORDER TO "BECOME" AND SO GIVING BIRTH TO THE PROCESS OF CREATION. THIS ADAM KADMON IS THE FIRST BORN "SON-DAUGHTER OF SOURCE " WHO IS WHOLE AND INTEGRATED IN THE BEGINNING OF TIME. A UNIT THAT IS COMPOSED OF TWIN HALVES AND IN IT CONTAINS ALL THE DREAMS AND POTENTIAL AND POSSIBILITIES.

HOWEVER A SELF SUSTAINING UNIT ADAM KADMON IS SELF-CONTAINED AND SO NOTHING HAPPENS. THERE IS ONLY THE "ORIGINAL SON-DAUGHTER" AND THE GREAT MOTHER BINAH AND THE GREAT FATHER CHOCHMA AND GRANDPARENT KETER. BY THIS POINT THE UNIVERSE IS JUST A DREAM. IT DOES NOT EXIST YET. IT'S ONLY A DREAM IN-POTENTIA IN THE MIND AND SOUL OF ADAM KADMON. AT A CERTAIN POINT HOWEVER, THE DIVINE SON AS ANY CURIOUS CHILD WOULD BE, BECOMES BORED AND "WANTS TO LIVE AND TO LEAVE." AS A CREATIVE SPIRIT ADAM KADMON WISHES TO EXPAND OR EVOLVE IN MANY DIFFERENT WAYS WHICH IS SIMILAR TO THE PROCESS OF EVOLUTION WE HUMANS GO THROUGH. A PERIOD OF ACTION WHERE YOU MUST RISK AND LEAVE THE COMFORT OF YOUR HOME AND FAMILY UNIT AND EMBARK ON A JOURNEY OF SELF-DISCOVERY ON YOUR OWN. WONDERING WHAT YOU CAN DO AND HOW YOU CAN EXPRESS YOURSELF.

AND THIS BEGINNING IS WHAT ADAM KADMON EMBARKS ON. LEAVING THE COMFORT OF THE HEAVENLY FAMILY UNIT BEHIND AND STARTING A NEW JOURNEY. BUT TO START THIS JOURNEY SOMETHING WOULD HAVE TO HAPPEN TO ADAM KADMON. HIS STATE OF BEING WILL HAVE TO CHANGE DRAMATICALLY BECAUSE WITHOUT "SACRIFICE" OF A CERTAIN TYPE THIS PROCESS CANNOT HAPPEN. AS A SELF-CONTAINED FUNCTIONAL UNIT ADAM KADMON REMAINS FIXED IN PLACE AT THE ORIGINAL HEAVENLY HOME. IT CANNOT "MOVE." HOWEVER, WHEN ADAM KADMON DECIDES

TO BREAK FREE S-HE BREAKS APART AS THE ANDROGYNOUS SPIRITUAL PRINCIPLE S-HE IS AND WHICH IS MADE UP OF THE BINARY CODE OF CREATION AS ONE UNIT. MALE AND FEMALE AS ONE "SON OF MAN."

WHEN ADAM KADMON DECIDED TO BREAK FREE AND GO ON HIS-HER JOURNEY SOMETHING AMAZING HAPPENS. SOMETHING OF COSMIC PROPORTIONS. S-HE LEAVES BEHIND ITS FORMER STATE OF PERFECT SELF CONTAINED BALANCE AND EQUILIBRIUM SEPARATING ITSELF FROM ITSELF. WHAT WAS ONCE FUSED TOGETHER AS ONE IS NOW TWO PARTS OR TWINS NO LONGER JOINED TOGETHER PHYSICALLY. THIS CREATES WHAT IS KNOWN AS A TZIM TZUM OR AN IMPLOSION AND EXPLOSION OF ENERGY WHERE THE INDEPENDENT NEGATIVE EVE ENERGIES AND THE INDEPENDENT POSITIVE ADAM ENERGIES CAN NOW INTERACT AND BECOME ACTIVE WITH EACH OTHER GIVING PLACE TO AN ETERNAL COSMIC DANCE AND COITUS. AND THROUGH THAT COSMIC DANCE IN WHICH BOTH ENERGIES INTERACT WITH EACH OTHER, THEY GIVE BIRTH TO CREATION AND THE UNIVERSES. HOW DOES THIS CREATION TAKE PLACE????

WELL, BOTH THE EVE PRINCIPLE AND THE ADAM PRINCIPLE REPRESENT THE NEGATIVE AND POSITIVE ENERGY PRINCIPLES AND AS SUCH THEY EXCHANGE AND INTERACT WITH EACH OTHER GIVING BIRTH EVENTUALLY TO A THIRD ENERGY PRINCIPLE WHICH IS EQUIVALENT TO ANOTHER DIVINE CHILD THIS TIME BORN OF ADAM KADMON DIVIDED. THIS DIVINE CHILD ENERGY PRINCIPLE IS THE RECONCILER THAT ATTACHES THE NEGATIVE WITH THE POSITIVE PRINCIPLES MAKING CREATION A POSSIBILITY. THESE THREE PRINCIPLES ARE THE BUILDING BLOCKS OF LIFE. AND AS THE TZIM TZUM OCCURS AND THE EXPLOSION OF ENERGY HAPPENS, THIS EXPLOSION OF ENERGY BEGINS THE INTERACTION AND EXCHANGE OF BOTH THE YIN AND THE YANG PRINCIPLES AND AS SUCH THEY BEGIN THE PROCESS OF CREATING LIVING BEINGS, WORLDS AND UNIVERSES AS THESE ENERGY PRINCIPLES ARE CONCIOUSNESS ITSELF.

IT'S STILL ADAM KADMON BUT NO LONGER AS ONE SELF CONTAINED ANDROGYNOUS UNIT BUT AS A PLETHORA OF CREATIVE WORKS AND EXPRESSIONS. ADAM KADMON'S DREAM COMES FINALLY ALIVE AND BECOMES A REALITY IN CREATION ITSELF.

NOW, WHAT DOES MY PRESENT PAINFUL SITUATION HAVE TO DO WITH THE STORY OF CREATION???? WELL, THIS STORY OF CREATION IS ABOUT THE FALL FROM THE FORMER STATE OF GRACE OR INTEGRATION AND WHOLENESS TO ONE OF SEPARATION. AND THIS SEPARATION BETWEEN WHAT WAS FORMERLY "ONE" GAVE BIRTH TO THE CONCEPT OF SIN OR IMPERFECTION OR MAKING MISTAKES. WE LIVE IN THE PLANE OF MATTER.

IT IS ONE OF THE DENSEST UNIVERSES AND THE FARTHEST AWAY FROM THE ORIGIN OR FINEST SPIRITUAL PLANES OF EXISTENCE. THEREFORE IN THIS PLANE OF EXISTENCE WHERE THE MAIN STATE IS MATERIAL AND IS OF A DENSER ASPECT AND MORE AKIN TO THE NEGATIVE EVE REALM, MAKING MISTAKES IS PART OF THIS REALM.

AND SO JUST LIKE ADAM KADMON'S GREAT FALL INTO CREATION, SO IS MY GREAT FALL OF WHICH I AM TRYING TO GET UP WITH DIVINITY'S HELP. AFTER ALL, THE GREAT FALL OF ADAM KADMON IS A JOURNEY AND A PROCESS OF CREATION AND SELF LEARNING. AND AT THE END OF TIMES THE UNIVERSE IS SAID TO CONTRACT BACK AS ADAM KADMON FINISHES HIS JOURNEY AND LIFTS HIM-HERSELF UP AGAIN BACK TO THE ORIGINAL DIVINE HOME AND SO THE PROCESS GOES BACK TO THE BEGINNING. AND SO IT IS WITH WHAT I AM GOING THROUGH AND WITH WHAT MANY LIKE MYSELF ARE GOING THROUGH RIGHT NOW. THIS FALL IS JUST ANOTHER BEGINNING TO START OVER AGAIN AND TO RISE. THERE'S NO OTHER WAY.

MAKING MISTAKES IS PART OF THE JOURNEY AND OF LEARNING MORE ABOUT LIFE AND ONESELF. HOW WILL I EVER LEARN WHAT TO DO OR WHAT NOT TO DO; WHAT IS NEGATIVE FROM WHAT IS POSITIVE; WHY I SHOULD NOT DO SOMETHING FROM THAT WHICH I SHOULD DO IF I DON'T MAKE MISTAKES? ITS INHERENT IN THE INTERPLAY OF BOTH THE NEGATIVE AND POSITIVE FORCES AND WE ARE HERE TO LEARN TO DANCE IN THE MIDDLE OF THIS DANCE.

AND SO LIKE ADAM KADMON WHOM HAD TO FALL GREATLY IN ORDER TO BRING ABOUT A NEW EXPERIENCE, SO I FELL AND I'M LEARNING A GREAT DEAL FROM THIS GRAND FALL THAT DOES NOT ALLOW ME TO STAY WITHIN MY OWN COMFORT ZONE AND SAFETY AND IS POINTING AT SOMETHING ELSE. IT IS POINTING AT MY NEGATIVE PATTERNS AND LETTING ME KNOW I NEED TO BRING THE POSITIVE OUT OF THOSE NEGATIVE EXPERIENCES AND TURN THE NEGATIVE INTO POSITIVE.

SINCERELY,
"THE DIVINE SON- DAUGHTER"

---

8.  **THE TREE OF LIFE AND DUALITY AS A "BALANCE WITH SCALES" REPRESENTING THE CONCEPT OF "COSMIC JUSTICE" OR "CAUSE AND EFFECT!" —BINAH AND CHOKMAH IN RELATIVE BALANCE AND EQUILIBRIUM**

THE TREE OF GOOD AND EVIL AND OF KNOWLEDGE ALSO REPRESENTS THE DIAGRAM OF A SCALE AS IN A BALANCE THAT WEIGHS BOTH GOOD

AND EVIL ACTIONS AND WHICH TAKES ALSO INTO ACCOUNT THE GRAY AREAS IN BETWEEN. BY GRAY AREAS WE MEAN THOSE AREAS OF HUMAN ACTIVITY THAT ARE HARD TO DECIDE WHETHER THEY ARE BENEFICIAL OR DESTRUCTIVE OR ARE NEUTRAL OR ARE BOTH GOOD OR EVIL DEPENDING ON THE PARTICULAR SITUATION.

SOLOMON "THE SERPENTINE BIPOLAR" JUDGE CONCEPT OCCUPIES THE POSITION OF THE MIDDLE PILLAR OR —DA-AT–. HE IS THE ONE THAT BY HIS WISDOM/ ILLUMINATION AND ENLIGHTENED STATES IS ABLE TO DECIDE WITH RELATIVE ACCURACY THE DIFFERENCE BETWEEN THE SCALES OF GOOD AND EVIL AND MAKE JUST DECISIONS. BEING ABLE TO METE OUT JUSTICE BY MAKING THE BEST CHOICE POSSIBLE FOR THE PARTICULAR SITUATION. KING SOLOMON IS AN ARCHETYPE OF THE SERPENTINE SHAMAN - KING ARCHETYPE IN UNIVERSAL STORY AND MYTH.

THESE ARE THE SCALES OF THE GODDESS MA-AT IN EGYPTIAN TRADITION. BINAH BEING ONE SCALE AND CHOKMAH BEING THE OPPOSITE SCALE AND DA-AT THE CENTER PILLAR OF THE TRIAD THAT MAKES SURE THE SCALES AND BALANCES STAND AND FUNCTION EQUALLY AND PROPERLY IN RELATION TO ONE ANOTHER.

AS YOU WILL RECALL, THE "FORMATION OF THE UNIVERSE" AS IN THE "YIN AND YANG" PRINCIPLES SPLITTING AND FUSING AND SO FORTH FOLLOWS A SIMILAR PATTERN. THIS COSMIC - ENERGETIC PATTERN RESEMBLES "THE COSMIC SCALES OF JUSTICE" SO THAT THE COSMOS REMAINS IN A RELATIVELY BALANCED STATE OR ELSE THE ENTIRE MATRIX OF THE UNIVERSE WOULD BE A CHAOTIC MESS UNABLE TO SUSTAIN ITSELF AS WELL AS LIFE ON EARTH AND OTHER PLANETS AND LIFE SYSTEMS.

THE CENTER PILLAR IS ACTIVATED BY THE PREFRONTAL CORTEX AND ITS AJNA CHAKRA AND THE HEART CHAKRA AS ONE UNIT IN A HUMAN BEING. THE ACTIVE FUNCTIONING OF BOTH IS KEY TO THE "JUSTICE" PRINCIPLE OF THE MIDDLE PILLAR SINCE WITHOUT INTUITION OR INNER VISION AND WITHOUT EMPATHY AND AN OPEN HEART IT IS VERY DIFFICULT TO MAKE WISE JUDGMENT AND DECISIONS THAT TAKE INTO CONSIDERATION THE FACTS AS WELL AS THE MOTIVES. THE PREFRONTAL CORTEX ALSO INFLUENCES MAN'S ABILITY TO TELL RIGHT FROM WRONG.

BEING ABLE TO CONNECT BOTH THE MIND AND THE HEART AS IN BINAH AND CHOKMAH RESPECTIVELY, ALLOWS FOR A JUST AND MEASURED APPLICATION OF THE LAW WITH MERCY WITHOUT BECOMING "A TYRANT." BEING CAREFUL NOT TO "CAUSE UNJUST AND UNNECESSARY HARM AND SUFFERING."

THE UNIVERSE IS AN ACCOUNTING SYSTEM WITH DEBITS AND CREDITS THAT HAPPENS AUTOMATICALLY AS IN THE PROCESS OF "CAUSE AND EFFECT." WHICH MEANS THAT WHATEVER ONE DOES WILL EVENTUALLY CAUSE A GOOD, NEUTRAL OR EVIL EFFECT ON THE PERSON OR ENVIRONMENT. THESE ARE THE SCALES OF "JUSTICE" OF THE COSMOS. IT IS VERY IMPORTANT TO WATCH OUR ACTIONS AND THE INNER MOTIVATIONS RESIDING IN OUR SHADOW OR UNCONSCIOUS SELF THAT MOVE US TO CARRY OUT CERTAIN ACTIONS OR NOT.

SOURCE IS BOTH YIN AND YANG AND "THE MOVER OF ALL CAUSES." THEREFORE, WE ARE ALL LINKED TO THE SOURCE AND TO THE "FIRST" CAUSE AND EFFECT WHICH IS DESCRIBED IN METAPHORICAL AND SYMBOLIC WAYS IN THE BOOK OF GENESIS OR THE ANDRO-GENESIS AND "THE FALL OF ADAMEVA KAD-M-ONE." THEREFORE, THAT FIRST "CAUSE AND EFFECT" EVENTUALLY LED TO THE FORMATION OF THE COSMOS. THEREFORE "CAUSE AND EFFECT" AND THE CONCEPT OF "JUST MEASURES AND WEIGHTS" ARE RELATED AND ARE AN INTRINSIC AND INHERENT PART OF THE ENTIRE SYSTEM OF LIFE IN MATTER AND THE COSMOS OR THE MATRIX.

SINCERELY, "KARMA CHAMELE-ONNE, THE FIRST CAUSE AND THE LAST EFFECT"

---

## 9.  THE TREE OF LIFE, UNION AND INTEGRATION (1-29-2021)

SO THE TREE OF LIFE, AS OPPOSED TO THE TREE OF GOOD AND EVIL THAT WAS OPENLY ACCESSIBLE TO ADAM AND EVE, WAS KEPT AWAY FROM ADAM. ISN'T THAT INTERESTING? IF THE TREE OF GOOD AND EVIL WHICH IS THE TREE OF DUALITY, SEPARATION AND OPPOSITES WAS ALL THAT EVIL THEN IT WOULD HAVE MADE MORE SENSE FOR GOD TO KEEP THAT TREE AWAY AND INACCESSIBLE FROM ADAM AND EVE. BUT THAT WAS NOT THE CASE ACCORDING TO THE LITERAL INTERPRETATION OF THE STORY. BUT ON THE OTHER HAND, THE TREE OF LIFE WHICH IS OF UNION, AND INTEGRATION WAS NOT MADE ACCESSIBLE TO ADAM? WOULD NOT IT MAKE MORE SENSE TO MAKE THE TREE OF LIFE ACCESSIBLE IN THE FIRST PLACE AND THE TREE OF GOOD AND EVIL NOT AT ALL???

WELL, THIS STORY OF THE TREE OF GOOD AND EVIL REALLY MAKES ONE END UP WITH MORE QUESTIONS THAN ANSWERS.

SO WHAT'S UP WITH THIS TREE OF LIFE AND WHAT DO I MEAN IT IS THE TREE OF UNION AND INTEGRATION???

WELL, THE TREE OF LIFE IS REALLY THE OPPOSITE OF THE TREE OF GOOD AND EVIL. WHAT PEOPLE DO NOT REALIZE IS THAT THE TREE OF GOOD AND EVIL AND TREE OF LIFE ARE NOT ONLY OPPOSITES BUT ARE THE SAME TREE BUT VIEWED FROM A DIFFERENT ANGLE OR PERSPECTIVE. MEANING THAT IT IS EITHER "GOOD AND EVIL" OR "OF LIFE" DEPENDING ON YOUR PERCEPTION.

IN THE DIAGRAM OF THE TREE OF GOOD AND EVIL WE SEE A TREE WITH THREE PILLARS. ONE ON THE LEFT AND ANOTHER ON THE RIGHT AND ANOTHER ONE IN THE MIDDLE. AS WE CAN SEE HERE THIS TREE HAS TWO PARTS AS IN A DUAL BIPOLAR TREE WHICH IS ALSO TRI-DIMENSIONAL.

AND SO, THE TREE OF GOOD AND EVIL IN THE GENESIS STORY IS MORE THAN A LITERAL TREE WITH EYE OPENING FRUIT. IT POINTS TO A STATE OF CONSCIOUSNESS AND THE PERCEPTION OF THIS TRI-DIMENSIONAL PLANE OF EXISTENCE. THEREFORE, THE TREE OF LIFE THAT WAS KEPT AWAY FROM ADAM AND EVE IS THE SAME TREE OF GOOD AND EVIL BUT LOOKING AT IT FROM BELOW. IN OTHER WORDS, THE TREE OF GOOD AND EVIL IS A TREE OF DESCENT INTO THE WORLD OF MATTER AND DUALITIES AND OPPOSITES. IT'S A TREE ABOUT A STATE OF BEING WHERE YOU ARE FALLING DOWN INTO A LOWER STATE OF CONSCIOUSNESS AND THE TREE OF LIFE IS THE SAME TREE BUT RISING UP TO A HIGHER STATE OF CONSCIOUSNESS. GOING UPWARDS BACK TO THE HEAVENLY PLACES FROM WHICH WE FELL DOWN IN THE BEGINNING OF TIME. THESE SPARKS OF DIVINITY TRAPPED IN MATTER IS A COSMIC PROCESS THAT HAS BEEN HAPPENING SINCE THE BEGINNING OF TIME OR THE COSMIC TZIM-TZUM.

AND SO BOTH THESE TREES WORK IN COMBINATION IN ORDER TO ACHIEVE A PARTICULAR GOAL FOR THE BETTERMENT OF HUMANITY. AS YOU MIGHT RECALL, ADAM AND EVE WERE INCAPABLE OF GROWTH IN THE VERY BEGINNING AS THEY WERE IN A STATE OF PERPETUAL INNOCENCE AND JUST FOLLOWING THE INSTRUCTIONS IMPOSED BY ELOHIM'S RULES AND REGULATIONS. THEY WERE IN A STATE OF PERPETUAL CHILDHOOD WITHOUT A DEEPER SENSE OF REALITY AND UNDERSTANDING AS DIVINITY POSSESSES BEING CONSCIOUS OF BOTH THE GOOD AND THE EVIL OR THE TOTALITY OF REALITY.

AFTER EATING OF THE FORBIDDEN FRUIT THEIR EYES OF PERCEPTION EXPANDED OR OPENED. NOW INSTEAD OF JUST SEEING SUPERFICIALLY AND LIMITEDLY, THEY COULD SEE IN A MORE PANORAMIC AND BROADER AND DEEPER VIEW. AN IN DEPTH OF UNDERSTANDING SO THAT NOW THEY BEGAN TO NOTICE WHAT THEY HAD NOT BEEN ABLE TO NOTICE BEFORE, THE EVIL AND THE FLAWS WITHIN THE MATERIAL PLANE AND THE UNIVERSE. AS THE UNIVERSE IS NOT ONLY LIGHT BUT ALSO DARKNESS

AND NOT ONLY GOOD BUT ALSO EVIL. AFTER FALLING FROM THAT INITIAL STATE OF GRACE, THEY WERE ABLE TO EXPERIENCE AND SEE AND NOTICE EVIL AND GOOD AND TO LEARN FROM BOTH.

THROUGH CONSTANT EXPERIENCE ONE GROWS IN UNDERSTANDING AND WISDOM AND EMPATHY. BECOMING AFTER THE IMAGE AND LIKENESS OF ELOHIM WHO CAN NOTICE BOTH THE DARK AND THE LIGHT AND THE IN-BETWEEN STATES OF CONSCIOUSNESS. THE TRI-DIMENSIONAL ASPECT OF REALITY WHICH ADAM AND EVE HAD ACCESS TO WHEN THEY METAPHORICALLY ATE FROM THE TREE OF DUALITY, SEPARATION AND POLARITIES. MEANING THAT AFTER EATING FROM THAT TREE OF SEPARATION, ADAM AND EVE WERE ABLE TO MAKE DISTINCTIONS BETWEEN ONE THING AND ANOTHER. BEFORE THAT, EVERYTHING WAS LIKE ONE WHOLE THING WHICH THEY COULDN'T UNDERSTAND OR ASSIMILATE, YET.

AND SO THIS TREE OF THE KNOWLEDGE OF GOOD AND EVIL IS THE PATH TOWARDS INTEGRATION AND HEALING. IT IS THE TREE OF GOOD AND EVIL SEEN FROM BELOW MOVING UPWARDS AND UNITING ALL THE DUALITIES OR POLARITIES FOUND IN BOTH SIDES OF THE TREE OF LIFE AND UNIFYING OR TURNING WHOLE WHAT BECAME SEPARATED IN THE FALLING DOWN OR DESCENT DOWN THE TREE OF GOOD AND EVIL. THIS TREE OF DIVISION AND SEPARATION BECOMES THE TREE OF LIFE AS IT MOVES UPWARDS AFTER HAVING A DESCENT AND REACHING "THE KINGDOM" OR SEPHIRA OF MALKUT WHERE OUR MATERIAL PLANE IS FOUND. THIS PROCESS POINTS TO THE JOURNEY OF HUMAN EVOLUTION AND CONSCIOUSNESS THAT TAKES PLACE HERE IN MALKUT AND THAT TAKES US BACK TO THE HEAVENS, TO THE STARS AND TO A STATE OF WHOLENESS, INTEGRATION, AND UNION WITHIN THAT IS INNATE IN OUR OWN BROKENNESS. IN OTHER WORDS, OUR BROKEN AND FLAWED HUMAN LIFE AND PAIN EXPERIENCE IS THE PATH ITSELF THAT WILL TAKE US BACK TO HEALING AND INTEGRATION AND BACK TO THE HEAVENLY PLACES.

THEREFORE, THE TREE OF LIFE REMINDS US THAT THERE IS GREAT VALUE IN OUR TREE OF GOOD AND EVIL EXPERIENCE. IN OTHER WORDS, WE CANNOT REACH THE TREE OF LIFE UNLESS WE GO THROUGH THE TREE OF GOOD AND EVIL FIRST WITH ALL ITS COLORS AND CHARACTERISTICS AND EXPERIENCES.

WE ARE DOWN HERE TO WORK OUT OUR PARTICULAR LIFE LESSONS WHICH WE BRING WITH US BEFORE WE ARE BORN. THESE LIFE LESSONS ARE PLACED IN OUR PATH AS OBSTACLES AND CHALLENGES THAT WE ARE TO EVENTUALLY OVERCOME AND THROUGH THEM GROW IN OUR OWN

PARTICULAR WAY IN THIS LIFE. IT IS FOR THIS REASON THAT THIS LIFE IS A SCHOOL AND THE MAIN REASON WE ARE PLACED HERE IN MALKUT OR THE MATERIAL KINGDOM OF THE DIVINE. ANOTHER REASON WE ARE HERE IS TO BECOME THE BEST VERSION OF OURSELVES BY TACKLING ALL THESE INNATE FLAWS AND TRANSGRESSIONS AND GROW UP AFTER THE IMAGE AND LIKENESS OF ELOHIM WHO ARE BOTH MALE AND FEMALE, DARK AND LIGHT, GOOD AND EVIL, THE SOURCE OF ALL. TO WALK THE PATH OF THE TREE OF LIFE IS NOT TO REGRESS AND STAY STUCK IN THE TREE OF GOOD AND EVIL "PLANE OF BEING" AND EXISTENCE, BUT TO REACH AN UNDERSTANDING OF IT AND MOVE FORWARD TO THE TREE OF LIFE OR OF HIGHER CONSCIOUSNESS.

HOW FAST WE ASCEND THE TREE OF LIFE HAS TO DO WITH HUMILITY. IT INVOLVES REACHING A PLACE OF FULL AND RADICAL ACCEPTANCE OF OUR OWN FLAWS AND LIMITATIONS AND STRENGTHS AND TALENTS WHICH WILL ENABLE US TO OVERCOME THESE OBSTACLES ALONG THE WAY. WE ARE BASICALLY HEALERS ALONG THE LIVING PATH OF LIFE AS WE BECOME OUR OWN HEALERS AND SAVIORS BY CORRECTING THESE FLAWS AND BECOMING AFTER THE IMAGE AND LIKENESS OF ELOHIM. ELOHIM, WHO BRING ORDER TO THIS EARTH AND COSMOS BY "CORRECTING" REALITY THROUGH ESTABLISHED RULES AND REGULATIONS OR COSMIC LAWS. THAT'S WHY ELOHIM HAVE PLACED IN US, IN OUR CONSCIENCES, THE SPIRITUAL COMMANDMENTS, LAWS AND PRECEPTS THAT HELP GUIDE US ALONG THE WAY. THESE ARE RECOMMENDATIONS THAT HELP US ASCEND THE TREE OF LIFE TOWARDS A MORE WHOLE, HEALED, INTEGRATED, LIFE -AFFIRMING STATE. THIS IS WHY THE TREE OF LIFE IS ABOUT AFFIRMING AND MAKING A PROMISE TO LIVE A LIFE AFTER GOOD AND HOLINESS. HOLINESS WHICH IS NOT TO DO WITH RELIGIOSITY BUT WITH BEING IN A STATE OF RELATIVE HEALTH IN MIND, SPIRIT, HEART, BODY, ETC. AFTER THE IMAGE AND LIKENESS OF THE ELOHIM.

AND SO THIS TREE OF GOOD AND EVIL REPRESENTS THE FLAWED MATERIAL PLANE IN WHICH WE LIVE AND MOVE. IT IS OUR JOB TO REACH FOR THE TREE OF LIFE BUT NOT RIGHT AWAY JUST AS IT WAS IN THE STORY OF ADAM AND EVE IN GENESIS. WE ARE SUPPOSED TO REALIZE THAT WE HAVE FALLEN SHORT AND REACH AN UNDERSTANDING EVENTUALLY OF WHY WE HAVE TRANSGRESSED REPEATEDLY.

WE CAN ONLY CHANGE THE PATH FROM FALLING DOWN ENDLESSLY BY UNDERSTANDING WHY AND THEN CHANGING OUR FLAWED ACTIONS AND THOUGHTS INTO THOSE OF THE LIGHT. OTHERWISE WERE WE TO REACH THE TREE OF LIFE IMMEDIATELY, WITHOUT GOING THROUGH THE PROCESS OF TRANSGRESSING AND FALLING AND FEELING PAIN, SUFFERING AND REMORSE FROM OUR OWN MISTAKES, WE WOULD

BE UNABLE TO UNDERSTAND THIS PROCESS AS IT PLAYS OUT IN OUR PARTICULAR LIVES. WE WOULD NEVER LEARN THE LESSONS AND GROW UP AFTER THE IMAGE AND LIKENESS OF ELOHIM. WE WOULD REMAIN THE SAME AS BEFORE AND PERHAPS BECOMING MORE EVIL. DO YOU SEE? THE PAIN IN SUFFERING CONTAINS ITS OWN HEALING ANTIDOTE. THE PAIN PRODUCED BY MAKING MISTAKES IS THERE TO TEACH US THAT IF IT HURTS WE HAVE MOVED AWAY FROM THE TREE OF LIFE PATH AND THAT WE NEED TO DO SOMETHING TO CORRECT THAT MISTAKE AND ACTION AND MOVE BACK TOWARDS OUR OWN ASCENSION UP THE TREE OF LIFE. THE TREE OF LIFE IS LIKE A COSMIC LADDER MOVING UPWARDS. A STAIRWAY TO HEAVEN.

ACTUALLY, WE CANNOT REACH TREE OF LIFE STATES OF CONSCIOUSNESS WITHOUT FIRST UNDERGOING THE NECESSARY TRIALS AND LESSONS INHERENT IN THE TREE OF THE KNOWLEDGE OF GOOD AND EVIL.

THEREFORE, OUR LIFE AS HUMANS IS HOLY AND IT'S A COSMIC PROCESS THAT HAS HEALTH AS ITS GOAL. I'M NOT SPEAKING HERE ABOUT BEING A SAINT. THIS IS ABOUT BEING IN HARMONY AND BALANCE WITHIN AND WITH OTHERS AND THE ENVIRONMENT. THIS PROCESS OF CONSTANT GROWTH AND AWARENESS SHAPES US LIKE A RAW DIAMOND INTO OUR BEST VERSIONS OF OURSELVES. THERE IS A DIVINE SPARK IN US AND THAT DIVINE ASPECT IN US REMIND US WHERE WE REALLY BELONG WHICH IS UP THERE AND WHAT OUR INNATE STATE IS. THAT DESPITE BEING HUMANS WE ARE INNATELY GOOD. LET US WORK THAT GOODNESS AND MAKE IT MORE ABUNDANT. LET US TRANSFORM OUR INNATE EVIL AND LET'S WALK BACK HOME TO OUR HEAVENLY PLACES. A HOLY PROCESS THAT GIVES TRUE MEANING AND PURPOSE TO HUMAN LIFE.

LET'S TURN AND TRANSFORM THE TREE OF GOOD AND EVIL INTO THE TREE OF LIFE, UNION AND INTEGRATION IN OURSELVES AND IN THE WORLD WE LIVE IN.

SINCERELY,
ELOHIM

## 10. THE TREE OF LIFE AND OF GOOD AND EVIL: DIVISION AND INTEGRATION

WHAT MOST PEOPLE TODAY DO NOT REALIZE IS THAT THE BOOK OF GENESIS IS A QABALISTIC MYSTICAL WRITING RATHER THAN A LITERAL ONE. IN FACT, THE TREE OF GOOD AND EVIL IN THE GARDEN OF EDEN IS A TEMPLATE OF THE UNIVERSE AND ITS NATURE. IT REPRESENTS THE PLANE OF EXISTENCE WE INHABIT WHICH IS CHARACTERIZED BY DUALITY, THUS THE NAME OF IT AS BOTH "GOOD AND EVIL." IT REPRESENTS DIVISION AND SEPARATION.

THE TREE OF GOOD AND EVIL REPRESENTS THE FIRST BORN ADAM KADMON OR THE FIRST COSMIC CHILD BORN OF THE ORIGINAL POWERS OF CREATION OR THE "DIVINE COUPLE" THROUGH WHOM ALL THINGS IN THE UNIVERSE WERE MADE. IN OTHER WORDS, THE UNIVERSE AND "THE CHILD OF THE DIVINE" ARE THE SAME. THE UNIVERSE IS POSSIBLE ONLY THROUGH ADAM KADMONS SACRIFICE WHERE HE FALLS OR DESCENDS FROM HIS STATE OF GRACE AND UNITY TO BREAK UP INTO DIVERSE PARTS AND SO BECOME THE UNIVERSE AND ALL LIVING AND INANIMATE BEINGS AND THINGS. WE HUMANS LIVE AND MOVE WITHIN THE MIND, BODY AND WILL AND ENERGY GRID OF ADAMEVA KADMON.

THEREFORE AS THIS TREE OF GOOD AND EVIL AND "THE SON OF MAN" ARE INTERCHANGEABLE, SO IS THE CONCEPT OF THE TREE OF LIFE. IN FACT, BOTH THE TREE OF GOOD AND EVIL AND THE TREE OF LIFE ARE ACTUALLY THE SAME TREE. ONLY THAT THE TREE OF GOOD AND EVIL DESCENDS WHILE THE TREE OF LIFE ASCENDS OR IS THE INVERSE OF THE OTHER. WHAT I MEAN TO SAY IS THAT IN THE TREE OF GOOD AND EVIL THE BASIC UNITS OF LIFE AND CREATION SEPARATE FROM EACH OTHER AND BRING ABOUT DUALITY AND SEPARATION AND CHAOS. WHILE IN THE INVERSE, IT BECOMES THE TREE OF LIFE IN WHICH THESE SAME BASIC UNITS OF LIFE ATTACH TO EACH OTHER OR BECOME ONE AND SO IT TURNS INTO THE TREE OF LIFE WHICH REPRESENTS UNION AND INTEGRATION WHICH IS THE SAME THING AS BEING IN A STATE OF WHOLENESS AND HEALTH.

ANOTHER WAY TO SEE THIS DIVINE DICHOTOMY IS BY REALIZING THAT BOTH "LIFE AND DEATH OR SEPARATION" COME TOGETHER AS ONE UNIT IN THIS MATERIAL DUALISTIC REALM.

FOR CENTURIES THE TREE OF GOOD AND EVIL AND THE TREE OF KNOWLEDGE OR LIFE HAVE BEEN CONSIDERED SEPARATE FROM EACH OTHER AS INTERPRETED FROM THE BOOK OF GENESIS. HOWEVER, BOTH

TREES ACTUALLY REPRESENT TWIN TREES WHICH FORM ONE UNIT. THE MOTHER SPHERE OF BINAH AND THE FATHER SPHERE OF CHOKMAH IN THE TREE OF DUALITY WHICH REPRESENT RESPECTIVELY BINAH OR THE NEGATIVE FEMININE ARCHETYPE AND STATE OF BEING; AND, CHOKMAH, THE POSITIVE MASCULINE ARCHETYPE AND STATE OF BEING. AND FROM BOTH OF THESE TWIN ENERGIES THAT ARE SEPARATE BUT THAT COMPLEMENT EACH OTHER, ARE BORN ALL THE DUAL QUALITIES IN THE UNIVERSE AND TRI DIMENSIONALITY. IN OTHER WORDS, EVERY QUALITY COMES IN TWOS. FOR THERE TO BE A POSITIVE QUALITY, THERE HAS TO BE ITS OPPOSITE AND COMPLEMENTARY QUALITY IN THE UNIVERSE, THE NEGATIVE.

THE TREE OF LIFE BELONGS TO THE FATHER PRINCIPLE WHILE THE TREE OF GOOD AND EVIL BELONGS TO THE MOTHER PRINCIPLE.

AND SO AS THESE DUAL ENERGIES SEPARATED FROM EACH OTHER FROM THEIR STATE OF UNITY, THE DUAL MATERIAL UNIVERSE AND OTHER PLANES OF EXISTENCE BEGAN TO TAKE SHAPE AND FORM. AND SO THIS IS THE MAIN REASON WHY YOU AND I LIVE IN THIS UNIVERSE THAT IS DUAL IN NATURE AND IN WHICH BOTH GOOD AND EVIL RESIDE. AS BEINGS WHOM ARE OF THIS PLANE AND WHOM ARE CREATED AFTER THE IMAGE AND LIKENESS OF "THE SON OF MAN" OR ADAM KADMON, WE ARE ALSO LIKE THAT TREE OF GOOD AND EVIL, BOTH GOOD AND EVIL. WHICH ALSO MEANS THAT WE POSSESS ALL THOSE GOOD AND EVIL QUALITIES AND ATTRIBUTES FROM UP ABOVE AND BELOW. MOST IMPORTANTLY, IT MEANS THAT WE ARE ALSO "THE TREE OF LIFE" WHICH IS OUR GOAL AND OUR HUMAN REASON TO BE HERE. TO TRANSFORM OUR TREE OF GOOD AND EVIL SELVES —OR OF SEPARATION AND FRAGMENTATION AND CHAOS— INTO THE TREE OF UNION AND HEALTH AND INTEGRATION WHICH IS LOVE AND PEACE AND HEALTH.

AS EARTH IS A SCHOOL THAT EXISTS TO HELP US REACH THIS GOAL OF RETURNING TO OUR HIGHER SELVES OR TRUE SELVES AS TREES OF LIFE, THE OBJECTIVE OF HUMAN CIVILIZATION AND SPIRITUAL TRADITION ALONG WITH ITS INSTITUTIONS SHOULD BE TO HELP EACH ONE OF US REACH THIS INCREDIBLE AND INHERENT HUMAN STATE AND OPPORTUNITY. SADLY IN A CORRUPT WORLD WHERE THE MAIN GOAL AND SACRIFICE HAS BEEN MATERIALISTIC, HUMANITY HAS MOVED AWAY AND FAR AWAY FROM THIS GOAL. A DIVINE GOAL THAT IS EQUIVALENT TO HUMANITY'S SURVIVAL IN THIS PLANET, FOR A HUMANITY WHO IS IN PERPETUAL CHAOS AND SEPARATION INTERNALLY, IS A HUMANITY THAT GIVES BIRTH TO AN ENVIRONMENT AND SOCIETY IN A PERPETUAL STATE OF CHAOS, DIVISION, WAR AND DISEASE.

IT IS THIS PROCESS OF HUMAN EVOLUTION THAT BEGAN WHEN "ADAM AND EVE PARTOOK OF THE FORBIDDEN FRUIT OF THE TREE OF GOOD AND EVIL AND THEIR EYES OF UNDERSTANDING BEGAN TO OPEN AND SEE AND ….NOTICE." THEY LOST THEIR INNOCENCE AND FELL FROM A STATE OF GRACE BUT THEY WERE GIVEN THE OPPORTUNITY TO GET UP AGAIN AND TO BEGIN EXPERIENCING THIS DUAL AND TRIPLE WORLD WITH BOTH ITS GOOD AND EVIL ASPECTS AND BY WHICH THEY WOULD GROW UP IN UNDERSTANDING AND WISDOM IN EVERY SENSE OF THE WORD. OR SO IT WAS EXPECTED.

SINCERELY,
"ADAM AND EVE – THE RISEN ONES"

---

## 11. THE MAYA "LA CEIBA" TREE OF LIFE AND THE 5 ELEMENTS REPRESENTING THE 4 RIVERS IN GENESIS STORY AND THE TREE OF LIFE —-THE LA CEIBA "PENTA-GRAMMATON" AND THE DIVINE "ANDRA-GENESIS" THE "5" "---LA CEIBA, HONDURAS

IN THE MAYAN MYTHOLOGY OF CREATION THERE ARE FOUR TREES THAT ARE FOUND IN THE FOUR CORNERS OF THE WORLD. THESE ARE THE RED, BLACK, YELLOW AND WHITE TREES. MMMM…. DOES NOT THIS SOUND LIKE THE HOPI MYTH OF THE "4 BROTHERS" WHO HAPPEN TO GO TO THE FOUR CORNERS OF THE WORLD AND ARE AS WELL RED, BLACK, YELLOW AND WHITE? THE TETRAGRAMMATON!

AND IN THE MIDST OF THE 4 TREES IS THE "LA CEIBA TREE," THE HOLY OR SACRED TREE THAT CONNECTS THE HEAVENS AND THE UNDERWORLDS WITH THE MIDDLE WORLD OR OUR WORLD. HERE WE HAVE ONCE AGAIN THE NUMBER "5." THE PENTAGRAMMATON OR "THE CEIBA PENTA-ANDRA." THE PENTA-ANDRA WORD HAS TWO ROOT WORDS AS IN "PENTA ===5" AND "ANDRA" WHICH IS ANDRO-GYNE!!! THE CEIBA TREE THEREFORE REPRESENTS "YIN-YANG" AND THE PRIMORDIAL WO-MAN WHO IS "5" AND WHO SACRIFICES ITSELF SUCH AS IN THE "CHRISTIAN MYTH" TO BRING ABOUT THE "WHOLE UNIVERSES AND COSMOS." AND FROM THAT "TREE" OR "YAXCHE" FLOWS EVERYTHING ELSE. THE 5 PENTA STANDS FOR THE FIVE ELEMENTS WHICH INCLUDES …SPIRIT.

THIS REMINDS ME OF THE STORY OF THE "LA CEIBA" SACRED TREE IN THE CITY OF LA CEIBA, HONDURAS THAT SERVED AS WELL AS A PHAROS OR LIGHTHOUSE. SHIPS WERE ABLE TO SEE THIS TREE FROM FAR AWAY OUT INTO THE SEA AND KNEW THAT LAND WAS CLOSE BY. AND SO IT IS INTERESTING IN THAT IT WAS HERE WHERE THIS "GIANT CEIBA TREE" STOOD THAT THE CITY OF "LA CEIBA" WAS FOUNDED AND GOT ITS NAME

AND THAT DURING THE BOOM OF THE BANANA INDUSTRY PEOPLE FROM ALL OVER THE WORLD CAME TO THESE SHORES AND TO THE CITY OF "LA CEIBA." THE FOUR BROTHERS OF ALL RACES COMING BACK TO "THE SACRED TREE." THE INDIGENOUS AND GARIFUNA PEOPLES OF LA CEIBA BELIEVED THAT THIS PARTICULAR SACRED CEIBA TREE CONNECTED HEAVEN TO EARTH AND THAT GOD DESCENDED TO EARTH THRU THIS MASSIVE TREE LIKE A HEAVENLY LADDER. LATER THE SACRED TREE WAS CHOPPED DOWN IN ORDER TO MAKE WAY FOR DEVELOPMENT, THE PEOPLE OF LA CEIBA CRIED. AND AT SOME POINT AFTER THAT TRAGIC INCIDENT A STORM CAME AND FLOODED THE BUILDING THAT NOW STOOD WHERE THE CEIBA TREE USED TO BE. CEIBA TREES WERE GROWN BY THE INDIGENOUS PEOPLES IN PLACES THAT HELD A STRONG SPIRITUAL VALUE AND PRESENCE.

AND SO IT SEEMS THAT SOMETHING SIMILAR BEGAN HAPPENING ALL OVER THE CONTINENT. THE ARRIVAL OF PEOPLES FROM ALL OVER THE WORLD SEEKING NEW HORIZONS RETURNING TO "LA CEIBA" TREE JUST AS THE HOPI AND MAYA BELIEVED WOULD EVENTUALLY HAPPEN.

THIS MAYAN MYTH AND PENTAGRAMMATON IS SIMILAR TO THE GENESIS STORY. BUT IN IT WE FIND 4 RIVERS WATERING THE WORLD TREE. THE FOUR ELEMENTS WHICH ARE FIRE, EARTH, WATER, AIR AND IN THE MIDST THE "ORIGIN OF THE FOUR ELEMENTS WHICH IS ...SPIRIT OR "QI-ETER AKASHA." WE HAVE THE FOUR TREES OR "HUMANS" WHO ARE THE MICROCOSM OF THE "LA CEIBA TREE" WHICH REPRESENTS THE MACROCOSM. "THE TREE OF LIFE" DIVIDING ITSELF INTO FOUR BRANCHES OR FOUR ELEMENTS UNITED BY THE ORIGINAL SPARK OF LIFE AND BY WHICH ALL WORLDS ARE CREATED SUCH AS ARE THE "4 WORLDS OF THE QABALAH."

WHAT THE MAYA TREE OF LIFE OR WORLD TREE IS IN RELATION TO THE OTHER 4 TREES IS THAT THE OTHER 4 TREES REPRESENT HUMANITY AS A WHOLE AND ARE BORN FROM THE MIDDLE TREE AND ARE LINKED TO IT. IN OTHER WORDS, HUMANITY IS IN UNION WITH SOURCE ALL THE TIME.

AS WE KNOW "TREES" HELP PRODUCE WATER:

Trees serve as natural sponges, collecting and filtering rainfall and releasing it slowly into streams and rivers, and are the most effective land cover for maintenance of water quality.(AMERICANFORESTS)

THE FOUR RIVERS IN THE GENESIS STORY FLOW OR FIND THEIR ORIGIN IN THE MIDDLE TREE OF LIFE!!! WITHOUT THE TREE, THE RIVERS WILL DRY AND WITHER. THIS IS THE BASIS OF ECOLOGY AND THE WEB OF LIFE THAT HUMANS ARE A PART OF. INTERCONNECTEDNESS WITH SOURCE AND THE

WEB OF LIFE. AT THE SAME TIME, THE RIVERS GIVE WATER TO THE TREE. THEREFORE IT'S ALL ABOUT CONNECTION AND INTERDEPENDENCE. WHAT I DO TO THE TREE WILL AFFECT THE WATER AND WHAT I DO TO THE WATER WILL AFFECT THE TREE OR "LIFE." THIS COSMOS IS A CONSTANT "GIVE AND TAKE." ALL VARIABLES DEPEND ON EACH OTHER AND ARE INTERCONNECTED. JUST AS THE FOUR RIVERS FLOW FROM THE TREE, SO THE 4 ELEMENTS FLOW NATURALLY FROM THE "PRIMORDIAL WO-MAN" OR "BIG BANG" IN ORDER THAT THE GARDEN OF EDEN OR ECOLOGY AND NATURE AND THE WORLD COME TO BE. NATURE IS THE BASIS OF ALL MATTER ON EARTH AND THE LAWS OF NATURE ARE A REFLECTION OF THE LAWS OF THE COSMOS!!!

IF YOU LOOK AT THE PICTURE OF THE YAXCHE IN MESOAMERICAN ART, YOU WILL NOTICE THE DIVINE TRIAD WITH ADAM KAD-M-ONNE IN THE MIDDLE. HE ALSO REPRESENTS THE "SHAMAN" OR ELDER OF THE COMMUNITY AS A REPRESENTATION OF THE TREE OF LIFE, THE GIVER OF KNOWLEDGE TO THE TRIBE. PAK-"AL." AS THE SHAMAN TRAVELS TO THE WORLDS OR DIMENSIONS, S-HE CONNECTS TO THOSE WORLDS USING AS WELL THE BARK OF LA CEIBA TREE USED IN MAYAN TRADITION FOR VISION WORK.

SINCERELY,
"PENTA-ANDRA" THE 5 ELEMENTS AS THE PRIMORDIAL WO-MAN MADE FLESH

---

## 12. THE GARDEN OR PARDES OF "ED-ENNU:" THE DIVINE ANDRO-GENESIS AND ITS STATE OF UNION AND FUSION BEFORE THE SPLITTING IN HALF AND THE BIRTH OF "TRANSGRESSION" – THE FALL OF ADAM KAD-"MAN"

KAD==== RELATED TO THE LATIN FOR "TO FALL" OR "CAD-ERE"

MON/MEN/MAN==== SANSKRIT FOR MENOS AND MENS AS IN "THINKING AND MIND AND MAN"

ADAM KAD-MAN === THE FALLEN ADAM, THE FIRST PRIMORDIAL MAN OR ENERGY SYSTEM HAVE YOU NOTICED THE NAME OF THE GARD-ENNE OF ED-EN? IF YOU SPLIT THE NAME IN HALF YOU GET "ED" AND "EN." AS YOU MIGHT KNOW THE SYLLABLE "EN" IS RELATED TO THE CONCEPT OF "UNO OR ONE" IN LATIN AND SANSKRIT.

"UN" ——--IN LATIN WHICH DERIVES FROM MUCH OLDER LANGUAGES.

Ekam is the Sanskrit for "one, single, solitary" (neuter gender), as a noun meaning "unity". WIKIPEDIA NOW NOTICE THAT EVEN IN THE OLDER SANSKRIT, THE TERM FOR UNITY IS CALLED "EKAM" WHICH SOUNDS A LOT TO "EDEN and OM." AND IS "GENDER NEUTRAL" WHICH MEANS AS WELL THAT ITS IS ALSO "ALL GENDERS IN ONE" JUST AS THE PRIMORDIAL ANDROGYNOUS COSMIC WO-MAN.

WHAT WE ARE TALKING HERE ABOUT ARE "IDEAS." THE FIRST CONCEPT IN COSMIC MIND. WHEN WE SPEAK ABOUT A GARDEN OF EDEN IS NOT A LITERAL GARDEN SOMEWHERE ON EARTH BUT A "STATE OF CONSCIOUSNESS AND ENERGY." THE GARDEN CONCEPT IS USED TO MAKE THIS DIFFICULT AND COMPLEX CONCEPT MORE UNDERSTANDABLE.

AS YOU WILL RECALL, AS "THE PRIMORDIAL BEING OF ENERGY" IS BORN AS IN "BOTH BINAH AND CHOKMAH" FUSIONING A HALF OF EACH OTHER TO CREATE A THIRD PRINCIPLE —-- WHO IS BOTH "YIN-YANG," THESE TWO FORCES EXIST IN A STATE OF PERFECT UNION AND EQUILIBRIUM AND BALANCE JUST AS IT IS IN THE CASE OF "MEDITATION PRACTICES TO FOCUS AND CALM AND TRANSCEND THE FRAGMENTED OR SPLIT MIND."

BOTH ENERGIES ARE IN A STATE OF UNITY WHICH REPRESENTS DA-AT OR ADAM KADM-EN THE "ONE WHO IS TWO WHO IS THREE." ADAM "KAD-MEN" AS IN ADAM THE MAN OR PRIMORDIAL CONSCIOUS AND THINKING BEING. THE COSMIC MENOS AND MIND. THE GENDER NEUTRAL BEING WHO BECOMES –MALE + FEMALE —OR —YIN + YANG —UNTIL IT SPLITS AND DESCENDS OR EXPANDS OR FALLS AND —FRAGMENTS ITSELF IN ORDER TO BUILD THE COSMOS. THE "WO-MEN" IN THE FORM OF HUMAN THAT HAVE FALLEN INTO THIS REALM OF MATTER IN ORDER TO COME BACK UP AGAIN "SHINING BRIGHT LIKE DIAMONDS."

THIS STATE OF FRAGMENTATION IS WHAT IS REFERRED TO AS THE "FALL" OF ADAM KAD-MAN OR THE FIRST ADAM!! OR THE FIRST "COSMIC MAN" OR ENERGY BEING WHO HAD TO FALL OR FRAGMENT ITSELF IN ORDER TO BRING ABOUT LIFE. WITHOUT THAT SPLIT AND FRAGMENTATION THERE WOULD BE NO ACTIVITY AND EXCHANGE OF ENERGIES AND IDEAS. NO POSSIBILITIES!!!

THIS IS WHAT IS REFERRED TO AS THE "ORIGINAL FALL OF ADAM KAD-MAN" WHICH HAS NOTHING TO DO WITH "ORIGINAL SIN." . REMEMBER THAT "YIN STANDS FOR DEATH AND YANG FOR LIFE!!! EACH IDEA COMES IN DUALITIES. AND SO AS THE YIN AND YANG ENERGIES FALL — THE CONCEPT OF MAKING MISTAKES AND DEATH AND CHANGE IS BORN — AS WELL AS ITS OPPOSITE AS IN LIFE AND NOT MAKING MISTAKES AND STABILITY. IT'S JUST THE WAY IT IS!!!

THEREFORE, THE UNION WHICH DENOTES PERFECTION ENDS AND GIVES WAY TO — FRAGMENTATION AND IMPERFECTION. IT IS "HUMAN NATURE" AND THE NATURAL WAY EVERYTHING IS BUILT.

AND SO THE MEN-ORA AND TREE OF LIFE AND Y-ESH-WA AND DA-AT AND ADAM KAD-MAN REPRESENT THE SAME —CONCEPT— OF THE TREE OF DUALITIES OR THE "DESCENT OF THE ENERGIES" THAT BRING ABOUT THE MATERIAL - SPIRITUAL PLANE.

THE DIVINE SPARKS TRAPPED IN MATTER STAND FOR THE "ENERGY TRAPPED IN THIS MATERIAL - ENERGETIC MATRIX." WHICH IS EVERYTHING IN THIS WORLD AND COSMOS AS CONDENSED ENERGY IN VIBRATION MANIFESTING AS MATTER ACCORDING TO THE IDEAS OF THE MOTHER PRINCIPLE.

ED-ANNU STANDS FOR "THE STATE OF UNION" AND THE PARDES OF THE ANNU ENERGIES ALSO KNOWN AS ...THE GODS AND GODDESSES ...OR THE PRIMORDIAL ENERGIES OF LIFE AND CREATION. .

SINCERELY,
ADAMEVA EKAM — THE FIRST ORIGINAL "FALLEN WO-MAN"

---

## 13. "AND YOUR EYES WILL OPEN" AND BE AS "ELOHIM" KNOWING GOOD FROM EVIL —THE PROCESS OF OPENING ONE'S INNER VISION IN BINAH AND CHOKMAH—THE THIRD EYE OF HORUS

AND SO THIS DIARY IS ABOUT THE GENESIS STORY AFTER ADAM AND EVE "EAT" OF THE FRUIT OF GOOD AND EVIL AND THEIR EYES ARE "OPENED!!!" AND SO —WHAT DOES IT MEAN THAT THEIR EYES "OPENED AND WERE LIKE ELOHIM, ABLE TO TELL THE DIFFERENCE BETWEEN ONE THING AND ANOTHER?"

WELL, AS YOU WILL RECALL, THIS VERSE POINTS TO A HUMAN'S ABILITY TO "NOTICE" NOT ONLY LITERALLY BUT INTERNALLY. ABLE TO DISTINGUISH BETWEEN "CHOICES AND OBJECTS." THIS IS WHAT THE WORLD OF DUALITY IS ABOUT.

WE HAVE EXPLAINED ABOUT THE FUNCTIONS AND QUALITIES OF BOTH "BINAH THE DARK FIERCE MOTHER ENERGY" AND "CHOKMA THE LIGHT SOFT FATHER ENERGY" IN THE TREE OF GOOD AND EVIL OR OF DUALITY AND OPPOSITES AND CORRESPONDENCES.

"THE SYMBOL OF THE –EYE" IS KEY HERE AS —WE MEAN —THE ONE EYE —-BECAUSE WHEN BOTH BINAH AND CHOKMAH ARE IN SYNC AND "ACTIVE"

IN A HUMAN, THEY ACT AS "ONE EYE IN UNION AND INTEGRATION." THIS "INNER EYE" OR "OCULUS" LET'S YOU NOTICE BOTH "THE DARK CONTENTS OF YOUR OWN SHADOW SELF AND CHARACTER FLAWS" AS WELL AS "THE LIGHT IN YOU AND THE GOOD QUALITIES AND TALENTS YOU POSSESS!!!"

WHEN YOU ARE ABLE TO ——-SEE AND NOTICE BOTH CLEARLY!!!, YOU ARE INTO SOMETHING… VERY SPECIAL. BOTH YOUR "MASCULINE EYE AND YOUR FEMININE INNER EYE" WHICH CORRESPOND TO BOTH CHOKMAH AND BINAH RESPECTIVELY, ARE IN SYNC AND WORKING TOGETHER ENABLING YOU TO "KNOW AND SEE YOURSELF MORE CLEARLY" AND "THE WORLD AROUND YOU TOO." YOU HAVE BECOME "THE ALL SEEING EYE OF HORUS!!!"

AND SO WHAT HAPPENS WHEN ONLY "ONE EYE IS OPEN, BUT NOT THE OTHER" IN A PSYCHOLOGICAL MANNER? WELL, WE END UP NOTICING ONLY THE BAD IN OURSELVES AND DENY THE GOOD IN OURSELVES OR, WE END UP NOTICING ONLY THE GOOD IN OURSELVES AND DENYING OUR DARK SIDE OR SHADOW. THE "INNER VISION" IS INCOMPLETE WHICH CAUSES IMBALANCES SUCH AS — BEING IN THE DARK ALL THE TIME OR MOST OF THE TIME AS IN BEING PESSIMIST OR ACTING OUT OUR OWN SHADOW;" OR, JUST "BEING OVER OPTIMISTIC AND FAILING TO NOTICE THE DANGERS THAT LURK AROUND US OR SIMPLY GIVING TOTALLY INTO PLEASURE."

AND SO AS YOU CAN SEE WE NEED TO HONE AND OPEN BOTH "OUR INNER BINAH AND CHOKMAH" WHICH CORRESPOND TO THE HUMAN EYES RESPECTIVELY AND BRING BALANCE AND COMMUNICATION BETWEEN BOTH. THE ONE CASTING LIGHT ON THE OTHER, AND THE OTHER CASTING THE SHADOW UPON THE LIGHT AT THE SAME TIME. BOTH TEMPERING EACH OTHER AND ACKNOWLEDGING EACH OTHER'S EXISTENCE.

BOTH EYES IN A STATE OF SEEING AND NOTICING EACH OTHER CONTRIBUTE TO ONE'S ABILITY TO NOTICE BOTH THE GOOD AND THE BAD AND THE —IN BETWEEN STATES – WHERE THINGS MIGHT NOT BE TOTALLY GOOD OR BAD BUT BOTH AT THE SAME TIME OR NEUTRAL.

Taoism teaches that the third eye, also called the mind's eye, is situated between the two physical eyes, and expands up to the middle of the forehead when opened. (WIKIPEDIA)

SINCERELY,
THE "ALL SEEING EYE OF HORUS"

---

**14.** **"AND MY EYES WERE OPEN" WHEN I REACHED OUT FOR THE "TREE OF KNOWLEDGE" OF "GOOD AND EVIL" AND BEGAN TO NOTICE THE "GOOD AND EVIL IN THE HEATHENS" AND THE "GOOD AND EVIL IN THE BELIEVERS"**

PLEASE, DO NOT TAKE THIS AS AN ATTACK. IT IS JUST A STUDY AND REFLECTION ON MY EXPERIENCES WITH BOTH PEOPLES AND MY OBSERVATIONS THRU PERSONAL AND NON PERSONAL EXPERIENCE.

WHEN I WAS "WITHIN THE CONFINES OF THE ENCLOSURE" I WAS "WARNED" THAT PEOPLE IN GENERAL WHO DID NOT "BELONG" TO MY GROUP WERE "DANGEROUS AND EVIL HEATHENS." HEATHENS JUST BECAUSE THEY DID NOT BELIEVE WHAT I BELIEVED AND READ WHAT I READ AND DID NOT BELONG TO "THE RIGHT PEOPLE." AND SO "BY AN ACT OF GOD" LATER ON IN MY LIFE I FOUND MYSELF" ON THE OTHER SIDE OF THE FENCE" AND LABELED — ONE OF THE MANY STIGMAS —SUCH AS "BAD ASSOCIATION," HERETIC, APOSTATE, POSSESSED, FORSAKEN BY GOD, ETC. AND SO JUST LIKE "MARIA OWENS" WHO ENDED UP "SHUNNED" BY THE RELIGIOUS COMMUNITY IN SALEM, SO WAS I.

AND SO "I BEGAN TO NOTICE THE DISCREPANCY BETWEEN THE GOSPEL ACCOUNT OF YESHUA'S APPROACH AND ATTITUDE TOWARDS THE OUTCAST WHOM HE ADVOCATED FOR" WHICH IS THE TOTAL OPPOSITE OF THAT WHICH I WAS EXPERIENCING BY THE ONES CLAIMING TO STAND UP FOR "JESUS AND CHRISTIAN LOVE." AND SO AS I BEGIN MY "EXILE" AWAY FROM "THE COMMUNITY" AND LIVING IN THE MARGINS OF "SALEM, MASSACHUSETTS," I END UP MEETING ALONG THE WAY "SO CALLED HEATHENS AND OUTCASTS AND REGULAR FOLK" WHO ARE NOT RELIGIOUS OR WHO FOLLOW ALTERNATIVE SPIRITUAL PATHS BUT THAT ACTUALLY — GET TO TREAT ME "LIKE A FELLOW HUMAN." I WAS SHOCKED TO NOTICE THAT "RELIGIOUS DOGMA" WAS ACTUALLY GETTING IN THE WAY FOR "THE RELIGIOUS COMMUNITY" TO REALLY LIVE AND UPHOLD THE "CHRISTIAN LOVE." AS YESHUA HIMSELF STATED — THERE IS NO MERIT IN LOVING OR SHOWING CONSIDERATION TO ONLY THOSE WHO "ARE LIKE YOU AND WHO LOVE YOU BACK."

DO NOT GET ME WRONG. I HAVE MET VERY NICE PEOPLE IN ALL TRADITIONS, INCLUDING THE MONOTHEISTIC. AND JUST LIKE "MARIA OWENS" ONCE YOU LEAVE, YOU ARE ALSO MOURNING THE PROCESS OF LEAVING BEHIND YOUR FRIENDS. FRIENDS WHO MIGHT OTHERWISE STILL

REACH OUT TO YOU IF IT WASN'T BECAUSE OF THE "RULES, LAWS AND REGULATIONS" OF THOSE INTERPRETING AND APPLYING THE SCRIPTURE IN A CERTAIN WAY. THE "AUTHORITY" OF THE CHURCH OR SYNAGOGUE OR MOSQUE.

SO THE POINT I WOULD LIKE TO MAKE IS THAT — THERE IS "GOOD" PEOPLE WITHIN ALL RELIGIONS AND THERE ARE ALSO "THOSE INCLINED TOWARDS CRUELTY" THAT WOULD JUSTIFY THAT CRUELTY ON THE BASIS OF RELIGIOUS DOCTRINE. BUT THE SAME GOES FOR THOSE ON THE OTHER SIDE OF THE FENCE. THERE ARE "THOSE SO-CALLED HEATHENS INCLINED TO CRUELTY" AS WELL AS THOSE WHO UNKNOWINGLY AND DESPITE HAVING NO RELIGION AT ALL, TREAT THEIR FELLOW HUMAN BEING WITH AUTHENTIC "CHRISTIAN LOVE" UNLIKE THE "CHRISTIAN" NEXT DOOR.

SO THIS EXPERIENCE MADE ME THINK ABOUT SOMETHING VERY INTERESTING WHEN I BEGAN TO NOTICE THAT "I HAD MET CERTAIN PEOPLE" ALONG THE WAY THAT DO NOT FOLLOW ANY TRADITION BUT THAT CARRY THEMSELVES AND TREAT OTHERS IN AN ETHICAL AND MORAL AND CONSIDERATE WAY. SINCE THEY DO NOT FOLLOW A RELIGION OR CARE ABOUT ANY GOD, WHERE DOES THAT "GOODNESS AND INCLINATION TO TREAT THEIR FELLOW MAN AS THEY WOULD LIKE TO BE TREATED" COMES FROM?

AND SO THIS BRINGS ME BACK TO THE "BUDDHIST TEACHING" THAT — WE ARE ALL INNATELY "GOOD." WE ARE BORN WITH BASIC GOODNESS. AND THAT "THAT GOODNESS EVENTUALLY IS COVERED UP ALONG THE JOURNEY OF LIFE THROUGH OUR OWN EXPERIENCES AND TRAUMAS AND EVILS AND CONDITIONINGS AND RELIGION AND FAMILY AND SOCIETY AND EVERYTHING ELSE."

IT HAS TO DO WITH "THE BELIEFS" WE HAVE BEEN PROGRAMMED WITH. IF YOU ARE TAUGHT THAT "OTHERS UNLIKE YOU ARE EVIL" FROM A VERY YOUNG AGE, THAT IS WHAT YOU WILL BELIEVE AND YOU WILL VIEW THE WORLD FROM A LENS OF "FEAR." YOU WILL GO THROUGH LIFE SEEING OTHERS AS DIFFERENT FROM YOURSELF AND "REACTING WITH FEAR AND MISTRUST" AT "THE OTHER" CREATING "PERCEIVED ENEMIES THAT ARE NOT REALLY THERE." ON THE OTHER HAND, IF YOU ARE RAISED AS A CHILD TO "EMBRACE THE WORLD AS IT IS AND TO EXTEND RESPECT AND CONSIDERATION TOWARDS OTHERS" THAT IS THE APPROACH YOU WILL HAVE TOWARDS PEOPLE AND THE ENERGY OF INCLUSION YOU WILL PUT OUT.

THIS IS WHY "IT IS IMPORTANT TO QUESTION AND REFLECT" ON THE "BELIEFS" THAT WE ARE PROGRAMMED WITH BY SOCIETY, FAMILY,

CHURCH, INSTITUTION, POLITIC, ETC. BECAUSE "THIS PARTICULAR BELIEF" WILL HAVE AN IMPACT ON OUR LIVES AND THE WORLD AROUND US. AN IMPACT THAT CAN BE FOR GOOD AND WELL-BEING OR FOR EVIL AND PAIN AND CHAOS.

THEREFORE, IT'S ALL RELATIVE. A RELIGIOUS TRADITION DOES NOT GUARANTEE THAT YOU WILL APPROACH THE WORLD IN A TRULY SPIRITUAL WAY AND NEITHER DOES HAVING NO RELIGION GUARANTEES YOU WILL BE AN "EVIL PERSON." WE MUST LOOK AT THE WHOLE PICTURE AND LOOK AT HUMANITY COLLECTIVELY. WE ALL—RELIGIOUS AND NON RELIGIOUS—ARE BORN WITH THE INCLINATION TO BOTH GOOD AND EVIL. AND IT IS AN INTRINSIC AND INHERENT PART OF THE HUMAN CONDITION AND THE PLANET ITSELF. EVERYONE HAS THE POTENTIAL TO DO GREAT THINGS AS WELL AS TO DO HORRIBLE ONES GIVEN THE "BELIEFS AND CIRCUMSTANCES" THAT WILL TRIGGER THIS PART TO COME OUT. THEREFORE THE "LABELING OF PEOPLE IN GENERAL AS EVIL" BY THOSE WHO CLAIM TO BE "GOOD" IS NOT ACCURATE BECAUSE" THE EVIL YOU SEE IN OTHERS ALSO RESIDES WITHIN YOU" NO MATTER HOW PURE AND PERFECT YOU TRY TO BE. IT'S LIKE BY SEEING THE EVIL IN OTHERS YOU ARE SEEING AS WELL THE EVIL IN YOURSELF.

THAT IS WHAT AUTHENTIC SPIRITUAL TRADITION AND PHILOSOPHY AND TEACHING IS POINTING TO US — TO REMIND US OF OUR "INNATE GOODNESS" IN RELATION TO OUR OWN SHADOW. WHEN WE BECOME "AWARE" OF THAT EVIL IN OURSELVES, WE START TO "LEARN ABOUT OUR WHOLE SELF" AND TO CHANNEL THAT STRONG DARK ENERGY FOR GOOD AND PRODUCTIVE PURPOSES. IT'S ALL ABOUT ENERGY AFTER ALL.

THE "TREE OF GOOD AND EVIL" IS A DIAGRAM OF "A HUMAN BEING AS WELL AS THE COSMOS." MEANING THAT EVERYONE IS "MADE UP OF THE LIGHT AND THE DARK." MANY RELIGIOUS AND NON RELIGIOUS PEOPLE COMMIT ATROCITIES BECAUSE THEY ARE NOT AWARE OF THEIR OWN EVIL INCLINATION. THEY COMMIT EVIL DEEDS BUT "LACK THE AWARENESS" TO BE ABLE TO NOTICE AND TELL "GOOD ENERGY FROM EVIL ENERGY" AND SO END UP DOING EVIL BELIEVING THAT THEY ARE DOING THE RIGHT THING OR NOTHING DESTRUCTIVE AT ALL. IT IS THE PURPOSE OF TRUE SPIRITUAL TEACHING TO HELP PEOPLE DISTINGUISH AND DISCERN ONE ENERGY FROM ANOTHER SO THAT THEY ARE "AWARE" OF BOTH ENERGY QUALITIES AND DO NOT END UP CONFUSING ONE THING WITH THE OTHER. THAT IS WHAT "AND YOU WILL BE LIKE US KNOWING GOOD FROM EVIL" IN A PHILOSOPHICAL SENSE MEANS.

THEREFORE, SOMEONE WHO IS UNABLE TO TELL THAT" MURDER AND HATE "FOR INSTANCE ARE EVIL ENERGIES AND RENDERS THESE "GOOD"

IS NOT A "SPIRITUALLY ATTUNED" PERSON REGARDLESS OF HOW MUCH RELIGION AND DOCTRINE AND HOURS HE OR SHE SPENDS PRAYING. "THEIR EYES ARE NOT YET OPEN" AS THESE "EYES" ARE NOT ONLY LITERAL BUT STAND FOR "UNDERSTANDING AND DISCERNMENT" OR THE "INNER SPIRITUAL EYES OF UNDERSTANDING AND WISDOM TO TELL THE DIFFERENCE."

SINCERELY,
H-ORUS

---

**15. IF THE CLERGY HAVE ACCESS TO "GOD" LIKE THEY CLAIM, SO DO I AND —-YOU TOO. HOW COME I CAN ALSO INTERPRET THE SCRIPTURES: THE CASE OF ADAM AND EVE AND THE TREE OF GOOD AND EVIL (2012)**

YOU KNOW "WHAT HAS BEEN HAPPENING" SINCE 2012, RIGHT? SINCE I BECAME "MANIC" AND I BEGAN TO "CHANNEL AND WRITE AND INTERPRET" ALL SORTS OF INFORMATION AND SCRIPTURES. AND THE FIRST "SCRIPTURE" I WAS ABLE TO INTERPRET / CHANNEL ACCORDINGLY TO "MY" OWN UNDERSTANDING WAS WHAT WAS COMING THRU ME OR WAS BEING CHANNELED THRU ME" WAS THE STORY OF GENESIS OF ADAM AND EVE. AND SO HERE I WILL GIVE A BRIEF INTERPRETATION ACCORDING TO HOW THE "DIVINE MANIA OR MADNESS" WAS ENABLING ME TO SEE AND TO UNDERSTAND THINGS I WAS NOT ABLE TO SEE AND UNDERSTAND BEFORE.

ADAM AND EVE .... AND THAT WONDERFUL TREE OF "DUALITY OR OF POLAR OPPOSITES" THAT COMPLEMENT EACH OTHER IS A DIAGRAM OR SYMBOL THAT REPRESENTS THE MATERIAL UNIVERSE IN WHICH WE FIND OURSELVES AND WHICH IS — RULED BY THE LAWS OF POLARITIES AND DUALITIES AND OPPOSITES THAT ALSO COMPLEMENT ONE ANOTHER.

THE FACT THAT –ADAM AND EVE—-

.......ARE SAID TO BE "IN A STATE OF INNOCENCE" BEFORE "EATING OF THE TREE OF DUALITY OR OPPOSITES" POINTS TO A STATE OF INFANCY AND UN-CONSCIOUSNESS. IF THE SCRIPTURE STATES THAT THEIR EYES OPENED AFTER EATING OF THE FRUIT OF "DUALITY AND POLARITY" IT MEANS THAT THEY WERE UNABLE TO "NOTICE THE DIFFERENCE BETWEEN GOOD AND EVIL BEFORE THAT EVENT AND "THEIR STATE OF CONSCIOUSNESS OR UNDERSTANDING WAS LIMITED JUST LIKE CHILDREN" BEFORE EATING OF THAT "FRUIT."

IN OTHER WORDS, BEFORE THE FALL, DEITY HAD TO TELL ADAM AND EVE WHAT TO DO AND WHERE TO GO AND WHAT TO THINK ETC. JUST LIKE CHILDREN. THE FACT THEY WERE NOT ABLE TO TELL "ONE THING FROM ANOTHER" BEFORE EATING OF THE TREE OF POLARITY MEANS THAT "THEY WERE NOT ABLE TO MAKE DECISIONS AND MAKE CHOICES" BECAUSE IN ORDER TO BE ABLE TO MAKE DECISIONS, YOU NEED TO BE ABLE TO TELL THE DIFFERENCE BETWEEN "TWO DIFFERENT OPTIONS" AND UNDERSTAND WHAT THOSE DIFFERENCES ARE ABOUT AND TIL THEN THAT WAS NOT THE CASE BEFORE THE SO CALLED "FALL" OF ADAM AND EVE.

THEREFORE, THEY HAD "NO FREE WILL" EITHER BECAUSE IN ORDER TO HAVE "FREE WILL" YOU NEED TO HAVE THE ABILITY AND FREEDOM TO MAKE CHOICES, TO MAKE DECISIONS BASED ON THOSE PAIRS OF OPPOSITES AND THE ABILITY TO TELL THE DIFFERENCE BETWEEN "GOOD AND EVIL." GOOD AND EVIL —SIMPLY REFERS TO ALL DUALITIES SUCH AS BLACK AND WHITE, SAD AND HAPPY, UP AND DOWN, ETC. ETC. ETC.

THEREFORE HUMANITY WAS IN A STATE OF "IGNORANCE AND INNOCENCE" BEFORE THE "FALL." THEY WERE BASICALLY "CLUELESS" AND THEIR "HUMAN EVOLUTION" WAS LIMITED TO FOLLOWING ORDERS AND THE INABILITY TO "SEE THIS REALITY AS IT TRULY IS."

AND SO ADAM AND EVE EVENTUALLY "EAT FROM THE TREE OF DUALITY" AND THEIR "EYES OPEN" AND THEY ARE ABLE TO SEE LIKE THE DIVINE!!! THE SERPENT THEREFORE WAS NOT LYING!!! THIS IS ALL METAPHORICAL AND SYMBOLIC FOR THE "EVOLUTION OF MAN." AND SO, THEY FALL AND ARE ABLE TO FINALLY "NOTICE" THE NATURE OF REALITY AS BEING A REALITY OF POLAR OPPOSITES THAT ALSO COMPLEMENT EACH OTHER. THANKS TO THE DARK, THEY ARE ABLE TO FINALLY NOTICE THE LIGHT. ETC. ETC. ETC.

YOU WILL NOTICE THAT "BOTH THEIR EYES OPEN" WHICH POINTS TO "TWO EYES" AND SO IT ALL POINTS TO THE ABILITY OF HUMANS TO BE AWARE OF THIS DUALITY THROUGH THE DUAL NATURE OF HUMAN VISION THROUGH THE TWIN EYES OF UNDERSTANDING AND WISDOM."

AFTER THE "FALL," ADAM AND EVE ARE NO LONGER LIKE "CHILDREN" BUT ARE NOW IN A PATH OF HUMAN EVOLUTION AND INDEPENDENCE. NOT HAVING SOMEONE TELLING THEM ALL THE TIME WHAT TO DO AND WHAT TO THINK BUT ....GAINING THE ABILITY AND FREEDOM OF MAKING CHOICES THANKS THAT NOW THEY CAN NOTICE DIFFERENCES AND GRADATIONS AND DUALITIES. AND SO THEY ARE ABLE TO —MAKE DECISIONS BASED ON TWO OR MORE OPTIONS. AS A RESULT OF THIS EVOLUTIONARY PROCESS, NOW ADAM AND EVE CAN MAKE THEIR OWN

MISTAKES AS WELL AND ACCORDING TO THOSE MISTAKES, BEGIN THE LEARNING PROCESS OF FALLING AND GETTING UP AND BY DOING SO ACCRUING AND GAINING "WISDOM, KNOWLEDGE AND UNDERSTANDING" OF THE MATERIAL-SPIRITUAL REALM AROUND THEM AND IN THEM.

YOU SEE, WITHOUT THE SO CALLED "FALL" THEY WOULD HAVE BEEN UNABLE TO "EVOLVE AS HUMAN BEINGS!!!" AND TO MAKE DECISIONS FOR THEMSELVES AND LEARN FROM THEIR OWN MISTAKES.

THIS IS THE INTERPRETATION THAT CAME THROUGH BACK THEN AND IT MAKES MORE SENSE THAN THE SO CALLED "ORIGINAL SIN." BASICALLY, ACCORDING TO THIS INTERPRETATION, IT WAS ALL SUPPOSED TO HAPPEN THIS WAY. AGAIN, THIS STORY IS "METAPHOR AND SYMBOLIC" AND NOT A LITERAL EVENT ABOUT EATING FROM AN APPLE OR FIG TREE. IT REPRESENTS OR POINTS TO THE "DUALITY OF OUR WORLD AND UNIVERSE" AND "THE EVOLUTIONARY PROCESS OF HUMAN BEINGS AND THEIR ALSO ...DUAL NATURES JUST LIKE THE COSMOS THEY INHABIT."

SINCERELY,
"THE SERPENT" OF THE TREE OF GOOD AND EVIL AND OF "KNOWLEDGE"

---

## 16.  THE "FIRST CAUSE AND EFFECT" AND THE "COSMIC SYSTEM OF CHECKS AND BALANCES:" THE EVOLUTION OF THE HUMAN SOUL

THEREFORE, LIKE WE EXPLAINED BEFORE, THE FIRST "CAUSE" IS DA-AT OR THE PRIMORDIAL DIVINE ANDROGYNE WHO IS "TWO AS ONE." THE ONE SPLITS IN TWO AND FRAGMENTS FROM ONE ANOTHER IN ORDER FOR THE COSMIC COITUS BETWEEN DUALITIES YIN AND YANG TO TAKE PLACE. THE DIVINE MASCULINE AND DIVINE FEMININE ARE BORN OF THE "DIVINE BISEXUAL ANDROGYNE WO-MAN" INTERDEPENDENT ENERGETIC SEED AND SYSTEM.

THE "FIRST CAUSE" BECOMES "THE FALL OR SPLIT OR FRAGMENTATION OF ADAMEVA KAD-M-UNNI" FROM WHICH EVERY OTHER CAUSE IS PRODUCED FROM THAT COSMIC "PRIMORDIAL FALL." AND SO AS HUMANS ARE BORN OF THIS PRIMORDIAL EFFECT OR TZIM-TZOOOOMMM EFFECT, THEY ALSO SHARE OF THIS PATTERN OF "CAUSE AND EFFECT" THAT IS INHERENT IN CREATION FROM THE VERY BEGINNING AND THAT SPREADS LIKE A RIPPLE EFFECT EVERYWHERE HERE AND IN ALL OTHER WORLDS AND UNIVERSES.

AND SO "HUMAN ACTION AND ACTIVITY" IS PART OF THIS CONDITION OF "CAUSE AND EFFECT" AS MIND AND ENERGY FROM BINAH AND CHOKMAH

THROUGH THE DIVINE ANDROGYNE PASSES ON LIKE A —DNA— TO HUMAN BEINGS AND ALL LIVING FORMS.

WHAT WE ARE TRYING TO SAY IS THAT .....

THE CAUSE AND EFFECT PATTERN IS THERE FOR EVOLUTIONARY PURPOSES AS THESE LEAD TO CONTINUOUS CHANGE AND CHANGE CAN BE FOR THE BETTER IF WE LEARN FROM IT. IT IS BECAUSE OF MISTAKES AND FALLING DOWN THAT WE GET UP AND LEARN FROM THAT MISTAKE OR CAUSE SO THAT WE CHOOSE WISELY NEXT TIME. AND SO WE GET TO LEARN TO TELL RIGHT FROM WRONG. THE CAUSE AND EFFECT PROCESS IS NOT ONLY A PATTERN OF LEARNING AND COSMIC EVOLUTION BUT ALSO A "COSMIC JUSTICE SYSTEM." IT'S THE SOURCE OF "UNDERSTANDING" THIS REALITY AND THE CAUSE AND EFFECTS OF THINGS AND ACTIONS AND THEIR INTERDEPENDENCE AND INTERACTIONS.

WHAT WE MEAN TO SAY IS THAT ... EVERYTHING IN THE UNIVERSE AND IN THE EARTH IS INTERCONNECTED IN A WEB OF LIFE AND SO WHEN ONE THING GOES DOWN OR UP EVENTUALLY ALONG THE WAY, SOMETHING ELSE HAS TO GO UP AND DOWN AS WELL IN ORDER TO COMPENSATE FOR THE EFFECT SO THAT THE SYSTEM OF COSMIC DEBITS AND CREDITS BALANCES ITSELF AND THE WHOLE THING DOES NOT END UP BECOMING A CHAOTIC MESS AND CRASHING.

THEREFORE, WHEN I HARM SOMEONE I CAN EXPECT SOME SORT OF JUSTICE MECHANISM TO HAPPEN SOONER OR LATER IN MY ACTIONS THAT WILL CAUSE AN EFFECT; AND, BECAUSE OF THAT EFFECT I WILL LEARN THAT WHAT I DID WAS NOT COOL AND I MIGHT END UP TAKING ANOTHER ROAD AND WORKING FOR LOVE AND JUSTICE. JUST AN EXAMPLE. AND SO —COSMIC JUSTICE WAS SERVED.

AND SO LIKE THE MAXIM SAYS — AS ABOVE SO IS BELOW AND AS BELOW SO IS ABOVE OR THE INTERDEPENDENCY AND INTERCONNECTEDNESS BETWEEN HUMAN AND COSMOS.

SO HERE IS WHERE —DABBLING WITH MAGIC FOR SELFISH AND UNETHICAL PURPOSES —OR WANTING TO CHANGE AND CONTROL LIFE AND CIRCUMSTANCES COMES IN AS IT SABOTAGES THE ENTIRE PROCESS AND SYSTEM AND HUMANS NEVER LEARN THE LESSONS THEY MUST LEARN IN ORDER FOR THEIR SOULS TO KEEP EVOLVING!!!

SINCERELY,
ADAMAS THE WIZ-ARD

## 17. "THE FEAR OF GOD" VS. "THE FEAR OF OUR ACTION'S CONSEQUENCES"--WE ARE BOTH THE CAUSE AND THE EFFECT IN THE SPIDER GRANDMOTHER'S WEB OF LIGHT AND ENERGY (A REFLECTION AND INTERPRETATION)

LIKE WE SAID BEFORE, THE BIBLE IS A BOOK OF STORIES AND THE DEITY IN THE TANAKI AND THROUGHOUT THE HEBREW BIBLE REPRESENTS THE "YIN YANG" ENERGIES HAVING AN EFFECT IN THE LIVES OF PEOPLE. THIS IS NOT LITERAL BUT SYMBOLIC AND METAPHYSICAL. THE FACT THAT THE DEITY IN THESE BOOKS "CHANGES CONSIDERABLY" IN ITS INTERACTIONS WITH THE PEOPLE FROM "ANGRY TO HAPPY" AND FROM "HURT TO JOYFUL" POINTS TO US THAT WE ARE SPEAKING OF THE "DUAL NATURE OF REALITY, OUR HUMAN AND COSMIC REALITY."

IN THE TANAKI "GOD PUNISHES AND GOD REWARDS" WHICH POINTS TO THE CONCEPT OF "DIVINE JUSTICE "BUT IT IS SYMBOLIC AND METAPHORICAL TO WHAT WE WILL REVEAL LATER. GOD IS ALSO A PERSONIFICATION OF THE "TREE OF GOOD AND EVIL" ITSELF."

BASICALLY, THE "YIN-YANG" ENERGIES ARE THE BASIC UNITS OF EXISTENCE AND THE "PRIMORDIAL CAUSE AND EFFECT." THEREFORE, IT IS LIKE AN INTERCONNECTED WEB OF ENERGY LIKE A SPIDERWEB IN WHICH ONE SILKY THREAD IS TOUCHED AND AS A RESULT THE REST OF THE WEB MOVES AND RESPONDS. THE SPIDER IN THE MIDDLE OF THE WEB REPRESENTS THE "YIN-YANG" ENERGIES OR THE SOURCE THAT KEEPS THE ENTIRE WEB SYSTEM ALIVE AND FUNCTIONING. THAT SPIDER REPRESENTS THE "PRIMORDIAL EFFECT" IN THAT WHEN SOMETHING HAPPENS IN ONE LINK IT NATURALLY AFFECTS THE REST OF THE WEB. AS A RESULT OF THIS MOTION AND ACTION IN THE WEB, THE SPIDER OR THE EFFECT MOVES TO THE POINT OF MOVEMENT AND ACTION BECOMING A "CAUSE" WHICH STARTS A CHAIN REACTION" OF CAUSES AND EFFECTS.

THERE IS NO PUNISHMENT AND REWARD INVOLVED SINCE IT IS THE NATURAL LAW THAT ANY ACTION WHETHER GOOD OR EVIL WILL CAUSE A NATURAL REACTION ON THE REST OF THE WEB OF LIFE WHICH WILL COME BACK TO THE POINT OF ACTION OR THE CAUSE. IT'S A SYSTEM OF DEBITS AND CREDITS!

AND SO IMAGINE THAT "YIN-YANG," THE FIRST CAUSE, LEADS TO A CONTINUUM OF EFFECTS THAT REPRESENTS THE TIME - SPACE -MATERIAL CONTINUUM. YOU AND I THEREFORE ARE A NATURAL "EFFECT" OF THIS FIRST "CAUSE" OR POINT OF ORIGIN. THEREFORE WE ARE ENERGETICALLY LINKED DIRECTLY. AN ENERGY WEB THAT CONVERGES

AND INTERSECTS WITH EVERYBODY ELSE'S INCLUDING NATURE. AND SO WHEN I MAKE A MISTAKE I BECOME A CAUSE THAT WILL REVERBERATE ENERGETICALLY IN ORDER TO BRING THE WEB OR SYSTEM BACK TO BALANCE AND SO SOMETHING" GOOD OR EVIL" WILL COME BACK TO ME WHETHER IN THIS LIFE OR THE NEXT IN ORDER TO MAKE SURE DIVINE LESSON AND DIVINE RECTIFICATION TAKES PLACE.

WHAT WE MEAN TO SAY IS THAT AS "YOU AND I" ARE "IMAGES AND LIKENESSES" OF THE POINT OF ORIGIN AND LINKED AND CONNECTED TO IT, WE BECOME AS WELL "CAUSES" SUCH AS THE POINT OF ORIGIN ITSELF AND SO WE WILL EVENTUALLY PRODUCE EFFECTS OF OUR OWN." FOR INSTANCE. IF THE "TIGER ATTACKS A HUMAN, THE CAUSE OF THE PAIN WILL HAVE AN EFFECT ON HUMAN WHO WILL TURN AROUND AND GO AFTER THE TIGER." DID THE TIGER SIN? NOPE! IT IS THE WAY THE TIGER IS AND AS ITS ACTION REVERBERATED IN A NEGATIVE WAY ON THE REST OF THE WEB, IT WILL HAVE AN EFFECT SOONER OR LATER." ONE OF THE REASONS SOME MONKS MEDITATE DAILY FOR 24 HOURS IN ORDER TO DISCONNECT FROM THE "CAUSE AND EFFECT" PROCESS BY STAYING STILL AND QUIET AND NOT INTERACTING WITH THE WEB THEREFORE THE ACTION - REACTION NATURAL RESPONSES ARE SUSPENDED BY OUR NON-ACTION AND NON-ATTACHMENT.

FOR INSTANCE, THE HOLOCAUST WAS A TERRIBLE EVENT THAT REVERBERATED ALL OVER. THE ACTION WAS EVIL AND YOU DID NOT SEE THE HEAVENS OPEN LIKE IN THE MOVIES AND DIVINE BEINGS COMING DOWN TO STOP IT. THE NATURAL REACTION TO THE EVIL WAS BOTH AN EQUAL REACTION FROM THE WEB AS IN "FIERY ATTACK FROM THE ALLIES" AND THE WEB OR SYSTEM WAS BROUGHT BACK TO RELATIVE BALANCE BY "THE LIBERATION OF THE OPPRESSED AND THE INSTITUTION OF THE 1948 HUMAN RIGHTS UNIVERSAL DECLARATION" IN EUROPE.

THE FOLLOWING ARE THE PRINCIPLES THAT ARE THE NATURAL LAWS OF SPIDER GRANDMOTHERS WEB OF LIFE AND ENERGY. THESE ARE THE 7 PRINCIPLES OF THE KYBA-LION:

- The principle of mentalism.
- The principle of correspondence.
- The principle of vibration.
- The principle of polarity.
- The principle of rhythm.
- The principle of cause and effect.
- The principle of gender.

SO THERE IS INDEED "DIVINE JUSTICE" BUT NOT IN THE SENSE OF GOD PUNISHING AND REWARDING PEOPLE AS HE OR SHE LIKES. IT'S ABOUT A JUST SYSTEM "OF CHECKS AND BALANCES" THAT STARTS WITH US AND ENDS WITH US ACCORDING TO THE 7 PRINCIPLES OF THE KYBALION WHICH INCLUDES THE "LAW OF KARMA."

BY THE WAY THE TERM "KYBA" MEANS:

Kyba name meaning is Inspiring, Master of their own DESTINY, Intuitive and Kyba is a Boy name. The Numerology Number for the name Kyba is 3. Below, you will learn how to pronounce Kyba and discover interesting details such as name popularity, numerology reading and more specific to the name Kyba.(NAMES LOOK)

AS WE CAN SEE FROM THE NAME KYBA ABOVE, WE FIND THAT KYBA MEANS TO BE A "MASTER OF YOUR OWN DESTINY" BY MEANS OF ONE'S ACTIONS WHETHER "GOOD OR EVIL" OR THROUGH NON-REACTION! THEREFORE, WE ARE BEINGS WITH GREAT POWER TO "BLESS AND OR TO CURSE." BUT AS WITH EVERYTHING, EVERY ACTION WILL CAUSE A REACTION AND EVERY CAUSE, AN EFFECT. JUST AS ADAM-KAD-M-ONNE aka THE "YIN-YANG" TWINS, WE ARE BOTH A "CAUSE AND AN EFFECT" AS WELL TO OURSELVES AND TO OTHERS. THE WEB OF LIFE OF ENERGY IS ACTIVE IN US AND AROUND US!

THERE IS A POINT WHERE "DIVINE ENERGIES" DO MANIFEST BUT THAT WILL BE FOR ANOTHER TIME.

SINCERELY, "SPIDER GRANDMOTHER" OR BINAH THE "BLUEPRINT" OF THE WEB OF LIFE AND "THE SUN" OR CHOKMAH ENERGIES ANIMATING THE BLUEPRINT WITH LIVING ENERGY

---

## 18. THE "TETRA-GRAMMAT-ONE" AND THE "MALE TO FEMALE, FEMALE TO MALE" ===4!!!

TETRA === 4!
GRAMMA== LETTER (GREEK)
T-ONNE ==THE ONE OR UNION OF THE 4

AS WE HAVE EXPLAINED ALREADY THE NUMBER "4" IS THE NUMBER OF THE TETRA-GRAMMAT-ONE OR THE NAME GIVEN TO "DEITY" IN THE TANAKI.

ALL TRADITIONS HAVE BEEN POINTING TO THE SAME COSMIC CONCEPTS WHICH BECOME VERY CLEAR IN THE "TREE OF DUALITY" DIAGRAM OR BLUEPRINT OF THE UNIVERSE FROM ITS MACROCOSM DOWN TO THE MICROCOSM. THE MICROCOSM BEING A HOLOGRAM OF THE MACROCOSM. WE CAN OBSERVE FROM THE "SACRED UNIVERSAL TREE" ARCHETYPE THAT WE ARE ALL INTERCONNECTED TO THE "TREE OF LIFE OR WORLD TREE." AS ABOVE ARE THE BRANCHES OF THE TREE OF THE WORLD TREE, SO IT IS AS BELOW IN THE ROOTS OF THE TREE—AND SO IS THE TRUNK OF THE TREE REPRESENTING THE "MIDDLE WORLD" WHICH IS FED AND SUSTAINED BY THESE DUAL COSMIC POWERS AND ENERGIES.

TETRAGRAMMAT-ONE IS REPRESENTED BY FOUR HEBREW LETTERS AND THESE "FOUR HEBREW LETTERS" ARE A "CYPHER" AFTER THE "YIN -YANG SYMBOL" OF TAOISM. THE YIN-YANG SYMBOL HAS A VALUE OF 1, 2, 3, 4 AND 5. LIKE THE YIN -YANG SYMBOL, THE TETRAGRAMMATON IS A SYMBOL OF INTERDEPENDENT AND INTERCONNECTED CREATIVE FORCES — REPRESENTED BY THE WHITE OR MASCULINE YANG WHICH IS INHERENT IN THE FEMININE OR BLACK YIN ...AND... THE BLACK FEMININE YIN WHICH IS INHERENT IN THE WHITE MASCULINE YANG. DO YOU SEE HERE THE ... VALUE OF ....4?

AS IN .... MASCULINE - FEMININE, FEMININE - MASCULINE ==== 4!!!

THEREFORE, TWO OF THE LETTERS OF TETRAGRAMMATON REPRESENT THE YIN ENERGIES AND TWO OF THE LETTERS REPRESENT THE ...YANG ENERGIES OR FORCES OF NATURE AND COSMOS.

AND SO AS WE WERE SAYING IN THE PREVIOUS DIARY, MARIAMNE WAS A "GIRL" WHO WANTED TO BE A "BOY" IN ORDER TO BE TREATED WITH THE SAME RIGHTS AND DIGNITIES AND OPPORTUNITIES AS THE BOYS. AND THEN SHE IS REBORN AS A "BOY" WHO IS A "GIRL" WITHIN THE BODY OF A BOY AS IN REINCARNATION. AND SO HERE WE SEE THE "YIN IN THE YANG AND THE YANG IN THE YIN ====4. AND SO THE TETRAGRAMMATON HAS A VALUE OF —4 WHEN YOU TAKE INTO ACCOUNT THE 4 LETTERS AND THE YIN-YANG SYMBOL WITH ITS 4 PRINCIPLES. 2 + 2 ===4 AND AS A WHOLE AS IN ITS CIRCLE FORM IT HAS A VALUE OF ...5...OR AN INTEGRATED WHOLE!!!

THEREFORE WE HAVE IN THE TETRAGRAMMATON THE PSYCHOLOGY BEHIND CARL JUNG'S ANIMA AND ANIMUS. THE FEMALE WITH THE MASCULINE ANIMUS AND THE MALE WITH THE FEMININE ANIMA ====4. THE SHADOW ALONG WITH THE LIGHT AND THE LIGHT ALONG WITH THE SHADOW. AS TWO OF THE LETTERS IN TETRAGRAMMATON ATTRIBUTED TO THE FEMALE ARE —THE SAME — WHILE THE MALE LETTERS ARE DIFFERENT, THE FEMALE SHADOW HAS A VALUE OF ONE AND THE MALE

HAS A VALUE OF TWO. 2 PLUS 1 ===3!!! THE TRIAD OF — THE TREE OF GOOD AND EVIL AND OF —LIFE.

AS THE TETRAGRAMMAT-ONE IS —4 PRINCIPLES AS —ONE UNION, WE CAN INFER THAT THE MONO-DEISTIC CONCEPT IS "ONE" ON THE SURFACE BUT —4 WITHIN. BASICALLY, THE —UNUMI IS IN REALITY AN .......E PLURIBUS 4!!!

SINCERELY,
THE "5"

---

### 19. EMBRACING OUR "INNER CHILD" AS OUR "DIVINE SELF:" WE ARE ALL ADAMEVA KAD-M-ANNU COSMIC SPARKS OF ENERGY EXPERIENCING A MATERIAL LIFE AND WORLD — DA-AT IS ALL OF "US!"

YOUR "INNER CHILD" OCCUPIES THE MIDDLE PILLAR IN THE "TREE OF LIFE." THE DA-AT MIDDLE PILLAR POSITION OCCUPIES THE PLACE OF THE "DIVINE CHILD" ADAM KADMON AND SO AS WE ARE HOLOGRAMS OF THE UNIVERSAL MIND AND ENERGY BODY MANIFESTING AS ONE IN ADAM KADMON, WE ARE ALSO "THE DIVINE CHILD OF THE UNIVERSE" MANIFESTING AS MANY FRAGMENTS OF THE ONE.

ENERGY SPARKS OF THE COSMIC ENERGY BODY OF ADAM-EVA KADMON GOING THROUGH A MATERIAL EXPERIENCE.

"THE CHILD" ARCHETYPE IS —SACRED! — AND THIS SACREDNESS IS NOT LIMITED ONLY TO ACTUAL CHILDREN AND CHILDHOOD BUT IT ENCOMPASSES AS WELL EVERYONE'S INNER - CHILD. THIS "INNER CHILD" IS THE —DIVINE SPARK— WHICH IS EVENTUALLY COVERED AND BURIED OVERTIME BY LIFE'S TRAUMAS AND EXPERIENCES AS WE MOVE THROUGH THIS TIME-SPACE-MATTER CONTINUUM AND PLANE OF PHYSICAL EXISTENCE. BY UNCOVERING OUR "INNER CHILD" WE ARE RECLAIMING OUR ORIGINAL DIVINE SPARK AND SANCTITY.

DOES THE "BE AS LITTLE CHILDREN" RING A BELL?

IS IT NOT A CORE TENET OF TRADITIONS WORLDWIDE THAT "CHILDREN GO TO HEAVEN" AND SHOULD BE PROTECTED AND NURTURED IN LOVE?

AFTER ALL, IT'S LOVE THAT NURTURES A CHILD'S SELF-ACCEPTANCE AND SELF - LOVE WHICH MAKES FOR A STABLE ADULT WHO WILL NOT BE STRUGGLING AND CONSUMED BY TRAUMA AND OTHER PSYCHO-EMOTIONAL PHYSICAL CHALLENGES AND NEUROSIS BASED ON NEGLECT

AND ABUSE BY ADULTS. TRAUMA AFTER ALL CAN GO BOTH WAYS IN ITS EFFECTS IN A PERSON AS IN —SHOWING A PERSON THE PATH OF EMPATHY AND HEALING OR, GIVING BIRTH TO HUMANS OVERWHELMED BY TOO MUCH PAIN AND RESENTMENT AND HATE AND REVENGE. IT'S THIS HEALTHY LOVING CHILDHOOD THAT IS THE —KEY—TO HEALTHY AND LOVING WORLDS AND HUMAN BEINGS WHO LOVE THE PLANET AND ALL LIVING BEINGS.

IT'S THE "INNER CHILD" WHO BECOMES WOUNDED AS WE PASS THROUGH THE MATERIAL PLANE OF EXISTENCE IN WHICH WE FALL METAPHORICALLY FROM A RELATIVE STATE OF INNOCENCE, TO A STATE OF PSYCHOLOGICAL FRAGMENTATION AS A RESULT OF THE FRAGMENTED NATURE OF THE MATERIAL WORLD AND ITS DUAL NATURE, BOTH "GOOD AND EVIL AND IN BETWEEN."

THEREFORE THE CONCEPT OF "CHILDHOOD" IS SACRED AND IS THE MIRROR OF THE COSMIC ANDRO-GYNE CHILD WHO MANIFESTS AS MANY GENDERS AND SEXES AND SEXUAL ORIENTATIONS AND COLORS ETC. ETC. ETC. AND PEOPLES AND LIVING BEINGS INCLUDING PLANTS AND ANIMALS AND INANIMATE THINGS. BASICALLY, IT'S ALL AN INTERDEPENDENT NETWORK AND WEB OF ENERGY THAT RECYCLES ITSELF OVER AND OVER AGAIN SPRINGING NEW LIFE. ADAM KADMON'S ENERGY BODY MANIFESTING IN AN INCREDIBLE VARIETY OF FORMS.

AS IT WAS DESCRIBED BEFORE, BINAH AND CHOKMAH UNITE "IN LOVE" THANKS TO KETER WHO REPRESENTS THE FIFTH BINDING ELEMENT OF LOVE. AND FROM THIS UNION OF COSMIC POWERS, THE "DIVINE ANDROGYNE CHILD ARCHETYPAL ENERGY" IS BORN. AN ENERGY THAT IS SACRED AND REPRESENTS "EVERY HUMAN AND LIVING BEING" IN THIS MATERIAL - ENERGY COSMOS. THE TRIPLE CHORD IS "L-O-V-E." AND IT IS BECAUSE OF THAT "HIGHER ENERGY OR L-O-V-E" THAT EVERYTHING IS POSSIBLE AND EVERYONE IS —ALIVE!

AS PARENTS EMULATE LOVE SO THE CHILD WILL LEARN AND FEEL WHAT LOVE IS AND SO WILL KNOW HOW TO SPREAD LOVE TO THE WORLD.

SINCERELY,
THE DIVINE ANDRO-"GENIE IN A BOTTLE"

## 20. "THE SUBSTANCE OF ALL THINGS" THAT PERVADES ALL LIVING BEINGS AND NATURE IS "QI" —THE CROWN OF QI--ETER (KETER) – THE FIFTH ELEMENT OF SPINOZA

THE TERM KETER HAS TWO SOUNDS AND ROOT WORDS AS IN "K" WHICH IS EQUIVALENT TO THE "QI" OR MANA OR PRANA OR LIFE FORCE IN THE TAOIST AND YOGIC TRADITIONS. AND THE WORD —ETER— WHICH IS ALSO KNOWN AS "AETHER OR AKASHA" IN THE VEDIC TRADITION AND WHICH REPRESENTS THE FUNDAMENTAL ELEMENT AND SOURCE OF ALL EXISTENCE.

IN BOTH YOGA AND IN TAOIST QI GONG TRADITIONS BREATHING IS THE KEY AND CORE PRACTICE. IT'S A BASIC TEACHING AND CONCEPT OF QI GONG THAT "ONE OBTAINS OR ABSORBS —QI— OR LIFE FORCE ENERGY FROM BREATHING!!!

THE ABOVE SOUNDS AS IF —QI IS IN THE AIR— AND QI IS WHAT ANIMATES LIVING BEINGS. QI IS ACTUALLY EVERYWHERE. SO THE WORD K-ETER IS COMPOSED OF TWO CONCEPTS WHICH ARE THE BASIC LIVING FORCE OR "K" (QI) AND … ETHER OR AKASHA.

THEREFORE SPINOZA'S "THE SUBSTANCE OF ALL THINGS" IS SIMILAR TO THE "QI THAT PERVADES AND ANIMATES ALL THINGS" AND THE "BASIC LIVING FORCE." THIS QI-ETER FORMS THE "5TH" ELEMENT IN THE TREE OF DUALITY OR OF LIFE ( THE WORLD TREE) BY WHICH ONE CAN SEE HOW K-ETER / AKASHA GIVES BIRTH TO BINAH (THE DIVINE FEMININE) AND TO CHOKMAH (THE DIVINE MASCULINE) AND HOW BOTH DIVINE CHILDREN OF AKASHA JOIN ENERGY FORCES TO CREATE THE DIVINE ANDROGYNOUS CHILD "DA-AT" WHO IS THE "3" WHO IS ALSO A "4" YIN-YANG UNITED PRINCIPLE OR THE "FOUR PRIMORDIAL NUMBERS."

THESE 4 PRIMORDIAL NUMBERS IN "DA-AT" REPRESENT THE "FOUR PRIMORDIAL ELEMENTS" IN THEIR SPIRITUAL- ENERGETIC ESSENCE UNITED BY THE "MIDDLE PILLAR." THESE 4 ELEMENTS COME TOGETHER AT —KETER'S OR AKASHA'S—MIDDLE PILLAR WHICH IS THE "FUNDAMENTAL ENERGY CURRENT THAT ANIMATES AND BINDS ALL THINGS TOGETHER AS ONE." QI-ETER / AKASHA IN THE TREE OF LIFE IS THE "CROWN" REPRESENTING THE SOURCE OF CONSCIOUSNESS AND ENERGY, THE ORIGINAL COSMIC WOMB.

THE KI-ETER POSITION IS EQUIVALENT TO "LOVE" BECAUSE IT IS THE STRONGEST FORCE THAT SEEKS TO BRING ELEMENTS AND COSMIC PRINCIPLES TOGETHER AND TO MANIFESTATION. JUST AS HUMAN BEINGS

COME TOGETHER, AND ANIMALS COME TOGETHER, AND CELLS COME TOGETHER TO FORM LIVING BEINGS, ETC. SO IS WITH EVERYTHING ELSE WHICH IN THEIR ESSENCE IT'S ALL ATOMS AND MOLECULES THAT COME TOGETHER BECAUSE OF THIS ALL PERVADING SUBSTANCE OF ALL THINGS AND FUNDAMENTAL ENERGY OR L-O-V-E.

LOVE …IS THE PRIMARY AND FUNDAMENTAL ENERGY AND THE BINDING FORCE OF THE UNIVERSE.

THEREFORE, THE INVISIBLE AIR IS TEEMING WITH LIVING—QI— OR BASIC LIFE FORCE. WHICH IS A REASON WHY TREES BREATH AND ANIMALS AND PLANTS AND HUMANS BREATHE THIS —QI— ENERGY WHICH IS EVERYWHERE.

THEREFORE…

TAKE A BREAK… RELAX… PLACE YOURSELF IN A COMFORTABLE POSITION … CLOSE YOUR EYES AND FOCUS ON THE —BREATH!!!!

PLACE YOUR HAND ON YOUR LOWER TUMMY AND THE OTHER HAND ON THE HEART AREA, AND, BREATH DEEPLY UNTIL THE AIR REACHES YOUR LOWER TUMMY. AND FROM YOUR TUMMY EXPAND TO YOUR DIAPHRAGM AND CHEST AREA….. THEN BREATHE OUT SLOWLY AND FEEL THE CHEST AREA CAVE IN FIRST AND THE DIAPHRAGM AND TUMMY NEXT. INDEED BY DOING THIS BREATHING YOU ARE FEEDING —QI—ENERGY OR PRANA TO YOUR LUNGS AND INTESTINES AND CELLS AND EXPELLING STRESS AND STAGNANT ENERGY. THIS IS GREAT AS IT REINVIGORATES YOUR INSIDES AND ALSO RELAXES THE MIND AND NERVES.

SINCERELY,
A-MARIE-KA'S OXYGEN aka "QI"-CA DA SILVA

---

## 21.  THERE'S ONLY ONE EARTH: THE FOUR ELEMENTS THAT COME TOGETHER AS ONE TO FORM "ONE HUMAN RACE" AND THE HOLINESS OF THE "ENTIRE EARTH AND LANDS"

HAVE YOU NOTICED THAT WHEREVER YOU GO ON EARTH YOU FIND YOURSELF ON…..LAND? DUHHH…. LAND OR — THE ELEMENT EARTH— WHICH IS BASICALLY THE SAME EVERYWHERE YOU GO. IN OTHER WORDS, ALL EARTH IN THIS PLANET IS THE SAME AND MADE UP OF THE SAME MINERALS AND COMPOUNDS NO MATTER HOE DIFFERENT THAT SOIL MIGHT LOOK.

THE EARTH PRODUCES THE SAME COMBINATIONS OF ELEMENTS WHICH MANIFEST AS THE "PRODUCTS AND FOODS OF THE EARTH." THESE FOODS OF THE EARTH ARE NOT INDEPENDENT FROM THE "LAND AND SOIL" ITSELF. THEY ARE AN EXTENSION OF THE LAND OR SOIL WHICH MIRACULOUSLY THE "HOLY QI" TRANSFORMS INTO FLOWERS, PLANTS, FRUITS,NUTS, HERBS, ETC. ETC. ETC. NO MATTER WHERE YOU GO YOU WILL FIND THE SAME "PRODUCTS" AND YOU WILL BE ABLE TO EAT THEM. AND WHEN YOU EAT THEM YOU WILL BE ABSORBING THE NUTRIENTS AND ELEMENTS OF THE EARTH WHICH SUSTAIN AND MAKE OUR BODIES. OUR BODIES WHICH ARE AN "EXTENSION OF THE NATURAL WORLD."

WHAT WE ARE SAYING HERE IS THAT WHETHER YOUR SKIN IS BLACK OR WHITE OR BROWN OR RED OR YELLOW IT IS THE SAME "EARTH, SOIL AND ELEMENTS" MANIFESTING IN DIVERSE COLORS AND FORMS JUST AS THAT SAME ENERGY MANIFESTS AS THE "DIVERSE FRUITS OF THE EARTH." AND REGARDLESS WHERE YOU GO AND THE EXTERNAL DIVERSITY OF CREATION ........

......THE SAME FOUR ELEMENTS "EARTH/SOIL, FIRE/ SUN, WATER AND AIR" KEEP FORMING AND MAINTAINING AND SUSTAINING YOUR BODY AND EVERYONE ELSE'S BODY. AS YOU CAN NOTICE, THE DIVERSITY IS PART OF THE NATURAL PROCESS AND BEHIND THIS DIVERSITY THE SOURCE OF IT ALL IS THE SAME OR "A UNION OR ONE" COSMIC PRINCIPLE OR ORIGIN. THIS IS WHAT THE FOUR LETTER NAME OF DEITY IN ABRAHAMIC LORE IS POINTING AT AS IN—ULTIMATE REALITY—WHO REPRESENTS THE "UNION OF THE FOUR ELEMENTS COMING TOGETHER AS ONE TO FORM HUMANS AND ALL LIVING BEINGS AND INANIMATE THINGS AS WELL."

PLEASE REFLECT ON THESE METAPHYSICAL TRUTHS AND "SCIENCE" AND YOU WILL REALIZE THAT —--- THE FOUR LETTERS YHVH IN HEBREW ONE ON TOP OF THE OTHER COMBINE TO FORM THE FIGURE OF A HUMAN WHO REPRESENTS THE "DIVINE ANDROGYNE OR THE VETRUVIAN MAN" WHICH IS THE TEMPLATE FOR THE HUMAN BEING AND OTHER BEINGS IN THE UNIVERSE.

SO IT IS NOW THE DAY TO REALIZE THAT THE "BODY" IS ALL THE SAME REGARDLESS OF THE COLOR AND FORM IT SHOWS UP IN THIS PLANET EARTH. WE NEED TO MOVE BEYOND THE "VEIL OF MAYA OR ILLUSION AND DELUSION" TO FINALLY SEE THE TRUTH BEHIND THE "DIVERSE" WAYS IN WHICH HUMAN BEINGS MANIFEST PHYSICALLY ON THIS EARTH. SO AS YOU CAN NOTICE HERE, THE EARTH IS ALL "ONE THING" AND AS YOU ARE BORN AND FORMED OF THE EARTH ITSELF, EACH ONE OF YOU IS AN EXTENSION OF THE NATURAL WORLD DEPENDENT ON THAT NATURAL

WORLD FOR LIFE AND SURVIVAL AND NOT —-INDEPENDENT OR SEPARATE FROM IT AS MANY OF YOU BELIEVE TODAY.

IF THE NATURAL WORLD COLLAPSES AND DIES, YOU MATERIAL - PHYSICAL SELF WILL ALSO DIE WITH IT. AS STRAIGHTFORWARD AND SIMPLE AS THAT.

AS YOU CAN SEE FROM THE ORDER OF THINGS IN THIS PLANET AND NOT AS MANY OF YOU BELIEVE TODAY, YOU DO NOT COME FIRST IN THE NATURAL WORLD. FIRST IS SPIRIT ENERGY, THEN ARE THE FOUR FOUNDATIONAL ELEMENTS, THEN THE "FRUITS OF THOSE ELEMENTS" MANIFESTING AS "FOODS AND EDIBLES" AND LAST BUT NOT LEAST THE "MOVING LIVING BEINGS" OF THE PLANET THAT DEPEND AND ARE FORMED AND BORN OF THOSE FRUITS OF THE EARTH WHICH IN TURN ARE BORN OF THE ELEMENTS.

AND SO AS WE CAN SEE FROM THIS ANALYSIS ON "HUMAN NATURE" FROM "UP HERE" IT IS ALL "THE SAME" DOWN THERE ON EARTH. WE DO NOT SEE DIFFERENCES AS YOU SEE THEM. TO US IT IS ALL AN UNIFIED WHOLE. THIS TEACHES US TWO THINGS IN THAT >>>>>>>> ALL OF YOU HAVE BEEN CHOSEN BEFORE YOU WERE BORN ON EARTH TO BE HERE ON EARTH IN ORDER TO "GROW SPIRITUALLY —-NOT RELIGION —-- BUT IN SPIRIT AND TO BECOME COMPASSIONATE BEINGS AND BECOME ONCE MORE CHANNELS OF "UNIVERSAL LOVE" WHICH IS THE BASIS OF THE "UNION OF THE ELEMENTS." AND THE SECOND THING TO REMEMBER IS THAT — ALL THE EARTH "IS THE HOLY LAND!!!!!!!!!!!!!!!!!!!!!!!!!!!!!!!!!!!!!!!!!!!!!!!!!!!!!!!!!!!!!

BASICALLY, THE "12 TRIBES" ARE SYMBOLS THAT REPRESENT THE "CONFEDERATION OF 12 STAR NATIONS" AND THE "HOLY LAND" ARCHETYPE STANDS FOR THE "ENTIRE LAND OR EAR TH!!!!!!!!!!!!!!!!!!!!!!!!!!!!!!!!!!!!!!!!!!!!!!!!!!!!!!!!!!!!!!!!!!!!!!! AS YOU CAN SEE ALL THESE CHARACTERS AND CONCEPTS ARE SYMBOLS AND ARCHETYPES THAT STAND FOR UNIVERSAL PRINCIPLES SUCH AS "HUMANITY AND ITS RELATIONSHIP TO NATURE AND ITS FOUR ELEMENTS WHICH MAN IS A PART OF."

THEREFORE, THE TIME TO EMBRACE EACH OTHER IS HERE AND WE HOPE THAT BY KNOWING THESE FACTS YOU WILL STOP MURDERING AND KILLING AND HATING EACH OTHER ON THE BASIS OF "EXTERIOR COLORS AND FORMS AND DIFFERENCES" AND FINALLY LEARN TO LOOK BEYOND THE VEIL OF THE FLESH COVERING AND INTO THE ESSENCE OF WHAT AND WHOM YOU ALL ARE WHICH IS "ORBS OF DIVINE LIGHT FILLED WITH CONSCIOUSNESS" WHO YEARN TO COME "BACK HOME." BUT FOR THAT TO HAPPEN YOU HAVE TO RAISE YOUR VIBRATIONS AND THE EARTH'S THROUGH AND WITH "LOVE."

SINCERELY,
"THE WORLDS OF THE ELEMENTALS SPEAKING THRU THE BIPOLAR GATES"

---

## 22. THE "TETRA-GRAMMAT-ONNE" AND THE "PENTA-GRAMMAT-ONNE:" THE FOUR BECOME 5 UNITED AND LINKED IN AND AS —LOVE —!

AND SO THE PREVIOUS TWO DIARIES INTEND TO EXPLAIN AS SIMPLE AS POSSIBLE THE PROCESS OF THE "FORMATION AND MANIFESTATION" OF THE UNIVERSE. AND AS HUMAN IS A HOLOGRAM OF THE UNIVERSAL ENERGIES MANIFESTING IN HIM/HER AS A HUMAN, THE CREATIVE PROCESS THAT BIRTHS HUMANS IS AFTER THE UNIVERSAL PROCESSES THAT GIVE BIRTH TO THE COSMOS AND EVERYTHING AND EVERYONE IN IT.

AND SO THE "UNION OF 4" WITHOUT KETARI OR KETER, WHICH IS THE FIFTH ELEMENT, IS NOT IN A STATE OF UNION BUT ONLY EXISTS AS PURE ENERGY AND OR PURE MIND IN A SEPARATE STATE IN BOTH CHOKMAH AND BINAH RESPECTIVELY. WITH THE "BINDING UNION OF LOVE" IN THE MIDDLE PILLAR, THE 4 BECOME 5 AND THE UNION IS COMPLETE!!!

AND SO WE CAN NOTICE FROM THE PREVIOUS DIARIES THAT THE 4 REPRESENT TETRA-GRAMMA-D-ONE. OR —DA-AT BUT IN A STATE OF INCOMPLETION. THERE IS SOMETHING THAT IS MISSING AND WHICH IS THE FIFTH BINDING ELEMENT OR "LOVE" AS IN —THE PENTA-GRAMMA-D-ANNU. FINALLY AND AT LAST THE 4 LETTERS OR ELEMENTS OR NUMBERS REACH BALANCE AND EQUILIBRIUM AND CAN BE DIRECTED IN A FOCUSED AND CONSTRUCTIVE WAY WITH THE BINDING ELEMENT OF —LOVE!! THEREFORE, "LOVE" BECOMES THE CROWN THAT MAKES THE MANIFESTATION OF THE MATERIAL - ENERGY UNIVERSE A REALITY.

THEREFORE, WE SHOULD BE THANKFUL EVERYDAY THAT THIS "BINDING FORCE WE CALL L-O-V-E" IS THE POWER THAT ALLOWS EVERYTHING TO EXIST AND TO LITERALLY STICK TOGETHER. THUS, WHEN WE EMBODY AND NURTURE LOVE IN OURSELVES AND SHARE IT WITH OTHERS, WE ARE LIVING AND MOVING IN THE HIGHEST VIBRATIONAL FREQUENCY WHICH LEADS TO UNION AND TO WHOLENESS, INTEGRATION AND HEALING.

THE SYMBOLISM AND STORY BEHIND THE "GOSPEL" IS ABOUT THE DESCENT AND FALL OF ADAMEVA KAD-M-ANNU WHO "SACRIFICES" HIS-HER EXALTED POSITION OF UNION AS A YIN-YANG UNIT AND DECIDES TO SPLIT IN ORDER THAT THE FUSION PROCESSES BEGIN AND THE TAPESTRY OF LIFE BECOMES A REALITY. THIS IS THE SECRET AND

SYMBOLISM AND METAPHOR BEHIND THE "SACRIFICE" OR "SPLITTING AND FRAGMENTATION" PROCESS WHICH IS STILL HAPPENING SINCE IT IS LOVE THAT COMPELS THE UNIVERSAL AND COSMIC ENERGIES TO GO THROUGH THIS PROCESS IN ORDER THAT EVERYTHING EXIST AND COMES TO LIFE. ADAMEVA KAD-M-ONNE REPRESENTS — TETRAGRAMMATON BECOMING PENTAGRAMMATON AND BRINGING EVERYTHING AND EVERYONE TO LIFE IN THE NAME OF "LOVE."

THEREFORE, WHEN WE ASCEND IN "LOVE" WE ARE — IN UNION WITH OURSELVES AND WITH OUR ENVIRONMENT. LOVE —BINDS US TO WHOLENESS AND INTEGRATION AND MAKES OUR DIVERSE BODIES EXIST IN A PLACE OF RELATIVE HEALTH AND—HARMONY.

PENTAGRAMMATON OCCUPIES THE POSITION OF —PRESERVATION— IN THE HINDU "TRIMURTI" OR DIVISION OF ENERGIES BELONGING TO BINAH AND CHOKMAH AND — DA-AT THE ANDROGYNOUS –INTEGRATED— DIVINE CHILD AND PRESERVER IN THE NAME OF LOVE!! Y-ESH-UA IN THE CHRISTIAN TRADITION.

SINCERELY,
"VENUS, WHO IN THE NAME OF LOVE COMES DOWN"

---

## 23. THE —0— OF KETARI AND THE "COSMIC PRINCIPLE OF LOVE" THAT UNITES ALL TOGETHER AS "ONE" THE HIGH 5!!!

AND SO AS WE WERE ABLE TO NOTICE IN THE DIARY ABOUT THE 4 ELEMENTS AND BI-NOMIAL MANIFESTATIONS OF BOTH YIN AND YANG, THERE IS THE —0— "ELEMENT" THAT REPRESENTS "KETARI" AND THAT "REPRESENTS THE BINDING FORCE."

AND SO AS WE HAVE EXPLAINED BEFORE, WE HAVE THE FOUR BASIC ENERGIES OF BOTH YIN AND YANG MANIFESTING AS FOUR PRIMORDIAL VIBRATIONS OF ENERGY TYPES THAT DESCEND OR FALL CREATING THE TIME-SPACE-MATTER CONTINUUM AND UNIVERSE. HOWEVER, "WHAT" KEEPS THESE ENERGIES TOGETHER AND COMING BACK TO RELATIVE BALANCE AND UNION IN ORDER TO BRING ABOUT CHANGE AND THE MATERIAL-ENERGY "TREE OF LIFE" OR UNIVERSE?

WELL, AS WE EXPLAINED SOME TIME AGO, THE "UNITING PRINCIPLE AND VALUE"? IS THE —0—! IF WE LOOK AT THE MIDDLE PILLAR, IT FORMS A STRAIGHT PILLAR OR LINE CONNECTING KETARI DIRECTLY TO DA-AT AND DA-AT DIRECTLY TO MALKUTA THROUGH BOTH TIFERET AND YESOD. IN DA-AT, THE CONCEPT OF "UNIVERSAL LOVE AND BONDING" COMES TO EXISTENCE. IT IS IN DA-AT THAT BOTH THE FATHER AND MOTHER

PRINCIPLE COME TOGETHER TO "TAKE A RIB OR PORTION OF EACH OTHERS' ENERGY" AND –SHARE OR FUSION EACH PORTION— TO BECOME ONE ANDROGYNOUS UNIT MADE UP OF BOTH YIN AND YANG aka ….DA'AT.

YOU WILL SEE THAT THIS UNION OF OPPOSITES AND COMPLEMENTS IS ABLE TO HAPPEN THANKS TO "KETARI" WHO IS IN THE MIDDLE ABOVE BINAH, CHOKMAH AND DA-AT. THE KETARI ENERGY THAT BINDS AND UNITES THE DIVINE TWINS OR YIN-YANG ENERGIES IS THE STREAM OR CURRENT OF KETARI. THIS CURRENT —0— REMAINS IN PLACE AS THE DA-AT CENTER OR MIDDLE INDEFINITELY AND PERPETUALLY SPLITS AND FUSIONS MAKING THE MATERIAL-TEMPORAL-ENERGETIC PLANE OF EXISTENCE A POSSIBILITY. EACH TIME DA-AT BREAKS APART AND BECOMES A BINAH AND CHOKMAH, THE DA-AT CREATES A SHADOW OF ITSELF IN THE MIDDLE PILLAR BY WHICH THE "KETARI" BINDING FORCE REMAINS AND TRAVELS AT THE SAME TIME WITH THE CURRENTS OF YIN AND YANG OR BINAH AND CHOKMAH RESPECTIVELY.

AS DA-AT IS THE "4 ELEMENTS" IN ACTUAL MANIFESTATION AND FORMATION, IT IS THIS INVISIBLE BINDING FORCE WE WILL CALL —LOVE— THAT MAKES THE UNION POSSIBLE DESPITE THE SEPARATION OF THE TWINS. IT IS THE BIRTH OF THE CONCEPT OF INTERDEPENDENCE.

AND SO AS THE 4 PRIMORDIAL ELEMENTS BECOME THE 4 MATERIAL ELEMENTS IN MALKUTA, THE KETER CURRENT OR —BINDING LOVE AND UNITY— TRAVELS AS WELL UNITING THE COSMIC DUALITIES UNTIL IT REACHES AND BECOMES MALKUTA OR THE MATERIAL-ENERGETIC UNIVERSES. AND SO AS WE CAN SEE, THIS UNIVERSE AND WORLD AND EVERY HUMAN IS BOUND TOGETHER — BY — LOVE!!! THE 4 BECOMING AN INTEGRATED AND WORKING WHOLE OR A NUMBER —–5!!!

"5" AS IN "UNITED WE STAND IN THE POWER AND ENERGY OF —L-O-V-E!"

SINCERELY, THE 4 COMING TOGETHER TO THE "0" AS THE —HIGH 5!!!

---

## 24. THE COSMIC DIVISION OF POWERS AND THE REALMS OF" GOOD" AND "EVIL" AND OF "BOTH GOOD… AND EVIL"

"And GOD saw that everything he created was GOOD!" (GENESIS) "And then there was LIGHT!" (GENESIS)

I always asked myself if GOD is all GOOD then why is there EVIL? It made no sense. And when I asked this to religious people specifically they either gave me some silly answers or answers that made no sense whatsoever and that left me with more questions or more confused.

Thanks DIVINITY that came to the rescue and EXPLAINED to me how it works or at least showed me a simple diagram that makes this a little more clear. If you see the first sentence above, it says in GENESIS that GOD created EVERYTHING and he saw that it was good. This makes more sense when we realize that there are TWO creation stories in GENESIS. The one that pertains to THE HEAVENLY FATHER ADAM AND HEAVENLY MOTHER EVE aka CHOKMAH THE FATHER AND BINAH THE MOTHER as separate and individual concepts independent of each other.

The second creation story is the one pertaining to the creation of the LESSER HEAVENLY ADAM AND LESSER HEAVENLY EVE aka ADAMEVA KADMON OR THE DIVINE ANDROGYNE. ADAM KADMON BEING THE UNIVERSAL ENERGETIC TEMPLATE after whom humanity was fashioned and in whom both the YIN AND THE YANG ENERGIES ARE UNITED AND DEPENDENT ON EACH OTHER.

Since WE know now that ADAM means EARTH MAN in general and EVE represents SPIRIT that gives ANIMATION to HUMAN, we are referring here to ALL OF HUMANKIND and to THE COMING TOGETHER OF MATTER and SPIRIT.

1. A well-known Hebrew name, Adam means "son of the red Earth." Its meaning comes from the Hebrew word adamah meaning "earth," from which Adam is said to be formed. Adam is also the name of the first man created by God in the Old Testament.(PARENTS.COM).

2. Eve /iːv/ is an English given name for a female, derived from the Latin name Eva, in turn originating with the Hebrew חַוָּה, (Chavah/Havah – chavah, to breathe, and chayah, to live, or to give life). The traditional meaning of Eve is life or "living". It can also mean full of life and mother of life. Eve. (WIKIPEDIA)

At the end when ELOHIM DIVIDES THE HEAVENS it is not only referring to heaven as in the Earth's natural canopy but TO THE DIVISION OF "HEAVENS" or REALMS OF SPIRIT AND MATTER. And so here is where WE need to clarify and affirm once again the verse in GENESIS where ELOHIM, FORMS EVE FROM THE "SIDE" OF ADAM, in this case the HEAVENLY HERMAPHRODITE PRIMORDIAL SON/DAUGHTER OF GODHEAD. In other words, GODHEAD separates HEAVENLY ADAM or "YANG ENERGY" FROM HEAVENLY EVE or "YIN ENERGY" and that way CREATION begins to take place. "YIN + YANG" ARE NOW SEPARATE UNITS AND NO LONGER A UNION, ABLE TO HAVE "COSMIC SEX" OR "RELATIONS" WHICH CREATES A "THIRD PRINCIPLE" that is also YIN-YANG that further divides itself PERPETUALLY creating the BUILDING BLOCKS of CREATION. ENERGY IS THE BUILDING BLOCK OF EVERYTHING!

And so when GENESIS speaks of THE DIVISION OF THE HEAVENS it is referring to this DIVISION BETWEEN YIN AND YANG!!! And as both are DIFFERENT ENERGIES THAT OPPOSE AND COMPLEMENT EACH OTHER AT THE SAME TIME, there has to be a SEPARATION between both or everything WOULD NOT EXIST. This ENERGETIC SEPARATION creates a SPACE IN BETWEEN where both ENERGIES can be together and relate to each other AS IN OUR WORLD!!!

And so THIS IS THE ORIGINAL SEPARATION OF POWERS!!! That happened in the beginning of this cycle and creation. And so as you will recall, there is the TREE OF GOOD AND EVIL which is also THE TREE OF UNION AND LIFE. When you turn the DIAGRAM HORIZONTALLY you can notice that THERE ARE THREE REALMS OF BEING with THE MIDDLE PILLAR SANDWICHED IN BETWEEN. Humans are SANDWICHED in the MIDDLE between the REALM OF BINNAH AND THE REALM OF CHOKMAH.

The realm of CHOCKMA is the realm of LIGHT AND THE ANGELIC BEINGS. And guess WHO is the GUARDIAN OR OVERSEER OR SUSTAINER OF THE REALM OF DARKNESS AND DEMON BEINGS??? Yep, you got it …its…. B-INNAH!!!!

WE will explain in a later diary what is the FUNCTION AND PURPOSE of the realms of CHOCKMA and B-INNAH and of THE ONE WHO OVERSEES AND SUSTAINS OUR "MIDDLE WORLD" THE REALM OF ADAM KAD-M-ONNE THE "FALLEN" ONE.

SINCERELY,
"YIN AND YANG, UNITED AS ONE IN THE DIVINE CHILD"

---

## 25. "ANGELS AND DEMONS:" THE "ANGEL-DEMON" ENERGY COMPONENTS IN EACH HUMAN BEING AND BASIC ANDROGYNOUS STRUCTURE OF THE COSMOS ACCORDING TO THE PRIMORDIAL FEMALE BEING OF LIGHT!

THE "ANGELS AND DEMONS" ARE BASICALLY DIFFERENT NAMES TO DESCRIBE THE SAME ENERGY MANIFESTING AS "TWIN" ENERGIES AFTER THE CONCEPT OF YIN AND YANG.

THE "SEPARATION OF POWERS" IN THE COSMOS FOLLOWS THE SAME "TRIPARTITE" DIVISION ACCORDING TO THE "TREE OF LIFE." IT IS CALLED THE "TREE OF LIFE" BECAUSE IT IS A TEMPLATE OR BASIC BLUEPRINT OF THE "PROCESS OF LIFE." IT IS A "SCIENTIFIC TEMPLATE." THESE PROCESSES ARE MORE COMPLEX THAN DESCRIBED IN A DIAGRAM BUT IT IS A METAPHYSICAL APPROXIMATION.

THE BINAH ENERGIES WOULD CORRESPOND TO THE "DEMON" ENERGIES AND THE CHOKMAH ENERGIES WOULD CORRESPOND TO THE "ANGEL" ENERGIES. BOTH ARE DESCRIBED IN QI-NESE TRADITION AS THE "YIN AND THE YANG."

THE DEMON ENERGIES AND THE ANGEL ENERGIES ARE "TWINS" CORRESPONDING TO THE FEMININE AND THE MASCULINE ENERGIES RESPECTIVELY. THEY ARE NOT—GOOD OR EVIL– PER SE BUT IN RELATION TO EACH OTHER JUST AS THEY ARE MEANT TO BE IN ORDER TO BE ABLE TO PRODUCE / BUILD / GIVE BIRTH TO EVERYTHING. BOTH ENERGIES, EITHER DEMONIC OR ANGELIC BECOME DYSFUNCTIONAL WHEN THEY GO INTO "EXTREMES" WHICH THEN CAUSE DAMAGE.

BOTH ARE INTERTWINED AND INTERCONNECTED AND SO FOR EACH ANGEL ENERGY THERE IS A CORRESPONDING DEMON ENERGY.

HUMANS OCCUPY THE "DA-AT" OR MIDDLE PILLAR OF THE TREE OF DUALITY OR LIFE WHICH IS IN THE POSITION OF "ADAM KADM-UNO THE COSMIC ANDROGYNE." IN THIS POSITION BOTH —ANGEL AND DEMON — ENERGIES CO-EXIST WITH ONE ANOTHER AT THE "SAME TIME." BEING MADE UP BY THE "FUSION" OF BOTH "ANGEL AND DEMON" ENERGIES. THIS IS THE BASIS OF THE ATOMIC ENERGY.

AND SO ...

AS EVERYTHING IN THE COSMOS IS PRODUCED BY THE "WILL TO POWER" OF ADAMEVA KAD-M-UNO, EVERYTHING IN THE COSMOS FOLLOWS THE SAME BASIC STRUCTURE OF BEING MADE UP OF BOTH —ANGEL AND DEMON—TWIN AND OPPOSITE-COMPLEMENTARY ENERGIES.

EVERYTHING IN THE COSMOS AND EVERY HUMAN BEING IS "ANDRO-GYNOUS" IN NATURE AND SO FOLLOWS THE SAME TEMPLATE AS THE "ORIGINAL PRIMORDIAL BEING" OR "ENERGY STRUCTURE."

THIS DUALITY IS THE REASON A PERSON CAN DO BOTH GOOD AND EVIL! HUMANS THEREFORE ARE TRI-DIMENSIONAL BEINGS AS IN BOTH DEMONIC, ANGELIC AND MATERIAL.

SOMETIMES IT IS NECESSARY TO BE "DEMONIC" AS IN THE CASE OF MEAN PEOPLE ABUSING YOUR DIGNITY, IN THIS CASE YOU NEED TO BE TOUGH AS DEMON ENERGY AND SET BOUNDARIES. ALSO, IT IS A BLESSING TO BE "ANGELIC" AS IN TREATING OTHERS WITH LOVE AND CONSIDERATION AND THAT WAY MAKING THIS WORLD A HEAVEN ON EARTH!!!

THEREFORE, WE NEED AS HUMANS TO BEGIN TO WORK ON BALANCING THESE "BASIC COMPONENTS" OF LIFE ENERGIES.

THIS IS THE BASIS OF —QI GONG — AND —TAI QI!!!

SINCERELY, "QI-QI RODRIGUEZ, THE ANDROGYNOUS ANGEL-DEMON OF LIGHT/DARK

---

## 26. THE 4 PRIMORDIAL NUMBERS PLUS —0— AND THE 12 SEFIROTIC POWERS OF THE "TREE OF LIFE" AND THE "VETRUVIAN MAN" OR THE "HANGED MAN NUMBER 12:"

WE HAVE TRAVELED THROUGH THE "PRIMORDIAL FAMILY" OR "PRIMORDIAL NUMBERS" AS IN KETER 0, BINAH AND CHOKMAH 1 AND 2, AND DA-AT BEING 3 AND 4. YOU WILL RECALL THAT DA-AT IS "CONJOINED TWIN ENERGIES" THEREFORE ARE EQUIVALENT TO A SECOND SET OF PRIMORDIAL NUMBERS JUST AS 1 AND 2. THESE ARE ABOVE AND REPEAT THEMSELVES BELOW AS IN 5 - 10 FROM GEVURAH AND CHESED ALL THE WAY DOWN TO MALKUTA.

AS WE CAN RECALL, THE UNIVERSE IS MATHEMATICAL AND IT BEGINS WITH THE NUMBERS 1 AND 2 or 1 AND 1 BEING BORN OF THE —0—. AND FROM THE 1 AND 2 ARE BORN THE 3 AND 4. 5 REPRESENTS THE UNION.

IF WE LOOK AT —0—-, THIS IS THE VOID OR THE DEEP WELL OR THE WOMB FROM WHERE THE "ESSENCE" OF THE ARCHETYPES AND ENERGY IS BORN. THE 1 IS BORN FROM KETER AND REPRESENTS THE WORLD OF PURE IDEAS, AND THE 2 OR ITS TWIN REPRESENTS THE WORLD OF PURE ENERGY. AND SO BOTH GET TOGETHER TO "CAUSE" A —COSMIC COMMOTION AS IN THE "BIRTH OF THE FIRST UNION OF CONCEPTS AND NUMBERS WHICH FORM THE BASIS FOR EVERYTHING ELSE.

AND SO WE HAVE FIVE CONCEPTS HERE AS IN KETER OR ORIGIN, AND BINAH AND CHOKMAH AND THE ANDROGYNE DA-AT WHO ARE "CONJOINED TWINS DA-AT." HERE WE HAVE AGAIN THE 0, 1, 2, 3, 4, WHICH MAKE UP 5. THEREFORE THE FIRST "4" SEFIROT" REPRESENT 5! AND WHEN YOU ADD THE REST OF THE SEFIROT, THE ENTIRE TREE OF LIFE ADDS UP TO —12!!!

12 AS IN THE "HANGED MAN!!!"

SO WE SEE THAT "THE TREE OF LIFE" REPRESENTS THE "HANGED MAN" OR THE "VETRUVIAN MAN" WHO REPRESENTS EACH AND EVERY HUMAN BEING WHO IS METAPHORICALLY NAILED TO THE CROSS OR TREE OF THE SPACE-TIME-MATTER CONTINUUM. AND SO AS WE REVEALED TO YOU BEFORE, THE "TREE OF LIFE AND DEATH" ALSO REPRESENTS THE "HUMAN BODY AND THAT BODY IS A HOLOGRAM OF THE COSMIC BODY"

OF THE ANDRO-GENESIS ADAMEVA KAD-M-ONE. Y-ESH-UA ON THE CROSS IS ANOTHER SYMBOL OF THIS PROCESS.

SO IF WE LOOK AT THE DIAGRAM — KETER WOULD BE "PURE CONSCIOUSNESS AND POTENTIAL" ITSELF THAT GIVES BIRTH TO "MIND AS IN BINNAH" AND "ENERGY AS IN CHOKMAH" AND BOTH FORM THE — BODY OF LIGHT AND THE BODY OF MATTER—WHO ARE ATTRIBUTES OF BOTH BINAH AND CHOKMAH DIVINE ANDRO-GYNE ADAMEVA KAD-M-UNO.

THEREFORE, WE ALL POSSESS A BODY OF LIGHT AND A BODY OF MATTER AND AS ENERGY IS THE ORIGIN OR CAUSE OF MATTER, YOUR HUMAN BODY CONCEALS WITHIN IT THE BODY OF LIGHT!!

SINCERELY,
ADAMEVA KAD-M-UNNO "THE MATTER AND THE LIGHT".

---

## 27. THE "WAR IN HEAVEN" AS ALLEGORY AND METAPHOR: THE CONSTANT STRUGGLE AND INTERACTION BETWEEN YIN AND YANG ENERGIES

Throughout the ages people have taken the WAR IN HEAVEN narrative LITERALLY which has been a HUGE MISTAKE and as a result the ORIGIN OF MUCH PAIN AND SUFFERING. As it has been misinterpreted and treated literally without asking THE RIGHT PHILO-SOPHICAL questions which that story wants to point to.

First of all, WHY would a LOVING GOD expel "SATAN" to Earth in the first place? The ACT OF EXPELLING "SATAN" TO EARTH —IS NOT —A LOVING ACT!!! Therefore, this story is an ALLEGORY AND METAPHOR with METAPHYSICAL MEANINGS. WHY would SATAN and his angels be in HEAVEN when that realm DOES NOT BELONG TO THE NEGATIVE ENERGIES? as these REALMS are SET UP ACCORDING TO "ENERGY QUALITY" where energies are separated according to QUALITY such as LIGHT versus DARK. As you were told before, THE ONLY PLACE IN WHICH THESE "GOOD AND EVIL" ENERGIES CAN COMMINGLE AND INTERACT WITH EACH OTHER IS "IN THIS MIDDLE WORLD" which is the REALM of BOTH "ENERGIES" COMBINED!!

Therefore the story IS POINTING AT SOMETHING ELSE more like a COSMIC PROCESS!

AS you were told before, when THE POWERS DIVIDED THEMSELVES each one ACCORDING TO ITS ENERGY VIBRATION AND FREQUENCY there was a SEPARATION OF ENERGIES between B-INNAH and CHOCKMAH. These energies TOOK THEIR RESPECTIVE PLACES as they cannot BE where they do not belong BECAUSE OF THEIR PARTICULAR NATURE. Therefore THIS VERSE in REVELATION 12: 7 -10 ....

1. And there was war in heaven: Michael and his angels fought against the dragon; and the dragon fought and his angels,

2. And prevailed not; neither was their place found any more in heaven.

3. And the great dragon was cast out, that old serpent, called the Devil, and Satan, which deceiveth the whole world: he was cast out into the earth, and his angels were cast out with him.

THE above verse is therefore referring to THE SEPARATION BETWEEN THE FORCES OR POWERS OR ENERGIES "OF LIGHT FROM THOSE OF THE DARK." Basically, it's another allegory of the GENESIS STORY of the SEPARATION OF THE HEAVENS or WATERS or UPPER HEAVENS FROM THE LOWER HEAVENS (HEAVENS AND HELLS). ST. MIK-AEL refers to the ARCHETYPE OF LIGHT AND GOOD or CHOKMAH. And SATAN, refers to the DENSER REALMS which are KEPT IN THEIR RESPECTIVE PLACES AND WHICH ARE KEPT FROM ABSORBING CREATION DUE TO THEIR RAW ENERGETIC CHAOTIC NATURES (THANKS TO ITS OPPOSITE AND TWIN HALF, THE LIGHT or CHOKMAH). This DARK B-INNAH ENERGY is AGGRESSIVE OR RAW IN QUALITY as in TOUGH AND ROUGH and THE LIGHT SERVES AS A NATURAL BOUNDARY.

It refers to the interplay between YIN AND YANG energies! Described clearly in ASIAN tradition and symbolism.

(BY THE WAY, THE "DRAGON AND SERPENT" DOES NOT REFER TO WHAT YOU THINK IT REFERS TO BUT TO —SOMETHING ELSE! This will be revealed in another diary later in the future IF —I AM—-STILL HERE).

Remember that usually in a war there are TWO parties fighting each other and the STRONGER ENERGY, in the case of CHOKMAH, being THE LIGHT OF A HIGHER VIBRATION, casts the DARKNESS or DENSER ENERGIES "BELOW" BECAUSE THESE DENSER ENERGIES VIBRATE AT A LOWER FREQUENCY.

And so the VANQUISHMENT of ASATANNA refers to the DIVISION OF LIGHT AND DARK according to each one's RESPECTIVE FREQUENCIES. At the same time THE STRUGGLE BETWEEN ST MIKAEL AND ASATANNA refers to the STRUGGLE OF YIN AND YANG IN OUR BIPOLAR WORLD AND REALM OF CONSCIOUSNESS and also to the STRUGGLE BETWEEN SPIRIT (ST MIKAEL) VS. MATTER (ASATANNA or MAYA). After all, MATTER IS A DENSER FORM OF ENERGY VIBRATING AT A LOWER FREQUENCY THAN SPIRIT.

Therefore, THE WAR IN HEAVEN REFERS TO THE DANCE OF LIFE!!!

This ST MIKAEL VS ASATANNA allegory and metaphor reminds US that HUMANS ARE BOTH "THE LIGHT AND THE DARK" and that THERE IS AN INHERENT, INTRINSIC AND NATURAL STRUGGLE IN HUMANS BETWEEN BOTH ENERGIES. And that the best way to LIVE THIS HUMAN LIFE TO THE FULLEST IS BY FINDING A HEALTHY BALANCE BETWEEN THESE TWIN ENERGIES. Therefore, this COSMIC STRUGGLE is taking place WITHIN EACH ONE OF us. As the maxim states: AS ABOVE, SO BELOW; AS BELOW, SO IS ABOVE!!! EACH human is a MINI COSMOS or MICROCOSM OF THE MACROCOSM.

What happens when we are out of BALANCE?

THE DENSER ENERGIES TAKE OVER AND MANIFEST AS — EVIL AND DESTRUCTIVE FORCES that manifest in man's world as A WORLD IN CHAOS AND DESTRUCTION WHERE THE FORCES OF LIGHT ARE MUCH NEEDED IN ORDER FOR IT TO SURVIVE AND KEEP THE DARKER ENERGIES IN BALANCE. AND IN THE CASE OF THE LIGHT, TOO MUCH OF IT WOULD LITERALLY BURN EVERYTHING OUT OF EXISTENCE IN THIS REALM. THEREFORE,

EMBRACE IN A HOLISTIC WAY BOTH YOUR LIGHT AND YOUR "SHADOW."

SINCERELY, "THE COSMIC DANCER OF LIGHT AND SHADOW"

---

## 28. THE LEFT VS. THE RIGHT BRAIN: "THE WAR OF THE BRAINS" — A VERITABLE WAR IS GOING ON AND MOST ARE NOT AWARE OF IT

ARE WE NOT TIRED OF THE "LEFT" VS. "RIGHT" AND VICE VERSA? AND IN THE MIDST OF ALL THE "CHAOS" PEOPLE ARE NOT "AWARE OR AWAKE" TO WHAT IS REALLY TRANSPIRING BEHIND THE IDEOLOGICAL WAR GOING ON HERE. BASICALLY GUYS, IT IS A "WAR OF THE BRAINS" TAKING PLACE.

WE CAN SEE THAT IN SOME THE LEFT BRAIN IS MOST PREDOMINANT THAN THE RIGHT BRAIN AND IN SOME THE RIGHT IS MOST PREDOMINANT THAN THE LEFT BRAIN. BUT PEOPLE HAVE FORGOTTEN THAT "WE ALL HAVE BOTH A LEFT AND A RIGHT BRAINS!!!!!"

WHAT THIS WAR OF THE BRAINS POINTS AT IN THIS ENDLESS TIT FOR TAT GOING ON HERE BETWEEN THE "RIGHT BRAINERS VS. THE LEFT BRAINERS" IS THAT — BOTH BRAIN LOBES NEED TO BE ACTIVATED!!!

PEOPLE ARE BASICALLY AND MAINLY LIVING AND INTERPRETING LIFE FROM ONE LOBE OF THE BRAIN OR THE OTHER; WHICH IS A PARTIAL AND INCOMPLETE VIEW OF THE WHOLE PICTURE. IN ORDER TO BE IN THE

MIDDLE AND BE ABLE TO SEE "BOTH POINTS OF VIEWS" AND CHOOSE THE BEST FROM BOTH IS TO BE IN THE "MIDDLE BRAIN."

IN ORDER TO ACTIVATE BOTH LOBES ONE MUST CHALLENGE THE BRAIN BY DOING MORE ACTIVITIES AND EXERCISES THAT ARE OF THE LEFT AND THE RIGHT BRAIN. FOR INSTANCE, IF A PERSON IS MORE ANALYTICAL AND LEFT BRAIN S-HE WOULD NEED TO DO MORE RIGHT BRAIN ACTIVITIES SUCH AS ART AND MUSIC. AND IT WORKS THE OTHER WAY AROUND AS WELL.

AND SO — THE ELOHIM STATE THAT WE NEED TO START "WORKING THOSE LAZY BRAINS" 😄 AND GETTING THEM ACTIVATED BECAUSE BEING UNDER THE TOTAL CONTROL OF A HALF OF THE BRAIN IS LIKE BEING IN EXTREMISM AND ALSO "POSSESSED BY THAT PART OF THE BRAIN."

THE OTHER ISSUE TO TAKE INTO ACCOUNT IS THAT — ETHICS– OR A LACK OF IT IS ONE OF THE MAJOR ISSUES TODAY. THE ETHICS IS LIKE THE MIDDLE BRAIN OR THE CONTROL CENTER OF THE WHOLE STRUCTURE THAT LET US CHOOSE "FROM BOTH LOBES THE BEST AND MOST ETHICAL" CHOICE.

THEREFORE, WHEN THE BRAIN IS HALF ASLEEP AND THE ETHICAL PRINCIPLE NON OR DYS-FUNCTIONAL, THE WHOLE BRAIN SYSTEM IS CHAOTIC AND SO WE GET THE CHAOS HAPPENING EVERYWHERE TODAY.

THE HUMAN BRAIN IS AFTER THE "TREE OF LIFE." WE WILL EXPLAIN THIS MORE IN DEPTH IN A FUTURE DIARY.

SINCERELY,
"A BEAUTIFUL COSMIC MIND"

---

## 29. ST. MIKA-EL AND ASAT-ANNA: THE INNER STRUGGLE BETWEEN THE CHRIST AND THE ASAT-ANNA

The symbols representing ST. MIKA-EL OVER THE ASAT-ANNA in CHRISTIAN SYMBOLISM represents the BATTLE OF OPPOSITES OR DUALITIES. Not only as YIN AND YANG, but also as LIGHT AND DARK, etc. etc. etc. In regards to people, it is THE SYMBOL AND REPRESENTATION OF THE LOWER SELF AND THE HIGHER SELF. The constant battle of the MIND and EMOTION in regards to NEGATIVE AND POSITIVE.

The ARKANA representation of the ST. MIKA-EL AND ASAT-ANNA is the battle between THE SAT-ANNA and the ASAT-ANNA. THE STRUGGLE between TRUTH OR SAT-ANNA IN VEDIC TERMINOLOGY AND THE MATERIAL PLANE AND ITS

MAYA OR ASATANNA. As you know MATTER IS RULED BY THE SENSES and SPIRIT IS RULED BY INTUITION AND THE HIGHER ENERGY FREQUENCIES. As we are MATTER IN BODY and in close contact to it and nearer to it, THE PULL OF MATTER IS STRONGER as in the case for example of GRAVITY. Meanwhile, SPIRIT IS CONCEALED BEHIND MATTER AND MORE SUBTLE and "farther" away from us in the sense that WE HAVE TO WORK ON OUR SPIRIT much harder in order to GET IN TOUCH WITH IT.

And so ST. MIKAEL and ASAT-ANNA is the STRENGTH CARD number 8 in THE SACRED TAROT in which ONE PRINCIPLE tames or balances the OTHER principle so that both are in relative balance and the HIGHER SELF OR YOUR INNER ST. MIKAEL IS IN CHARGE OF YOUR INNER DEVIL OR LOWER SELF.

After all, HUMAN NATURE is BIPOLAR just as the ARK OF THE COVENANT. Which is what it represents as these are the ENERGIES OF THE GALAXY AND THE EARTH which are active in humans. Therefore, we are all made up of both WHAT YOU REFER TO AS HEAVEN AND HELL. It's the COSMIC "DIVISION OF POWERS" which in the case of humans manifests as the DARK SELF AND THE LIGHT SELF. Whichever you feed, that is what will be IN CHARGE in your mind and emotions. Like MOTHER THERESA used to say, there is a HITLER AND A JESUS in all of us humans. When you finally peek into your dark unconscious and REALIZE your dark self then is when you realize things about yourself you had not realized before. Whether these are GOOD CONTENTS or DYSFUNCTIONAL ONES. When ST. MIKA-EL places his SPOTLIGHT ON YOUR DARKNESS OR SHADOW then you HAVE CHARGE OVER YOUR INNER "DEMON." At that point you have reached a state in which you are more AWARE and that MOVES YOU TO SEEK THE LIGHT WITHIN YOUR OWN SHADOW than just running constantly from both. YOU CAN'T UNDERSTAND WHAT YOU CANNOT SEE.

Basically, humans are HYBRID "ANGEL-DEMON" beings with the capacity of BEING —BOTH. Therefore, humans have the FREE WILL to choose which to feed and focus on as in either THE ANGEL IN YOU or the DEVIL IN YOU. Both ENERGIES manifest in diverse GRADATIONS which mean that YIN and YANG are —BOTH — part of NATURE AND THE MAKE UP OF HUMAN AND SO – THE KEY — IS TO LEARN TO —PROCESS THESE ENERGIES such as in the case of THE ASIAN TAOIST AND MARTIAL ARTS which HELP TEMPER THE HOLY INNER FIRE OF MAN OR "QI," BOTH THE YIN AND YANG ENERGIES in constructive ways that lead to health and BALANCE.

HUMANS are MULTIFACETED BEINGS made up of — SPIRIT, MATTER, SOUL, BODY, MIND, EMOTIONS etc. or composed of MANY "BODIES" IN ONE which are interconnected and which intersect with one another. Therefore, disease of the body might affect the MIND and the disease of MIND might affect the EMOTIONS and the BODY, etc. etc.etc. it is an INTEGRATED UNIT made up of diverse parts that complement each other and depend on each other to FUNCTION PROPERLY.

WE are glad that some religious people feel that they are SAVED and healed already in the name of Jesus. That is wonderful. However, the moment of excitement might fade overtime and the OLD DEMONS might manifest back in other ways and obsessions and so WORKING ON THYSELF regularly is necessary whether that is through psychology, therapy, hobbies, etc. etc. etc. Just an observation as WE have seen cases of SPONTANEOUS "HEALINGS" only for the disease or condition to reappear again down the road or MANIFEST DIFFERENTLY. THE SPIRITUAL PATH IS — LIFE LONG. Of course this is the case in regards to those who have a harder time reaching catharsis.

ST. MIKA-EL REFERS TO "TRUTH" SLAYING — UNTRUTH OR ILLUSION— BRINGING ABOUT CLARITY AND THE ABILITY TO —SEE —WHERE YOU ARE STANDING AND GOING. THE LIGHT TEMPERING AND TRANSFORMING THE FIERCE RAW ENERGIES OF THE MOTHER WHICH ARE PART OF HUMAN NATURE.

SINCERELY,
"MIGUELITO" FROM TEX-GALPA ARKANGEL ST. MIKAEL

---

## 30. IT'S NOT ABOUT SEX OR GENDER— IT IS ABOUT "ENERGY!" YIN AND YANG AS "ADAM AND EVE" AND THE "ENERGY GRID OF THE TREE OF LIFE OR THE LIVING GRID/ DIAGRAM!!!"

ENERGY DOES NOT HAVE A SEX OR GENDER! ENERGY DOES NOT HAVE A SEX OR GENDER! ENERGY DOES NOT HAVE A SEX OR GENDER!

YIN AND YANG —ARE "GENDER NEUTRAL" BY THEMSELVES ON THEIR OWN IN ENERGY TERMS. BOTH ARE NAMED OR DESCRIBED OR REPRESENTED BY THE ICONIC ADAM AND EVE HUMAN PERSONIFICATIONS OF YIN AND YANG!!!

ADAM AND EVE ARE NOT TWO LITERAL PEOPLE BUT REFERS TO "ENERGY SYSTEMS" AND REASON BOTH ARE TIED AND LINKED TO THE "ENERGY GRID DIAGRAM OF THE TREE OF LIFE OR OF THE LIVING!!!" MEANING THAT, THE SAME GOES FOR "AND ELOHIM CREATED THEM MALE AND FEMALE AFTER THE IMAGE AND LIKENESS OF ELOHIM." WHICH IN TECHNICAL AND SCIENTIFIC TERMS TRANSLATES AS:

"AND (KETER) AND CHOKMAH AND BINAH CREATED THE ENERGIES OF YIN AND YANG AFTER THEIR OWN IMAGES AND LIKENESSES, YIN AND YANG CREATED THEY CREATED THEM."

IMAGE === REFERS TO THE WORLD OF ARCHETYPES OF BINAH OR YIN!!! (THAT REPRESENT THE IDEAS AND SYMBOLS AND CONCEPTS THAT FORM THE BASIS OF THE ARCHETYPES AND THE UNIVERSAL BLUEPRINT).

LIKENESS ==== IS AFTER THE COSMIC FIRE AND ENERGY AND ELECTRICITY THAT FORMS LIVING BEINGS AND THINGS (PHYSICAL, MENTAL, EMOTIONAL, PSYCHIC, SPIRITUAL ETC.) WHICH ARE ALL FORMS OF THE SAME ENERGIES MANIFESTING SIMULTANEOUSLY AND AT DIFFERENT GRADES AND LEVELS OF VIBRATION. BELONGING TO CHOKMAH OR YANG!!!

THEREFORE THE MISINTERPRETATION HERE THAT EXTREME FUNDAMENTALISTS HAVE OF GENESIS IS A BAD MISTAKE!!!... THAT HAS CREATED SO MANY PROBLEMS AND PAIN AND SUFFERING AS A RESULT.

AS HUMANS ARE FORMED AFTER THE "ARCHETYPES AND ENERGY" OF SOURCE, EACH AND EVERY HUMAN OCCUPIES THE MIDDLE PILLAR OF DA-AT THE "DIVINE ANDRO-GENE" IN THE SENSE THAT EACH PERSON IS BOTH —AN ARCHETYPE MANIFESTING AS ENERGY BORN OF A DIVINE CONCEPT AND IDEA!!! AND SO EACH PERSON IS INHERENTLY AND INTRINSICALLY BOTH ——----FEMALE AND MALE OR TO DEPICT IT MORE ACCURATELY, BOTH YIN AND YANG.

IT HAS NOTHING TO DO WITH PHYSICAL SEX AND GENDER BUT WITH "ENERGIES" WHICH ARE DESCRIBED AS "MALE AND FEMALE" IN ORDER TO MAKE IT MORE UNDERSTANDABLE TO HUMANS. EACH HUMAN BOTH WOMAN AND MAN IS —-YIN AND YANG!!! ANDROGYNOUS. IF A HUMAN WAS NOT AN ANDROGYNOUS BEING S-HE WOULD STILL BE A SINGLE CELLED AMOEBA AND WOULD NOT BE A COMPLETE DUAL HUMAN BEING AS EACH ONE OF YOU IS TODAY.

THE CLOSEST TYPE OF SEXUAL MATURATION IN A PERSON IS THE "BISEXUAL" AS BOTH ENERGIES ARE LITERALLY ACTIVE AND IN SYNC WITH ONE ANOTHER. IN THE BISEXUAL, BOTH ENERGIES ARE IN CONSTANT INTERACTION WITH EACH OTHER JUST AS IN THE "ARK OF COMMUNION" WHERE THE YIN AND YANG ENERGIES ARE REPRESENTED BY THE TWIN HEAVENLY BEINGS. BY THE WAY, THIS PROCESS IS NOT LEARNED BUT — YOU ARE BORN WITH IT. WHEN IT IS YOUR TIME TO BE BORN THIS WAY, IT'S YOUR TIME TO BE THIS WAY. THEREFORE, SEXUAL ORIENTATION AND ATTRACTION DEPENDS ON THE PARTICULAR COMBINATION OF YIN AND YANG ENERGIES A PERSON IS BORN WITH.

SINCERELY,
THE ANDRO-GENE "YIN AND YANG"

## 31. "COME, COME EAT OF MY FLESH AND DRINK OF MY BLOOD" – THE PARTAKING OF THE ELEMENTS OF LIFE

John 6:53-58 New International Version (NIV)

Jesus said to them, "Very truly I tell you, unless you eat the flesh of the Son of Man and drink his blood, you have no life in you. Whoever eats my flesh and drinks my blood has eternal life, and I will raise them up at the last day.

IT IS UTTERLY RIDICULOUS TO BELIEVE OR THINK THAT THIS GOSPEL VERSE IS ABOUT "DRACULA" OR "CANNIBALISM." IT IS PROHIBITED IN THE TRADITIONAL JEWISH LAWS ANYWAYS TO EAT HUMAN FLESH AND DRINK BLOOD. THEREFORE THIS VERSE MUST BE POINTING TO SOMETHING TOTALLY DIFFERENT.

AS WE HAVE SEEN ALREADY, THE BIBLE IS A BOOK OF SYMBOLS AND CONCEPTS AND IDEAS AND METAPHORS, ETC. ETC. ETC. AND SO EACH "IDEA" IN IT IS LIKE A CLUE ONE HAS TO DECIPHER IN ORDER TO GET A GIST OF WHAT THE TEXT IS TRYING TO CONVEY. IN THIS CASE, IT IS ABOUT —-THE FOUR ELEMENTS AND IN PARTICULAR THOSE ATTRIBUTED TO THE FEMALE ASPECT OF UNIVERSAL REALITY.

AS WE HAVE STATED BEFORE, THE ENTIRE GENESIS AND THE BINDING STORIES OF ISAAC IN JUDAISM AND ISHMAEL IN ISLAM AND OF THE DEATH OF CHRIST ARE SYMBOLS AND STORIES THAT REPRESENT THE "COSMIC ORIGIN OF THINGS AND THE PROCESS OF CREATION" CALLED BY SOME THE "BIG BANG" AND AND BY OTHERS THE "TZIM TZOOOM." JESUS REPRESENTS IN THE GOSPEL STORY AN "OVERCOMING" OF THIS WORLD AS AN ACT OF REMEMBRANCE NOT ONLY OF HIS "DIVINE SELF" BUT ALSO THE INNER "WISDOM" IN CONNECTION TO THAT HIGHER SELF. AS A RESULT, BECOMING A LIVING CHRIST OR BECOMING INFUSED WITH THE FACULTY OF "REASON AND KNOWLEDGE." HE REPRESENTS ADAM KADMON INCARNATED!!!

AS SUCH HE REPRESENTS AS IN THE MAXIM —AS ABOVE SO BELOW, AND AS BELOW SO IS ABOVE —- THE "PRIMORDIAL FALLEN WO-MAN ADAMEVA KAD-M-ONNE", AND SO HE HAS RISEN METAPHORICALLY ABOVE THE WAYS OF THIS WORLD AND FOUND REDEMPTION. JUST AS IN THE TREE OF GOOD AND EVIL BECOMING THE TREE OF LIFE, UNION AND INTEGRATION PROCESS. THEREFORE, AS WE HAVE EXPLAINED BEFORE, ADAMEVA KAD-M-ONNE STANDS FOR THE SEPARATION INTO "YIN AND YANG" AND FROM THIS SEPARATION, THE BIRTH OF ENERGIES MANIFESTING IN MATTER SUCH AS FIRE, AIR, WATER AND EARTH.

THEREFORE, THE "BREAD OR FLESH" REPRESENTS THE ELEMENT OF MATTER OR EARTH AND THE BLOOD REPRESENTS THE ELEMENT OF WATER. INTERESTINGLY BOTH ARE ATTRIBUTED TO THE DIVINE FEMININE PRINCIPLE. SINCE Y-ESH-UA IS A SYMBOL FOR ADAMEVA KAD-M-ONNE AS A CHRIST FIGURE, THE SHE-KI-INNA MANIFESTS WITH THE CHRIST PRINCIPLE WHO IS LIKE "THE BRIDE OF CHRIST." IN METAPHYSICAL TERMS. AND SO SHE SPEAKS THRU HIM, WHICH MEANS THAT ANYTHING THAT Y-ESH-UA SAYS MIGHT NOT BE COMING FROM HIM PERSONALLY BUT FROM THE SHE-KI-INNA HERSELF.

THEREFORE, COME AND EAT OF MY ELEMENTS! EARTH AND WATER REPRESENTING —

The symbolism of earth Element

It symbolizes prosperity, fertility, stability, orderliness, groundedness, sustenance, creativity, physical abundance, nourishment, solidity, dependability, security, permanence, intuition, introspection, and wisdom.(FITSRI)

Water popularly represents life. It can be associated with birth, fertility, and refreshment. In a Christian context, water has many correlations. Christ walked on water, and transmuted it into WINE, thus these acts can be seen as a transcendence of the earthly condition. (UNIVERSITY OF MICHIGAN)

AND SO AS WE CAN NOTICE FROM THE ABOVE DESCRIPTIONS OF THE ELEMENTS, THE EATING OR PARTAKING OF THE EMBLEMS OF BREAD AND WINE STANDS FOR THE "BODY OF CHRIST" OR THE "4 ELEMENTS MANIFESTING AS THE BODY OF ADAMEVA KAD-M-ONNE. SO EATING THESE IS A RITUAL IN WHICH I AM STATING THAT — I AFFIRM FOR MYSELF GOODNESS AND PROSPERITY AND FERTILITY AND GROUNDEDNESS AND CREATIVITY ..... ETC... AS WELL AS ... LIFE AND REFRESHMENT. I AM AFFIRMING THE INTERDEPENDENCE OF MY BODY WITH THE EARTH'S ELEMENTS AND THE UNION OF IT ALL.

IN THE BREAD ALL THE FOUR ELEMENTS COME TOGETHER TO FORM THE BODY AND THE WINE IS THE BLOOD. AND BOTH ARE POINTING TO THE PRIMORDIAL BODY OF LIGHT OF ADAM KADMON WHICH IS THE FOUNDATION FOR THE PHYSICAL EARTHLY BODY.

SINCERELY,
"THE BODY OF ADAMEVA KAD-M-ONNE AND THE 4"

### 32. THE "GOLEM" CONCEPT: THE OPPOSITE OF THE "CHRIST PRINCIPLE OR THE STATE OF BEING AWAKE"--- WHEN MEN BECOME "MONSTERS" PART I

THE "CHRIST" MEANS THE "ANOINTED ONE" AND TO BE ANOINTED IS NOT ABOUT RELIGION EITHER.

CHRIST REFERS TO THE "HUMAN BECOMING AWAKE" TO HIS / HER OWN DIVINE HIGHER SELF. S-HE BECOMES "A FULLY CONSCIOUS AND RESPONSIBLE" HUMAN BEING. CONSCIOUS OF HIS/ HER ACTIONS TOWARDS EVERYTHING AND EVERYONE INCLUDING HIM/HERSELF. THE "WISE HUMAN" AND HIS /HER RELATIONSHIP WITH THE WHOLE.

THE ARCHETYPE OF THE "CHRIST" IS RELATED TO THE ARCHETYPE OF THE "QI-KI-INNA" AND "KETER" WHO COMPLEMENTS THE FOUR ELEMENTS IN THE METAPHYSICAL SENSE AND MANIFESTS AS AN INTEGRATED HUMAN BEING WHOSE FACULTIES OF REASON AND THINKING ARE IN SYNC AND IN ALIGNMENT WITH THE HEART CHAKRA OR HIS /HER EMOTIONAL CORE AND CENTER.

IT IS THE LINKING AND ACTIVATION AND FUNCTION OF THE MAIN CENTERS OF THE HUMAN ORGANISM SUCH AS THE MIND OR BRAIN CENTER AND THE HEART OR CARDIAC BRAIN CENTER WITH THE BELLY. ALIGNING BOTH EMOTIONS AND THOUGHTS AND THE INTUITIVE CENTER FULLY AND IN SYNC WITH EACH OTHER!!!

THE EMOTIONALLY AWAKENED PERSON HAS "EMPATHY AND DOES NOT RUN AWAY FROM HIS / HER EMOTIONS AND FEELINGS" AND SO IS NOT NUMB TO THE PAIN IN OTHERS. THE MIND IN SYNC WITH THE "LOVING HEART" ALIGNS HIS / HER ACTIONS ACCORDING TO THESE EMOTIONS AND ACTS IN A RESPONSIBLE WAY. IT'S A STATE OF BEING IN WHICH ONE CHOOSES TO HARBOR THOUGHTS THAT ARE IN ALIGNMENT WITH TENDER EMOTIONS THAT PROMOTE HARMONY, BALANCE AND WELL BEING. THAT IS HOW THE "SYSTEM" WORKS.

AND THAT IS THE BASIS FOR THE "CHRIST" PRINCIPLE ACTIVATION IN A PERSON!!!

WHEN THE OPPOSITE HAPPENS YOU HAVE THE "GOL-EM" STATES IN WHICH THE HUMAN IS OUT OF TOUCH WITH HIS /HER EMOTIONAL CORE AND THEREFORE FEELS NO EMPATHY FOR OTHERS BECOMING AN IRRESPONSIBLE AND - OR VIOLENT HUMAN BEING. HIS HEART AND MIND BECOME DISCONNECTED FROM EACH OTHER ACTING ONLY FROM THE INTELLECT OR MIND ALONE OR FROM RAW EMOTION WITHOUT INTELLECT.

WHICH IS EQUIVALENT TO BEING IN A STATE OF DISCONNECTION WIRHIN SINCE IN THIS CASE, THE MIND AND HEART ARE NOT ALIGNED TO EACH OTHER. IN THE "GOLEM" STATE, THE HUMAN HAS NO EMPATHY AND SO DOES NOT FEEL ANY REMORSE OR HAS NO —INNER COMPASS–THAT WILL PREVENT HIM OR HER FROM CAUSING HARM ONTO ANOTHER PERSON OR TO OTHER LIVING BEINGS AND THE PLANET. WHEN A PERSON HAS EVIL EMOTIONS FED BY EVIL THOUGHT PROCESSES AND VICE VERSA, THERE IS NOT AN EMOTIONAL INNER COMPASS TO PREVENT HIM OR HER FROM DOING THE UNTHINKABLE. S-HE CANNOT PUT HIM OR HERSELF IN ANOTHER PERSON'S SHOES.

THIS STATE OF "GOLEM" LEADS TO MEN BECOMING LIKE "VORACIOUS BEASTS WHO FEEL NO REMORSE AT HURTING OTHERS AND EMBRACING VIOLENCE."

SINCERELY, "THE LIGHT OF CHOCHMA" aka "THE CONSCIOUS CHRIST"

---

## 33.  THE "GOL-EM" CONCEPT: THE OPPOSITE OF THE "CHRIST PRINCIPLE OR THE STATE OF BEING AWAKE"--- WHEN MEN BECOME "MONSTERS" PART II

IN THE "GOLEM" LEGEND, THE "HUMANOID OF DUST AND EARTH" HAS NO CONSCIOUSNESS. IT ONLY FOLLOWS ORDERS LIKE A ROBOT. THE GOLEM IS ORDERED TO CAUSE HARM LIKE A MONSTER FEELING NO REMORSE OR UNABLE TO ACCOUNT FOR ITS ACTIONS OR "THINK" ABOUT WHAT IT IS DOING.

THIS "GOLEM" IS MADE UP OF ONLY THREE ELEMENTS AS IN — AIR, WATER AND EARTH AND —ELECTRICITY!!! BUT IS MISSING THE "KETER" ELEMENT AS IN — LOVE WHICH IS SPIRITUAL DIVINE FIRE AND CONSCIOUSNESS.

HUMAN BODY IS A GOLEM PROTOTYPE THAT HAS BEEN ACTIVATED WITH UNIVERSAL ENERGY. AND ENDOWED WITH LOVE IN HUMAN AND THE "FACULTIES OF REASONING, THINKING AND FEELING." ALTHOUGH, THESE CAN BE THWARTED BY CONDITIONING, BRAINWASHING AND TRAUMA WHICH MIGHT LEAD TO GOL-EM STATE AT TIMES WHEN NEGATIVITY TAKES OVER AND THE PERSON'S INNER LIGHT IS FURTHERMORE BURIED IN NEGATIVITY AND RESENTMENTS. .

THEREFORE, THE RAMPANT VIOLENCE TODAY AND CORRUPTION IS DUE TO THIS "GOL-EM" PROCESS AND STATE. AND SO —WE RECOMMEND AND ENCOURAGE "TO WHOM THIS DIARY MAY CONCERN" TO — START NURTURING AND DEVELOPING THEIR INNATE EMOTIONS AND MENTAL

FACULTIES. TO STRIVE TO BE IN SYNCHRONICITY WITH ONES OWN HIGHER DIVINE SELF FOR THE WELL BEING AND CONTINUED LIFE OF THIS BEAUTIFUL PLANET.

BECOME "THE CHRIST IN YOU!!!"

SINCERELY,
THE COSMIC CHRIST

---

## 34. "MENTAL ILLNESS" VS. "666" AND "EVIL INCLINATION" —- THE TIME FOR HEALING AND LIBERATION

Right now there is serious SCAPEGOATING taking place upon VULNERABLE AND PROTECTED GROUPS in order to DEFLECT from the real ILLNESS taking over here and the NEGLECT OF PERSONAL RESPONSIBILITY towards the PEOPLE.

IRRESPONSIBLE persons rather than ACCEPTING AND ACKNOWLEDGING how their decisions and actions CONTRIBUTE TO THE VIOLENCE everywhere, they SCAPEGOAT EVERYTHING ON A CERTAIN GROUP OR GROUPS in order to SHIFT BLAME and have someone else take the hits for their own EVIL INCLINATIONS. This is very much EVIL taking over.

As WE explained before, many so called MENTALLY ILL are actually experiencing EMOTIONAL ISSUES, PSYCHOLOGICAL ISSUES and or ARE UNDERGOING A TRUE PROCESS OF SPIRITUAL AWAKENING!!! These processes here DO NOT EQUATE A PERSON WITH —BEING EVIL! Perhaps there might be a case here and there but for the most part SO CALLED "MENTALLY ILL" are actually VULNERABLE AND GOOD PEOPLE who have GREAT EMPATHY FOR THE PAIN OF OTHERS BECAUSE THEY KNOW EVERY DAY WHAT IT IS TO LIVE WITH PAIN!!! UNLIKE other people who are NUMB AND LACK EMPATHY because they have not experienced pain or shy away from pain all the time looking to live in comfort and obsessed with feeling secure all the time.

Now WE have the (-) 6+6+6= (-) 18 GROUPS all over the world who will cast blame on the VULNERABLE OF SOCIETY because it is a way of deflecting personal responsibility of the "(-) 6+6+6 types." Basically it is the PERSECUTION all over again of the MOST VULNERABLE by those with the "MARK OF THE BEAST." As WE explained before, the MARK OF THE BEAST is a SYMBOL representing the stunted BRAIN and the PREFRONTAL LOBE which is where the ABILITY TO TELL GOOD FROM EVIL is found and where the feeling of EMPATHY is born is a person.

In GOLEM TYPES this pre-frontal lobe is in a dormant or messed up state. In the (-) 666 group this ability has been NUMBED OR HAMPERED because of diverse factors and so remains dormant in some way. Thus, the person is unable to feel any EMPATHY AND UNABLE TO TELL THE DIFFERENCE BETWEEN GOOD AND EVIL. This is a very DANGEROUS COMBINATION in which people have NO SENSE OF THE EVIL THEY ARE DOING because to them EVIL LOOKS GOOD, AND GOOD LOOKS EVIL. Therefore, they have no EMPATHY whatsoever for the PAIN AND SUFFERING THEY CAUSE WITH THEIR ACTIONS or are INDIFFERENT TOWARDS IT. As WE explained before ... (-)6+6+6= (-) 18 IS "THE MOON CARD" in the ARK-ANNA of the TAROT which is linked to the SUBCONSCIOUS PROCESSES AND THE SHADOW ASPECTS OF THE HUMAN MIND.

In other words the (-) 666 see and FEEL NOTHING WRONG IN DOING BAD!!! Meanwhile the so called MENTALLY ILL as they can FEEL PAIN UNLIKE THE (-) 666 GROUP, can still tell the difference between one thing and the other, and even if they fail they DO FEEL REMORSE FOR THEIR ACTIONS AND —CHANGE. On the other hand, the - 666 are those labeled today as having PSYCHOPATHIC AND NARCISSISTIC PERSONALITY disorders.

HAVING A SO CALLED MENTAL ILLNESS "DOES NOT AUTOMATICALLY MAKE A PERSON EVIL!!!" EXCESS TRAUMA THOUGH CAN CAUSE THE PREFRONTAL BRAIN TO MALFUNCTION IN ALL TYPES OF PEOPLE. However, those who claim to be NOT TRULY ILL FROM THE BRAIN, WILL USUALLY SHIFT BLAME ON THE POOR VULNERABLE ONES WHO CANNOT DEFEND THEMSELVES AND — THE (-) 666 WILL BEGIN TO CAST STONES ON THE VULNERABLE TYPES IN ORDER TO COVER AND CONCEAL HIS HER TRUE "DEGENERATE" STATE.

Do you see that happening today? every time something bad happens automatically SOME will CAST BLAME ON THE "MENTALLY ILL"!!! When the REAL SOURCE OF EVIL THAT SUSTAINS THE EVIL IS SOMEWHERE ELSE LOOKING as "HEALTHY AND NORMAL" BUT is not. And this (-) 666 process is happening and has been happening for a very long time and it is happening EVERYWHERE. As violence and hate have overtaken the entire WORLD.

Prime examples of this process of the - 666 are NAZI GERMANY and HITLER and today ZIONISTS and their SCAPEGOATING OF GROUPS. It seems that "HE IS BACK" or THAT FOUL AIR that had corrupted "him" is back.

Therefore, WE are here NOT to DEFLECT but to POINT TO THOSE WHO NEED TRUE HEALING to ACTIVATE — THE PREFRONTAL LOBE AND ACTIVATE THE CAPACITY TO BE EMPATHIC AND ABLE TO TELL THE DIFFERENCE BETWEEN GOOD AND EVIL. Because it is here where THE TRAUMA AND IMBALANCE IN SOCIETY BEGINS which ends up causing other peoples

"MENTAL- EMOTIONAL BREAKDOWNS AND PRODUCING MORE IMBALANCE IN SOCIETY. Because MOST OF THE (-) 666=(-) 18 are NON-EMPATHIC they have the capacity of FACING challenges much easier since they are INSENSITIVE TO PAIN. This characteristic of the (-) 666 makes it easy for them to reach the TOP in the areas of POWER AND MATERIAL INFLUENCE AND PROSPERITY!!! And so it is very detrimental to have PEOPLE WITHOUT EMPATHY AND THE INABILITY TO SEE THE DIFFERENCE BETWEEN GOOD AND EVIL IN PLACES OF RESPONSIBILITY that are supposed to oversee the CARE AND WELL BEING OF OTHER PEOPLE. How is a person going to make WISE DECISIONS that benefit the well being of the PEOPLE when they FEEL NO EMPATHY FOR THE PLIGHT AND SUFFERING OF THE PEOPLE THEY ARE ENTRUSTED TO LOOK AFTER???!

THE TIME IS COME TO "TURN THE PAGE" — and to begin the HEALING WORK of those who are really in need of healing and those in need of LIBERATION.

SINCERELY, THE ++++ 666 or the +18 = 9 HERMIT CARRYING THE LIGHT OF REASON

---

## 35. CURSES!!!: THE EVERYDAY POWER EACH ONE OF US HAS TO "BLESS" OR TO "CURSE!!!"

PEOPLE THINK FOR THE MOST PART THAT "CURSES" ARE BASED ON "HOCUS POCUS" AND "ABRAHADABRAS." IT IS POSSIBLE BUT THERE IS ANOTHER EASIER WAY TO—CURSE PEOPLE —FOR LIFE THAN BY HOCUS POCUS. AND HERE IS WHERE THE CONCEPT OF PERSONAL RESPONSIBILITY HAS TO BE TAKEN INTO ACCOUNT. LET US EXPLAIN.

HUMANS ARE MAGICAL BEINGS IN THE SENSE THAT THEY ARE ANIMATED BY "LIVING...QI..ENERGIES." EMOTIONS AND THOUGHTS ARE MANIFESTATIONS OF ENERGY IN VIBRATION WHETHER THESE ARE POSITIVE OR NEGATIVE. THESE THOUGHT AND EMOTIONAL ENERGIES LEAD TO ACTION AND MANY TIMES THESE ACTIONS BORN OF THESE ENERGIES CAN BE EITHER FOR GOOD AS IN "BLESSING" OR CAN BE REALLY "BAD AND MESSED UP AS IN ...CURSE!!!!"

THIS IS WHY THE WAY WE TREAT EACH OTHER IS OF UTMOST IMPORTANCE AND LIKE SOME RELIGIOUS PEOPLE CLAIM TODAY ...TREATING OTHERS AS YOU WOULD LIKE TO BE TREATED...IS NOT A SIGN OF WEAKNESS BUT OF REAL STRENGTH AND WELL BEING BECAUSE ONE IS "BLESSING OTHERS THROUGH ONE'S WORDS AND ACTIONS." BUT THE OPPOSITE HAPPENS AS WELL, AS IN CURSING OTHERS THROUGH EVIL WORDS AND ACTIONS. WE COULD BE "SPREADING EVIL AND CURSES" UPON OTHERS

IN THE FORM OF TRAUMA AND PSYCHO-EMOTIONAL DAMAGE THAT CAN LAST A LIFETIME AND SPREAD HARM TO ENTIRE COMMUNITIES. WE DO POSSESS PERSONAL POWER TO BESTOW GOODNESS AND HEALTH OR DESTRUCTION, CHAOS AND...DEATH THROUGH OUR OWN WORDS AND ACTIONS.

TO GIVE A SIMPLE EXAMPLE, LET US SAY THAT A PARENT TREATS THE CHILD WITH NEGLECT AND BAD WORDS. THIS PARENT WITHOUT REALIZING IT IS "CURSING HIS/HER CHILD!!!" THESE WORDS AND ACTIONS WHICH ARE ALL FORMS OF TOXIC ENERGY IS BEING PASSED ONTO THE CHILD AS IN "TRANSFERENCE" WHICH HE SHE ENDS UP ABSORBING AND BECOMING PART OF HIS BAGGAGE. BAGGAGE THAT S-HE CARRIES IN THE FORM OF TRAUMA AND SELF HATE AND OTHER DYSFUNCTIONS BORN OF THE CURSE THAT PARENT PLACED ON THE CHILD; WHICH IN TURN MIGHT HAVE BEEN PLACED UPON THE PARENT BY THE ANCESTORS. AND SO HERE WE HAVE A CURSE BEEN PASSED FROM GENERATION TO GENERATION.

LET US SAY THEN THAT THIS CHILD IS CARRYING THIS EVIL CURSE AND THAT S-HE IS UNABLE TO PROCESS IT AND GET THE LOVE AND SUPPORT TO HEAL AND UNDERSTAND WHAT THIS STATE OF BEING "WOUNDED ENTAILS;" THEREFORE, S-HE ENDS UP PROJECTING THE CURSE ONTO OTHERS AND LASHING OUT AT PEOPLE IN VIOLENT WAYS IN ORDER TO COMPENSATE FOR THE EVIL THAT WAS DONE TO HIM OR HER. AND SO THE CURSE IS PASSED ONTO OTHERS IN THE COMMUNITY.

SO AS WE CAN SEE HERE, US HUMANS CARRY GREAT "POWER" AND WE DO NOT REALLY NEED TO GET INTO HOCUS POCUS OR ABRACADABRA. SINCE WE ALREADY IN OUR DAILY LIFE HAVE THE POWER THRU OUR OWN THOUGHTS, WORDS AND ACTIONS TO "BLESS OR TO CURSE" OTHERS!!! THEREFORE, WE MUST TAKE CARE AND WATCH OUT HOW WE TREAT OURSELVES FIRST AND OTHERS. WE NEED TO SEEK HEALING FOR INNER PEACE AND HELP SO THAT WE DO NOT END UP SPREADING OUR CURSES ONTO OTHERS AND MAKING OUR SITUATION EVEN WORSE AND THAT OF THE WORLD.

EVERYTHING WILL BE OKAY. LOVE IS IN THE WAY! LOVE IS HERE! IT'S ALREADY IN YOU!

SINCERELY, "THE SCAPEGOAT WHO IS NO LONGER CARRYING THE BLEMISHES OF ANYONE"

**36. THE "CYPHER" OF THE "666" AS POINTING TO "STATES OF UNCONSCIOUSNESS —- AND THE DANGERS OF "NOT BEING AWARE OF OUR OWN SHADOW"--- MOVING FROM THE "DARK SIDE OF THE MOON TO THE BRIGHTER SIDE"**

—-THE TRUE MEANING OF: YOU GET TO CHOKMAH THROUGH THE SON AND THE SON IS DA'AT.

—-THE TRUE MEANING OF THE PROMISED LAND AS IN ARRIVING TO CHOKMA HIGHER STATES OF CONSCIOUSNESS.

AS WE EXPLAINED "LONG TIME AGO" THE 666 IS A "CYPHER" AND —NOT—A LITERAL NUMBER THAT SOMEONE WILL COME AND PLACE ON YOUR FOREHEAD AS SOME PEOPLE LIKE TO INTERPRET. IT IS A —CYPHER—OR A CODE FOR:

6 +6 + 6 ===18 THE MOON CARD IN THE TAROT, IN BOTH ITS NEGATIVE OR POSITIVE INTERPRETATIONS THE MOON CARD REPRESENTS "STATES OF CONSCIOUSNESS OR UNCONSCIOUSNESS." IN THE REVERSE OR NEGATIVE INTERPRETATION, IT POINTS AT "NOT BEING AWARE OF OUR OWN SHADOW AND SO BEING UNDER THE CONTROL AND MANIPULATION OF THESE FORCES IN YOUR UNCONSCIOUS/ SUBCONSCIOUS WHICH WOULD BE EQUIVALENT TO BEING UNDER THE IMPOSITION, CONTROL AND MANIPULATION OF YOUR OWN PERSONAL "TYRANT" OR UNCONSCIOUS FORCES OR OF BEING ....POSSESSED.

THE UNCONSCIOUS FORCES OR THE DARK SIDE OF THE MIND IS EQUIVALENT TO THE DARK SIDE OF THE MOON. MEANWHILE THE LIGHT THAT HELPS DISSIPATE THE STATE OF BEING IN THE DARK IS EQUIVALENT TO ACHIEVING "ILLUMINATION/ ENLIGHTENMENT" OR REACHING TO THE BRIGHT SIDE OF THE MOON OR THE FULL MOON THANKS TO CHOKMAH THE SUN PRINCIPLE.

IF YOU LOOK VERY CLOSELY AT THE "TREE OF LIFE / DUALITY" YOU WILL NOTICE THAT THIS PROCESS OF MOVING FROM THE DARK TO THE LIGHT IS REPRESENTED IN THE DIAGRAM. LET US EXPLAIN FURTHER.

BINAH WOULD REPRESENT THE "DARK SIDE OF THE MOON" AND TO GET TO THE OTHER SIDE AS IN THE BRIGHT SIDE OF THE MOON WHICH IS LINKED TO THE FATHER PRINCIPLE OR CHOKMAH— YOU HAVE TO PASS THRU THE —MID-BAR OR MIDDLE PATH OR POINT OF TRANSITION. WHO IS —DA-AT—!!! WHICH IS BASICALLY ...."WHO?"

REMINDER: "YOU CANNOT GET TO THE FATHER WITHOUT THE "SON... (-DAUGHTER" ADAM KAD-M-ONNE "). (GOSPEL)

THE ABOVE IS WHAT Y-ESH-UA "MEANT. IT IS NOT A LITERAL MEANING AS IN—WITHOUT Y-ESH-UA–YOU CANNOT GET TO THE FATHER WHO REPRESENTS THE BRIGHT SIDE OF THE MOON OR ILLUMINATION AND ENLIGHTENED STATES OF CONSCIOUSNESS.

AS YOU WILL RECALL, THE TRANSITION SPACE BETWEEN ONE POINT AND ANOTHER IS A PLACE OF "TRIAL AND IMPROVEMENT. AS A RESULT OF THOSE LIFE TRIALS" IS THAT ONE GETS LIFE EXPERIENCE AND LEARNING AS MAKING MISTAKES LEADS EVENTUALLY TO UNDERSTANDING AND WISDOM. THEREFORE, EGYPT OR MIZRAIM OR THE PLACE OF CONSTRICTION IS REPRESENTED BY BINAH, WHILE THE PLACE OF MID-BAR OR TRANSITION IS OCCUPIED BY DA-AT OR THE HEAVENLY "SON-DAUGHTER AS IN LESSER YIN AND YANG" AND THE PROMISED LAND REPRESENTS THE BRIGHT SIDE OF THE MOON AND THE SUN IN CHOCKMAH. THE MOTHER OR "UNDERSTANDING" CANNOT UNITE TO THE FATHER OR "WISDOM" WITHOUT THE CHILD IN ARCHETYPAL TERMS.

THE MID-BAR OR DA-AT WOULD BE EQUIVALENT TO THE —WAXING CRESCENT MOON—OF THE MOTHER PRINCIPLE.

THEREFORE, NOT ONLY IS THE "YOU DON'T GET TO THE FATHER WITHOUT THE SON" A METAPHOR FOR THE ABOVE PROCESS OF HUMAN ENLIGHTENMENT BUT ALSO THE PROMISED LAND IS NOT REFERRING TO SOME GEOGRAPHICAL TERRITORY ON EARTH BUT TO A HIGHER STATE OF CONSCIOUSNESS IN CHOCHMA!!!

AND SO WE SEE HERE THE — DARK MOON STATE OF UNCONSCIOUSNESS AND THE CRESCENT MOON PROCESS OF LEARNING THRU TRIAL AND ERROR — LEADING EVENTUALLY TO THE "EUREKA MOMENT OF UNDERSTANDING AND WISDOM TO KNOW THE DIFFERENCE BETWEEN DUALITIES OR ILLUMINATION REPRESENTED BY THE FULL MOON!!!

THEREFORE THE 666 OF REVELATIONS IS ANOTHER "CYPHER" AS IN —6+6+6=== 18 THE MOON CARD OF THE TAROT WHICH REPRESENTS THE DEEP UNCONSCIOUS AND THE PROCESS OF ILLUMINATION DESCRIBED ABOVE. BEING UNDER THE INFLUENCE OF (-) 666 MEANS THAT WE ARE NOT AWARE OF WHAT WE ARE DOING BECAUSE WE DO NOT UNDERSTAND AND KNOW OURSELVES YET!!

WHEN YOU MOVE FROM THE DARK MOON THRU THE CRESCENT PHASE ONTO THE BRIGHT ILLUMINATED MOON, YOU HAVE "GROWN UP" AS THE WORD "CRESCENT OR CRESCERE" MEANS TO GROW. AND SO YOU ARE IN BALANCE AND EQUILIBRIUM AS BOTH THE DARK AND THE LIGHT ARE ACTIVE AND YOUR LIGHT SIDE IS IN SYNC WITH THE DARK SIDE. NOW YOU UNDERSTAND YOUR BRIGHT SIDE AS WELL AS THE SHADOW IN YOU!!!

SINCERELY,
EVA L-UNA

---

## 37. The 144,000: "JEZEBEL'S" PERSECUTION AND MURDER OF ALL THOSE WHO BEAR CHRIST'S "TESTIMONY" TO THE HEALING OF EARTH AND PEOPLES I

There has been a lot of INTERPRETATION AND MIS-INTERPRETATION regarding the 144,000 in the symbolic book of Revelation. I have heard throughout the years the most interesting and the most ridiculous interpretations too. People forget that EVERYTHING about the Book of Revelations is SYMBOLIC and supposed to represent something HIDDEN. Until now uncovered by him/her who possesses the keys or understanding to decipher the codes and their meaning. Blessings to the LORD/LADY of HEAVENS! Amen!

As you will recall the ARK-ANNA OF THE TAROT is symbolic and PSYCHOLOGICAL which is what the symbols in the Book of Revelation are pointing at. Basically, THE SYMBOLS OF REVELATION ARE ARCHETYPAL AND BASED ON PSYCHOLOGY.

It's just funny that every religious person I know wants and swears to be one of the 144,000 because they claim to love god fervently and attend church all day long. However, that is not how it works in regards to the 144,000.

THE NUMBER IS —SYMBOLIC!!! It is not to be taken literally. THE 144,000 represents something else altogether than people dressed in white robes going up to heaven. The number 144,000 can be better UNDERSTOOD by reading the other verse in Revelation 17:6:

Revelation 17:6, NIV: I saw that the woman was drunk with the blood of God's HOLY people, the blood of those who bore TESTIMONY to Jesus. When I saw her, I was greatly astonished.

So THE REVELATION 17:6 VERSE is referring to the JEZEBEL TYPES THAT GO ON PERSECUTING THE "HOLY" ONES who GIVE TESTIMONY OF JESUS. Let me explain here what this is referring to. Being HOLY does not have anything to do with being religious. You can be non religious and be in a state of holiness.

As WE told you before, the term HOLY refers to being in relative INTEGRATION, BALANCE, HEALTH AND EQUILIBRIUM. For instance, when you are striving to find emotional, psychological and physical balance in order to have a happier and healthier life you are indeed pursuing a state of HOLINESS or being WHOLE. As you will recall, THE ABOVE IS WHAT THE GOSPEL OF YESHUA IS ALL ABOUT. IT IS NOT ABOUT RELIGION, CREED OR DOGMA BUT ABOUT WHAT REALLY COUNTS IN THE HEALTH AND STABILITY OF THE PLANET — PEOPLE'S OWN INNER STATES that eventually manifest and translate in the everyday world as A HEALTHY SUSTAINABLE WORLD as opposed to ONE IN THE BRINK OF ANNIHILATION. That is WHAT "BEARING TESTIMONY OF JESUS" REFERS TO. And as we all know because of history and today's unfortunate events, THOSE WHO WISH TO HEAL THE WORLD AND THE PEOPLE AND TO BRING THIS WORLD BACK TO BALANCE AND RELATIVE ORDER ARE THE ONES WHO HISTORICALLY ARE PERSECUTED AND MURDERED. YESHUA BEING THE FIRST FRUIT OF THOSE BEARING THE TESTIMONY OF THE "CHRIST."

And so after we understand that VERSE better, let's explain the 144,000. What does this 144,000 refer to?

Well, the answer is clear in the verse of REV 17:6. These 144,000 are those who are PERSECUTED, SILENCED AND MURDERED FOR THE SAKE OF THE WELL BEING OF THE PEOPLE AND THE WORLD. And this has always happened because THE WORLD OF MATTER IS "THE MATRIX" and is an ILLUSION that will make you believe that THIS IS IT and so some will be blinded by this ILLUSION and will MURDER THOSE WHO HOLD THE EARTH SACRED and who are trying their best to keep the planet healthy and the people as well. And so WHAT types of people are the 144,000?

TO BE CONTINUED....

---

### 38. The 144,000: "JEZEBEL'S" PERSECUTION AND MURDER OF ALL THOSE WHO BEAR CHRIST'S "TESTIMONY" TO THE HEALING OF EARTH AND PEOPLES II

Well, the VALUE OF THE NUMBER 144,000 reveals who these 144,000 are? As follows:

1 is the MAGICIAN ARCHETYPE. It is not referring to magicians or the like but refers to THOSE MEN AND WOMEN WHO HAVE THE ABILITY TO DO THINGS FOR THE WELL BEING OF EARTH AND PEOPLE BECAUSE THEY POSSESS THE WISDOM AND INSIGHT TO CREATE ORDER OUT OF CHAOS.

8 (4 + 4) is the STRENGTH ARCHETYPE. This refers to the ABILITY OF THESE MEN AND WOMEN TOWARDS SELF CONTROL AND LIVING IN MODERATION AND TEMPERANCE IN THEIR EMOTIONS AND PSYCHE. BASICALLY THEY ARE — NON VIOLENT and THEIR YIN ENERGIES ARE WELL TAMED AND IN BALANCE WITH AND BY THE YANG ENERGIES AND VICE VERSA.

000= 4+4+4= 12 is the HANGED MAN archetype that REFERS TO HAVING BEEN "LEFT HANGING" LITERALLY BECAUSE OF THEIR INABILITY TO BE ABLE TO CARRY OUT OR COMPLETE THEIR LIFE SAVING WORK AND MISSION AS THEY ARE MURDERED etc. etc. etc. or as in the GOSPEL STORY, BEING LITERALLY HANGED.

1 + 8= 9 THE 144,000 ARE LIKE "THE HERMIT CARD" and are CARRYING THE LAMP OF WISDOM AND INSIGHT BY WHICH THEY CAN HELP GUIDE HUMANITY FROM GOING ASTRAY AND SELF ANNIHILATION.

000 =4+4+4= 12 THE HANGED MAN again and THESE ARE THE HERMIT TYPES OR WISE MEN AND WISE WOMEN WHO FOR AGES HAVE BEEN PERSECUTED AND MURDERED BY THE MATERIAL POWERS OF THIS WORLD OF ASAT-ANNA.

9 + 12 = 21 REFERS TO THE END OF THE ROAD or OF THE WORLD as in the end of the entire CYCLE from "0" to "21." in this case it is referring to the END OF A CYCLE. 9 + 3 = 12 THE HANGED MAN. As in being in a state of suspension and or limbo not knowing WHICH ROAD TO CHOOSE— CORRUPTION or HEALTH— and so choosing the FORMER, CAN BE CATASTROPHIC AND SPELL THE END.

And so you might wonder what has happened to all those who have DIED to make things better for others and that have been unable to do so because THE LORD OF MATTER GETS ANGRY AND DOES THE UNTHINKABLE all the time which is to shed the HOLY BLOOD OF THOSE WHO GIVE TESTIMONY OF THE MESSAGE AND ADMONISHMENT OF THE HEALING OF THE WORLD AND ITS INHABITANTS. Examples of these MARTYRS IN CHRIST –are NOT necessarily Christian although some might be— but ARE FROM ALL PEOPLES AND TRIBES. A clear example of MARTYRS IN CHRIST are THE MURDERS OF BERTA CACERES and JANET KAWAS in Honduras for working to PROTECT MOTHER EARTH and its ANIMALS, PLANTS and ... THE HEALTH OF THE PEOPLE since humans live from and are sustained by MOTHER EARTH GAIA HERSELF.

1+4+4= 9 THE HERMITS OF THE EARTH

000 = 4 + 4 + 4 = 12 THE HANGED ONES OF THE EARTH

9 AND 12 == 21 THE HANGED HERMITS OR ILLUMINATED ONES OF THE DIVINE FROM THE BEGINNING UNTIL THE END OF THE CURRENT CYCLE.

SINCERELY, "THE 144-000 COMMUNICATING THROUGH OUR DIVINE GOAT OF MENDES"

---

## 39. THE "BEAST" ARCHETYPE AND THE "FALSE PROPHET" OF APOKA-L-IPSIS: THE CORRUPT SYMBIOTIC RELATIONSHIP OF POWER AND INFLUENCE JUSTIFIED BY EXTREMIST IDEOLOGICAL AND RELIGIOUS POSITIONS IN THE LAST DAYS OF KALI YUG!

The BEAST AND THE FALSE PROPHET are ARCHETYPES that come in PAIRS. As in a DUAL archetype. This archetype has many correspondences in our world in which the BEAST archetype represents GOVERNMENT or POLITICAL INSTITUTIONS and THE FALSE "PROPHET" represents IDEOLOGY, PHILOSOPHY, RELIGION, AND RELIGIOUS INSTITUTIONS.

As you can see from the explanation above, THE BEAST/ FALSE PROPHET ARCHETYPE sounds much like the CHURCH AND STATE combo or GOVERNMENTS SPREADING CERTAIN EXTREMIST IDEOLOGIES. What makes this HYBRID ARCHETYPE DANGEROUS AND DETRIMENTAL FOR EVERYONE is that it is a SYMBIOTIC "DYSFUNCTIONAL"

RELATIONSHIP in which BOTH the BEAST archetype and the FALSE PROPHET archetype HELP SUSTAIN AND SUPPORT EACH OTHER by evil and corrupt means.

As this relationship is DYSFUNCTIONAL, it becomes EVIL overtime and VERY DETRIMENTAL TO THE HEALTH OF THE PEOPLE, NATION and WORLD if / and when BOTH "RISE" and BECOME POWERFUL!!!

WE have seen this happening over and over again throughout history. A perfect example of this DYSFUNCTIONAL DUOPOLY was the BOLSHEVIK REVOLUTION of 1917 with its EXTREMIST IDEOLOGY and THE CHURCH-STATE set up of the middle ages to just name a few examples.

THE BEAST and FALSE PROPHET as you will recall are connected to MONEY and to THE POWER OF MONEY and so BOTH will AB-USE the concept of MONEY in order to GAIN POWER OVER THE SYSTEM AND MAINTAIN THEIR INFLUENCE OVER IT.

THE FALSE PROPHET many times represents EXTREMIST RELIGIOUS INSTITUTIONS AND IDEOLOGIES that just like MONEY, will CORRUPT the RELIGIOUS INSTITUTIONS and use the SACRED TEACHINGS AND SYMBOLS TO GAIN POWER AND INFLUENCE OVER THE PEOPLE and SUSTAIN the SYSTEMS OF POWER AND CONTROL AND INFLUENCE FOR THEIR OWN ADVANTAGE AND TO PROMOTE THEIR OWN AGENDAS. THERE IS NOTHING

"GODLY OR SACRED" ABOUT THEM BUT ACTUALLY "HAVE THE OPPOSITE EFFECT."

THE BEAST ENERGY is perfectly described by what happened in NAZI GERMANY in which the STATE CORRUPTED RELIGION IN ORDER TO JUSTIFY —GENOCIDE!!! And so this MALEVOLENT ENERGY is happening today at an alarming rate in many places of the WORLD and YOU SHOULD KEEP AN EYE OPEN AND NOT BE DECEIVED BY IT. The BEAST as the book of APOKA-L-IPSIS describes it SPEAKS GREAT WORDS A LA 1984 "SAYING ONE THING BUT DOING AND MEANING THE OPPOSITE." CORRUPTING "RELIGIOUS TEACHING" BY WAY OF THE POWER OF MONEY IN ORDER TO SUSTAIN ITS POWER AND INFLUENCE OVER PEOPLE, NATIONS AND THE WORLD. JUSTIFYING "EVIL AND MURDER" BY WAY OF "MISUSING" THE SACRED TEACHINGS IN ORDER TO ACCOMPLISH ITS TASK OF CORRUPTING THE WORLD FOR THE SAKE OF POWER.

THE BEAST and THE FALSE PROPHET archetypes are like JEZEBEL in that they BOTH "UNITE" AGAINST THE "PEOPLE OF GOD" who are those WHO PROMOTE JUSTICE AND HEALING OF THE WORLD as in the 144- 000 or the 9 / 12 RIGHTEOUS MEN AND WOMEN WHO UPHOLD THE DIGNITY AND HOLINESS OF LIFE AND THE PLANET.

As you can notice, that DYSFUNCTIONAL DUOPOLY has taken over THE WORLD by the DIRE CONDITIONS everywhere. IT'S A WAR being waged BETWEEN THOSE WHO "SERVE THE BEAST AND THE FALSE PROPHET" ARCHETYPAL ENERGIES VS. THE 144-000 SERVANTS OF THE DIVINE WHO UPHOLD THE HOLINESS OF THE PLANET AND THE DIVINE VALUES AND PRINCIPLES THAT AFFIRM LIFE AND TRUE SPIRITUAL VALUES.

Therefore, THE ELOHIM state to people today to BEWARE OF THIS MALIGNANT INFLUENCE; and, for THOSE IN PLACES OF RESPONSIBILITY and PEOPLE IN GENERAL, BEWARE OF EATING AND PARTAKING OF THE WAYS OF THE "BEAST AND FALSE PROPHET" for they will lead you to PERDITION.

THE BEAST WHO SPEAKS "GREAT WORDS" AND CLAIMS TO BE THE CHRIST PRESENCE, AND THE FALSE PROPHET WHO CLAIMS TO REPRESENT "THE PEOPLE" AND HIDES HIS EVIL CRIMES BEHIND "RELIGION" and BOTH "ARCHETYPAL ENERGIES" HAVE TAKEN CONTROL.

JUST LOOK AT WHAT IS HAPPENING!!!! DO WE NEED TO SAY MORE?

SINCERELY, "BINAH AND HER SHE-KI-INNA"

## 40. REVELATION 13: 15 AND THE BEAST ARCHETYPE AND HIS CULTURE OF DEATH AND VIOLENCE — OVERTAKEN, CONTROLLED AND MANIPULATED BY THE LOWER UNCONSCIOUS AND AFTER THE IMAGE AND LIKENESS OF THE BEAST

**15** And he had power to give life unto the image of the beast, that the image of the beast should both speak, and cause that as many as would not worship the image of the beast should be killed.

13 IS THE NUMBER OF THE "DEATH CARD" IN THE TAROT AND IN THIS VERSE IT REPRESENTS "LITERAL DEATH AND DEATH OF THE GOOD IN PEOPLE." THE NUMBER —15— IS THE "DEVIL'S CARD" AS IN THE ARCHETYPE OF BEING TRAPPED AND SHACKLED TO THE EVIL IMPULSE AND TO DELUSION AND UNTRUTH.

"THAT AS MANY AS WOULD NOT WORSHIP THE IMAGE OF THE BEAST SHOULD BE KILLED!!!"

WHAT DOES THE "AFTER THE IMAGE OF THE BEAST" SOUND LIKE? …DOES IT NOT SOUND LIKE THE GENESIS "AFTER THE IMAGE AND LIKENESS OF ELOHIM, ELOHIM CREATED THEM TO KNOW GOOD FROM EVIL JUST LIKE ELOHIM???"

BASICALLY, THE "IMAGE OF THE BEAST" IS NOT REFERRING TO SOME STATUE LIKE MANY RELIGIOUS FOLK CLAIM TODAY. IT REFERS TO "THOSE WHO ARE AFTER THE IMAGE OF THE BEAST" WHO IS IN OPPOSITION TO TRUTH AND IS —------UNLIKE—---- THOSE WHO ARE AFTER "THE IMAGE AND LIKENESS OF ELOHIM KNOWING BOTH GOOD AND EVIL AND ABLE TO TELL THE DIFFERENCE!!!"

SO BASICALLY "THERE ARE THOSE WHO ARE AWAKE AND AFTER THE IMAGE OF GOODNESS AND REASON AND ABLE TO DIFFERENTIATE BETWEEN GOOD AND EVIL" AND ON THE OTHER SIDE YOU HAVE THOSE WHO ARE "AFTER THE IMAGE OF THE BEAST AS IN ASLEEP AND UNABLE TO DIFFERENTIATE GOOD FROM EVIL AND WHO ARE IN A STATE OF UNCONSCIOUSNESS OVERTAKEN BY THE EVIL IMPULSE AND INCLINATION!!!' THESE DO NOT RESEMBLE "THE ELOHIM OR WISDOM" BUT RATHER RESEMBLE "THE BEAST ARCHETYPE OF IGNORANCE AND SPIRITUAL - PSYCHOLOGICAL BLINDNESS AND EVIL DEEDS SUCH AS HATRED AND VIOLENCE."

SO THOSE "AFTER THE IMAGE AND LIKENESS OF THE BEAST" —BREATHE POWER AND LIFE UNTO THE BEAST AND SO THE BEAST OBTAINS HIS

POWER FROM THE PEOPLE WHO ARE ATTRACTED TO THE BEAST ENERGIES SINCE "LIKE ENERGY ATTRACTS LIKE ENERGY." IN THIS CASE, "EVIL, CORRUPTION AND IGNORANCE."

SO THIS "BEAST ENERGY" AND ARCHETYPE IS UNLIKE THE "LIGHT OF THE WORLD" ARCHETYPE SINCE IT DRAWS ITS ENERGY LIKE AN IDOL FROM THE EVIL ENERGY OF THE PEOPLE UNDER ITS SPELL. THIS IS THE CONCEPT OF "THE AUTHORITARIANS AND EXTREMISTS AND VENGEFUL PEOPLE LIKE HITLER" TYPES THAT ARE POPPING UP ALL OVER AND ESPECIALLY IN THE JUDEO-XTIAN-ISLAMIC WORLD "TAKING THE PLACE OF DEITY AND THE LIGHT AND OF THE MASHIAH ARCHETYPAL ENERGIES."

THE BEAST ENERGY IS ABOUT —POWER, ABUSE, DELUSION, DECEPTION, LYING, VIOLENCE, NONSENSE, NO REASONING, ILLUSION, IMPRISONMENT OF THE MIND AND HEART, GENOCIDE AND PERSECUTION, BRAINWASHING AS A MEANS OF CONTROL AND MANIPULATION, ETC, ETC . ETC. AND THERE ARE PEOPLE UNFORTUNATELY THAT WILL FIND THESE ENERGIES "SAVORY AND DELICIOUS" BECAUSE THESE LOW FREQUENCY ENERGIES RESONATE WITH THEIR LOW LEVEL OF CONSCIOUSNESS AND EVERY DYSFUNCTION HIDING IN THEIR "SHADOW SELF."

SO WHEN PEOPLE IN POWER START CLAIMING THAT THEY WILL GO AFTER EVERYBODY THAT DOES NOT WORSHIP "THE BEAST ARCHETYPE" BELIEVE IT BECAUSE THIS VERSE IS TIED TO BOTH THE "DEVIL ARCHETYPE AND THE DEATH CARD ARCHETYPE."

BEWARE! MAY THE LIGHT OVERCOME THE BEAST AND HIS MINIONS!!!

JOHN 3: 19 This is the verdict: Light has come into the world, but people loved darkness instead of light because their deeds were evil.

SINCERELY, THE LIGHT OF THE W'OR"LD IN YOU (THE EMPRESS SHEKINA AND HER SON RIDING UPON THE WHITE HORSE OF KALKI)

---

## 41.  REVELATION 19: 19-20 THE BEAST AS "THE AUTHORITARIAN STATE" IN BED WITH THE "FALSE PROPHET OR THE CORRUPT EXTREMIST RELIGIOUS SYSTEM"

19 And I saw the beast, and the kings of the earth, and their armies, gathered together to make war against him that sat on the horse, and against his army.

20 And the beast was taken, and with him the false prophet that wrought miracles before him, with which he deceived them that had received the mark of the beast, and them that worshipped his image. These both were cast alive into a lake of fire

burning with brimstone.

THE NUMBER 19 IS THE "SUN CARD WHICH DEPICTS KALKI "THE JUST AND RIGHTEOUS" ARCHETYPE WHO REPRESENTS THE "ONE WHO THEY GATHERED TOGETHER TO MAKE WAR AGAINST THAT SAT ON THE HORSE, AND AGAINST HIS ARMY."

THE NUMBER 20 IS "THE JUDGMENT CARD" AND SO THE BEAST AND HIS FALSE PROPHET IS CAST ALIVE INTO A LAKE OF FIRE BURNING WITH BRIMSTONE. THEY BOTH, THE FALSE PROPHET AND THE BEAST ARE CAST OUT FROM THE LIGHT AND BANISHED TO THE WORLD OF DELUSION UNABLE TO WAKE UP AND FIND THE LIGHT.

THE BEAST REPRESENTS THE ARCHETYPE OF AUTHORITARIAN AND EXTREMIST POLITICAL IDEOLOGIES AND SYSTEMS. THE ENTIRE SYSTEM AND AUTHORITARIAN MACHINE THAT CORRUPTS INSTITUTIONS AND THE HEARTS OF PEOPLE IN ORDER THAT ALL THESE CONTINUE TO BREATHE "LIFE AND POWER" TO IT. THE BEAST IS INNATELY WEAK AND DRAWS POWER AND MIGHT FROM THOSE GIVING UP THEIR OWN INNER POWER TO GIVE IT TO THE BEAST. THE BEAST IS A MIRAGE OR MIRROR OF THE DYSFUNCTIONAL CONTENTS OF THE COLLECTIVE SHADOW BEING PROJECTED ONTO THE BEAST AS THEIR —IDOL!!! WILLING TO "SHED INNOCENT BLOOD" LIKE CAIN IN ORDER TO PRESERVE POWER AND CONTROL.

THE FALSE PROPHET ARE THOSE AFTER THE IMAGE AND LIKENESS OF THE PROPHETS OF BAAL IN TANAK. THIS DOES NOT REFER TO A STATUE. THE BEAST ITSELF IS AN IDOL FOR IT IS EMPTY AND ITS CLAIMS TO BE FOR DEITY AND THE LIGHT ARE FALSE! WHEN THE BEAST IS ACTUALLY FOR THE OPPOSITE AND ITS WORKS ARE THOSE OF EVIL. THE FALSE PROPHET IS AT THE CENTER OF THE "CHURCH AND STATE" CONCEPT. THE CORRUPT RELIGIOUS INSTITUTIONS AND LEADERS WHO WORSHIP AND SERVE THE BEAST VIOLATING THE SACRED CODES AND LOFTY SPIRITUAL VALUES, PRINCIPLES, ETHICS AND JUSTICE" ON BEHALF OF THE BEAST THEY SERVE. THIS RELIGIOUS SYSTEM IS IN A CORRUPT STATE AND SO ARE ITS LEADERS WHO ARE IN BED WITH THE BEAST SYSTEM AND BOTH WORK IN COLLUSION WITH EACH OTHER TO MAINTAIN THE "1984" STRUCTURE OF POWER AND AMBITION, BRAINWASHING, TERROR, VIOLENCE AND MANIPULATION IN ORDER TO KEEP THE LIGHT AWAY AND FROM SHINING THROUGH.

BOTH "THE BEAST AND THE FALSE PROPHET" REPRESENT THE AUTHORITARIAN AND CORRUPT RELIGIOUS-POLITICAL SYSTEM WHO CLAIM TO BE GOD AND THE WORD OF GOD. BOTH ARE TO BE CASTED TO THE "SYMBOLIC LAKE OF FIRE" WHICH MEANS "DIVINE JUSTICE

MANIFESTING AS HUMAN JUSTICE" WHICH MEANS THE "END OF THE CHURCH - STATE" SET UP AND THE AFFIRMATION OF MANKIND TO THE "UPHOLDING OF THE TRUE AND LOFTY DEMOCRATIC SYSTEMS AND VALUES."

BOTH THE BEAST AND THE FALSE PROPHET SPEAK "GREAT THINGS" AS IF THEY WERE SPEAKING ON BEHALF OF THE LIGHT AND THE GOOD. INSTEAD THEIR TEETH SHALL GNASH FOR USING THE SACRED TO SPREAD HATE, VIOLENCE AND FRATRICIDE WHICH IS CONTRARY TO "THE LIGHT AND TO HEALING OR WHOLENESS."

SINCERELY,
"JOSEPH" THE INTERPRETER OF DREAMS AND SCRIPTURE

---

## 42. 666 === 6 + 6 + 6 ====18 THE "MARK OF THE BEAST" AND "THE MOON CARD" AND THE "UNCONSCIOUS SELF" —-LEAD US FROM THE UNREAL TO THE "REAL IN US!" NAMASTE NARASIMHAYA

AS YOU WILL RECALL A SIGN OF BEING IN A STATE OF UNCONSCIOUSNESS IS NOT BEING AWARE OF THE CONTENTS AND PROCESSES TAKING PLACE IN THE UNCONSCIOUS MIND AND SO THESE TAKE OVER AND ONE ENDS UP BEING MANIPULATED BY THE LOWER INSTINCTS. BEING PULLED AND INFLUENCED BY THESE FORCES LIKE A PUPPET. EVENTUALLY, ONE ENDS UP PROJECTING WHAT ONE REFUSES TO SEE IN HIM-HERSELF ONTO OTHER PEOPLE AND LASH AT THEM IN HATEFUL AND VIOLENT WAYS.

THE 18 CARD IS THE MOON CARD WHICH HAS TO DO WITH THE PROCESSES OF THE UNCONSCIOUS AND THE SHADOW. IT'S ALL PSYCHOLOGICAL IN NATURE. THERE IS WHERE THE PROBLEMS ARE BORN. AND SO JUST AS THE MOON REPRESENTS THE DARK SHADOW AND THE UNCONSCIOUS CONTENTS, SO THE MOON REPRESENTS THE OTHER SIDE IN HER CRESCENT MOON WHICH IS THE PROCESS OF BRINGING TO LIGHT OUR OWN PSYCHOLOGICAL PROCESSES AND CONTENTS OF THE UNCONSCIOUS GRADUALLY UNTIL REACHING FULL MOON STATUS WHICH STANDS FOR ILLUMINATION AND ENLIGHTENMENT. THIS STATE IS WHEN WE ARE ABLE TO UNDERSTAND OURSELVES "NAKED BEFORE PROVIDENCE" AND WHY WE DO WHAT WE DO. WHEN THIS PROCESS TAKES PLACE, WE ARE CAPABLE OF MAKING THE NECESSARY CHANGES TO FREE OURSELVES FROM THE POWER OF THESE DESTRUCTIVE ASPECTS OF OUR HUMAN SELF AND COME BACK TO RELATIVE HARMONY IN WHICH BOTH OUR INNER DARK AND LIGHT WORK TOGETHER TO POLISH THE PHILOSOPHER'S STONE.

THIS IS WHAT THE "KEYSTONE" OR FOUNDATION STANDS FOR AS A-MARIE-KA BECOMING A NATION OF AWAKENING AND ILLUMINATION WHERE FREEDOM IS USED NOT TO ABUSE IT BUT TO — POLISH AND BRING OUT THE "BEST IN OURSELVES."

AND SO AS WE STATED BEFORE, THE "666" IS NOT A LITERAL NUMBER MARKED ON PEOPLE'S FOREHEADS LIKE SOME RELIGIOUS FOLK CLAIM. ACTUALLY SOME WHO CLAIM THE ABOVE, DESPITE BEING RELIGIOUS MIGHT BE UNDER THE INFLUENCE OF "THE BEAST AND BE SYMBOLICALLY WEARING HIS MARK." WHAT THE (-) 6+6+6===(-)18 REFERS TO IS BEING UNDER THE INFLUENCE OF DYSFUNCTIONAL SUBCONSCIOUS FORCES AND ALSO BEING IN A STATE OF "SLUMBER" UNABLE TO NOTICE WHAT IS EVIL AND BAD FROM WHAT IS GOOD AND RIGHTEOUS.

THE FOREHEAD OR THE PREFRONTAL CORTEX IS THE SEAT OF EMPATHY AND THE ABILITY TO TELL WHAT IS RIGHT FROM WHAT IS WRONG. WHEN THIS PREFRONTAL BRAIN IS DAMAGED OR ASLEEP, THE PERSON IS IN A STATE OF BEING UNDER THE CONTROL OF SHADOW FORCES AND UNABLE TO FEEL EMPATHY TOWARDS THE SUFFERING OF OTHERS. SO S-HE IS PRONE AND VULNERABLE TO VIOLENT IMPULSES AND ANGER, UNABLE TO UNDERSTAND THAT VIOLENCE AND AGGRESSION EVENTUALLY WILL AFFECT HIM OR HER AND THE COMMUNITY IN VERY DETRIMENTAL WAYS.

THE BEAST IS ASSOCIATED WITH A STATE OF IGNORANCE AND A DEPRAVED MIND OR THE "(-) 6+6+6" BECAUSE THESE ARE THE QUALITIES AND ATTRIBUTES OF THE BEAST WHO IS A MIRROR OR IDOL GIVEN BREATH BY THE PEOPLE AND SO IT IS FASHIONED AFTER THE IMAGE AND LIKENESS OF THE DYSFUNCTIONAL PSYCHOLOGICAL STATE OF THE PEOPLE THEMSELVES. IT IS LIKE A BLOODY MOLOCH AND BAAL THAT PEOPLE ARE WILLING TO SACRIFICE INNOCENT BLOOD TO BECAUSE THAT IS WHAT THAT IDOL REQUIRES IN ORDER TO KEEP PEOPLE UNDER ITS INFLUENCE AND IGNORANCE AND CONTROL. IT IS A VERY SYMBIOTIC DYSFUNCTIONAL CYCLE AND RELATIONSHIP.

<u>18.THE MOON--Hidden enemies, danger, calumny, darkness, terror, deception, occult forces, error.</u>

*Reversed:* Instability, inconstancy, silence, lesser degrees of deception and error. (WIKIPEDIA)

IS NOT THE ABOVE THE DESCRIPTION OF THE —MOON QUALITIES —IN ITS NEGATIVE-REVERSED INTERPRETATION EXACTLY AS THOSE "WEARING THE MARK OF THE BEAST?" AS IN SEEING HIDDEN ENEMIES EVERYWHERE AND IN EVERYONE THAT DOES NOT "FOLLOW AND WORSHIP THE BEAST?" TERROR AND FEAR THAT TAKE OVER BECAUSE OF BEING IN THE DARK AND GRIPPED BY SUCH NEGATIVE ENERGIES SUCH AS VIOLENCE, HATRED

AND AGGRESSION? THE "OCCULT FORCES OF THE UNCONSCIOUS TAKING OVER AND MANIPULATING" THE EMOTIONS AND THOUGHTS AND ACTIONS OF THOSE WEARING THE MARK? THE MISTAKES AND ERRORS MADE EVERYWHERE IN DECISION MAKING SINCE ONE CANNOT MAKE WISE DECISIONS IN SUCH A STATE OF BLINDNESS? SUCH AS CALLING FOR —CIVIL WAR AND VIOLENCE AS A SOLUTION TO EVERYTHING. AND THE POLITICAL AND ECONOMIC AND SOCIAL INSTABILITY AS A RESULT. ETC. ETC. ETC.

"FREE YOUR MINDS" FROM "THE MARK OF THE BEAST'S" HOLD ON YOU.

HE USES FEAR TO KEEP YOU IN THE DARK TELLING YOU THAT OTHERS WILL DO SUCH AND SUCH BUT IS ALL LIES. WHILE CASTING BLAME ON OTHERS, AND SO KEEPING THE ATTENTION ELSEWHERE WHILE DISMANTLING THE PROTECTIONS SET UP IN PLACE TO PREVENT THE "BEAST ARCHETYPE" FROM TAKING OVER A LA 1984!!!

SINCERELY,
EVA L-UNA

---

## 43. THE MARK OF THE BEAST 666 and THE POWER OF MONEY: THE DETERMINING FACTOR OF THESE LAST DAYS OF KALI YUG AND THE NEW "VALUES" OF SATYA

**REVELATION 13:16-17**

**16** And he causeth all, both small and great, rich and poor, free and bond, to receive a mark in their right hand, or in their foreheads:

**17** And that no man might buy or sell, save he that had the mark, or the name of the beast, or the number of his name.

WE already explained the meaning of the (-) 6+6+6=18 and the PREFRONTAL LOBE processes. THE BULLY archetype energy belongs to the 666= -18 NEGATIVE interpretation of the number and MARK OF THE BEAST. Just as HITLER was a BULLY, so was GOL-IATH. BULLY TYPES have NO EMPATHY towards anyone. The GOL root word as in GOL- EM or a MINDLESS HUMANOID OR ZOMBIE-LIKE BEING THAT BECOMES DANGEROUS BECAUSE IT LACKS THE CHARACTERISTICS OF INTELLECT AND HEART and EMPATHY AND THE FIFTH ELEMENT which is LOVE OR "KI-ETHER."

Look at past DIARIES for more detailed information pertaining to the GOL and GOL-EM and how these relate to the MARK OF THE BEAST archetypal energy.

In the Revelation "13" –16 - 17 — you will notice that the MARK OF THE BEAST is linked to the man-made concept of MONEY!!! MONEY is handled BY HAND!!! And many of the global troubles today or most are connected to THE POWER OF MONEY WHEN IT IS "USED" BY (-) 666 TYPES, be them GANGS or BANKERS or INDUSTRY or POLITICOS or RELIGIOUS INSTITUTIONS. It becomes a POWERFUL MEANS OF "CONTROL" BY THESE "(-) 666" TYPES that lack EMPATHY AND THE ABILITY TO KNOW THE DIFFERENCE BETWEEN GOOD AND EVIL.

As you will notice today, most of the ISSUES AFFECTING HUMANKIND have to do with MONEY!!! From rampant crime and violence to destruction of the planet to the disintegration of entire communities due to rampant poverty and so many social issues stemming from the concept of money. WHEN THOSE "LACKING IN EMPATHY AND THE ABILITY TO TELL THE DIFFERENCE BETWEEN GOOD AND EVIL" have POWER OVER MONEY, THEY WILL USE THAT MONEY NOT ONLY FOR CONTROL BUT ALSO TO SPREAD DISEASE AND GREED. It is the same case WE explained earlier as in the question... WHAT SENSE DOES IT MAKE TO ENTRUST THE WELLBEING AND CARE OF THE PEOPLE TO PERSONS WHO LACK EMPATHY AND WHOSE FRONTAL LOBE CAN'T TELL THE DIFFERENCE BETWEEN GOOD ACTION AND EVIL ACTION? They will end up making a mess and for the most part will make decisions BASED ON THEIR SELFISH NEEDS AND ENDS HAVING NO CAPACITY TO EMPATHIZE WITH THE HUMAN CONDITION AND THE PAIN AND SUFFERING OF OTHERS and how their misuse of money is contributing to these social - economic ills..

In regards to money, these persons who are all over the globe will TAKE CONTROL OF THE USE OF MONEY FOR SELFISH AND DETRIMENTAL PURPOSES because they lack THE EMPATHY TO FEEL FOR THE OTHER and so their decisions will not be based on HOW THEY CAN USE THE MONEY TO BENEFIT OTHERS, instead it will always be HOW THEY CAN USE THAT MONEY TO BENEFIT THEMSELVES AND THOSE LIKE THEMSELVES.

As MONEY AND THE POWER OF MONEY is being used for the most part not to REALLY MAKE THE LIFE OF THE PEOPLE BETTER but to CORRUPT INSTITUTIONS, BUY PEOPLE AND JUSTICE, FOR PERSONAL ENRICHMENT TO THE DETRIMENT OF THE WHOLE, etc. etc. etc. .... The QUALITY OF LIFE IN SOCIETY DECLINES AND THE PEOPLE BEGIN TO SUFFER ENDLESSLY MAKING LIFE MISERABLE AND A BURDEN WHICH CAUSES THE WHOLE SOCIETY TO —COLLAPSE!!!

This collapse contributes to MORE TRAUMA and to the THE MULTIPLICATION OF THE (-) 666 archetypal processes because PEOPLES HEALTH BEGINS TO DECLINE AND RESENTMENT TAKES OVER AND MORE FRONTAL LOBES START

TO MLFUNCTION AND EMPATHY GOES OUT THE WINDOW. At the end you get a society OUT OF CONTROL AND READY TO IMPLODE IN ITSELF!!!

Which is what is happening all over the world today by being OVER FIXATED IN A MAN-MADE INVENTION THAT WAS MEANT TO BE USED TO MAKE EXCHANGE EASIER AND TO MAKE LIFE BETTER. INSTEAD, IT HAS BEEN TURNED INTO A WEAPON OF CONTROL AND ABUSE. When that happens MONEY BECOMES THE CENTER OF MAN'S UNIVERSE AND ONE MORE CAUSE OF MAN'S MISERY and PROBLEMS.

THE MONEY SYSTEM NEEDS TO BE REFORMED AND "HUMANIZED" and made into a channel of BLESSING FOR THE PEOPLE AND A CHANNEL FOR HUMAN GROWTH,

FULFILLMENT AND WELL BEING. If that is not the case WE are afraid the situation will further erode and corrode and become AN UNHEALTHY MESS that will bring about the collapse of the entire world and perhaps NUCLEAR HOLOCAUST because of constant fighting over MONEY AND POWER.

In the new AGE OF SATYA — POWER IS NO LONGER IN THE HANDS OF MONEY BUT IN THE HANDS OF — TRUTH AND TRUE SPIRITUAL VALUES AND PRINCIPLES that WE have mentioned over and over again such as KINDNESS, PEACE, UNDERSTANDING, COOPERATION, LOVE, TRUE STRENGTH AND "NOT AFTER THE FALSE BULLY TYPE OF FORCE AND IMPOSITION," etc. etc.etc. WHOEVER, does not begin to move in that direction will not make it to SATYA and those who move towards THESE HIGH VIBRATIONAL ENERGIES will become "AS BEACONS OF HOPE AND LIGHT" like the ZI-ONNE MOUNTAIN TO WHICH ALL NATIONS WILL LOOK FOR COUNSEL AND GUIDANCE AND WISDOM.

THE TIME IS COME TO "CAMBIARE PAGINA."

SINCERELY, "KAL-KI, THE ONE WHO DISSIPATES IGNORANCE WITH THE LIGHT"

---

## 44. EASTER'S "THE CHRIST IN YOU" —-- "OVERCOMING" THE GOL-GOTHA (THE ATTITUDE OF THE GOL) AND EMBARKING ON THE ALKEMETICAL PROCESS OF TRANSFORMING "NEGATIVE" ENERGIES INTO "POSITIVE ONES"

And so the symbolism of the EASTER CRUCIFIXION has a very important message and it's about the VICTORY of LOVE OVER THE "GOL- GOTHA" or the ATTITUDE OF THE GOL-EM.

JOHN 16:33

I have said these things to you, that in me you may have peace. In the world you will have tribulation. But take heart, I have OVERCOME THE WORLD.

Y-ESH-UA on the cross is ATOP GOL-GOTHA!!! Meaning that HE WAS ABLE TO OVERCOME THE GOL - GOTHA attitudes and energies.

And so as WE explained before, it was due to the ATTITUDE OF THE GOL-EM that THE WORLD was cleansed in the story of NOAH. And both in the story of DAVID and in SODOM AND GOMORRAH it was this KIND OF EVIL ATTITUDE and the lack of EMPATHY and "WISDOM AND UNDERSTANDING" that led to the demise of the world.

Y-ESH-UA who represents LOVE, WISDOM AND UNDERSTANDING was able to OVERCOME THE WORLD by not "BECOMING" HIMSELF AFTER THE ATTITUDE OF THE "GOL" but rather REMAINING STEADFAST IN LOVE ENERGY UNTIL THE END. Y-ESH-UA ATOP GOL-GOTHA is equivalent to LOVE BEING ON TOP OF AND IN CONTROL OF THE DARK ENERGIES OF THE SHADOW. As in the ST MIKA-EL ATOP ASATANNA symbol. THESE DARK ENERGIES ARE NOT EVIL PER SE BUT ARE THE RAW UNFILTERED ENERGIES THAT NEED TO BE TAMED AND TRANSFORMED.

GOL-GOTHA IS TRANSLATED AS THE SKULL HILL for a reason because it is referring to the HEAD and BRAIN. Therefore, Y-ESH-UA represents HIGHER CONSCIOUSNESS WHO IS EMPATHIC AND CAN TELL THE DIFFERENCE BETWEEN GOOD AND EVIL. And so Y-ESH-UA'S DEATH — MARKS THE TIME WHEN — HIGHER CONSCIOUSNESS WOULD BE ATOP LOWER CONSCIOUSNESS. The SKULL is to do with KALI YUGA and so it is pointing to the END OF KALI YUGA when HIGHER CONSCIOUSNESS AND LOVE WILL BE "ON TOP" OR IN CONTROL OF "THE BEAST" ENERGY IN MAN.

Y-ESH-UA could have GONE THE OTHER WAY of BECOMING after the "GOL-GOTHA" but instead he ALCHEMICALLY "TRANSFORMED ALL THAT GOL ENERGY" into POSITIVE VIBRATIONAL ENERGY. He did NOT GIVE INTO "LOWER ENERGIES" but remained in CONTROL MAKING SURE "LOVE" WAS AND REMAINED — ON TOP. The opposite is what happened to DAR-TH VAD-ER in STAR WARS in which EVIL ENDS UP CORRUPTING HIM AND TURNING HIM TOWARDS THE DARK SIDE. Y-ESH-UA — despite everything that he had to go through — NEVER GAVE IN TO THAT — EVIL "TOXIC" ENERGY. Just like MLK and BERTHA CACERES and others throughout history that have OVERCOME THE WORLD.

And so ...

Y-ESH-UA, unlike what some people today are saying, was not WEAK and neither was he a FAILURE. The story is about the ABILITY AND CAPABILITY OF HUMANS TO CURB THEIR OWN EVIL IMPULSE and or NOT BE SOILED BY OTHER'S "EVIL."

THE 3 CRUCIFIED ATOP GOL-GOTHA represent CHOKMAH, B-INNAH and DA-AT IN THE TREE OF LIFE —--CRUCIFIED!!! Or rather SACRIFICED. In which THIS WORLD has TEMPORARY victory in the MATERIAL REALM but the CHRIST HAS LONG LASTING VICTORY IN ALL REALMS.

For the Greeks, In their eyes the number 3 was considered as the perfect number, the number of harmony, wisdom and understanding. It was also the number of time – past, present, future; birth, life, death; beginning, middle, end – it was the number of the divine. (WNO.ORG.UK)

Remember that WISDOM AND UNDERSTANDING are attributed respectively to both CHOCKMA and B-INNAH. And the MIDDLE PILLAR where Y-ESH-UA is nailed in GOL-GOTHA represents the HARMONY BETWEEN THE TWO. Therefore, the FACT THAT THESE 3 ASPECTS ARE ATOP GOL-GOTHA or the SKULL means that in order to OVERCOME falling into THE GOL-EM condition, HUMANS need to HARMONIZE or BALANCE "BOTH SIDES OF THE HUMAN BRAIN" so that both complement each other.

It is all about ALCHEMY AND HUMAN DEVELOPMENT and part of the SAT-YOGA process of reaching UNION, at last.

SINCERELY, "YESHUA, 2012"

---

## 45. SKULL MOUNTAIN AND GOL-GOTHA: THE END OF THE AGE OF "KALI-KATA" AND THE BEGINNING OF THE AGE OF "DIWALI" OR THE ENLIGHTENED MINDS FOR AN ENLIGHTENED WORLD

THE GOL-GOTHA OR SKULL MOUNTAIN IS A SYMBOL FOR THE "MIND."

"GOL" HAS MANY MEANINGS SUCH AS "RIVER" IN MONGOLIAN AND "NAKED/ BALD" IN PROTO-INDO-EUROPEAN; BOWL/ BASIN IN HEBREW SUCH AS THE BOWL BETWEEN THE TWIN PILLARS AT THE TEMPLE.

THE GUTTURAL "G" BECOMES A "KH" IN SOME LANGUAGES WHICH MAKES THE WORD SOUND LIKE "KHOLKOTA." AS IN "SKOL- KOTHA." THE NAME "GOL-GOTHA" OR "KOL-KOTA" SOUNDS MUCH LIKE THE NAME OF THE INDIAN CITY OF "KOLKATA" WHICH DERIVES FROM:

*Kolikata* is thought to be a variation of *Kalikkhetrô* (Bengali: কালীС$"ত্র [ˈkali̩kʰetrɔ]), meaning "Field of [the goddess] Kali". Similarly, it can be a variation of 'Kalikshetra' (Sanskrit: कालीक्षेत्र, lit. "area of Goddess Kali"). (WIKIPEDIA)

The name may have its origin in the words *khal* (Bengali: খাল [ˈkʰal]) meaning "canal", followed by *kata* (Bengali: কাটা [ˈkaʈa]), which may mean "dug" (WIKIPEDIA)

According to another theory, the area specialised in the production of quicklime or *koli chun* (Bengali: কলি চুন [ˈkɔliˌtʃun]) and coir or *kata* (Bengali: কাতা [ˈkata]); hence, it was called *Kolikata*). (WIKIPEDIA) LIMESTONE "QUARRY" (WIKIPEDIA)

AS WE EXPLAINED BEFORE, THE SKULL AS SYMBOL HAS TO DO WITH THE "DIVINE AND THE HUMAN MIND." IT IS THE HUMAN'S COMPUTER SYSTEM. THE "HEAD" IS WHERE THE "PREFRONTAL CORTEX" IS FOUND WHICH IS THE CENTER OF "EMPATHY AND THE ABILITY TO TELL RIGHT FROM WRONG." THIS IS THE BASIS OF THE "PENTAGRAM OF UNION" WHICH REPRESENTS THE COMPLETE FUNCTIONING OF THE PREFRONTAL CORTEX AND THE ABILITY OF A MAN TO FEEL AND THINK AND BEHAVE IN WAYS THAT UPHOLD THE BASIC MORAL AND ETHICAL LAWS OF CONDUCT AND BEHAVIOR SUCH AS "DO NO HARM."

ON THE OTHER HAND, A MAL-FUNCTIONING OR NOT FUNCTIONING PREFRONTAL CORTEX DUE TO TRAUMA OR ANY OTHER REASON ENDS UP AFFECTING PEOPLE TO THE POINT WHERE THEY FEEL NO EMPATHY FOR THE SUFFERING OF OTHERS, THEREFORE CARRYING OUT EVIL AND FEELING NO PAIN OR REMORSE FOR IT. AT THE SAME TIME, GOL-EM CANNOT TELL THE DIFFERENCE BETWEEN GOOD AND EVIL AND CONFUSE BOTH GIVING BIRTH TO VIOLENT AND PATHOLOGICAL TYPES OF PERSONALITIES.

THE "SKULL" SYMBOL IS LINKED TO THE GODDESS "KALI-KATA." HER SYMBOL IS A CHAIN OF SKULLS. AND THE AGE OF KALI WHICH IS THE AGE OF DEATH AND CORRUPTION AND WHICH IS PASSING AWAY IS NAMED AFTER THE DARK ASPECT. THE SHADOW ASPECT BELONGING TO BINAH MOTHER IN ITS UNENLIGHTENED STATE. THE STORY OF THE CRUCIFIXION IS POINTING TO THE BEGINNING OF THE END OF KALI YUGA AND THE BEGINNING OF THE AGE OF AQU-ARI-US OR ENLIGHTENMENT. THE WORLD IS IN A CORRUPT STATE BEGINNING WITH FAILING HUMAN INSTITUTIONS AND LEADERSHIP AND THE COLLAPSE OF THE ECOSYSTEM BECAUSE OF THE MALFUNCTIONING OF THIS PART OF THE BRAIN, THE PREFRONTAL CORTEX. THE SKULL OF KALI REPRESENTS THE DEATH OF THE OLD AND THE "REBIRTH" OF THE NEW.

THE NAME "KOL" OR "GOL" IS LINKED TO "RIVERS" SUCH AS THE JORDAN RIVER IN THE STORY OF Y-ESH-UA AND ALSO TO "BEING NAKED AND BALD" WHICH CORRESPOND WITH THE CONDITION OF Y-ESH-UA IN

THE CRUCIFIXION STORY BEING HANGED NAKED WITH ONLY THE UNDERGARMENTS AND —--- Y-ESH-UA WAS "A BALD MAN."

THE "BOWL" BETWEEN THE PILLARS AT THE TEMPLE IS SIMILAR TO THE "HOLY GRAIL" THEME AND MYTH IN THE MYSTICAL CHRISTIAN TRADITION. BOWL THAT HOLDS THE 4 ELEMENTS INCLUDING 'WATER" AS IN "WINE" OR — FIRE "AS IN THE ETERNAL FLAME" REPRESENTING THE "LIGHT WITHIN OR THE FLAME OF LIFE."

THE DIVINE SPARK!!!

THEREFORE, KALI-KATA MOUNTAIN LINKS THE INDIAN TRADITION WITH THE CHRISTIAN AND JEWISH AND ISLAMIC ONES. AGAIN, IT IS ALL ABOUT THE SYMBOLS. THE PLACE OF GOL-GOTHA WAS NEXT OR CLOSE TO THE GEHENNA BURNING PLACE WHICH IS BELIEVED TO HAVE BEEN LIKE A HUGE CANAL WHERE THE TRASH WAS BURNT AND ALSO NEAR LIMESTONE QUARRIES OUTSIDE THE CITY OF JERUSALEM.

THEREFORE, THE STORY AND SYMBOL OF "GOL-GOTHA" OR KALI-KATA REMINDS US TO BE AWARE OF OUR "HEADS AND MINDS" AND THAT WE "NURTURE AND CULTIVATE" OUR INTELLECTUAL FACULTIES AND EMOTIONS TO AVOID ENDING UP WITH "DANGEROUS MINDS" THAT KEEP REPEATING THE SAME SAD HUMAN STORY OVER AND OVER AGAIN AND SPREADING TRAUMA WHICH ENDS UP TURNING THIS WORLD INTO A HELLISH GEHENNA FIRE REALM.

SINCERELY, "SLEEPY BUT NOT HOLLOW"

---

## 46. KING D-AVI-D: THE KING CROWNED WITH "L-O-V-E" VS. THE "GOL"-EM "GOL-IATH — "CHOOSING OUR LEADERS WISELY!"

The name for D-AVI-D is made up of the word AVI which means: MY GOD, FATHER. DE -AVI-D therefore stands for OF GOD or OF FATHER. The name also stands for BELOVED and TO LOVE.

David (Hebrew: דָּוִד, Modern: *David*, Tiberian: *Dāwîḏ*) means "beloved", derived from the root *dôwd* (דוד), which originally meant "to boil", but survives in Biblical Hebrew only in the figurative usage "to love"; specifically, it is a term for an uncle or figuratively, a lover/beloved (it is used in this way in the Song of Songs: יל ידודו ידודל אנ׳, "I am for my beloved and my beloved is for me").[1] In Christian tradition, the name was adopted as Syriac: ܕܘܝܕ Dawid, Greek Δαυίδ, Latin *Davidus* or *David*. The Quranic spelling is دَاوُد *Dāwūd or Dā'ūd*. (WIKIPEDIA)

Therefore, the NAME stands for BELOVED OF THE FATHER!! And WHY does the FATHER loved D-AVI-D in Biblical myth??? What set D-AVI-D apart from his brothers which made him be CHOSEN BY THE FATHER according to BIBLE STORY? Because D-AVI-D was a MAN WHO "LOVED!!!" His REAL CROWN was not the golden crown but the CROWN OF LOVE!!!

Therefore, D-AVI-D was NOT chosen because of HIS LOOKS, BODY TYPE, SKIN COLOR, RELIGION, or other physical attributes and features based on SHAPES, FORMS AND COLORS. He was chosen to be KING OF ISRAEL BECAUSE HE WAS A "LOVING PERSON."

Like the BIBLE says— you cannot claim to LOVE GOD whom you cannot see when you don't LOVE THY BRETHREN whom you have NEXT TO YOURSELF.

Therefore, WHAT SET D-AVI-D apart from other kings was HIS EMPATHY FOR OTHERS!!! He was not the BULLY AND CRUEL AND VIOLENT type of MAN which is represented by GOL-IATH. The type of HU-MAN that PLEASES THE DIVINE is that one with TENDER EMOTIONS AND LOVE IN HIS HER HEART,

"GOL"-IATH shares the ROOT WORD for "GOL"-EM!!! Meaning that unlike the INTEGRATED WHOLE MAN THAT DAVID WAS having L-O-V-E in his HEART, GOL-IATH was like a DANGEROUS GOL-EM type of man who lacked EMPATHY FOR OTHERS. HE WAS A KILLING MACHINE!!! THAT IS WHY "THE STONE" HIT GOL-IATH "ON THE FOREHEAD!!!!!!!!!" Just like WE have explained recently, GOL-IATH was unable to TELL THE DIFFERENCE BETWEEN GOOD AND EVIL and to FEEL EMPATHY FOR OTHERS and so HE WAS STRUCK ON THE "PREFRONTAL LOBE." This story of D-AVI-D AND GOL-IATH is a METAPHOR for the STRUGGLE BETWEEN "LOVE" AND "HATE. The story links with the REVELATIONS symbols of THE MARK OF THE BEAST VS. THE MARK OF THE ELOHIM.

GOL-IATH therefore represents the GOL-EM STATE who becomes so DESENSITIZED TO THE PAIN OF OTHERS and who JUST FOLLOWS ORDERS without UNDERSTANDING whether these orders are good or outright evil. GOL-Y-ATH'S impulse is EVIL AND VIOLENT without any sense of REMORSE AND SHAME because HIS EMPATHIC ABILITIES ARE NUMBED OR DAMAGED. As WE have revealed before, the PREFRONTAL LOBE of the HEAD is the seat of CONSCIOUSNESS as in having the ability to tell the DIFFERENCE BETWEEN GOOD AND EVIL and is also the seat of EMPATHY in the human brain which links it to the HEART CHAKRA.

And this is WHAT HU-MANS have been doing for a very long time. PRAISING THE "GOL-EM" TYPES OF MANKIND while REJECTING THE "MAN" THAT BEARS THE "CROWN OF THE FATHER WHICH IS L-O-V-E!!!!"

And so NOW that WE have revealed to you the TRUTH behind the KING D-AVI-D STORY, now you know WHAT TYPE OF "LEADERSHIP" PLEASES THE UNIVERSE. WHAT is happening with the FASCISM taking place right now is equivalent to CHOOSING GOL-IATH BECAUSE OF HIS BULLYING and physical and material "STRENGTH. " People mostly are being DECEIVED by this evil energy meanwhile REJECTING "KING D-AVI-D" just because to you he seems WEAK BECAUSE OF "LOVE" when it is THAT LOVE THAT MAKES HIM STRONGER. Therefore, choose LEADERS WHO LOVE AND HAVE EMPATHY AND NOT — GOL-IATHS!!!

SINCERELY,
"THE LION OF JUDAH"

---

## 47.  VIOLENCE AND SINGLING OUT PEOPLE TO BE ATTACKED IS NOT THE WAY OF THE CHRIST AND THE PRIMITIVE CHURCH: ADMONISHMENT TO THE "CHRISTIAN A-MARIE-KI-ANNE CONGREGATION" ACCORDING TO SOPHIA AND HER CHRIST

FOR OUR "CHRISTIAN" CONGREGATIONS AS IN THE 7 CHURCHES ACCORDING TO JO-ANNA OF PATMOS. THE NUMBER 7 IS A CRYPTEX THAT STANDS FOR:

THE NUMBER 7 REPRESENTS AMONGST MANY THINGS "COMPLETION" AS IN THE 7 PLANETS AND THE 7 MUSICAL NOTES AND THE 7 DAYS OF THE WEEK AND THE 7 CHAKRAS AND THE 7 CANDELABRA OF THE MENORAH ETC. ETC. ETC. IT ALSO STANDS FOR:

*In numerology, the number 7 is often considered to be a symbol of mystery, knowledge and intuition. You're always seeking the truth at the heart of things. You are wise and intelligent, though this can sometimes leave you feeling indecisive, as you often overthink things.(BABYCENTREUK.COM)*

THEREFORE, WE CAN INFER THAT THE "7 CHURCHES" STAND FOR "THE COMPLETION" OR THE WHOLE OF THE PEOPLE REPRESENTED BY THE NUMBER 7. A PEOPLE THAT ARE AFTER "MYSTERY, KNOWLEDGE AND INTUITION." SEEKING THE TRUTH AT THE HEART OF LIFE AND THE UNIVERSE. PEOPLE WHO ARE AFTER THE CHRIST AND WISDOM AND INTELLIGENCE REPRESENTED BY THE HOLY SOPHIA OR SHE-KI-INNA. THEREFORE THE "WHOLE CONGREGATION" THAT ENCOMPASSES ALL THE CHURCHES SHOULD ABSTAIN FROM:

Ephesus (Revelation 2:1–7): known for having labored hard and not fainted, and separating themselves from the wicked; admonished for having forsaken its first love (2:4)

Smyrna (Revelation 2:8–11): admired for its tribulation and poverty; forecast to suffer persecution (2:10)

Pergamum (Revelation 2:12–17): located where 'Satan's seat' is; needs to repent of allowing false teachers (2:16)

Thyatira (Revelation 2:18–29): known for its charity, whose "latter works are greater than the former"; tolerates the teachings of a false prophetess (2:20)

Sardis (Revelation 3:1–6): admonished for – in contrast to its good reputation – being dead; cautioned to fortify itself and return to God through repentance (3:2–3)

Philadelphia (Revelation 3:7–13): known as steadfast in faith, keeping God's word and enduring patiently (3:10)

Laodicea, near Denizli (see Laodicean Church) (Revelation 3:14–22): called lukewarm and insipid (3:16)(WIKIPEDIA)

AS WE CAN SEE ABOVE, THE CONGREGATION MADE OF MANY CONGREGATIONS IS ADMONISHED TO RETURN TO THE "FIRST LOVE" AND REJECT "WICKEDNESS" WHICH INCLUDES MOSTLY HATRED AND VIOLENCE. ESPECIALLY THOSE WHO FOLLOW THE EXAMPLES AND ADMONISHMENTS OF "FALSE PROPHETS AND PROPHETESS" WHO DELUDE AND DECEIVE THE PEOPLE WITH TEACHINGS THAT CONTRADICT" THE TRUE SPIRIT OF THE GOSPEL AND THE EXAMPLE OF THE CHRIST. THE CHRIST PRINCIPLE INCLUDES TEMPERANCE AND LOVE AND NON VIOLENCE AND THE SETTING OF CLEAR BOUNDARIES WHEN IT COMES TO EVIL WORKS AND ACTIONS SUCH AS IN THE CASE OF PERSECUTING AND VILIFYING ENTIRE GROUPS OF PEOPLE. REJECTING THE INJUSTICE BASED ON "DIFFERENCES" SUCH AS RACE AND ETHNIC ORIGINS AND COLOR. SINCE IN CHRIST THERE IS NO MORE GREEK OR ROMAN OR MALE AND FEMALE BUT ARE "ALL AS ONE UNDER THE LIGHT OF CHRIST AND UNDER THE HOLY SHE-KI-INNA."

AS THE "CHRIST" PRINCIPLE AND ITS SHE-KI-INNA ARE THE HEAD OR "ROSH" OF THE PEOPLE, THE CHRIST SPIRIT TAKES PRECEDENCE OVER THE "DYSFUNCTIONAL SPIRIT OF SOME LEADERS AND HEADS OF CHURCHES" THAT SEEM TO LEAD THE PEOPLE BLINDLY ACCORDING TO THEIR OWN BIASES AND DYSFUNCTIONAL UNCONSCIOUS IMPULSES.

RETURN TO THE "FIRST LOVE" AS IN "LOVE ONE ANOTHER. " IT IS CLEAR THAT IT IS THE MOST DIFFICULT COMMANDMENT THERE IS AS IT ENCOURAGES ONE TO GO AGAINST THE EASIEST AND THE BASEST PART

OF OUR HUMAN SELF WHICH IS TO HATE AND BE VIOLENT. THEREFORE, IT TAKES MORE COURAGE AND STRENGTH TO "LOVE" THAN IT IS TO HATE AND BE VIOLENT. THEREFORE, STRENGTH IS MEASURED BY A MAN'S CAPACITY TO SUBDUE HIS BEASTLY AND SAVAGE SELF UNTO SOMETHING GREATER AS THE DIVINE HIGHER SELF WHICH IS BASED ON LOVE AND THE LIGHT.

THE ADMONISHMENT WARNS AGAINST "FALSE PROPHETS" WHO ARE EASILY IDENTIFIED BY BEING "LOVELESS AND SPREADING HATE AND VIOLENCE IN THEIR RHETORIC." THEY DO NOT FOLLOW THE EXAMPLE OF THE CHRIST AND THE SHE-KI-INNA BUT RATHER FOLLOW THE EXAMPLE OF JEZEBEL IN PROMOTING VIOLENCE AND BLOODINESS."

KEEPING "GOD'S WORD" OR —SOFIA—-IS REFERRING TO —

"Mystery, knowledge and intuition. You're always seeking the truth at the heart of things. You are wise and intelligent"(BABYCENTREUK.COM).

THE CONGREGATION IS ADMONISHED TO FOLLOW THE WISDOM OR PHILO-SOPHIA WHICH IS THE PROCESS OF "SEEKING THE TRUTH AT THE HEART OF THINGS." IT DOES NOT REFER TO BRAINWASHING OR CONDITIONING RELIGION AND DOGMA AND BELIEF ESPECIALLY AFTER THE TEACHINGS OF MOLOCH WHICH ARE BASED ON HATE AND VIOLENCE WHICH IS THE SAME AS SACRIFICING INNOCENT BLOOD TO MAN-MADE IDOLS AND THEIR FALSE IDEOLOGIES CREATED BY LAWLESS MEN OF FLESH AND BLOOD."

AS THE TERM CHRIST AND SOPHIA POINT AT, THE "CHRISTIAN" IS AFTER THE PROCESS OF ILLUMINATION AND ENLIGHTENMENT OR THE PROCESS OF AWAKENING WHICH IS AT THE HEART OF THE GOSPEL STORY AND ALL ITS SYMBOLS AND METAPHORS. WAKE UP CHURCHES AND EMBRACE THE LIGHT OF THE NEW WORLD.

SINCERELY, "THE LIVING CHRIST AND THE SOPHIA CALLING ON THE PEOPLE"

---

**48. "WHAT IT FEELS LIKE FOR A GIRL AND A ....BOY:" DO UNTO OTHERS WHAT YOU WOULD LIKE BE DONE UNTO YOU —IS THE LAW AND THE PROPHETS!**

MATTHEW 7:12

12 "So whatever you wish that others would do to you, do also to them, for this is the Law and the Prophets.

SUCH A SIMPLE CONCEPT AND YET SO DIFFICULT TO PUT INTO PRACTICE. YET, IT IS SUCH AN CORNERSTONE TEACHING IN THE GOSPEL TRADITION THAT IT REMINDS US THAT IT IS THE FULFILLMENT OF THE LAW AND EVERYTHING THE PROPHETS TAUGHT AND STOOD FOR. THIS "GOLDEN RULE" HOWEVER IS NOT JUST A JUDEO AND CHRISTIAN AND ISLAMIC TRADITION BUT IT BELONGS TO MOST WORLD TRADITIONS AS WELL.

HOW WOULD I FEEL IF I WAS "MISTREATED" LIKE THE PERSON NEXT TO ME? HOW WOULD I FEEL IF I WAS TOLD HORRIBLE HURTFUL THINGS OR HAVE OTHERS DO TERRIBLE THINGS TO MY PERSON? ETC. ETC. THIS "DO UNTO OTHERS AS YOU WOULD LIKE TO BE DONE UNTO YOU" WISDOM TEACHING IS ABOUT PUTTING OURSELVES IN THE SHOES OF ANOTHER PERSON SO THAT WE ARE ABLE TO "UNDERSTAND LIFE FROM THAT PERSON'S PERSPECTIVE AND EXPERIENCE" AND TO "EMPATHIZE" WITH "WHAT IT FEELS LIKE FOR A GIRL AND A …BOY."

HOW WOULD I FEEL IF I WAS INSULTED JUST LIKE THE PERSON NEXT TO ME? HOW WOULD I FEEL IF I WAS DEPRIVED OF MY FREEDOM AND BASIC HUMAN AND CIVIL RIGHTS? THINK ABOUT THAT FOR A MOMENT AND LET US PLACE OURSELVES IN THE PLACE OF THAT PERSON WHO MIGHT, OR IS ACTUALLY GOING THROUGH THAT EXPERIENCE. HOW WOULD I FEEL IF I WAS GOING THROUGH THESE NEGATIVE EXPERIENCES MYSELF?

HOW IS IT THAT BY DOING THIS SIMPLE BUT VERY DIFFICULT EXERCISE ONE CAN FEEL WHAT THE OTHER PERSON FEELS WITHOUT ACTUALLY GOING THROUGH THE ACTUAL EXPERIENCE? IT IS BECAUSE "BOTH" PERSONS ARE —HUMAN AND ALIKE. OUR COMMON HUMANITY MAKES US FEEL THE SAME THING UNDER THE SAME CIRCUMSTANCES AS THAT OTHER PERSON. WE ARE ALL THE SAME "UNDERNEATH IT ALL." REMEMBER THAT. AND SO WE CAN EMPATHIZE WITH THAT OTHER PERSON BECAUSE WE ARE HUMAN AFTER ALL AND SO WILL REACT IN SIMILAR WAYS WHEN UNDERGOING SIMILAR CIRCUMSTANCES AND SITUATIONS.

THIS EXERCISE IS USEFUL IN THAT IT HELPS US BECOME "AWARE" OF "WHAT IT FEELS LIKE FOR A BOY OR A …GIRL" AND WAKES US UP TO OUR "COMMON HUMANITY." MEANING THAT REGARDLESS OF OUR EXTERNAL DIFFERENCES, WE WILL REACT SIMILARLY TO CERTAIN EXPERIENCES BECAUSE WITHIN AND INSIDE WE ARE ALL "THE SAME." WITH THE SAME EMOTIONAL AND PSYCHOLOGICAL LANDSCAPES. DOING THIS EXERCISE REGULARLY AND REMEMBERING THE TIMES IN OUR LIVES WHEN WE HAVE BEEN MISTREATED" BY OTHERS AND HOW WE FELT, WILL HELP US "NOT CROSS THE LINE" INTO HATE AND VIOLENCE AND MURDER. CROSSING INTO FORBIDDEN TERRITORY LEADS US AWAY FROM OUR HUMANITY AND FROM OUR HIGHER SELF. INSTEAD IT LOWERS OURSELVES TO THE LEVEL

OF "DEMONS" WHICH ARE ARCHETYPAL ENERGIES OF THE LOWEST AND DENSEST VIBRATIONS. AS HUMANS WE ARE ALWAYS GIVEN A CHOICE WHETHER TO RISE ABOVE OUR LOWER SELVES OR WHETHER TO LOWER OURSELVES TO THE LEVEL OF DEMONIC INFLUENCES / DESTRUCTIVE ENERGIES.

PUTTING OURSELVES IN THE PLACE OF ANOTHER AFFIRMS OUR COMMON HUMANITY AND OUR "EQUALITY" SINCE REGARDLESS OF ETHNIC AND RACIAL AND RELIGIOUS DIFFERENCES AND DIVISIONS, "WE ALL BLEED THE SAME LIGHT" AND WILL SUFFER EQUALLY AND REACT EQUALLY UNDER OPPRESSION AND OR SIMILAR AND EQUAL CIRCUMSTANCES.

THEREFORE, "LET US DO UNTO OTHERS WHAT WE WOULD LIKE BE DONE UNTO US." THIS IS ANOTHER COSMIC VALUE AND PRINCIPLE IN THE KEYSTONE FOUNDATIONS AND ORDERLY SET UP OF THE UNIVERSE."

IT'S WISE TO REMEMBER THAT WHATEVER EVIL WE ALLOW TO HAPPEN TO OTHERS WILL EVENTUALLY CATCH UP WITH US AS WELL. IT IS TIME TO WAKE UP TO THIS FACT AND PLACE HEALTHY AND STRONG BOUNDARIES OF LIGHT THAT KEEP INJUSTICE AT BAY. NOT ONLY PROTECTING THE DIGNITY OF OTHERS BY DOING SO BUT ALSO PROTECTING OURSELVES AS WELL.

SINCERELY, Y-ESH-VA AND MA'AT AND HER SCALES OF JUSTICE"

---

### 49. NO PROPHECY IS SET ON STONE: "PEOPLE HAVE THE POWER" TO CREATE POSITIVE CHANGE AND CHANGE THE COURSE OF HISTORY FOR THE BETTER!

Because of EVERYTHING that is going on, people seem to be FREAKED OUT and expecting the WORSE forgetting that at the end THE DIVINE IS IN CONTROL. Like in the BOOK OF APOKA-L-IPSIS, ITS "ENDING" is A VERY REFRESHING AND POSITIVE ENDING taking us back to THE BEGINNING or to the GOLDEN AGE.

NO PROPHECY IS SET ON STONE. PEOPLE have the POWER TO BRING ABOUT POSITIVE CHANGE SINCE HEAVEN AND EARTH ARE IN A SYMBIOTIC RELATIONSHIP ALL THE TIME.

That any so-called PROPHECY predicts things will happen a certain way or another IS NOT A JUSTIFICATION TO JUST SIT DOWN AND DO NOTHING AND EXPECT THE DIVINE TO MANIFEST AND INTERVENE. Y-ESH-UA and the HEALING MOVEMENTS did not just stay put waiting for DIVINE INTERVENTION to HEAL THE WORLD. THEY were ACTIVE in spreading the MESSAGE OF "HEALING

AND RESTORATION" rather than just telling people to LEAVE IT TO GOD. THEY were ACTIVE in the STREETS and IN THE HOUSE AND THE MOUNTAINS telling people that THE KINGDOM OF THE LIGHT is WITHIN, BECAUSE THE LIGHT THAT IS WITHIN EACH PERSON WILL DICTATE THE LIGHT OUT THERE IN THE COMMUNITY AND THE WORLD. Keeping the LIGHT to ONESELF is EQUIVALENT TO "the BAD SERVANT" who kept the TALENTS OF THE MASTER HIDDEN RATHER THAN MULTIPLYING THEM. which stands for — ENABLING "EVIL" BY DOING NOTHING. PEOPLE CAN USE THEIR SKILLS AND ABILITIES TO "BRING A LITTLE LIGHT AND HELP UPLIFT THE WORLD IN THEIR OWN FAMILIES AND COMMUNITIES."

THE TIME for just PRAYING AND LEAVING IT ALL UP TO GOD TO FIX THIS IS NOT GOING TO HELP ANYONE.

WHAT WE are undergoing today is "THE SEASON" WHERE EVERYTHING IS COMING OUT TO THE LIGHT. That is what the term REVELATION means as in "TO REVEAL." Everything is coming out into the OPEN. And that is the BEGINNING OF THE ROAD TO MAKING THINGS RIGHT AND BETTER FOR THE WORLD AND PEOPLES. IF everything remains HIDDEN, how are you going to KNOW WHAT NEEDS — HEALING?

Remember the 144,000= 9 -12 THE WISE HERMIT TYPES WHO CARRY THE — GUIDING LIGHT— AND ARE "HANGED OR MURDERED?" And, did not WE tell you yesterday THAT THE DIVINE IS JUDGING THE "PHARAOHS" SUCH AS IN THE FOLLOWING QURANIC VERSE:

*"But it was OUR WILL to favor those who were OPPRESSED in the land, making them models of RIGHTEOUSNESS as well as SUCCESSORS .... In the NEW WORLD OR AGE" (S-URA-QASA)*

Thus, this is also an ADMONISHMENT TO THOSE IN POSITIONS OF RESPONSIBILITY TO REFUSE —CORRUPTION AND TO REFUSE TO PERSECUTE THOSE WHO ARE THE HEALERS OF THE WORLD OR THE — 144- 000 (9 - 12) which includes HEALERS, ACTIVISTS, VISIONARIES, CREATIVES, INTUITIVES, INDIGENOUS PEOPLES, etc. etc. etc.

You will notice from the above NUMBER CODE, that 9-12 comes after "9-11." 9+11 ADDS UP TO "20" THE JUDGMENT DAY or PERIOD. THE DAY AFTER — 9 -11, is "9-12" which ADDS UP TO "21" WHICH IS THE WORLD card and archetype that points to the END OF THE CURRENT WORLD WHICH BEGAN ON 9-11/ 9-12 THE DAY AFTER. THE JUDGMENT OF THE WORLD FOR THE PERSECUTION AND MURDER OF ALL THOSE WHO HAVE STRUGGLED TO PROTECT AND HEAL THE WORLD.

IF THE WORLD REFUSES TO "CHANGE" FOR THE BETTER AND TO CHANGE "THE ROAD YOU'RE ON" ... THEN "IT WILL ALL BE A ...ROLL AND NOT A ROCK." Like the song says.

SINCERELY, "DI-ANNU SAL-AZAR aka YESHUA"

---

## 50.  THE SEAL AND THE CODE: THE 13 CONSTELLATIONS AND INCARNATIONS OF AVA-T-ARA AND THE "THE NAME" ON OUR FOREHEADS I

REVELATION 7: 3 - 8

**5** From the tribe of Judah 12,000 were sealed, from the tribe of Reuben 12,000, from the tribe of Gad 12,000, **6** from the tribe of Asher 12,000, from the tribe of Naphtali 12,000, from the tribe of Manasseh 12,000, **7** from the tribe of Simeon 12,000, from the tribe of Levi 12,000, from the tribe of Issachar 12,000, **8** from the tribe of Zebulun 12,000, from the tribe of Joseph 12,000, from the tribe of Benjamin 12,000." (THEBIBLEGATEWAY)

Many take the numbers in the above verse to be LITERAL but they are not. These are a CODE in numbers that leads to other numbers and to the ARCHETYPAL meaning behind the value. Therefore:

"12,"000 = THE HANGED WO-MAN and THE HANGED MAN CARD NUMBER 12.
"1" "2",000 = 1 THE MAGICIAN #1 and THE HIGH PRIESTESS #2 and THE HANGED MAN
"12" ( 1 + 2),000 = 3 THE EMPRESS and THE HANGED MAN
12,000 = 1 + 2+ 4 + 4 + 4 = 15 THE DEVILS CARD and 6 THE LOVERS CARD ADAM/EVE

12 X 6 = 72 = 9 THE HERMIT and 14 TEMPERANCE and 5 THE HIEROPHANT =28= 10/16

12 X 6= THE "72" NAMES OF DEITY or ELOHIM and the 72 DISCIPLES OF YESHUA sent everywhere to help HEAL THE WORLD. THE "TRUE" DISCIPLES after the CHRIST are those WHO CARRY THE LAMP OF WISDOM, ARE IN TEMPERANCE or MODERATION AND RESTRAIN FROM DOING EVIL and FOLLOW AND UPHOLD DIVINE COSMIC LAW of JUSTICE and ETHICS. THE "LOVE THAT FULFILLS ALL LAW AND COMMANDMENTS." 7X2

= 14 AND THESE HERMIT TYPES OR ILLUMINATED ONES ARE IN A STATE OF BALANCE, HARMONY AND TEMPERANCE. 1 + 4= 5 THE HIEROPHANT AND THE UNITY OF THE 5 OR "THEY ARE THE INTERPRETERS OF THE LAW AFTER HIGHER CONSCIOUSNESS."

THE 12 TRIBES OF ISRAEL adds up to the number 3 ( 1 + 2) THE EMPRESS CARD OR THE DIVINE FEMININE. SHE REPRESENTS THE 13TH TRIBE OF D-INNA. THE TRIBES REPRESENT THE 13 CONSTELLATIONS FROM WHICH HUMANKIND ORI-GINATES AND WHICH RULE OVER HUMANITY. THE 13TH TRIBE RULES OVER THE 12. SIMILAR TO THE STRENGTH CARD IN WHICH THE HOLY SHEKINNA EMPRESS TAMES THE FIRE ELEMENT IN MAN FROM GOING WILD AND BECOMING DANGEROUSLY EVIL.

All the numbers point to HUMAN INCARNATIONS OF THE AVA-D-ARA or THE HEAVENLY EVE OF LIGHT and THE CHRIST PRINCIPLE. The 12 refers to COMPLETION AND HARMONY which is the COMPLETION OF A CYCLE and THE ARRIVAL OF THE AGE OF HARMONY. THE YIN and YANG represent the MAGICIAN AND HIGH PRIESTESS of the TEMPLE in the form of the CHRIST SOLOMON AND HIS SHEKINA. THE TEMPLE of the L-OR-D IS NOT THE ONE BUILT WITH ROCK THAT CRUMBLES ALL THE TIME BUT THE TEMPLE OF YIN-YANG OR — THE HUMAN — HIM-HERSELF AND THE PLANET EARTH ITSELF.

AVA-T-ARA refers to THE DESCENT OR AWAKENING OF A DIVINE SPARK OR ASPECT OF ADAM KAD-M-ONNE in the realm of matter. This process becomes activated when there's an imbalance between MATTER AND SPIRIT and as a result humankind has lost touch with HIS - HER INNER GUIDE AND COMPASS AND NOW HAS TURNED INTO A DANGEROUS GOL-EM READY TO DESTROY ITSELF AND THE PLANET. AVA is that DIVINE FEMININE INCARNATING AS THE HEAVENLY LIGHT OR "URI/ ARA" ON EARTH.

The overall message of the SCRIPTURE and code is one of LIBERATION from a state of entrapment and being overcome by the UNCONSCIOUS SHADOW FORCES which contribute to the planet's insanity. Examples of SHADOW UNCONSCIOUS FORCES OVERTAKING THE PLANET are HITLER, STALIN, FRANCO, AND OTHER MODERN DAY DYSFUNCTIONAL GOL-EM MINDS that "LEAD AND RULE THE WORLD" as in the DEVIL'S CARD number 15.

The more consumed by matter the people become, the more society NEGLECTS —SPIRIT and WE are not referring to religion but to THE DIVINE SPARK IN HUMAN WHICH MAKES A HUMAN AWARE OF ONE ANOTHER'S COMMON NAMASTE OR DIVINITY IN THE LIGHT. IT IS IMPERATIVE RIGHT NOW TO ENCOURAGE HUMANKIND TO NURTURE THE SPIRIT WITHIN AND NOT ONLY FEEDING THE URGES OF MATTER.

REVELATION 14: 1 Then I looked, and behold, on Mount Zion stood the , and with him 144,000 who had his name and his Father's name written on their foreheads. BIBLEGATEWAY

TODAY, THE "ELOHIM" wishes me to reveal THAT NAME.

"THE NAME" written on OUR foreheads is the NAME OF "SHEM-HAM-PH-ORA-ASH." The NAME is linked to YAKOV'S LADDER and the line of communication between HEAVEN AND EARTH of ALL the NATIONS AND EACH NATION'S ILLUMINATED BEINGS. This number IS NOT referring just to the JUDEO-CHRISTIAN-ISLAMIC FAITH BUT TO "ALL" NATIONS as all the ILLUMINATED ONES or HEALERS come from all NATIONS, TRIBES, RACES, SEXUAL ORIENTATIONS, RELIGIONS, TRADITIONS, SPIRITUALITIES, ETHNICITIES, GENDERS, etc. etc. etc.THEY are the ones who are striving to KEEP this world afloat and by WHICH THE WORLD IS "SAVED" AND IS ALSO "JUDGED" ON THEIR BEHALFS.

As Revelation 19:12 states:

His eyes were as a flame of fire, and on His head were many crowns; and He had a name written that no man knew, but He Himself.

TODAY, YOU KNOW WHAT THAT NAME IS.

THE ELOHIM STATE THAT THIS INFORMATION SHALL NOT BE USED FOR EVIL PURPOSES THAT CONTRADICT WHAT THE CHRIST IS AND HIS-HER MESSAGE. THERE ARE SERIOUS AND GRAVE KARMIC AND DIVINE CONSEQUENCES BY DOING SO, GOL-EM!

THE "TRUTH" OR "SATYA" WILL SET YOU FREE.

SINCERELY, THE 72 SPIRITS OF RENEWAL AND REBIRTH and Y-ESH-UA

---

## 51. THE INFATUATION WITH POWER ...VS... THE LOVE OF FREEDOM!---FEEDING THE BRUISED BIG EGO BY CURBING FREEDOM AND LIBERTY AND FEEDING THE NARCISSIST SELF

HAVE YOU NOTICED HOW THIS "WAR" AGAINST "CULTURE AND HEALING" IS ALL ABOUT "THE PERSECUTION OF GROUPS AND THE ERASURE OF HISTORY AND THE DECIMATION OF CULTURE?" IT IS NOT ABOUT ENLIGHTENING BUT RATHER ABOUT KEEPING EVERYTHING CONCEALED AND SENDING EVERYTHING AND EVERYONE BACK TO THE AGES OF IGNORANCE.

WHAT IS GOING ON "UNDERNEATH IT ALL" IS THAT THERE IS A STRUGGLE BETWEEN "THE LOVE OF POWER" VERSUS THE "LOVE OF FREEDOM" IN WHICH CERTAIN GROUPS AND PEOPLE ARE WILLING TO VIOLATE THE CONSTITUTION AND DECLARATION OF INDEPENDENCE AS WELL AS CURB BASIC FREEDOMS AND LIBERTIES AND PERSECUTE CITIZENS BECAUSE

THEY ARE DOING IT IN ORDER TO "KEEP AND HOLD TO POWER TOTALLY AND IN PERPETUITY!!" AND ALL BASED ON...FEAR!

THE DENIAL AND DEFLECTION IS CARRIED OUT IN ORDER TO OBSCURE THE TRUTH THAT THIS IS NOT ABOUT JUSTICE AND MAKING THE NATION GREAT BUT IT IS ALL ABOUT "THE INFATUATION WITH POWER" AT ALL COSTS WHICH IS BASICALLY "THE EGO WORKING HARD TO INFLATE AND AGGRANDIZE ITSELF EVEN MORE THAN IT SHOULD." IF THE PERSECUTION AND SCAPEGOATING WAS ABOUT JUSTICE AND THE GOOD OF THE NATION...THE ONES DOING THIS AFTER ABSOLUTE POWER AND STEPPING ON PEOPLE'S LIBERTIES/FREEDOMS AND VIOLATING THE CONSTITUTION WOULD NOT BE ACTING THIS WAY BUT THEY WOULD BE WORKING TOGETHER TO HEAL THE NATION AND THE PEOPLE RATHER THAN DOING THE OPPOSITE AS IN PUTTING THE NATION AGAINST ITSELF.

THE "BIG EGO" IS AT THE CENTER OF THIS BIG PROBLEM!!! THE "INFATUATION WITH POWER AND VALIDATION FROM THE OUTSIDE" WHICH HAS NOTHING TO DO WITH "LOVE" IS ABOUT THE SUSTAINMENT OF THE "HUGE EGO" AND ITS "DEFENSE MECHANISMS" BY MEANS OF LYING, DEFLECTION, PROJECTION AND DOING EVERY SORT OF MENTAL TRICKERY AND EMOTIONAL MANIPULATION IN THE BOOK IN ORDER TO PROTECT THAT "EGO." AND WE CAN SEE THIS PROCESS GOING ON BETWEEN THE "GRAND /MAIN EGO" OR THE FASCIST LEADERSHIP AND THE "LESSER BIG EGO" OR THE GROUP OF FOLLOWERS OF SUCH IDEOLOGIES.

"THINK ABOUT IT"...WOULD YOU LOVE YOUR COUNTRY IF YOU WERE PUTTING PEOPLE AT RISK OF KILLING ONE ANOTHER AND SACRIFICING THEM LIKE MOLOK FOR YOUR "BIG EGO???" THAT IS THE OPPOSITE OF LOVE. WOULD YOU LIE TO YOUR BRETHREN OVER AND OVER AGAIN TO KEEP THAT POWER RATHER THAN BEING HONEST IN YOUR SPEECH AND INTENTIONS? THAT IS NOT LOVE EITHER. HOW IS IT THAT THE BIG EGO AND LESSER BIG EGO "VIOLATE THE FREEDOMS AND LIBERTIES" THAT ARE REPRESENTED BY "THE ICON BY WHICH THE NATION IS KNOWN ALL OVER THE WORLD " AS IN "LADY LIBERTY" WHO REPRESENTS "FREEDOM AND LIBERTY" AND ENLIGHTENMENT, AND BE SAYING THAT YOU ARE FOR THE NATION AND FOR THE WELL BEING OF THE PEOPLE???

SOMEONE BE —LYING —REALLY BAD JUST LIKE THE "SATAN" IN THE JUDEO AND -CHRISTIAN TRADITION.

BASICALLY, THE "INFATUATION WITH POWER" BECAUSE OF FEAR AND THE WISH TO HAVE TOTAL CONTROL OF YOUR ENVIRONMENT BECAUSE OF THOSE FEARS BASED ON DYSFUNCTIONS AND BIASES SUCH AS "THE GREAT REPLACEMENT THEORY" ETC. ETC. ETC. IS WHAT IS BEHIND THE MOVE AND DESIRE TO IMPLEMENT TOTAL CONTROL OF EVERYTHING

AND EVERYONE. IT IS A MENTAL - EMOTIONAL / PSYCHOLOGICAL DYSFUNCTION. THIS IS THE TOTAL OPPOSITE OF WHAT FREEDOM AND LIBERTY IS AND OF COURSE "IF YOU ARE FREE TO THINK AND REFLECT" YOU ARE A GREAT DANGER AND CHALLENGE TO THE "INFATUATION FOR TOTAL POWER AND CONTROL AND THE BIG INFLATED EGO." AND SO THE BIG EGO FILLED WITH INNER INSECURITIES WILL TRAMPLE ON THE NATION AND ITS FOUNDATIONS AND SACRIFICE IT ALL NOT FOR THE LOVE OF IT, BUT TO SATISFY HIS OWN EGO AND EMPOWER IT EVEN MORE THRU THE TOTAL CONTROL OF THE CITIZEN AND ITS EVENTUAL CONDITIONING AND BRAINWASHING. AND GO —UNCHALLENGED!!! JUST LIKE —IN FASCIST POLITICAL SYSTEMS:(!

SINCERELY,
LADY LIBERTAS aka MARIAMNE

---

## 52. DEFLECTING BY "BLAMING AND TARGETING" CERTAIN GROUPS TO AVOID LOOKING AT YOUR OWN "SHADOW": THE MARK OF THE BEAST AND THE WORKS OF THE ANTI-CHRIST (-) 6+6+6= (-) 18

This is EXACTLY — WHAT– HITLER did. And you will NOTICE that he began with JEWS and later on the PERSECUTION AND GENOCIDE expanded to DISABLED, LGBTQ, PEOPLE OF COLOR, JW's, etc. etc. etc. AMERICA needs and must BEWARE OF THIS VERY DANGEROUS TREND. This TREND OF CASTING BLAME ON A CERTAIN AND PARTICULAR GROUP is a form of DEFLECTION IN ORDER TO AVOID "LOOKING AT YOUR OWN SHADOW AND FEARS AND INSECURITIES WITHIN THAT SHADOW." WHAT YOU SEE IN "THE OTHER" IS MOST PROBABLY A PROJECTION ONTO THE OTHER OF YOUR OWN SELF AND WHAT YOU DENY AND REFUSE TO ACKNOWLEDGE AND SEE ABOUT YOUR OWN SELF.

The CALLING FOR THE ERADICATION OF CERTAIN GROUPS POINTS TO THE "DYSFUNCTIONAL CONTENTS IN THE MIND OF THIS TYPE OF PERSONALITY" which are HATE, DISCRIMINATION, PERSECUTION, — MURDER" etc. As YOU can see THE "LIGHT OF REASON" COMES TO THE WORLD to "EXPOSE" the TRUE CONTENTS AND INCLINATIONS of the HEART. INNER DEMONIC ENERGIES concealed behind a FACADE OF DEVOTION AND SELF-RIGHTEOUSNESS AND SUPERIORITY are COMING OUT FROM BEHIND THE VEIL.

Have YOU noticed how these extremist elements as depicted in the AGORA movie are "CALLING FOR THE ERADICATION OF WOMEN AND CHILDREN?" It is because they are REACTING to the LIGHT and everything hidden is COMING TO THE FORE. Now WE wonder ourselves if BOTH FASCIST ELEMENTS ON

BOTH SIDES OF THE POND are actually LINKED SOMEHOW as WE KNOW that both have close ties. And so are both working together to SPREAD CHAOS AND HATE? Just an OBSERVATION.

And so as THE DARKNESS from them cannot do anything else but COME OUT AND REACT in a very NEGATIVE AND LOW VIBRATION, this is WHEN THOSE WHO HAVE "EYES AND EARS" perceive the TRUE NATURE of these people so that THE WORLD CAN AWAKEN AND REALIZE what truly LURKS behind the DISCRIMINATORY AND HOMICIDAL IMPULSES of THE FASCIST.

This ENERGY that TARGETS PEOPLE rather THAN TAKE RESPONSIBILITY FOR ITS OWN DYSFUNCTION, is what the BIBLE refers to as THE ANTICHRIST. Do you remember the NUMBER OF THE BEAST? It's called A BEAST because VIOLENT BEASTS usually REACT TO EVERYTHING AND ARE READY TO ATTACK!!! This BEAST archetype has the NUMBER (-) 666 which adds up to (-) 18!!! THE MOON CARD in the sense that WE explained yesterday in our DIARY ON THE "LUNAR CYCLE" OF "MOVING FROM THE DARK TO THE LIGHT" ONLY THAT IN THIS CASE THE WRONGDOER BASKS IN IGNORANCE.

And so RATHER THAN USING THE SCRIPTURE and PSYCHOLOGY to HELP ILLUMINATE THAT SHADOW SIDE OF THEMSELVES so that they are not UNDER THE INFLUENCE OF EVIL, they do PROJECT THEIR INSECURITIES UPON ANOTHER and so the BEAST MENTALITY AND ACTIONS follow as in PERSECUTION AND GENOCIDE. This is the difference between the Y-ESH-UA archetype who IS THE CHRIST OR LIGHT WHO SHINES LIKE THE SUN UPON EVERYONE 'S SHADOW and the BEAST who FUNCTIONS AND ACTS from the REALM OF THE UNENLIGHTENED SHADOW CATEGORIZING PEOPLE AND SINGLING THEM OUT FOR DESTRUCTION.

Now, OUR QUESTION TO YOU IS — ARE YOU GOING TO LISTEN TO "THE BEAST" or are you going to LISTEN TO "THE LIGHT?"

For the BEAST is after CHAOS AND HATE AND ANNIHILATION! But the LIVING CHRIST PRINCIPLE WHICH IS ILLUMINATION ASKS FOR –LOVE AND UNITY AND GOOD WILL AMONG ALL WO-MEN!!!

IS NOT TARGETING ANOTHER GROUP — UNJUST AND UNFAIR?? Aren't you DOING EXACTLY WHAT YOU CLAIM THOSE YOU ACCUSE OF DOING? And so here WE have the REACTIVITY we been talking about for awhile as in CLAIMING TO BE "NOT RACIST" but at the SAME TIME — CALLING FOR THE PERSECUTION AND ANNIHILATION of ANOTHER GROUP. It seems to US that it is similar to NOT BEING IN A STATE OF FULL AWARENESS SINCE YOU ARE ACCUSING OTHERS OF "THE SAME THING THAT YOU ARE DOING YOURSELF." WHICH IS EQUIVALENT TO BEING IN A STATE OF "SLUMBER."

And so MY BROTHERS AND SISTERS in CHRIST" THE ONE WHO IS TRUTH AND WHO LEADS US FROM UNTRUTH TO TRUTH," DURING THESE BEGINNINGS OF SAT-YA AND ENDINGS OF KALI YUG, it's time TO LISTEN TO THE "CHRIST OR LIGHT IN YOU" rather than to THE BEAST AND ANTICHRIST FOUL SPIRIT THAT IS FOGGING THE MIND OF SOME AND SPREADING THE "FRUITS OF HELL" RATHER THAN THOSE OF THE SPIRIT.

As for the DEFLECTION FROM PERSONAL RESPONSIBILITY OF THOSE INDIVIDUALS " WHO BLAME OTHERS FOR WHAT THEY THEMSELVES ARE DOING"— It is time to leave the CASTING OF STONES, take RESPONSIBILITY FOR YOUR "OWN EMOTIONAL AND PSYCHOLOGICAL HEALTH" and FOCUS ON "FINDING COMMON GROUND AND WORKING TOGETHER TO TACKLE THE REAL ISSUES OF THE DAY THAT ARE WHAT POLITICIANS ARE SUPPOSEDLY TRAINED TO DO AND SUPPOSED TO DO such as HOMELESSNESS, CRIME, INEQUALITY, RACISM, UNAFFORDABLE HOUSING, etc. etc.etc.

(-) 18 = (1+8)= (-) 9 is THE HERMIT CARD in its NEGATIVE INTERPRETATION as in THOSE WHO ARE SUPPOSED TO LEAD THE PEOPLE TO "THE LIGHT" BUT INSTEAD USE THEIR EVIL INCLINATION TO SPREAD MORE EVIL. THE DYSFUNCTIONAL KING AND HIEROPHANT ARCHETYPES.

SINCERELY, "THE CHRIST"

---

## 53. IF THERE IS "WOKE" THERE IS ALSO "ASLEEP:" CHOOSING TO BE IN A WAKEFUL STATE LIKE THE 5 VIRGINS OR TO BE ASLEEP AND BE LEFT BEHIND LIKE THE OTHER SLEEPY 5

MATTHEW 25:

Then shall the kingdom of heaven be likened unto ten virgins, who took their lamps, and went forth to meet the bridegroom. [2] And five of them were wise, and five were foolish. [3] Those that were foolish took their lamps, and took no oil with them: [4] But the wise took oil in their vessels with their lamps.(GOSPEL)

THERE IS THIS FUNNY AND TRAGIC OBSESSION WITH "WOKE" AND THINGS "WOKE." IT'S BECOME ONE OF THOSE WORDS USED FREELY LIKE "COMMUNISM, SOCIALISM AND OTHER …ISMS" IN ORDER TO DEFLECT AND SILENCE HEALTHY DISCOURSE ABOUT ISSUES THAT NEED TO BE CONFRONTED RATHER THAN IGNORED.

WELL, THERE ARE THESE ADS AND VIDEOS ABOUT "FINDING OUT WHO IS WOKE AND WHAT COMPANIES ARE WOKE SO THAT YOU DO NOT INVEST IN THEM" AND OTHER NONSENSE LIKE THAT. I MEAN, THE WORLD IS LITERALLY "UNDERGOING IMPORTANT CHANGES" AND WHAT MANY ARE

WORRIED ABOUT AND CLINGING TO IS IN CERTAIN "WORDS" IN ORDER TO KEEP PEOPLE ASLEEP.

OH WELL....

AND SO MY OVERACTIVE MIND AND IMAGINATION BEGAN TO THINK AND REFLECT ABOUT THE TERM "WOKE" WHICH COMES FROM "BEING AWAKE" JUST LIKE IN THE PARABLE OF THE VIRGINS THAT ARE "AWAKE" AND "WOKE" IN THE MIDDLE OF THE NIGHT WHEN ALL IS IN THE "THE DARK" AND IT'S HARDER TO SEE WHAT IS REALLY HAPPENING. SO WHEN THE BRIDEGROOM ARRIVES THE "WOKE ONES" ARE READY FOR THE FESTIVITIES. AND SO .... WHAT AM SAYING HERE IS THAT THE OPPOSITE OF THE WORD "WOKE OR TO BE AWAKENED" IS "TO BE ASLEEP!!!" THEREFORE, IF I AM NOT AWAKE, I MUST BE ASLEEP AND IN A SLUMBER... AVOIDING AND IGNORING PRESSING ISSUES GOING ON AND SO ... MY QUESTION IS .... WOULD I RATHER BE IN A STATE OF AWAKENING OR IN A STATE OF SLUMBER AND SLEEPINESS???

GOOD QUESTION, RIGHT!

AND LIKE THE PARABLE OF THE 10 VIRGINS, 5 WERE ABLE TO WELCOME THE BRIDEGROOM BUT THE OTHER 5 WERE ASLEEP LOSING THAT GREAT OPPORTUNITY. IN THOSE DAYS IT WAS TRAGIC FOR A WOMAN TO BE UNMARRIED SINCE MARRIAGE WAS SEEN AS A BENEFIT AND HAVING CHILDREN AS A SORT OF INSURANCE POLICY DURING OLD AGE.

THE NUMBER 10 IS THE "WHEEL OF FORTUNE" AND IT HAS "8 PARTS" AS IN THE "STRENGTH CARD" AND SO WHAT THIS IS ALSO INDICATING IS THAT THE 5 VIRGINS WHO WERE "WOKE" WERE "THE STRONG ONES" WHO WERE ABLE TO RECEIVE THE BRIDEGROOM IN TIME TO CATCH THE NEXT BUGGY AND GET OUT OF THE PLACE OF RESTRICTION AND CONSTRICTION THEY WERE TRAPPED IN. THE WOKE ONES WERE ABLE TO ESCAPE FROM A VERY LIMITED AND UNHEALTHY PLACE.

THIS PARABLE POINTS TO "MAKING WISE DECISIONS." WHILE THE SLEEPING ONES WERE LEFT BEHIND BECAUSE THEY REFUSED TO SEE WHAT WAS ACTUALLY HAPPENING AND FAILED TO TAKE NEEDED ACTION THE WOKE 5 SAVED THEMSELVES. 10 + 8 ===18 THE MOON CARD OR THE PROCESS OF GOING FROM BEING IN THE DARK TO BEING IN THE LIGHT OR AWAKE OR AWARE IS THE CHARACTERISTIC OF "STRONG PEOPLE."

THE NUMBER 5 IN THIS PARABLE REPRESENTS THE "KINGDOM OF HEAVEN" — AND SO THE HIEROPHANT CARD NUMBER 5 REPRESENTS:

5. THE HIEROPHANT. --Marriage, alliance, captivity, servitude; by another account, mercy, and goodness; inspiration; the man to whom the Querent has recourse.(WIKIPEDIA)

SO YOU CAN NOTICE FROM THE ABOVE THAT THE 5 AWAKENED VIRGINS WERE READY FOR MARRIAGE WITH THE HIEROPHANT IN ORDER TO ESCAPE CAPTIVITY BY FORMING AN ALLIANCE WITH THE BRIDEGROOM. THE OTHER 5 WOULD HAVE A REVERSED AND NEGATIVE MEANING. IN THOSE DAYS MARRIAGE WAS A WAY OUT. AND SO IT TELLS YOU THAT AN INTERPRETATION WOULD BE THAT THE "SLEEPING BEAUTIES" REMAINED CAPTIVE TO WHOMEVER THEY LIVED UNDER AND SO WERE NOT ABLE TO ATTAIN THE FREEDOM THEY CRAVED. THEY WERE NOT "STRONG" ENOUGH. THEY REMAINED IN SERVITUDE TO THEIR LOWER SELVES AND TO THE CORRUPT AGE OF KALI WHICH WE ARE LEAVING BEHIND AS WE SPEAK..

AND SO ... IN WHAT STATE WOULD YOU RATHER BE? AWAKENED AND WOKE OR ...ASLEEP? LIVING IN A FANTASY IN WHICH THE WORLD AROUND IS FALLING APART BUT BE SO ASLEEP THAT YOU ARE UNABLE TO REALIZE WHAT IS GOING ON OR TO PERCEIVE THE DANGEROUS SITUATION AND .... BE UNABLE TO FIND A WAY OUT!? UNABLE TO FIND A WAY OUT BY JOINING THE BRIDEGROOM WHO "UNDERSTANDS THE LAW" AND SO HE CAN PROVIDE SOLUTIONS TO THE DIRE CONDITION AND SITUATION OF THE VIRGINS.

5 REPRESENTS PENTAGRAMMATON OR "UNION AND INTEGRATION OF THE SELF." THEREFORE, THE PARABLE IS POINTING TO "ALCHEMY." THE 5 WERE IN AN INTEGRATED AND STATE OF WHOLENESS WHILE THE OTHER 5 HAD NOT WOKEN UP YET TO THEIR HIGHER SELVES. THEREFORE, WE HAVE HERE THE "MALE AND FEMALE" —YIN AND YANG — PRINCIPLES THAT NEED TO BE INTEGRATED IN ORDER FOR THE VIRGINS TO BE IN A STATE OF WAKEFULNESS. THERE IS MUCH ABOUT THIS PARABLE BUT THAT WILL BE FOR A LATER TIME. THE MASCULINE LIGHT ILLUMINATING THE FEMALE SHADOW AND SO LIBERATING THE LIGHT WITHIN AND GIVING BIRTH TO THE FACULTY OF DISCERNMENT.

THE 5 WOKE VIRGINS HAVE LAMPS LIKE "THE HERMIT CARD" IN THE SACRED TAROT, MEANING THAT THEY ARE IN A STATE OF "ILLUMINATION AND ENLIGHTENMENT" ABLE TO KNOW WHERE TO GO AND WHICH PATH TO TAKE. THIS POINTS TO THE CONCEPT OF "INTUITION" WHICH HAS TO DO WITH THEIR ABILITY TO PERCEIVE WHEN THE BRIDEGROOM HAS ARRIVED. WE ALSO HAVE THE CONCEPT OF A GUIDING LIGHT TO KNOW WHERE AND WHAT YOU ARE WALKING INTO AND THE CONCEPT OF "TAKING ACTION." WHEN ONE IS ASLEEP ONE DOES NOT TAKE CONSTRUCTIVE ACTION BUT

STAYS IN A STATE OF DEFLECTION AND THE IGNORING OF REALITY BY MEANS OF—DENIALISMS AND LABELING" WHICH KEEPS ONE STUCK IN THE SAME SITUATION AND CONDITIONS FOREVER.

THE BRIDEGROOM IS "1" AS IN "THE MAGICIAN" ARCHETYPE WHO REPRESENTS THE ABILITY TO MAKE THINGS HAPPEN. THE MAGICIAN REPRESENTS:

When the Magician appears in a spread, it points to the talents, capabilities and resources at the querent's disposal to succeed. The message is to tap into one's full potential rather than holding back, especially when there is a need to transform something.(WIKIPEDIA)

THERE IS NEED TO TRANSFORM THE WORLD FROM ITS CURRENT STATE OF COLLAPSE AND CHAOS INTO SOMETHING BETTER SO THAT LIFE CAN CONTINUE. THIS PARABLE IS LINKED TO THE ONE WITH THE "TALENTS" THAT ARE TO BE USED RATHER THAN BE HELD BACK LIKE THE 5 ASLEEP VIRGINS. MARRIAGE IS ABOUT "GIVING BIRTH" TO A NEW ERA.

"THE KINGDOM OF HEAVEN" THEN REFERS NOT TO A LITERAL PLACE NECESSARILY BUT TO A "STATE OF HIGHER CONSCIOUSNESS" THAT IS LIKENED TO "BEING AWAKE" AND CONNECTED TO "WISDOM." THE OPPOSITE OF THE "WISE" VIRGINS ARE THE "FOOLISH ONES" THEREFORE, "FOOLISHNESS" IS LINKED TO THE STATE OF BEING "UNAWAKE" OR UNAWARE AND AS SUCH UPHOLDING INJUSTICE AND SOCIAL EVILS AND PERPETUATING THESE DUE TO NOT BEING IN A CONSCIOUS STATE WHEREIN THE LIGHT ILLUMINATES THE SHADOW SELF AND SO PEOPLE BECOME AWARE OF THEIR DYSFUNCTIONAL ACTIONS AND INCLINATIONS AND HOW THESE CONTRIBUTE TO THE MESS EVERYWHERE.

"WOKE" = The quality of being ALERT to and concerned about social injustice and discrimination.

"ASLEEP" IN RELATION TO "WOKE" = The quality of "NOT BEING ALERT" and UNCONCERNED OR LACKING EMPATHY ABOUT SOCIAL INJUSTICES AND DISCRIMINATION.

THE FESTIVITIES OF THE BRIDE OR THE "CHRIST PRINCIPLE" HAVE TO DO WITH THE ALCHEMICAL MARRIAGE AND THE BIRTH OF SATYA YUGA, THE AGE OF TRUTH, LIGHT AND PEACE. THOSE WHO ARE ASLEEP WILL BE LEFT BEHIND. THE GROOM HAS ARRIVED AS PROMISED.

SINCERELY, "SOLOMON THE ARCHITECT AND MAGICIAN OF THE NEW AGE"

## 54. EL-E-AZAR: THE MIGHTY FIRE, WISDOM AND LIGHT OF THE KING or "ARI" OF Y-ESH-UA

I learnt today about EL-AZAR or the name ELEAZAR. There is some very interesting information that derives from the ETYMOLOGY of this name and its relationship with many biblical concepts. First of all, let us start with whom ELEAZAR was:

**Eleazar** (/ɛliˈeɪzər/; Hebrew: אֶלְעָזָר, Modern: *'El'azar*, Tiberian: *'El'āzār*, "El has helped") or **El'azar** was a priest in the Hebrew Bible, the second High Priest, succeeding his father Aaron after he died.[1] He was a nephew of Moses. (WIKIPEDIA)

Eleazar was involved in the creation of the ALTAR AND THE FIREPANS. And was involved in the ritual of the RED HEIFER which is as follows:

The red heifer offering instructions are described in the Book of Numbers. The children of Israel were commanded to obtain "a red heifer without spot, wherein is no blemish, and upon which never came yoke".[2] The heifer is then to be slaughtered and burned outside of the camp.[3] Cedar wood, hyssop, and wool or yarn dyed scarlet are added to the fire, and the remaining ashes are placed in a vessel containing pure water. (WIKIPEDIA)

The etymology of the name EL-E-AZAR is EL - Y - AZAR which means GOD IS MY HELP. However, if you look closely at different parts of this name you will notice that it is composed of 3 words as in the NAME OF GOD "EL" and "Y" as in AND, and the word AZAR. In turn the word AZAR can be divided into AZ-ARI.

What is interesting about the concepts behind the name if we start with AZAR is that AZ-ARI has to do with the LION OF JUDAH as in THE ARI!!! And as you already know ARI is a form of the word for FIRE, LIGHT, WISDOM as in URI / UR/ OR / AR/ ER/ IR. So here we notice that the word AZ-ARI has to do with FIRE, LIGHT, WISDOM and THE LION OF JUDAH or the ARI-EL.

*The word AZ in hebrew stands for עז 'az, az; from H5810; strong, vehement, harsh:—fierce, greedy, mighty, power, roughly, strong.(BLUELETTERBIBLE).*

Therefore, the name AZ-ARI refers to the FIERCE, MIGHTY, POWERFUL, STRONG "FIRE" "LIGHT" "WISDOM" "ARI." On the other hand, the AZ word is also related to the AZA which means MADE HOT, HEAT. Are you seeing the PATTERN here?

Now let US see what AZAR means in PERSIAN and other languages besides Hebrew: The NAME AZAR stands for A BOY NAME MEANING —HELP, FIRE, SCARLET, KING!!! Do you see the patterns here with the Hebrew as in FIRE and in the case of the ARI OR LION OF JUDAH and the concepts of HELP AND KING as in Y-ESH-UA THE KING THAT HELPS HUMANKIND!!! And who was SACRIFICED LIKE THE RED HEIFER which is red as the color of BLOOD and SCARLET.

Now something very interesting is that in the SPANISH language the verb AZAR exists. And guess what it means? It means to ROAST MEAT ON THE FIRE. As in CARNE "AZA"-DA. The verb ASAR according to the DICCIONARIO ETIMOLOGICO comes from the LATIN words ASSARE and ASUS and ARSUS which means TO BURN. AR-SUS as in ARI or UR as in B-UR-N and AR-DER IN CASTILIAN. Therefore the LATIN here is related to the HEBREW AZAR and to the PERSIAN etc. And, all this points to what EL-E-AZAR did at the ALTAR WITH THE RED HEIFER which was to BURN IT or ROAST IT to DEITY. Just as in Spanish CARNE DE HEIFER ASA-DA.

And so WE can conclude by all these related words from the word AZAR that ELI-AZAR stands for EL THE STRONG FIRE as in GOD IS THE STRONG DIVINE FIRE THAT CONSUMES and Y-ESH-UA IS THE KING THAT HELPS or THE ESH or FIRE THAT HELPS.

It all points to the element of SACRED FIRE! THE "DIVINE SPARK" IN EVERYONE!!! The term AZAR is also related to other concepts that WE will keep to ourselves for NOW.

SINCERELY, DI-ANNU SAL-AZAR

---

## 55.  THE "RETURN OF KALKI" AND THE "LIGHTNING STRIKE" WELCOMING THE YEAR OF THE HORSE 2014

ON A THURSDAY OF JANUARY OF 2014 THE JESUS CORCOVADO STATUE IN RIO DE JANEIRO BRAZIL WAS STRUCK BY LIGHTNING TO THE POINT THAT ONE OF ITS FINGERS WAS CHIPPED. THIS NIGHT HAD BEEN RECORDED AS ONE OF THE NIGHTS WITH MOST LIGHTNING STRIKES SINCE THESE HAVE BEEN MONITORED AND RECORDED IN BRAZIL.

THIS EVENT WAS TO WELCOME "THE YEAR OF THE HORSE" OF THE CHINESE CALENDAR.

BY NOW 2012 AND THE MAYAN CALENDAR CRAZE HAD PASSED AND THE LARGE METEOR HAD FALLEN ON RUSSIA. BY THEN I WAS BEGINNING TO CONNECT THE DOTS AND THE "SYMBOLS AND SIGNS." AND SO SOME LITTLE VOICE IN MY HEAD OR INTUITION WAS TELLING ME THAT GREAT CHANGES WERE ABOUT TO COME TO EARTH BECAUSE OF THESE CELESTIAL AND COSMIC EVENTS AND ENERGIES.

THEN YOU ADD THE YEAR OF THE HORSE AND THE LIGHTNING STRIKE UPON CORCOVADO AND YOU GET "KALKI ARRIVING TO EARTH ON A HORSE IN THE YEAR 2014" JUST AS THE MAYAN CALENDAR HAD PREDICTED.

AND SO ANOTHER INTERESTING THING HAPPENING HERE WITH THE SYMBOLS AND SIGNS OF THE TIMES IS THAT THE DAY OF THE LIGHTNING STRIKE WAS A "THURS-DAY NIGHT." AND SO … THE NAME IN ENGLISH FOR THURSDAY COMES FROM THE NAME OF THE GOD "THOR" WHO IS THE GOD OF THUNDER AND LIGHTNING IN THE TEUTONIC TRADITIONS!!! IN CASTILIAN THE NAME IS "JUEVES" AFTER GOD JUPITER WHICH IS ALSO LINKED TO LIGHTNING!!!

AND HAVE NOT THINGS CHANGED DRAMATICALLY EVER SINCE THESE INITIAL YEARS OF 2012 AND ONWARDS???

THE CLEANSING COSMIC ENERGIES ARE –HERE. 2014 ADDS UP TO 7 THE CHARIOT CARD WHICH HAS THE TWIN YIN YANG ENERGIES AS HORSES OR SPHINXES AND ALSO ADDS UP TO 11 WHICH IS THE JUSTICE CARD WHICH IS ASSOCIATED TO JUPITER AS IN "COSMIC LAWS."

THERE ARE MANY REASONS WHY EVERYTHING IS IN CHAOS SINCE 2012-2014 AND ONE OF THESE REASONS IS THAT WE ARE PASSING FROM ONE WORLD ONTO A NEW ONE AND SO THE OUTDATED WORLD IS IN RESISTANCE MODE WHILE THE NEW GENERATIONS AND THE NEW WORLD WISH TO MOVE FORWARD AND BE REBORN. ALSO, THE COSMIC ENERGIES ARE PUSHING OUT TO THE OPEN THE DYSFUNCTION AND BRINGING WHAT WAS HIDDEN TO LIGHT IN ORDER THAT THE COLLECTIVE SHADOW BE HEALED SINCE THAT IS WHAT IS KEEPING US FROM MOVING FORWARD INTO THE "NEW WORLD." AND A LACK OF ETHICS AND JUSTICE ALL OVER IS WHAT IS COMPOUNDING HUMANITY'S PROBLEMS EVERYWHERE AND ADDING TO THE TRAUMA AND INSANITY.

SINCERELY, "THE ONE WHO COULD READ THE STARS AND THE HEAVENS"

---

## 56.  KAL-QI, KAL-QI, KAL-QI- LEAH …. THE RETURN OF "KAL-QI" OF LEAH, THE JEWISH AND PALESTINIAN PEOPLE AND THE KALKI TRADITION OF THE LAND AND PEOPLE OF IN-DIA!!!

KAL- QI IS THE NAME FOR THE "ENERGY OR EMANATION" THAT BRINGS CHANGE AND RENEWAL TO THE PLANET AND WHICH IS DESCRIBED AS A REINCARNATED DEMI-BEING IN THE HINDU TRADITION.

THE TERM "KAL-QI" HAS THE WORD IN SANSKRIT FOR "TIME AND DARKNESS" WHICH IS "KALA" AS WELL AS "QI" AS IN LIGHT, GOLD,

ELECTRICITY AND FIRE. THE CONCEPT AND NAME AS A WHOLE POINT TO A "DARK TIME IN WHICH THE LIGHT WILL BE BORN AS IN A —NEW DAY!!!' K- "AL" - QI ALSO HAS THE "ROOT– AL" WHICH IS PART OF THE NAME AL-LA IN ISLAM THEREFORE K-AL-QI IS A DIVINE COSMIC EMANATION THAT CARRIES WITHIN IT THE HOLY "QI."

THE KAL-QI ARCHETYPAL ENERGY REMINDS US OF THE ALCHEMICAL PROCESS OF WORKING THE DARK AND THE LIGHT AND OF "THE ENERGY OR LIGHT OR —QI—THAT DISPELS THE –KAL—OR STATE OF IGNORANCE AND CORRUPTION OF THE AGE OF KALI.

THEREFORE, THE HINDU RETURN OF KAL-QI IS AN ARCHETYPE JUST AS QUETZALCOATL AND KUKULCAN AND YESHUA AND THE OTHERS. THESE ARE "ENERGIES" THAT BRING ABOUT RENEWAL AND RESTORATION. PEOPLE NEED TO UNDERSTAND THESE ENERGIES ARE NOT ABOUT "RELIGION!!!" THEY ARE ABOUT THE ASCENSION AND EVOLUTION OF THE "HIGHER SELF IN HUMANS."

QI — AS IT HAS ALREADY BEEN EXPLAINED IS RELATED TO THE TERM AND CONCEPT AND ARCHETYPE OF THE HOLY "QI"-KI-INNA" OR THE DIVINE PRESENCE THAT HEALS. QI IS ALSO THE BASIC SUBSTANCE OF LIFE PERVADING EVERYTHING.

AND SO ...

ISN'T IT KINDA "WEIRD" THINKING ABOUT THE MONOTHEISTIC AND POLYTHEISTIC BELIEF IN THE RETURN OF SOME ALIEN FROM SPACE WHO WILL COME TO SAVE THIS PLANET? HAS IT WORKED BEFORE? N-O-P-E!!!

AND THAT IS THE FLAW OF THE BELIEF AND EXPECTATION OF SOMEONE WHO WILL COME TO SAVE THE WHOLE THING. IT TENDS TO MAKE PEOPLE COMPLACENT IN THAT THEY LEAVE EVERYTHING TO BE SOLVED AS BY MAGIC TO THE SO CALLED "MESSIAH." MEANWHILE PEOPLE DISCARD ALL PERSONAL AND COLLECTIVE RESPONSIBILITY TO HELP SAVE THE PLANET AND SOCIETY AND THEMSELVES.

IRONICALLY ALL THESE RELIGIONS ESPECIALLY THE SO-CALLED "MONOTHEISTIC" EXPANDED GEOGRAPHICALLY BECAUSE THEY TRIED TO "SAVE THE WORLD" AND SO THEY THOUGHT THAT BY EXPANDING AND CONVERTING THE ENTIRE PLANET THEY COULD SAVE IT. WHICH CAN NEVER HAPPEN. PERFECT EXAMPLE OF THAT IS CHRISTIANITY IN WHICH DIFFERENT CHRISTIAN TRADITIONS HAVE FOUGHT WARS AMONGST EACH OTHER FOR CENTURIES. ISLAM, THE SAME THING. THIS "QAL-KI" WOULD BE THE 10TH REINCARNATION ACCORDING TO HINDUISM? THE THING IS THAT, IF IT'S THE TENTH, WHAT HAPPENED WITH THE OTHER 9

REINCARNATIONS? THE WORLD SHOULD HAVE ALREADY BEEN "SAVED" AT LEAST BY THE FIFTH ONE.

JUST THINKING ABOUT THIS MAKES ME FEEL "TIRED." I FEEL LIKE I HAVE GONE THROUGH THIS CRAZINESS FOREVER. LIFETIME AFTER LIFETIME. TIME AFTER TIME.

AND SO ... GOING BACK TO THE RETURN OF QAL-KI-LEAH OR QAL-KI-LYAH, AND THE "STORY" OF THE HOUSE OF BETHLEHEM... ISN'T IT "KRAZZZY" THAT IF SOMEONE WAS "TO RETURN" AS THE "TRADITIONS" CLAIM, THAT THIS BEING WOULD BE CONNECTED TO ALL PEOPLES AND WOULD ACTUALLY COME FROM BOTH "JEWRY" AS WELL AS THE "PALESTINIAN PEOPLE" AS ALL THE KEY NAMES AND CITIES FROM THE "RETURN OF "THE MESSIAH" " —OR THE HOUSE OF ANNA—-COME FROM THE WEST BANK/ PALESTINE MAINLY. ADD TO THAT ARABIA AND INDIA AND THE AMERICAS AND AFRICA AND SO AND SO AND SO ......

A REAL MELTING POT PACKAGED IN A HUMAN BEING OR BEINGS!!! LINKED TO ALL THE PEOPLES AND TO THE COSMIC ENERGIES. WHO BY HIS-HER/ THEIR PRESENCE THESE ENERGIES HELP USHER THE BEGINNING OF A NEW DAY OR DIA!!!

HOWEVER, AS MUCH AS I WOULD LOVE THIS TO BE THE REAL THING IT IS JUST AN ARCHETYPE THAT IS UNIVERSAL AND THAT ACTUALLY "LIVES IN EVERY ONE AND IN EACH ONE OF US." IT'S TIME TO ACTIVATE THIS ENERGY AND TUNE IT WITH THE COSMIC ENERGIES AND BRING ABOUT A POSITIVE CHANGE TO OUR CONDITION AS HUMANS, THE PLANET AND TO OTHER LIFE FORMS.

Kalki is described in the Puranas as the avatar who rejuvenates existence by ending the darkest and destructive period to remove adharma (unrighteousness) and ushering in the Satya Yuga, while riding a white horse with a fiery sword. The description and details of Kalki are different among various Puranas. (WIKIPEDIA)

SINCERELY, "QAL-KI OF LEAH" THRU THE BIPOLAR GATES OF COMMUNICATION

---

## 57. KUKUL-KI-ANNE: THE FEATHERED SERPENT and the MAYAN E PLURIBUS UNNU-M

KUKUL-"QI" -ANNE is the SAME QUETZAL-COATLICUE archetype as YESHUA. He's the PLUMED SERPENT or ENNO-QI character.

KUKUL-QI-ANNI 's name points back to the recurrent theme of the HEALING principle from the "QI" traditions which stand for THE OVERSEER OF HUMAN SOCIETY and NATURE ensuring that both remain in relative balance and prosperity. KUKUL-QI-ANNI is also SHA-M-INNA (SHAMAN/KA) or the vehicle of the VOICES of the SPIRITUAL WORLD to the MAYAN WORLD and UPHOLDER of the CIRCLE OF LIFE or THE "ONNE AND ONLY."

The cult of Kukulkan/Quetzalcoatl was the first Mesoamerican religion to transcend the old Classic Period linguistic and ethnic divisions.[4] This cult facilitated communication and peaceful trade among peoples of many different social and ethnic backgrounds.[4] Although the cult was originally centred on the ancient city of Chichen Itza in the modern Mexican state of Yucatán, it spread as far as the Guatemalan Highlands and northern Belize.[5] ( WIKIPEDIA)

As you can see from the above excerpt, THE CULT OF KUKUL-QI-ANNE follows the same TRADITION OF THE TOWER OF BAB-EL as in ONE PEOPLE OUT OF MANY. It eventually TRANSCENDED LINGUISTIC AND ETHNIC DIVISIONS and founded A MAYA PEOPLE AND CIVILIZATION. Therefore the MAYA was not a homogeneous people like it is believed but A PEOPLE OUT OF MANY. Although the MAYA had many gods and goddesses just as the other TRADITIONS AND PEOPLE WORLDWIDE, they believed in a CENTRAL DEITY who they called by many names who was known as THE GREAT SPIRIT. As their cosmovision was one about the UNNI-TY OF THINGS or the CIRCLE OF LIFE, they were well aware that despite the apparent MULTIPLICITY there is a UNIQUE CENTRAL UNITING FORCE BEHIND IT ALL.

SPIRIT after all is RUACH ELOHEEM and along with many traditions this GREAT SPIRIT FORCE IS THE RUACH behind all things and manifestation of LIFE.

The MAYAN PEOPLE or PIPOL or POPOL sacred writing was the POPOL VUH that speaks of the DIVINE TWINS archetype which it shares with other world spiritual traditions. It points to the YIN-YANG and the ADAM and EVE, etc, etc etc. or the interaction and interplay of the DUALITIES but represented in symbol and in story form. The word POPOL sounds much like the Latin word for PEOPLE which in Italian is POPOLO. VU sounds much like the Latin root word for to SEE as in VEDERE in Italian, VIO in Spanish, French VU and originating from the much older language of SANSKRIT. THE POPOL VUH therefore is a DIARY OF THE THINGS THAT THE POPOL or POPL MAYA SAW AND WAS GIVEN BY DEITY.

The DEITY KUKUL-KI-ANNE takes abode in a CHRIST figure just as YESHUA and so THE PLUMED SERPENTINE becomes the EMBODIMENT AND INCARNATION OF DEITY ON EARTH. Another SON OF GOD or GREAT SPIRIT recurrent theme or MAYAN CHRIST teacher, prophet and redeemer. That is WHY KUKUL-QI-ANNE was considered or treated as an EMANATION OF GOD HIMSELF.

KUKUL-QI-ANNU …IS…BACK!

SINCERELY, "BIRDIE"

---

### 58. COP-ANNE: THE COPA AND THE PAN (P-ANNE) OR THE CUP AND THE BREAD OF LIFE AND Q QUETZAL-COATLICUE'S CHRIST CONSCIOUSNESS COVENANT

COPAN is the Mayan city in Honduras. Where the MONKEY god symbols or statues are found. COP-ANNE was a city of UR or lights in the Mayan world as in A CENTER OF CULTURE, ART and CIVILIZATION.

H-ONNE-D-URA-S stands for DEPTHS as in deep valleys or deep OCEANS. The UNION OF CENTRAL AMERICAN STATES as it was envisioned to be in the beginning after Independence from Spain IS DEPICTED IN THE UNION OF THE 5 STARS FLAG. The union of 5 which reminds us of "PENTA-GRAMMA-ATON."

THE MAYA PYRAMID is the main symbol of COP-ANNE and has the same connotation as in the EGYPTIAN pyramid and that of the SEAL OF THE USA. It is pointing to a STAIRWAY TO HEAVEN or to the STARS. For the MAYA astronomy was very important and just like the other indigenous tribes elsewhere, they knew that HUMANKIND HAD ORIGINS in the STARS or constellations above.

The pyramid points up to MAN'S DIVINE SELF and ability to OVERCOME the challenges of this REALM OF MATTER and rise above them.

THE MAYA also believed in a QUETZAL-COATL being or KU-KUL-KI-ANNU. Who was to come from the EAST eventually to complete the CYCLE that was about to end and HELP begin the NEW CYCLE. As it has been explained before, the ENERGY of THE WINGED SERPENT is also that of the SERPENTINE or HANGED MAN 2000 years ago. As they say, the BIRDIE keeps moving and popping up from place to place when and where there is the most need.

And just as in the past, the SERPENTINE shows up in the MAYAN ICONOGRAPHY and symbolism. THE MAYA knew that this type of ENERGY is a HEALING energy that intends to restore BALANCE and bring RENEWAL and REBIRTH. It's a CIRCLE OF LIFE cycle like the OUROBOR-US or OURO-V-"URI"-US. GOLDEN as "ORO" or GOLD and FIERY LIKE THE LIGHT.

And the name COP-ANNE alluded not only to a MAYAN WORD and name but as well to another STORY BEHIND THE "STORY." As in COPA which is CUP OR GRAIL in Castilian Spanish. And the P-ANNE as in THE BREAD OF LIFE AND LIGHT or PAN also in Castilian. Both COSMIC DIVINE PRINCIPLES manifesting through the person of the SERPENTINE.

THIS IS THE "LAST SUPPER" between QUETZAL-COATLICUE and the 12 DISCIPLES who represent the 12 STAR CONSTELLATIONS or HUMANITY AS A WHOLE AND COLLECTIVELY. The 12 + 1 CRYSTAL SKULLS OF THE MAYA.

SINCERELY, "THE WINGED SERPENT, KUKUL-KI-ANNE"

---

## 59. THEO-TI-WA-QI-ANNI: WHERE THE THEO-TI-WAKANOS MEET THE GREAT MYSTERY OR THE TAO

WAK-ANNE -TANKA is the LAKOTA name for the DIVINE... THEO-T-WAKAN is the Mexican Indigenous Center named after the GREAT SPIRIT. NAMED BY NORTH AMERICAN INDIGENOUS TRIBES AS ...... WAKAN - TANKA. GOD, YOU THE WAKAN!!!

In Lakota spirituality, **Wakan Tanka** (Standard Lakota Orthography: **Wakȟáŋ Tȟáŋka**) is the term for the sacred or the divine.[1][2] This is usually translated as the "Great Spirit" and occasionally as "Great Mystery".*Wakȟáŋ Tȟáŋka* can be interpreted as the power or the sacredness that resides in everything, resembling some animistic and pantheistic beliefs. This term describes every creature and object as *wakȟáŋ* ("holy") or having aspects that are *wakȟáŋ*.[3][4] The element *Tanka* or *Tȟáŋka* corresponds to "Great" or "large". (WIKIPEDIA)

The GREAT MYSTERY is also the TAO as in the Eastern Tradition. The name of the MESOAMERICAN CITY of THEO-TI-WAK-ANNI has the root word for the TITLE of DEITY or GOD or THE MYSTERY or THE TAO or the "THEO." THEO-T-WAKAN as in TAO-THE -WAKAN or THEO THE GREAT MYSTERY. THE GREAT SPIRIT!!! THE GREAT TAO!!!

WAK-ANNU T-ANNE-KI ...THEREFORE IS A TITLE SIMILAR TO THE EASTERN "TAO" OR GREAT MYSTERY. AFTER ALL, "THE TAO THAT CAN BE NAMED IS NOT THE TAO."

And so this CITY was the CITY OF THE WAKAN - THEO or GREAT SPIRIT!!! And it was an IMPORTANT RELIGIOUS AND SPIRITUAL CENTER. Its culture is linked to that of the NORTHERN TRIBES that worshiped WAKA-T-ANNE-KA. THE ONNE AND ONLY as in the Mesopotamian ANNU or the Judeo INNA or the UNNO or —ONE— in Castillian. THE ORIGINAL PANTHEON of the DEITIES. Although the NATIVE TRADITIONS are not considered MONOTHEISTIC, they are, in the sense that THEY BELIEVE IN "GREAT" SPIRIT. And every other SPIRIT form emanates from and is subservient to the "ONNE" AND ONLY THE GREAT TANKA who is ANNU or ONE.

Just like the EGYPTIANS and other world traditions, some of the NATIVE AMERICAN TRIBES worshiped THE SUN as a representation or manifestation of

THE WAKAN-TANKA. This is where the SUN DANCE comes from. So you can see that there is a LINK or Spiritual connection between EGYPT AND THE WESTERN INDIGENOUS CULTURES AND TRADITIONS.

THEO-T-WAK-ANNI is sometimes translated as THE PLACE WHERE THE GODS ARE BORN. And so here we have the reference to the ANNU or ELOHIM. The myths and stories might be different but the CONCEPTS are similar or the same and pointing to the SAME DIRECTION as the other traditions. As we can notice here, all peoples are drawing the same or similar information from the SAME COSMIC SOURCE and ARCHETYPES and OBSERVATIONS.

Like it states in the article, some believe that THEO-T-WAKAN actually means CITY OF THE SUN. BOTH meanings are correct since for the indigenous spiritual tradition THE SUN REPRESENTED THE SOURCE AND SUSTAINER OF LIFE OR THE TAO. The sun being a symbol of the THEO, TAO, GREAT SPIRIT. And so just like the ROMANS on the other side of the world, the THEO-TI-WAKANU must also have had an observance or special date in which the BIRTH OF THE SUN or just THE CONCEPT OF THE BIRTH OF THE LIGHT was celebrated or observed. In the winter.

THEO-T-WA-KI-ANNI… do you see its similarities to TAOISM? "KI-ANNI," as in EVERYTHING IS INFUSED WITH THE SACRED "QI or KI" Thus, they had knowledge about the SACRED "QI" in everything just as in YESHUA'S "LIFT THE ROCK AND THERE YOU WILL FIND ME, SPLIT THE WOOD AND THERE, I AM" in the GOSPEL OF THOMAS. The one speaking through the person of YESHUA was THE HOLY QI-KI-ANNI or QI-KI-INNA. .

THEO-TI-WAKAN had the TEMPLE TO THE "SUN" representing the FATHER PRINCIPLE, and the Temple to the MOON representing the DIVINE FEMININE or MOTHER PRINCIPLE or the DIVINE PARENT ENERGIES. QUETZAL-COATLICUE or the FEATHERED SERPENTINE is the DIVINE CHILD PRINCIPLE and THE HUMAN VESSEL OR TEMPLE FOR BOTH ENERGIES. There you have the DIVINE TRIAD in the TREE OF LIFE which in the MAYA TRADITIONS is represented by the MAYAN CEIBA TREE. The FEATHERED SERPENTINE is the one coiled in the TREE OF GOOD AND EVIL AND OF UNION AND LIFE. So here we see how the GENESIS metaphors on the TREE OF GOOD AND EVIL also complement the MAYAN SYMBOLISM.

SINCERELY, "THE EAGLE MESSENGER OF WAK-ANNE T-ANNE-KA"

## 60. THE RETURN OF THOTH: THE ENERGY OF THE HOLY SCRIBE "CALLING OCCUPANTS OF INTERPLANETARY CRAFT" FOR THE RESTORATION OF HUMAN CIVIL-IZATION AND WORLD PEACE!

The sound of the name THOTH is similar to that of the Scots names TOT or TOTUM that has the meaning of "SMALL CHILD or TOT."

We can infer from the definition above that THOTH is after those who Y-ESH-UA said would be like LITTLE CHILDREN. LITTLE CHILDREN in the sense that WE have already explained.

THE THOTH archetype represents in the EGYPTIAN TRADITION "THE SCRIBE." A scribe is a record keeper or a person who copies out documents. The word and term SCRI-BE is from the same root word as the SAN-"SCRI" -T or HOLY WRITING and Latin SCRI-VERE/ ESCRIBIR. In the case of THOTH, the meaning of SCRI-BE-RE goes further than just COPYING TEXTS. It refers also to:

RECEIVING DIVINE INFORMATION or CLARIFICATION or COMMUNICATION FROM THE "WORLDS" AND PUTTING THIS INFORMATION INTO WRITING. Creating as a result a SANCTA SCRIT-URA or a WRITING/ SCRI-PTURE FROM THE REALMS OF "LIGHT, WISDOM AND FIRE." In order to do this THOTH is CALLED ON BY THE POWERS OF THE UNIVERSE and goes through the DIVINE INITIATION that "OPENS THE GATES OF THE HEAVENS" by which THOTH receives DIVINE INSPIRATION for the WELL BEING OF THE PEOPLES.

THOTH is also ENOCH or the same ENERGY manifesting over and over again when the FATE OF HUMANITY is in danger and THE DIVINE POWERS have to INTERVENE.

TODAY, we are once again undergoing the ending of another CYCLE and the beginning of a new one. The reason this is happening is because RELIGION HAS BECOME WEAPONIZED and has lost its ORIGINAL PURPOSE which was supposedly to BRING THE VERY BEST IN PEOPLE. Instead, for thousands of years religion has deteriorated itself into a mere system of BELIEFS that channel the ENERGIES OF HATE which are from the WORLDS BELOW, rather than the ENERGIES OF LOVE which are from the WORLDS ABOVE. And so BOTH WORLDS are reaching out to PEOPLE today. But at the end of the day it's up to the PEOPLE whether they want to LISTEN or IGNORE this message.

Humanity is living in the TECHNOLOGICAL- INDUSTRIAL ERA and this is NOT NEW. It is NOT the first time this has happened. IT happened back in PREVIOUS AGES or WORLDS and reason why the BOOK OF ENOCH explains how HUMANITY BECAME ADVANCED IN THESE AREAS but unfortunately, as it gained greater TECHNICAL-INDUSTRIAL ADVANCEMENT s-he began to REGRESS AND to DEVOLVE in other areas of human life and development such as in the areas of BASIC HUMAN ETHICS, VALUES AND PRINCIPLES. Which means that regardless of the ADVANCEMENT in the world of matter and technology, HUMANITY was going downhill in collapse mode due to the EROSION OF ETHICS AND HIGHER VALUES AND PRINCIPLES or its SPIRITUAL SELF. THE CORE OF MAN'S SPIRITUAL NATURE.

ENOCH and ANNE-KI are related and it could be said that ANNE-KI-DU or ENNE-KI is a DESCENDANT OF "ENOCH" or a version of ENOCH. Meaning that when THESE ENERGIES come back or MAKE THEMSELVES MANIFEST ONCE AGAIN, we are as a humanity at the DAWN OF A "NEW DAY."

ENOCH or THOTH is IDRIS in ISLAM.

THEY ARE ALL THE SAME ENERGY and when THEY are back THEY are back because of the same reasons they have been here before—- RAMPANT VIOLENCE AND WARFARE AND TRAUMA THAT HAS TAKEN OVER THE EARTH!!!!

WARFARE AND VIOLENCE to "solve" DIFFERENCES is the OPPOSITE of "CIVILIZATION!" CIVIL-IZATION is about CIVILITY!!! VIOLENCE IS A "DISEASE!!!" And so when the EARTH is OVERWHELMED WITH WARFARE AND VIOLENCE, overtime mankind becomes so DESENSITIZED that he or she ends up becoming a "MONSTER." Eventually, spreading THIS EVIL like the plague. When this happens, we are about to cross to the POINT OF NO RETURN and it is at that time that THE SHINING ONES come back to ISSUE WARNING, ADMONISHMENT AND — A STOP — BEFORE IT'S TOO LATE.

ANCIENT EGYPT is the PINNACLE OF CIVIL-I-ZATION in ancient history. And so THOTH THE SCRIBE is one of its CENTER FIGURES AND ENERGIES that have made a COMEBACK as he is a representation of the ELOHIM.

THEREFORE, THOTH is a CHANNEL AND INSTRUMENT FOR "TRANSFORMATION" of ourselves and of OUR WORLD into one of LOVE AND PEACE AND HARMONY!!!

SINCERELY, THOTH

---

## 61. AKHEN-AT-ONNE and THE EGYPTO- M-ONNO-DEISTIC TRADITION of the S-UN

AKHEN-AT-ONNE did what all the others have done including ABRAHAM, YAKOV, YESHUA, MOHAMMAD and in the case of ancient EGYPT, AKHEN-AT-ONNE. AKHENAT-ONNE was the ONE who TOOK ALL THOSE GODS AND

GODDESSES that represented the FRAGMENTATION OF REALITY or MAYA and MULTIPLICITY and CONDENSED THEM ALL INTO ONE DIVINE PRINCIPLE. He was basically AFFIRMING THE "ONNE"-NESS OR "UNNI- TY" of THE CIRCLE OF LIFE.

He worshiped the "ONE" behind the VEIL OF MAYA and MULTIPLICITY. The UNIFIED REALITY BEHIND THIS VISUAL FRAGMENTED ONE.

He called that REALITY or THE ONE the ATEN or ATON or AT-ONNE. As in English to be "AT - ONE" or in a state of UNION WITHIN AND WITH THE UNNI-VERSE. And the SYMBOL for that AT-ONNE which is also L-OR-D of FIRE AND LIGHT or ORI-GENES was the S-UN!!! As in English "IS UN or IS ONE." Therefore the S-UN represents the UNITY or UNNI-TAS BEHIND EVERYTHING.

"AKEN-(IS) AT - ONE" WITH THE "ANNU" or DEITY.

AKHEN was his TITLE and THE PHARAOH called himself the ONE of the "HOLY UNION" or AKH-ENNE OF THE ONE or of GOD OR DEITY.

And so AKEN OF THE ONE DIVINE PRINCIPLE is another TEACHER-PRIEST In the line of the M-ONNO-DEISTIC TRADITIONS who affirm the UNITY OF ALL THE CREATIVE-

ENERGETIC POWERS depicted traditionally all over the world PAN-THEO-NS as MANY gods and goddesses or DIVINE ENERGIES OR ESSENCES BORN OF THE ONE AND ONLY.

AKEN in Egyptian means RAM-HEADED, THEREFORE ... AKEN -AT-ONE .... STANDS FOR "THE RAM OF THE ONE AND ONLY." And this tradition is linked to the HEBREW tradition of the archetype of the RAM as a representative of DEITY such as YESHUA is in CHRISTIANITY. THE "BIPOLAR" HORNED RAM OF MENDES who also stands for the UNION OF YIN AND YANG or of POLAR OPPOSITES and BI-POLAR ADAM KAD-M-ONE..

SINCERELY, "THE RAM OF THE ONE, THE HORNED ONE OF MENDES"

---

## 62. THE WINGED SERPENT: THE BI-POLAR SERPENTINE THAT DELIVERS DIVINE KNOWLEDGE AND WHOSE TOTEM IS THE "BIRD" — ENOC AT "LA ISLA BONITA" OF LAKE TEX-COCO

DO YOU RECALL THE OFFICIAL SYMBOL OF THE AZTECS IN T-ENOC-TI-TEL-ANNE IS AN EAGLE THAT EATS AND ABSORBS THE SERPENT ENERGY!!!

BOTH THE EAGLE AND THE SERPENT FORM AN UNDIVIDED UNION AND ARCHETYPE. THE EAGLE WHO REPRESENTS "AIR" OR DIVINE MIND IS ATTRIBUTED TO BINAH AND THE COSMIC BLUEPRINT WHICH IS THE BASIS

FOR "THOUGHT." MEANWHILE THE SERPENT IS ATTRIBUTED TO CHOKMAH WHO IS THE BASIS FOR THE DIVINE SERPENTINE ENERGY. BOTH AS A UNIT STAND FOR —- DIVINE ENERGY OR YIN AND YANG INTERTWINED TOGETHER. AND WORKING TOGETHER IN HARMONY IN ORDER TO MAKE LIFE A LIVING REALITY. ONE IS MIND AND IDEAS AND THE OTHER IS ENERGY WHICH FORMS THE IDEA INTO MANIFESTATION.

THE EAGLE IS THE TRADITIONAL BIRD FOR THE "ONES CONNECTED TO THE DIVINE SPHERES" AND CALLED SHAMAN OR SHAMANKA. IF YOU THINK ABOUT IT, BOTH THE "AIR AND THE FIRE" REMINDS US OF THE "CHERUBIM OR SERAPHIM" IN JUDEO AND CHRISTIAN AND ISLAMIC TRADITION. AND — TO THE "BAFO-OMET" AS IN —- BREATH OR AIR + MY LIGHT + OMET/ EMET, TRUTH. AS IN "THE SPEAKING SERPENT OF FIRE SPEAKS TRUTH!!!

THAT IS WHY ALL TRADITIONS VENERATE THE SERPENT!!! THE COBRA IN INDIA, THE DRAGON IN CHINA, AND OTHER TYPES OF SERPENTS IN OTHER TRADITIONS. BIRDS ARE ALSO VENERATED SUCH AS THE EAGLE AND THE QUETZAL AND THE PAHANA (WHICH IS RELATED ALSO TO THE CASTILIAN WORD FOR —BIRD—PAH-ARO!!!)" PAH-ANA THE ONE WITH THE FEATHERED HEADDRESS WHO IS LIKE A BIRD AND A SERPENT IN HOPI TRADITION.

THE ANCIENTS WERE NOT MAKING THINGS UP AND IMAGINING NONSENSE. EVEN CARL JUNG THROUGH THE STUDY OF THE MIND PROVED THAT THE ARCHETYPES ARE ALIVE AND THAT PSYCHOLOGY IS NOT DIVORCED FROM SPIRITUALITY.

I AM CONFIRMING WITH THIS DIARY THE NATIVE AMERICAN TRADITION WHICH ALSO SHARES THE SAME CONCEPTS WITH OTHER WORLD TRADITIONS AS THEY ARE ALL POINTING TO THE SAME UNIVERSAL TRUTHS AND SCIENCE THROUGH STORY AND ICONOGRAPHY.

T-ENOK-TI-TEL-ANNU STANDS FOR "YOU ENOCH AND YOUR MOUND OR ISLA BONITA IN THE MIDDLE OF LAKE TEXCOCO." ENOCH IS ALSO A SERPENTINE ASSOCIATED WITH ENKI IN THE MESOPOTAMIAN TRADITION AS WELL AS WITH HERMES IN THE GREEK TRADITION ALL BEING "ARCHETYPES!!!"

HERMES HAS THE WINGS AND THE STAFF SIMILAR TO MOSES AND HIS CADUCEUS AND THE HEALING SERPENT IS COILED AROUND IT. ALL THESE SYMBOLS POINTING TO THE HEALING POWER THAT IS INHERENT IN HUMANITY.

DO YOU SEE HOW ALL THESE SYMBOLS FIT INTO EACH OTHER TELLING A "STORY THAT ACTUALLY LOOKS SIMILAR FROM ALL ANGLES???"

AND SO THE GENOCIDE OF THE INDIGENOUS TRIBES WAS A GLOBAL TRAGEDY AND A GREAT LOSS BORN OF IGNORANCE, RELIGIOUS FANATICISM AND NONSENSE. THE BURNING OF THE INDIGENOUS SACRED TEXTS AND FORMULAS FOR HEALING INSCRIBED IN THOSE SACRED TEXTS AND CODEX WAS UNCALLED FOR. IRONICALLY, THE INDIGENOUS PEOPLES WERE TEACHING THE SAME OR SIMILAR CONCEPTS AND OBSERVATIONS AND TRUTHS AS THE OTHER TRADITIONS SEEN FROM THE NATIVE A-MARIE-KI-ANNE TRADITION AND POINT OF VIEW. THEY DESERVE AN APOLOGY AND RESTITUTION.

SINCERELY, "THE TRUTH SHALL SET YOU FREE aka PAH-ANNA"

---

## 63. THE "NATIVE AMERICAN" WERE WAITING FOR "US" AND INSTEAD "OUR RIGHTFUL PLACE" WAS STOLEN AND THE PERSON OF THE "HOLY SHE-KI-INNA" DESECRATED

AS THEY STATED BEFORE THINGS BEGAN TO GO SOUR BACK IN 1492. THE NATIVE AMERICANS WERE EXPECTING "US" TO COME BACK TO OUR PLACE OF REFUGE AND PARADISE. INSTEAD, THE CHURCH AND STATE ARRIVED, LOOKING AFTER GOLD AND THE MATERIAL THINGS OF THIS WORLD WHICH SET UP THE SYSTEM OF THINGS TODAY.

THE FRIENDLY AND WELCOMING "TREATMENT" THE EUROPEANS RECEIVED ON BEHALF OF MOST INDIGENOUS PEOPLES "WAS MEANT FOR THE HOLY SHE-KI-INNA"

AS THE INDIGENOUS PEOPLES BELIEVED ERRONEOUSLY THAT THE EUROPEAN WAS THE "ONE THEY WERE WAITING" FOR. INSTEAD, THE EUROPEAN TOOK ADVANTAGE OF THE "HOSPITALITY AND CARE" THAT WAS MEANT TO BE FOR THE "HOLY SHE-KI-INNA AND HER MESSENGER" SO THAT A "NEW WORLD" WOULD BE SET UP ACCORDING TO AND IN ALIGNMENT WITH THE "SPIRITUAL VALUES" THAT QUETZAL-COATL WAS SUPPOSED TO DELIVER.

INSTEAD...THE LAND BEGAN TO BE COMMODIFIED AND THE NATIVE PEOPLES MURDERED IN "OUR NAMES." HAVING BEEN TAKEN ADVANTAGE OF IN ORDER TO SET UP THE WORLD OF MATTER UPON THE LANDS THAT WERE "FOR THE HOLY SHE-KI-INNA AND HER NEW WORLD BASED ON HIGHER STANDARDS AND ETHICAL AND SPIRITUAL VALUES."

AND SO ... THE EUROPEAN GETS THE "GRAND RECEPTION." THE INDIGENOUS TAKING THE EUROPEAN TO BE "QUETZALCOATLICUE" or "KUKULKAN" etc. AND INSTEAD THE LAND IS FORCEFULLY TAKEN NOT FOR

THE "HOLY PRESENCE" BUT TO SERVE THE INTERESTS OF MATTER AND FOR PROFIT OF THE NEWCOMERS. IN OTHER WORDS, FOR THE SERVICE OF …GREED.

DO YOU SEE …THE BIG MISTAKE?

WE ARE TALKING HERE OF "THE DIVINE PRESENCE" AS IT MANIFESTS IN THE PERSON OF QUETZALCOATLICUE FOR WHICH THE CITY OF—--T-"ANNOKI"- TI-TEL-ANNU (T-ENOCH-TITLAN)—--HAD BEEN FOUNDED IN THE MIDST OF THAT BEAUTIFUL LAKE. 500 HUNDRED YEARS PASS BY "AND WE COME BACK AND SHOW UP AGAIN LIKE THIEF IN THE NIGHT" AND OUR ENTIRE LAND HAS BEEN "PRICE TAGGED" AND THE "HOLY SHE-KI-INNA AND HER DIVINE MESSENGER" HAVE NO PLACE TO REST AND WITH LITTLE OR NO HOSPITALITY EXTENDED TO THEM. INSTEAD— AS WE — MAKE OUR PRESENCE KNOWN — WE ARE IGNORED AND VILIFIED AND PERSECUTED TO THE POINT WHERE WE ARE CHASED EVERYWHERE WE GO — HAVING SPIES —SPYING ON US AND INTIMIDATING US THE "HOLY PRESENCE." ALL IN THE NAME OF "MATTER AND GREED, CORRUPT RELIGION AND TAINTED GOVERNMENTS.".

AND SO AS "THE PEOPLE" REFUSE TO LISTEN AND THE "DIVINE PRESENCE" BEGINS TO EXPERIENCE VEXATION AND "THE EVILS OF THIS WORLD, " A WORLD THAT HAS "LOST" ITS WAY, DIVINE "JUDGMENT IS PASSED!!!" AS IT HAS CROSSED THE LINE NOT KNOWING ANYMORE THE DIFFERENCE BETWEEN THE "DIVINE" AND THE "MUNDANE." KNOWING WELL THAT HAD "WE" ARRIVED 500 YEARS AGO TO "OUR" AMERICAN LANDS, THE "HOLY SHE-KI-INNA" WOULD NOT HAVE UNDERGONE ALL THIS TRIBULATION TO THE POINT OF "DESECRATION."HAVING HER PERSON "THREATENED WITH GUNS AND MACHETES AND INDUCING HER TO COMMIT SUICIDE BY MEANS OF STRESS AND PERSECUTION" BY THOSE POWERS OF THIS WORLD THAT HAVE BEEN MARKED TO SUFFER "KARMIC CONSEQUENCES" AS THE "HOLY SHE-KI-INNA IS THE APPLE OF GOD'S EYE."

THE DIVINE SENDING "US" ALL OVER THE LANDS TO LOOK AT THE PLIGHT OF THE PEOPLE EVERYWHERE … NOTICING THAT THE COMMON FACTOR ALL OVER IS — MONEY AND HOW TRAPPED THE PEOPLE HAVE BECOME BY IT OR CORRODED BY IT. AND SO … HERE WE ARE… DELIVERING "DIVINE ADMONISHMENT" LETTING PEOPLE KNOW THAT IT IS BETTER TO "BUILD TREASURE IN HEAVEN" THAN IN THIS TRANSIENT AND TEMPORARY WORLD.

THIS WORLD IS STILL STANDING—ONLY—BECAUSE OF THE INTERCESSION AND MERCY OF THE HOLY SHE-KI-INNA". BUT THAT STANDING WILL ONLY CONTINUE DEPENDING ON HOW PEOPLE "CHANGE THEIR HEARTS" TO …. LOVE AND COMPASSION…. FROM NOW ONWARDS.

SINCERELY, "THE ANNU"

## 64. Y-ESH-UA, THE TOMB AND A ROCK ROLLING: THE PHILOSOPHER'S STONE AND THE PROCESS OF SPIRITUAL DEVELOPMENT

It's a SHAME that because of RELIGIOUS EXTREMISTS the SPIRIT of the GOSPEL story is being DISTORTED and many are BUILDING HATRED TOWARDS IT. People need to SEPARATE the GOSPEL STORY from RELIGION as these are two VERY different things. And so thanks to THESE RELIGIOUS EXTREMISTS who are tainting the MESSAGE with their HATE, they are actually TURNING PEOPLE AWAY from it. Like WE stated before, these RELIGIOUS EXTREMISTS have the opposite effect they intend to make as in TURNING PEOPLE AWAY FROM ANYTHING RELIGIOUS AND EVEN —SPIRITUAL.

Like those claiming to BE CHRISTIAN and calling for the ANNIHILATION OF TRANS. Which is what was taking place back in ROMAN JUDEA PALESTINA 2000 years ago when RELIGIOUS EXTREMISTS would condemn people to DEATH BY STONING them because they were not KOSHER ENOUGH. It is a SHAME and a BLEMISH CAST UPON Y-ESH-UA BY THESE SO CALLED "RELIGIOUS PEOPLES" who bear the same attitudes and EVIL INCLINATION as those back 2000 years ago. Ironically, they claim to uphold and represent the Gospel spirit but rather are trashing it.

The EASTER STORY might be RIDICULOUS for some people but it is not all — STORY. Just like the GENESIS STORY, it is a METAPHOR AND ALLEGORY about COSMIC TRUTHS that later will be revealed. Like WE stated before, THE GOSPEL MESSAGE is to LOVE regardless of SHAPES, FORMS AND COLORS or what the Hindu refer to as MAYA OR ILLUSION. Where the TANAKH is EXCLUSIVE to some people, the GOSPEL is INCLUSIVE to all peoples. But the Gospel has been MISINTERPRETED unfortunately and so here WE are to fill in the blanks and gaps behind the story. And so the HATE OF THE RELIGIOUS EXTREMISTS TODAY IS BEING TRANSFERRED ONTO THE NON-RELIGIOUS PEOPLE who eventually end up causing a chain reaction of HATE AND RETRIBUTION against those religious fanatics causing the hate in the first place.

THEREFORE HERE WE HAVE THE "CONSTITUTION AND THE DECLARATION OF INDEPENDENCE" and THE SEPARATION OF CHURCH AND STATE to prevent EXTREMISMS FROM TAKING OVER IN THE FORM OF EITHER SECULAR OR RELIGIOUS ABUSE.

The EASTER STORY is to do with the DEATH AND TRANSFORMATION Card number 13!! Y-ESH-UA was KNOWN as the SERPENTINE for a —REASON. And that REASON "WE CANNOT REVEAL YET — but WE will at a later date. For now suffices to say that THE EASTER DEATH IS ABOUT –THE ALCHEMICAL PROCESS in humans or the PHILOSOPHER'S STONE!!! As you know SERPENTS

HIBERNATE in order to SHED THE OLD and BRING ABOUT THE NEW PERSON as in TRANSFORMATION from one state of being into a NEW ONE.

For instance the 3 DAYS IN THE TOMB is a SACRED NUMBER "3" which in CHINESE CULTURE represents:

The number 3 (三, pinyin: sān; Cantonese Yale: sāam) sounds like 生 (pinyin: shēng; Cantonese Yale: sāang), which means "to live" or "life" so it's considered a good number. It's significant since it is one of three important stages in a person's life (birth, marriage, and death). WIKIPEDIA

It stands for THE SACREDNESS of LIFE and  TO LIVE and to DIE TO THE OLD to be REBORN TO THE NEW!!

The reason that these RELIGIOUS EXTREMISTS throughout history have gone into GENOCIDAL MANIA is because they do not understand the REAL MESSAGE behind the STORY but take everything literally. THESE RELIGIOUS EXTREMISTS have not tasted of the PHILOSOPHER'S STONE as the Y-ESH-UA story points out and instead they end up becoming not agents of TRUE REBIRTH AND TRANSFORMATION but rather agents of  DESTRUCTION AND EVIL AND CORRUPTION which actually contradicts the spirit of EASTER.

Y-ESH-UA "DIES" IN THE FLESH TO BE REBORN "IN SPIRIT" which is basically telling us NOT TO BE FIXATED ON THE FLESH as in THE SUPERFICIAL WORLD OF SHAPES AND FORMS AND COLORS BUT TO LOOK WITHIN AT THE DIVINITY AND SPIRIT IN EACH PERSON. And so WE have these extremist peoples believing they are carrying THE DIVINE WILL when in reality they are STILL FIXATED TO MAYA AND TO THE WORLD OF SHAPES, FORMS AND COLORS although they are full of themselves in RELIGION.

Therefore, THOSE PROMOTERS OF DEATH ARE "FALSE FOLLOWERS OF CHRIST" BECAUSE rather than affirming the DIVINITY WITHIN EACH PERSON, they IGNORE IT AND RATHER THAN ASSIGNING SPIRITUAL VALUE TO EACH PERSON,  THEY PERSECUTE AND JUDGE PEOPLE ACCORDING TO " THE SHAPE, FORM AND COLOR" OF PEOPLE.  This DISCRIMINATION AND ABUSE is totally against the SPIRIT OF THE GOSPEL OF THE CHRIST which WE— HAVE COME TO "RECLAIM" FROM THE HANDS OF THOSE WHO ARE REALLY "STANDING IN THE SPIRIT OF LAWLESSNESS AND DEATH!!!"

ON BEHALF OF "THE SPIRIT OF THE CHRIST" WE APOLOGIZE FOR THE SUFFERING AND PAIN THAT "RELIGIOUS EXTREMISTS" HAVE BROUGHT UPON HUMANKIND AND STILL DO TO THIS DAY.

SINCERELY, "YESHUA"

**65. "YESHUA" - THE ARCHETYPE OF THE "SCAPEGOAT" OF HUMANKIND: CASTING ALL BLAME FOR THE DYSFUNCTIONS AND EVILS OF SOCIETY ON THE "DEVIL HIMSELF!"**

YESHUA IS AN "ARCHETYPE!!!"OR IS HE FOR REAL? OR BOTH?

THE "SCAPEGOAT" IS THE "OUTCAST" WHO HAS LIVED THROUGHOUT THE HISTORY OF MANKIND OSTRACIZED AND PERSECUTED FOR "POINTING OUT THE TRUTH" IN COMMUNITY, FAMILY, NATION, AND WORLD. USUALLY THE OUTCAST AND SCAPEGOAT HAS THE "VISION" OR "INNER SIGHT" WHICH IS REFERRED TO IN MANY TRADITIONS AS THE "SEER" WHO CAN SEE AND NOTICE THE DETAILS AND WHAT TRANSPIRES BEHIND THE MECHANISMS OF PEOPLE AND SOCIETY THAT MOST ARE UNABLE TO PERCEIVE.

HE OR SHE IS CONDEMNED TO THE "SHADOWS OF BRIMSTONE, CROSSES AND FIRE" BY THE MASSES WHO FOR THE MOST PART HAVE BEEN CONDITIONED AND BRAINWASHED BY THE "FORCES OF THIS WORLD" THAT THRIVE AND SUSTAIN THEMSELVES ON THE ACQUISITION OF EXTERNAL WORLDLY POWER AND BY MANIPULATING THE MASSES AT THEIR OWN CONVENIENCE AND TO THEIR OWN DETRIMENT AND THAT OF THE WORLD AS WELL.

AS WE CAN SEE TODAY, MANY ARE BEING SCAPEGOATED SUCH AS THE "WITCH" AND THE "LGBTQ" AND THE "TRANS" AND "ALL THOSE CONSIDERED '"OTHERS AND DIFFERENT" OUT OF "FEAR" BASED ON IGNORANCE. THESE RELIGIOUS EXTREMISTS ARE UNABLE TO REACH OUT TO THE OTHER BECAUSE IN THEIR INFANTILE MIND THE "OTHER" IS "THE DEVIL HIMSELF."

AND SO "YESHUA" IS THE ARCHETYPE OF THE "SCAPEGOAT" —THE "ONE" RENDERED MAD, ECCENTRIC, UNUSUAL, DIFFERENT, —OHHHH, THE DEVIL HIMSELF INCARNATE, THE BLACK SHEEP OF THE ENTIRE WORLD!!! THE ONE WHO POINTS OUT THE INCONSISTENCIES AND DYSFUNCTIONS OF THOSE WHO "ARE LIKE WOLVES IN SHEEP'S CLOTHING" AND WHO PERSECUTE "MARIA THE WISE" FOR FALLING IN LOVE WITH NATHANIEL, WHILE NATHANIEL THE PURITAN HEAD OF THE CHURCH HAS COMMITTED ADULTERY AND GOTTEN AWAY WITH IT JUST BECAUSE "HE IS IN A POSITION OF POWER AND PRIVILEGE AND IS A .... MAN CONCEALING HIS DYSFUNCTION BEHIND RELIGION!!!"

AND SO AS THE STORY GOES AND AS IT HAPPENS THROUGHOUT HISTORY, THE "DEVIL" IN THE PERSON OF "THE SCAPEGOAT" HAS TO SUFFER ALL

THE INJUSTICES OF THE MOB AND THE MASSES. SOCIETY EVENTUALLY CASTING ALL BLAME ON HIM/HER AND THAT WAY DEFLECTING FROM THEMSELVES FULL OWNERSHIP AND RESPONSIBILITY FOR THEIR INNATE DYSFUNCTION, EVIL INCLINATION, DYSFUNCTIONAL THOUGHTS AND EMOTIONS AND ACTIONS…!!! AND SO WHAT HAPPENS?

THAT THE "STATUS QUO" CONTINUES TO ROT TO THE POINT WHERE THE ENTIRE SYSTEM COLLAPSES DUE TO THE SILENCING OF THE "WISE SEER" WHILE GIVING POWER AND ATTENTION AND OBEDIENCE TO THE ARCHETYPE OF "IGNORANCE AND THE DYSFUNCTIONAL AGGRANDIZED EGO."

IT TAKES A "REAL GOAT" TO NOTICE "THE GOLEM" IDENTITY. MEANING THAT, THE "GOAT" IS THAT ONE WHO IS "WIDE AWAKE AND CAN NOTICE" WHAT THE "NICE OBEDIENT SHEEP CANNOT SEE FOR THEMSELVES" WHO ARE BEING DECEIVED AND MANIPULATED TOWARDS EVIL AND WHO ARE BEING LED BY THE BLIND TOWARDS THEIR OWN DESTRUCTION. THE BLIND …ARE THOSE LACKING THE "SIGHT."

HOW CONVENIENT TO BLAME THE — DEVIL AND THE DEMON AND THE — MARGINALIZED IN SOCIETY, PROJECTING ONTO THEM ALL THE "DYSFUNCTION" THAT HAS TAKEN POSSESSION OF THE MIND OF THE ACCUSER WHO IS POSSESSED" BY ALL THOSE "DARK ELEMENTS LURKING WITHIN THE SHADOW SELF" READY TO STRIKE AT "THE UNTOUCHABLES" OF THE WORLD. BLAMING THESE "UNTOUCHABLES" FOR "THEIR" OWN BAD DECISIONS, EVIL ACTIONS AND PREJUDICES. MANY A TIME, "DRESSING" ALL THESE "DARK SHADOW CONTENTS" AS RELIGION AND PIETY THAT IS READY TO SEND "THE SCAPEGOAT YESHUA BACK TO GOLGOTHA AT ANY TIME" BECAUSE THEY CANNOT BEAR TO LOOK IN THE MIRROR AND SEE THE TRUTH ABOUT THE QUALITY AND HEALTH OF THEIR OWN SOULS.

FROM THE "DIARIES OF …MARIA, CONSORT OF "YESHUA" THE SCAPEGOAT"

---

## 66. ISSA-BEL TRAS-TAMAR-A: THE HOUSE OF JUDAH and THE RETURN OF ISSA THE BEL

So as you can tell from what WE have revealed, NAMES have secret MEANINGS and represent SYMBOLS and ARCHETYPES. And so it is with QUEEN ISSA-BEL of CASTILLE and LEON in SPAIN. CASTILLE is THE TOWER and LEON is after the LION OF "JUDAH." Her card is THE STRENGTH CARD number 8 where EMPRESS energy tempers the MALE FIERY PRINCIPLE.

Isn't it interesting that 1492 has a numerical value of 16 or THE TOWER CARD in the SACRED TAROT which represents irreversible and unexpected changes, catastrophe and destruction in its negative interpretation? Isn't that what 1492 brought to the Americas and to the INNE-DIGENOUS PEOPLES? The weird thing about all this is that the AZTECS AND OTHERS were expecting T-ENNO-QI aka QUETZALCOATL, KUKULKAN and "YESHUA" to come from the East across the waters. The AZTEC knew by their astronomical predictions and calendar that the TIME FOR HIS APPEARANCE was near and about to happen around that time.

Sadly, it was not YESHUA who showed up but ISSA-BEL'S "LA NINA, LA PINTA Y LA SANTA MARIA" representing the SPANISH MONARCHY. Ironically, Queen ISSA-BEL of SPAIN name is after YESHUA WHO IN ARABIC IS CALLED "ISSA." In other words her name stands for ISSA OR YESHUA THE BEAUTIFUL or BEL.

As you might know, Spain was MUSLIM FOR 700 years. And the high nobility in the Jewish, Christian and Islamic Spanish societies of those days would intermarry for dynastic and strategic reasons amongst themselves. They would adopt each other's religions and or culture and customs. The CHRISTIANS did that a lot in order to advance in their aim of taking over AL-ANDALUS from the MUSLIMS. And so you get a nobility of the times mixing strategic bloodlines which would include WISIGOTHICA and JEWISH and CHRISTIAN and MUSLIM, etc. Therefore from ISSA-BEL'S name we can infer that she was a mixture of CHRISTIAN AND JEWISH AND MUSLIM regal bloodlines.

She must have been so fervent in her religion that she must have thought of herself as YESHUA'S BRIDE in the book of Revelation who would spread the GOSPEL throughout the world to bring about the NEW AGE OF AQUARIUS. Remember that not only were NATIVE AMERICANS astronomers but also the EUROPEAN who also saw change coming.

And so came 1492 and the end of an old ERA TO BEGIN A NEW ONE. The date has the number 14 in it which represents the Tarot card of TEMPERANCE which becomes 5 or the HIEROPHANT Tarot card (when you add 1 + 4). ISSA "THE HIEROPHANT archetype who is in a state of TEMPERANCE." 92 adds up to 11 or the JUSTICE CARD in the sacred Tarot which in turn adds up to 2 or the HIGH PRIESTESS CARD which represents in the case of YESHUA HIS HOLY SHE-QI-INNA. Both here to remind humanity about the FOUNDATIONS OF THIS REALITY WHICH SIT UPON "JUSTICE and MERCY."

Now, you might be asking yourself why do WE say that ISSA-BEL was not only CHRISTIAN and MUSLIM but also of "JEWISH" origins? Well, it's in her LAST NAME!!! TRAS-TAMAR-A which stands not only for BEYOND or after THE WATERS or THE OCEANS as in the icon of MOTHER MARY of whom she was a fervent devotee. The name MARIA is related to the word MAR or OCEAN. Do you see the NAME? Well, it's right there as in TRAS TAMAR or AFTER "TAMAR" who is THE WIFE OF JUDAH IN THE BIBLE. And as you will recall ISSA-BEL'S coat of arms is the TOWER and the LION OF JUDAH. TAMARA is also ARABIC after JUDAH'S TAMAR.

Although 1492 ended up being a disaster, the NAME "ISSA-THE-BEL" and the multicultural history behind that name stands for UNION AND COEXISTENCE as in AL ANDALUS GOLDEN AGE in which JEW, CHRISTIAN AND MUSLIM coexisted and lived together in a cultural GOLDEN AGE "together" in peace.

SINCERELY, "ISSA THE BEL"

---

## 67. ISSA-BELLA OF CASTILLE and 1492: THE TOWER and the WATER CHARIOTS OF "THE SHE-KI-INNA"

Well, 1492 is one of those dates where THE WORLD CHANGED IN UNAVOIDABLE WAYS just what TOWER CARD number 16 of the TAROT represents. (1492 ADDS UP TO 16) 16 THE TOWER CARD is also the 1 + 6 = 7 or THE CHARIOT CARD which stands for TRANSPORTATION AND MOVEMENT (JOURNEY) and MOVING FROM ONE PLACE TO ANOTHER. And is not a BOAT or SHIP a water vessel or WATER CHARIOT such as the NINA, PINTA AND SANTA MARIA?

And so as we have stated before, perhaps people today are not that religious like in the past or do not believe in religion anymore but the FACT does not change that THE ENTIRE CONQUEST WAS CARRIED OUT WITH THE CHRIST-Y-ANNE CROSS and BIBLE in hand. It was all done in the NAMES and SYMBOLS considered sacred and which are LINKED TO ARCHETYPAL FORCES that have a life of their own.

What then was the first thing done when ISSA-BELLA'S WATER CHARIOTS arrived on the shores of the AMERICAN CONTINENTS? They blessed and claimed THE LAND for the THRONE OF "ISSA" THE BEL "KINGDOM OF HEAVEN," as the name of the QUEEN OF SPAIN stands for ISSA or JESUS. And the CROWN + CHURCH also claimed THE WHOLE THING in the name of CHRIST and for the CROSS of YESHUA. The entire landmass is therefore dedicated to YESHUA THE CHRIST WHO IN TURN REPRESENTS ADAM KADM-ONE WHO IN TURN REPRESENTS THE DIVINE PRESENCE AND ULTIMATE REALITY OR PENTA-GRAMMA-"ATON."

Similarly, the NATIVE AMERICANS who also revered the same land had dedicated it to WAKAN TANKA or GREAT SPIRIT who is the same ULTIMATE REALITY and GREAT MYSTERY representing the UNITY BEHIND EVERYTHING AND EVERYONE. Therefore the entire AMERICAN CONTINENT has been blessed and dedicated to THE ULTIMATE REALITY by EAST AND WEST alike.

And so the name ISSA-BEL comes from the ARABIC language that SPAIN inherited from its 700 years of MOORISH presence in the Peninsula. ISSA is the name of YESHUA in Arabic who is "BEL" OR THE PRETTY OR HANDSOME ONE. And "CASTILLE" is Spanish for CASTLE and castles have "TOWERS" just as MARIA MAGDALENE OR THE "FEMALE TOWER OF THE GNOSTIC JESUS MOVEMENTS."

The ships or water chariots that landed here in the name of YESHUA THE BEL were 3 as in LA NINA, LA PINTA and LA SANTA MARIA. All 3 form a TRINITY that describes the HOLY PRESENCE or SHE-K-INNA and SOPHIA who is the original ROSE OF SHAR-ONNE. The ROSE OF THE ONE AND ONLY or THE ROSE OF UNION. This TRINITY of names becomes "QUE PINTA TIENE LA NINA SANTA MARIA." Translated roughly as "HOW FINE IS THE GIRL SAINT MARY." it can also mean … LA PINTA or THE COLORED ONE!!! And if you do not realize yet, the SANTA MARIA vessel's original name is the MARIA GAL-ANTE or the GALLANTE ONE and the GALLEGA. Therefore the name MARIA THE HOLY ONE and the entire SHIP UNIT collectively refer to the DIVINE PRESENCE or the HOLY SHE-K-INNA who is symbolized by MOTHER MARY, MAGDALENE and the other FEMALES IN THE ABRAHAMIC TRADITIONS. The SHE-KI-INNA therefore is A "PRINCESS" OF THE DIVINE and is A YOUNG MAIDEN dressed in RED AND YELLOW just as are the national colors of SPAIN and who was dressed in those colors when she appeared to me back in VALENCIA STREET in the 2010's. SHE'S THE GALLANT ONE.

And so WHAT do you expect is gonna HAPPEN? THE CHARIOT CARD indicates that THE WHEELS AND DIALS OF DESTINY HAVE BEEN SET INTO MOTION for this entire world.

THERE IS H-O-P-E for this world hopefully. AND ISSA and MARIA GAL-ANTE ARE BACK!!!

---

## 68. THE GENESIS ACCOUNT: "GNOSIS" VS. "ORTHODOXY AND TRADITION"---THE WAR BETWEEN OPPOSITES AND HOW THEY ALSO RECONCILE THEMSELVES (IT'S ALL SYMBOLIC OF HUMAN STATES OF CONSCIOUSNESS AND MIND)

WHAT DOES THE "SYMBOL" OF "GOD OR DEITY OR ELOHIM" REPRESENT IN GENESIS? HOW ABOUT THE SERPENT?

IF DEITY IS ALL KNOWING –WHY WOULD DEITY PLACE THE TREE OF GOOD AND EVIL IN THE MIDDLE OF THE GARDEN AND ON TOP OF THAT —POINT IT OUT OUT OF ALL THE TREES IN THE GARDEN TO INNOCENT ADAM AND EVE –WHO HAD NO IDEA WHAT GOOD AND EVIL WAS?

IT SEEMS THAT "SOMEONE" WANTED TO PIQUE THE INTEREST AND CURIOSITY OF BOTH ADAM AND EVE!

ON TOP OF THAT ....WHY WOULD DEITY ...CREATE THE "SERPENT" AND ALLOW THE SERPENT TO BE IN THE TREE? AND MOST OF ALL...TO "DECEIVE" ADAM AND EVE?

IF DEITY IS ALL KNOWING WHY WOULD DEITY NOT STOP THE SERPENT IN THE FIRST PLACE IN ORDER TO PROTECT HIS CHILDREN JUST AS A HUMAN PARENT WOULD?

... WE CAN NOTICE HERE THAT TAKING THIS STORY LITERALLY MAKES NO SENSE BUT INDEED SETS HUMANS EVIL INCLINATION ABLAZE WITH DESIRES TO KILL AND DESTROY REAL AND LITERAL SNAKES WHO ARE PART OF THE EARTH'S ECOSYSTEM AND PERSECUTE OTHERS AS BEING "SNAKES" AND ALL SORT OF NONSENSE.......! IRONICALLY, WE END UP BECOMING LIKE "CAIN" WHO WAS THE FIRST ONE TO MURDER IN GENESIS.

AND SO ...WHAT DOES "DEITY AND THE SERPENT" REPRESENT?

WE HAVE ON ONE SIDE OF THE RING —DEITY — AND ON THE OTHER SIDE OF THE RING "THE SERPENTINE." OR ARE BOTH ACTUALLY WORKING TOGETHER TO REACH A COMMON AIM OR DO BOTH REPRESENT TWO FACES OF THE SAME COIN?

AND SO ANOTHER WAY OF INTERPRETING THE STORY OF GENESIS IS ONE IN WHICH DEITY STANDS FOR "TRADITION AND ORTHODOXY" AS IN — NOT THINKING FOR ONESELF BUT JUST BEING TOLD WHAT TO DO, WHAT TO THINK, WHAT TO BELIEVE IN, WHAT TO WHAT TO WHAT TO. IT REPRESENTS "ORTHODOXIA AND PATRIARCHY" AT ITS BEST. THE OVERPROTECTION OF CHILDREN IN WHICH WE ARE NOT ALLOWED TO THINK AND DECIDE FOR OURSELVES BUT RATHER OBEY WITHOUT THOUGHT OR INQUIRY. THIS IS A VERY SUPERFICIAL WAY TO EXPERIENCE THIS REALITY. AT THE CENTER OF THIS IDEOLOGY IS ""FEAR""" OF DISOBEYING THE AUTHORITARIAN KING, THE INSTITUTION, THE IDEOLOGY, THE GROUP MENTALITY, ETC. ETC. ETC. IT'S A STATE IN WHICH OTHERS DO THE THINKING FOR OURSELVES. AND IT'S ALL BASED ON...FEAR! ALWAYS TRYING TO KEEP OURSELVES SAFE BUT IN EXTREMIS AND TO OUR OWN DETRIMENT.

ON THE OTHER HAND, THE "SERPENTINE ENERGY" IS "FEMALE!!!" IT REPRESENTS "GNOSIS" AND THE OPPOSITE OF "BLIND OBEDIENCE". IT REPRESENTS THE PROCESS OF KNOWING FOR OURSELVES BY REACHING OUR OWN UNDERSTANDING AND BY MAKING OUR OWN CHOICES AND DECISIONS AND "MISTAKES" OR "GETTING IT RIGHT." THE SERPENT REPRESENTS "THINKING FOR OURSELVES" IN ORDER TO LEARN

BY EXPERIENCE THROUGHOUT THIS LIFE JOURNEY. LIKE THE BUDDHIST STATE — THE SPIRITUAL PATH IS THE PATH OF LIFE ITSELF WITH THE ROCKS AND THE MUD AND THE PISS AND THE CRAP AND EVERYTHING ALONG THE WAY. HOW DO WE ACQUIRE WISDOM AND EMPATHY FOR THE HUMAN CONDITION? BY GOING THRU THE UPS AND DOWNS OF LIFE ITSELF IN OUR OWN. THIS IS MORE OF AN OPEN WAY OF VIEWING LIFE AND OF APPROACHING LIFE WHICH INVOLVES —COURAGE –AS IN COURAGE TO MAKE MISTAKES BECAUSE WE LEARN FROM THESE AND BECOME BETTER AT KNOWING OURSELVES AND UNDERSTANDING BETTER HOW THE REAL WORLD AROUND US WORKS.

AND SO … WHO DO WE HAVE IN BETWEEN THE OPPOSITES OF "TRADITION/ ORTHODOXY/BLIND OBEDIENCE VS. GNOSIS/FREEDOM/THINKING FOR OURSELVES AND MAKING MISTAKES THRU PERSONAL CHOICES ????

WE END UP WITH "THE COMBINATION OF BOTH" CONCEPTS AS IN —TAKING THE BEST OF BOTH. IN OTHER WORDS, I WILL OBEY THE LAW BUT I WILL ALSO FOLLOW MY INTUITION WHEN THINGS DON'T SEEM RIGHT. DON'T SEEM RIGHT AS IN —WHEN SOMEONE IS TELLING ME IN "THE NAME OF DEITY' TO HATE AND BE VIOLENT AND EMBRACE EVIL DOING. THE PRIME EXAMPLE OF THE PATRIARCHY "OBEY" WITHOUT QUESTIONING IS "HITLER AND OTHER FASCIST AUTHORITARIAN TYPES !!!" THOSE WHO HAD THE VALOR AND COURAGE TO QUESTION "HITLER, STALIN, FRANCO, ETC." KNEW THE DIFFERENCE BETWEEN GOOD AND EVIL AND FOLLOWED THEIR OWN INTUITION. THEREFORE, EMBRACING THE EXTREME POSITIONS LEADS TO CHAOS BOTH WAYS— THE ONE KILLS THE SPIRIT OF GROWTH AND THE OTHER ONE LEADS TO CHAOS.

THE KEY IS FOUND IN THE —MIDDLE GROUND—BETWEEN BOTH TRADITION AND PROGRESS. IN WHICH I HAVE THE FREEDOM TO CHOOSE FROM BOTH ACCORDING TO THE CIRCUMSTANCES OF A PARTICULAR SITUATION AND THE CONSEQUENCES TO BE FACED BY THE CHOICES I MAKE.

SINCERELY, YESHUA THE SERPENTINE

---

## 69. THE "CLAIM" THAT JESUS' REAL FATHER WAS A ROMAN SOLDIER AND THE "MULTI-RACIAL" ETHNIC ORIGINS OF THE JEWISH PEOPLE TODAY

"HANNA REINA DIAS" SECOND DAUGHTER OF "MARIA" WITH SAMUEL THE SEPHARDIC JEW IN THE "PRACTICAL MAGIC SERIES" IS A PERFECT EXAMPLE OF THE PROCESS OF ETHNIC AND CULTURAL EXCHANGE AND

INTEGRATION THAT HAS HAPPENED THROUGHOUT THE CENTURIES BETWEEN JEWS AND NON-JEWS. THE "HANNA" NAME REMINDS ME OF THE "HOUSE OF ANNA" AND THE "SERPENTINE BLOODLINE" AND JESUS WHO JUST LIKE "MARIA OWENS" AND HER "BLOODLINE" WAS ACCUSED BY THE RELIGIOUS AUTHORITIES OF THE PERIOD OF BEING A "WITCH, WIZARD OR MAGICIAN." JUST LIKE MARIA WHO WAS BORN WITH THE "GIFT OF HEALING AND ENERGY" SO WAS JESUS WHO ENDED UP BEING ACCUSED BY THE RELIGIOUS AUTHORITY OF BEING WICCE IN ORDER TO VILIFY AND PERSECUTE HIM. MAGIC WHICH WAS PROHIBITED BY THE "MOSAIC LAW" BUT WAS PERFECTLY FINE "WHEN MOSES USED IT AGAINST PHARAOH" IN EXODUS AND WHEN PRACTICED BY JEWISH QABALISTS.

AND SO, ALONG WITH THE CLAIM SOME "BOOKS" MAKE THAT MARY WAS A HARLOT AND JESUS A BASTARD AND A MAGICIAN, ONE CAN ALSO FIND THE CLAIM THAT HIS FATHER WAS A ROMAN SOLDIER. WHETHER THAT WAS TRUE OR SIMPLY A WAY FOR THE AUTHORITIES OF THE TIME TO SLANDER AND DISCREDIT JESUS, WHO KNOWS. HOWEVER, IF THE ROMAN SOLDIER STORY WAS EVEN TRUE THAT WOULD HAVE MADE JESUS "BI-RACIAL" AND STILL A "JEW BORN OF A JEWISH MOTHER SINCE JEWISHNESS WAS PASSED FROM THE MATRILINEAL LINE ANYWAYS.

AND SO, THIS IS THE TREND IN ALL THREE MONOTHEISTIC TRADITIONS TODAY IN WHICH ALL THREE ARE IN A COMPETITION TO DISCREDIT ONE ANOTHER DUE TO THE HISTORICAL ENMITY THAT HAS BEEN EXACERBATING IN RECENT YEARS AMONG THEM. AND SO "IF JESUS WAS OF A ROMAN FATHER WHAT IS THE BIG DEAL?" HE WAS STILL A "HEBREW" AND ON TOP OF THAT OF THE LINE OF "HANNA."

AND SO, TODAY THE CONTROVERSIAL STORY IS COMING OUT AND USED TO CAUSE A STIR AND TO QUESTION THE VALIDITY OF THE GOSPEL MESSAGE THROUGH JESUS QUESTIONNABLE ORIGINS. HOWEVER, HAVING A JEWISH AND A NON JEWISH PARENT IS NOT UNIQUE TO YESHUA AND IS SOMETHING THAT HAS BEEN HAPPENING WITH ALL THE JEWISH COMMUNITIES SINCE THE BEGINNING OF THE EXISTENCE OF A "JEWISH OR HEBREW PEOPLE." AND THIS CULTURAL AND RACIAL MELANGE MANIFESTS CLEARLY IN THE PRESENT TIME IN THE DIVERSITY OF THE JEWISH PEOPLE THEMSELVES.

"JEWISHNESS" IS UNLIKE "NAZI GERMANY'S ARYAN PURE RACE IDEOLOGY" IN WHICH EVERYONE WAS SUPPOSED TO BE WHITE AND TO LOOK THE SAME. THE JEWISH PEOPLE JUST LIKE CHRISTIANS AND MUSLIMS ARE NOT A "PURE RACE" BUT A MELANGE OF DIVERSE PEOPLES AND ETHNIC ORIGINS. IN THE CASE OF THE JEWISH PEOPLE, YOU HAVE THE HEBRAIC SIDE AND THE NON-HEBRAIC ORIGINS. AND THIS CAN BE

PROVEN THROUGH DIRECT OBSERVATION OF THE "JEWISH PEOPLE" THEMSELVES IN THAT THEY ALL COME IN DIFFERENT COLORS AND PHYSICAL CHARACTERISTICS. IF THAT WAS NOT THE CASE AND IT WAS A "PURE RACE" THEN ALL THE JEWISH PEOPLE WOULD LOOK THE SAME OR SIMILAR. INSTEAD, YOU HAVE "SEPHARDIC JEWS WHO LOOK SPANISH, ASIAN JEWS WHO LOOK ASIAN, MIDDLE EASTERN JEWS WHO LOOK MIDDLE EASTERN, AFRICAN JEWS WHO LOOK AFRICAN,

EUROPEAN JEWS WHO LOOK…EUROPEAN. AND SO IT GOES. THE REASON WHY JEWS COME IN DIVERSE COLORS AND PHYSICAL CHARACTERISTICS THAT RESEMBLE THE INHABITANTS OF THEIR PLACES OF ORIGIN, IS BECAUSE THE "HEBREW" SIDE MIXED WITH THE "PARTICULAR PEOPLE OR ETHNICITY" OF THE PARTICULAR COUNTRY OF ORIGIN OR THE ANCESTORS CONVERTED TO JUDAISM.

THEREFORE, BY THE ART OF SIMPLE OBSERVATION WE CAN INFER THAT "JEWISHNESS" IS NOT A "PURE RACIAL COMPOSITION" AS SOME EXTREMIST IDEOLOGIES AND OTHERS WANT TO CLAIM.

SEPHARDIC JEWS FOR INSTANCE ARE BOTH "HEBREW AND IBERIAN" IN ORIGIN AND THEIR LADINO LANGUAGE AND CULTURE IS A COMBINATION OF HEBREW AND SPANISH AND ANDALUSIAN CUSTOMS AND TRADITIONS WHICH THEY HAVE INHERITED FROM THEIR MIXED ANCESTRY.

THE SAME HAPPENS WITH THE MUSLIM PEOPLE IN WHICH AS ISLAM EXPANDED AND CONQUERED LANDS, IT BEGAN TO ABSORB THE DIVERSE ETHNICITIES AND PEOPLE OF THOSE LANDS WHO WOULD BECOME MUSLIM AND ADOPT THE MUSLIM OFFICIAL TRADITION WHILE AT THE SAME TIME INTEGRATING THEIR PARTICULAR CULTURAL AND LINGUISTIC PATTERNS INTO THAT MUSLIM CULTURE AND ARABIC LANGUAGE. REASON WHY THE MUSLIM PEOPLE ALSO SHOW UP IN DIVERSE COLORS AND PHYSICAL CHARACTERISTICS INCLUDING BLONDE BLUE EYED PEOPLE AND DARKER ONES. LIKEWISE, THEIR MUSLIM CULTURES AND ARABIC DIALECTS HAVE ABSORBED ELEMENTS AND WORDS FROM THE "ORIGINAL CULTURES AND LANGUAGES" OF PRE-ISLAMIC MIDDLE EAST AND ASIA.

AND SO IT GOES WITH THE "CHRISTIAN" AND SO AND SO AND SO. THEREFORE, WE CAN CONCLUDE BY SAYING THAT THERE IS NO "PURE CHRISTIAN OR JEWISH OR MUSLIM RACE" AS MANY PEOPLE LIKE TO ERRONEOUSLY CLAIM.

AND THAT YESHUA WAS INDEED HEBREW AND SO MUCH MORE EVEN IF HIS REAL FATHER WAS NOT.

SINCERELY, YESHUA REINCARNATED

## 70. IKS-SVA-KU IN THE LAND OF KALA-APA: UPPER KALI-FORNIA "THE GARDEN OF EDEN" OF KALA-FIA WHERE THE GIANT BIRDS NEST

IKS=To see, behold, view, perceive, observe, look or gaze at

SVA = own, one's own, self, the human soul".

KU= represents the number 1 (one) in the "word-numeral system

So here we go again to the story of IKSVAKU who lives in the LAND OF KALA-APA and who is of the LINE OF THE SUN KING or M-ANNU and receives DIVINE MESSAGE to deliver to the world before the return of KALKI. According to the VEDIC TRADITION.

And so this LINE OF THE VEDIC SCRIPTURE is similar to the one in the ZOHAR that the ELOHIM pointed to me back in 2012 when THEY began to MANIFEST through IKS-SVA-KU IN THE LAND OF KALA-APA or APAR (UPPER) KALI-FORNIA. That line in the ZOHAR is:

*At that time, the Messiah King will awaken to come out of the Garden of Eden, from the place called "the bird's nest," and will appear in the land of the Galilee. And on the day when the Messiah goes out there, the whole world will be angered and all the people in the world will hide in caves and in crevices in stones and they will not know how to be saved. It is written about that time, "And men shall go into the caves of the rocks, and into the holes of the earth, from before the terror of the Lord, and from the glory of His majesty, when He arises to shake mightily the earth."(KABALAHINFO.COM)*

Do you remember it was at the time WHEN WE sent you a message NOT TO MAKE WAR with "IRAN" and which you answered by sending "SOMEONE" to check US out? And so WE will clarify WHAT the message refers to again in regards to IKS-SVA-KU OF KALA-PA. You can reach YOUR OWN CONCLUSIONS.

TO "AWAKEN" is to wake up from the long sleep and dream states or REINCARNATION and become conscious of who YOU ARE and YOUR MISSION ON EARTH according to DIVINE WILL. MASHIACH will come out of THE GARDEN OF EDEN which is called KALI-FORNIA, the GARDEN PARADISE where according to the MYTH of KALIFORNIA the amazon women fly on GIANT BIRDS!!! IKS-VA-KU who appeared in the LAND OF GALILEE in 2000 by DIVINE WILL to start the process of AWAKENING AND OF REVELATION and link with the ancient PAST.

And his name is IKS-SVA-KU "SON OF E-"MANNU" -EL" from the LINE OF ARI-EL of JUDAH AND THE HOUSE OF ANNA. IKS as in the French letter —X— as in SON OF THE X-IST —-THE ONE WHO VALUES THE HUMAN SPIRIT AND THE DIVINE UNITY BEHIND THE MANIFESTATION OF THINGS. THE "FIRST SOUL" OR THE DIVINE EMANATION MANIFESTING AS IKS-SVA-KI PREPARING "THE WAY" FOR —FATHER KALKI IN SPIRIT.

IKS-SVA-KI lives in the land of KALA-APA or of KALA-FIA OR APAR (UPPER) KALA-FORNIA BY THE WATERS OF THE PACIFIC OCEAN who is said to be KALKI AND KUKULK-ANNE.

SANSKRIT "APA" also means to "remove from" or "to move" as in LATIN - SPANISH — "APA"-RTAR. As in ELOHIM APA-RTA (SEPARATES) THE WATERS ABOVE FROM THOSE BELOW.

KALA-APA as in THE SIGN OF THE PASSING AWAY OF THE OLD ERA, SEPARATING THE OLD ERA of KALA YUG FROM THE NEW ERA OF SAT YUG. AS IN TRAVERSING THE WATERS OF THE SEA OF REEDS TO THE OTHER SIDE ONTO THE NOV-US "OR" DO SECLORUM. KALA- IS SEPARATING OR "APA"RTANDO THE "FALSE FROM ... THE REAL."

GIANT BIRDS represent AIRPLANES!!! And IK-SHVA-KU or the ONE WHO CARRIES THE DIVINE QI and who CRIES (KU IN CHINESE) before THE ELOHIM on behalf of humanity and all living beings, has arrived.

SINCERELY, X-SHVA- KU in APA-R KALA-FORNIA

---

## 71.  QUETZAL-COATLICUE TONANTZIN

So in and around 1492 the Native Americans were expecting YESHUA a.k.a. QUETZALCOATL, THE SERPENT-INNE. There is a symbol in Mexican culture that links the Native American story with the story at the other side of the world. Basically what the church FAILED to realize and recognize back in 1492 and onwards was that the Indigenous peoples and the Europeans were referring to the same ARCHETYPE and PERSONS but with different names, dress and religion. Both were observing the same PROPHET!!!

The name QUETZALCOATL and COATLICUE form an archetype composed of two concepts related to each other. At least that is what "the tongues of fire" told me. If you join both names they make one name that fits perfectly well. It would be "QUETZALCOATLICUE." What does that name sound like to you with what you have been told already about QUETZALCOATL?

QUETZAL-COATL is a BIRD!!! And COATLICUE IS FEMALE, THE MOTHER ARCHETYPE!!!

WHO is the BIRDIE THAT IS FEMALE in Judeo -Christian - Islamic tradition??? Yep, you got it!!!! Bravo! ----------- THE HOLY SHE-KI-INNA or HOLY SPIRIT or THE SOPHIA OF THE NATIONS!!! COATLICUE is in Native American culture the MOTHER GODDESS and WHO is the SPIRITUAL MOTHER of JESUS who showers YESHUA with knowledge and wisdom? THE HOLY SUKINA or BINAH IN THE TREE OF LIFE THROUGH HER SOPHIA! .

And so the Aztecs were expecting QUETZALCOATL AND THE RETURN OF THE HOLY MOTHER THROUGH HER SHE-KI-INNA!!! BOTH YESHUA AND THE SOPHIA OF THE NATIONS whose name is also COATLICUE in the NATIVE AMERICAN TRADITION. Making YESHUA the SON OF THE HOLY MOTHER SHE-KI-INNA!!! THE SHEKINAH IS THE MOUTHPIECE OR REPRESENTATIVE OF THE "DARK MOTHER" UNIVERSAL PRINCIPLE OR BINAH IN THE "TREE OF LIFE."

And the symbol regardless of whether it happened by miracle or not is the painting in the Basilica of Mexico City who is MOTHER MARY representing the Spiritual mother of YESHUA or the HOLY SHE-KI-INNA whose name is also COATLICUE in the Indigenous tradition of Mexico.

SHE IS THE DIV-INNE PRESENCE of the DIVINE COSMIC PRINCIPLES in her NATIVE AMERICAN ASPECT.

SINCERELY, WADA-LUPE

---

## 72. Y-ORU-BA: THE OMMO AND CHILDREN OF "I, THE LIGHT, FIRE AND GOLD OF THE FATHER AND L-OR-D "UBA."

The Y-ORU-BA people are:

The **Yoruba people** (Yoruba: *Ìran Yorùbá, Ọmọ Odùduwà, Ọmọ Káàárọ̀-oòjíire*[21]) are a West African ethnic group that mainly inhabit parts of Nigeria, Benin, and Togo. The areas of these countries primarily inhabited by the Yoruba are often collectively referred to as Yorubaland. The Yoruba constitute more than 50 million people in Africa, are over a million outside the continent, and bear further representation among members of the African diaspora. (WIKIPEDIA)

The Y-ORU-BA also go by the name of the IR-ANNE Y-ORU-BA, and the OMO ODUDUWA and OMO KAA"ARO"- OOJ"IRE." The Y-ORU-BA are the "OMO" as in OMMO (sapiens) or MEN OF ODUDUWA or OMO or MEN OF KA"ARO" - OJ "IRE" —AS IN THE ANCIENT TERM FOR LIGHT AND FIRE —-URI—-or the MEN or OMO OF THE LIGHT, F- "IRE" AND GOLD in AFRICA.

The "IR-ANNE" refers to the UR/ IR of KAL-DEES and the ANNU tradition that the Y-ORU-BA tribe took with them after the MESOPOTAMIAN dispersion. Similar to the dispersion of the AR-I-ANNE peoples. They all carried with their languages the concept of the LIGHT OF UR and BAB-EL even though the term or word lost its original meaning over time but remained as part of their respective languages.

In SANS-KRIT-URA the term "IO" refers to "I" as in NA HA IO which roughly stands for DO NOT BECOME or NA as in —NO— BECOME — "I." And so you have a similar meaning in the term for YO-ORU-UBA as in IO - ARU-UBA as in — I - LIGHT, FIRE, GOLD - UBA. Therefore the YO-ORU-UBA stands for I, THE LIGHT AND FIRE AND GOLD OF "UBA."

UBA is an AFRICAN NAME meaning:

The name Uba is primarily a male name of African origin that means *Father, Lord*. (BABYNAMES .COM)

Therefore, the YO-ORU-UBA are the CHILDREN OF THE FATHER OR L-OR-D OF LIGHT,

FIRE AND GOLD whom refers not only to the name of a PATRIARCH but also to the name of FATHER HEAVEN who is L-OR-D OF LIGHT, FIRE AND GOLD. and HIS name is UBA which is a form of the term ABBA or FATHER in the SEMITIC LANGUAGES.

The Y-ORU-UBA religion or the religion of UBA is based on the ORI-SHA IFA deities. The name of these deities tells clearly the NATURE of these energies which are BASED ON FIRE. ORI-ISHA is referring to THE SOULS or ISH of FIRE. Central to the ORI-ISHA tradition is the concept of the SHE-QI-INNA as in THE HOLY "QI" which in YO-ORU-BA tradition is known by the name of —ASE. ASE is the encompassing energy or LIFE FORCE that permeates ALL OF CREATION just as it is found in the NATIVE AMERICAN TRADITION and in THE "QI" of ASI-ANNE TRADITION and in YESHUA's "Lift a rock and you will find me, split a piece of wood and I AM there" in the Gnostic Tradition. ORI is URI and ISHA is SOUL! SOULS OF FIRE!

The YORUBA religious tradition is POLY-THEISTIC just as the other PANTHEONS elsewhere which describe THE FRAGMENTATION OF THE UNITY INTO THE MANY WHO ARE AS ONE. Y-ORU-UBA believe in a distant SUPREME CREATOR FORCE THAT ENCOMPASSES THE WHOLE UNIVERSE whom in ALL TRADITIONS IS "THE FATHER or L-OR-D" of THE LIGHT, FIRE AND GOLD or — ABBA aka UBA. WE CAN OBSERVE HERE THE MONOTHEISM WITHIN THE POLYTHEISM.

SINCERELY, "UBA, THE L-OR-D THRU THE BIPOLAR GATES OF COMMUNICATION"

---

### 73. "THE BRIGHT ONE AND THE TOWER:" JUDGMENT BY AWA-TER ELEMENT AND THE ON-D-"INNA" YEM-AYA

Berta CACERES stands for BERTA "THE ONE WHO GOES AFTER THE LIGHT." However, the name can also be translated as in BERTA WHO IS "HUNTED DOWN FOR HER LIGHT AND HER GOLD!" And so it was back in MARCH 2, 2016, in the year of JUDGMENT and THE TOWER. 3 + 2 + 20 + 7 === 3 + 2 +2 +7 = 14 TEMPERANCE CARD — when the world began to be JUDGED for a LACK OF "TEMPERANCE and MODERATION and "RESTRAINT" in terms of HUNTING DOWN AND TAKING OUT "THE LIGHT" or ERE(URI) of BERTHA and LIFE ON EARTH IN GENERAL. The date has the numerical value of — 18 or THE MOON CARD, which stands for ACTING UNCONSCIOUSLY or DRIVEN BY THE DARK FORCES WITHIN THE MIND that lead to the hunting down of THE LIGHT or ERE and to the IRE (FIRE and ANGER) OF HEAVEN TOWARDS A WORLD that no longer fears PERPETRATING EVIL. 5 is the HIEROPHANT archetype which stands for SPIRITUAL WISDOM, RELIGIOUS BELIEFS, INSTITUTIONS. In the case of BERTHA THE BRIGHT ONE, "INSTITUTIONS: failed her as she should have BEEN PROTECTED just as those swimming in POWER AND LUXURY ARE PROTECTED AT ALL COSTS BY THIS WORLD. She deserved protection since SHE REPRESENTED THE VOICE OF THE ANNU OF THE WATERS.

BERTA communicated and protected MOTHER EARTH and her RIVERS. RIVERS which are alive with the SPIRITS OF THE UN-D-INNES and other SPIRITUAL BEINGS born of QI that are the SAFEKEEPERS AND GUARDIANS of the element of WATER. UNDI-INNES are also linked to the Latin root word for ONDO or DEPTHS. THE ANNU DEITIES OF THE WATERS OR DEPTHS OF THE RIVERS AND OCEANS, the H-ONNE-DURAS!!!

March has the numerical value of 3 which is THE EMPRESS CARD or the MOTHER EARTH archetype. And the day of her death is THE HIGH PRIESTESS or HOLY SHE- –QI—-INNA number 2 card and archetype. In addition to the JUDGMENT 20 card and the THE TOWER 16 card — which are mainly FEMALE ARCHETYPES both in their MATERIAL AND SPIRITUAL sense. Therefore 20-16 is JUDGMENT BY THE TOWER.

The GODDESS OF THE WATERS or ON-D-INNA is depicted in the STARBUCKS (the symbol which is an UNDINE) coffee shop at 700 CANAL STREET. THE L-OR-D took me there years ago TO SEE HER and explained to me about the SHIPS painted on the wall and THE LADY OF THE WATERS. L-OR-D or ELOHIM explained to me that she was ANNU OF THE WATERS named by the Africans YEM-AYA. And that she is BOTH "BLACK AND WHITE or MULATTO." BUSINESS AND ENTERPRISE created a crisscrossing throughout the oceans and the world like a SPIDER'S WEB in which MONEY AND SLAVES AND GOLD were transacted IN THE NAME OF YESHUA and by which the MODERN FOUNDATIONS OF THIS WORLD WERE SET UP and DEMOCRATIC SYSTEMS OF GOVERNMENT as well. Including the entire WESTERN HEMISPHERE BANKING SYSTEMS. There was supposed to be an actual CANAL OF WATER built where Canal Street is but at the end it was not built.

700 is equivalent to the 7 and the 00 = 8 (4+4). The CHARIOT CARD which can be a SHIP or VESSEL and the 8 STRENGTH CARD in which the FEMALE ENERGY tames the LION and MASCULINE ENERGY. The BLACK AND WHITE become ONE as in YEMAYA. YEMAYA stands for:

THE COSMIC SOUP that began in the OCEANS: Yemaya is the goddess of the living ocean, considered the mother of all. She is the source of all the waters, including rivers. Yemaya is a shortened version of Yey Omo Eja, which means 'Mother whose children are fish'.As all life is thought to have begun in the sea, all life is held to have begun with Yemaya.(YEMAYACOLLECTIONS.COM).

Do you understand the SYMBOLISM behind the term YEMAYA and how it is pointing to COSMOS AND TO —SCIENCE?

8 + 7 = 15 the DEVIL'S CARD which represents BEING SEDUCED BY THE MATERIAL WORLD AND PHYSICAL PLEASURES. LIVING IN FEAR, DOMINATION AND BONDAGE. BEING CAGED BY AN OVERABUNDANCE OF LUXURY, DISCRETION SHOULD BE USED IN PERSONAL AND BUSINESS MATTERS. (WIKIPEDIA)

From these symbols and relationships between them we can infer that "THE DEVIL" archetype represents MEN LACKING IN "TEMPERANCE" led to the HUNTING OF THE LIGHT OF BERTA. VIOLATING "YEMAYA" and HUNTING DOWN "HER REPRESENTATIVE AND VOICE" in exchange for LUXURY AND MATERIAL BONDAGE AND BUSINESS interests.

15 is "6" THE LOVERS CARD — being before THE DIVINE PRESENCE and BEFORE THE "TREE OF GOOD AND EVIL AND OF LIFE" to be JUDGED BY HEAVEN again. Eventually, man will benefit by changing course by CHOOSING THE TREE OF LIFE and becoming FREE from the bondage to DARK FORCES that move MAN TO DO EVIL.

BERTHA name means BRIGHT ONE, BRIGHT GIFT, BRIGHT JOY. CACERES from ARABIC AL-QASR which means CITADEL. A CITADEL IS A FORTRESS AND A TOWER!!! Therefore, the BRIGHT ONE IS —THE TOWER 16!

YEM in HEBREW means "LIFE" and is also a form of the root word YAM or OCEANS. AYA in Japanese and Arabic means BEAUTIFUL, WONDERFUL, AMAZING, MIRACLE. Therefore YEM-AYA stands roughly for BEAUTIFUL, WONDERFUL, AMAZING —LIFE— that of BERTHA THE TOWER. And, BEAUTIFUL OCEANS OF YEMAYA OUR LADY OF THE WATERS WHERE —LIFE BEGINS.

SINCERELY,
YEM-AYA THRU THE BIPOLAR GATES OF COMMUNICATION

## 74.   ISSA-Y-YAH'S DIV-INNE CALL FOR JUSTICE and RIGHTEOUSNESS: SI-ONNE THE JUST

SI-ONNE stands for the ROCK OF JUSTICE AND RIGHTEOUSNESS. SPIRITUALITY or RELIGION lacking in JUSTICE AND RIGHTEOUSNESS is not religion and neither spirituality but something else that IS NOT FROM THE MOST HIGH or THE HIGHER SELF. FOR THE HIGHER SELF does not condone VIOLENCE AND INJUSTICE.

ISSA -Y- YAH or the MESSAGE OF YESHUA aka ISSA and "YAH" CHAPTER 1: 11 - 17 is the following:

"The multitude of your sacrifices—what are they to me?" says the Lord. "I have more than enough of burnt offerings, of rams and the fat of fattened animals. I have no pleasure in the blood of bulls and lambs and goats.**12** When you come to appear before me, who has asked this of you,this trampling of my courts?**13** Stop bringing meaningless offerings!Your incense is detestable to me, New Moons, Sabbaths and convocations— I cannot bear your worthless assemblies.**14** Your New Moon feasts and your appointed festivals I hate with all my being.They have become a burden to me; I am weary of bearing them.**15** When you spread out your hands in prayer, I hide my eyes from you;even when you offer many prayers, I am not listening, Your hands are full of blood!**16** Wash and make yourselves clean. Take your evil deeds out of my sight;stop doing wrong. **17** Learn to do right; seek justice. Defend the oppressed.[a]Take up the cause of the fatherless; plead the case of the widow.(GOOGLE)

There it is and more CLEAR than that it cannot be. Here ADAM KADMON makes it clear that any outward modes of religion are useless because rather than focusing on JUSTICE AND RIGHTEOUSNESS people are embracing EVIL ACTION IN THEIR HEARTS WHICH TRANSLATES AS THE WAY THEY TREAT OTHERS AND EACH OTHER. I cannot say I LOVE GOD AND turn around and TREAT OTHERS LIKE if they were not DIV-INNE LIGHTS OF GOD incarnated as HUMAN. Once again "NAMASTE" THE DIVINE IN ME IS ALSO IN —YOU!!!

And so as it is clear in the Bible verses above that, all type of religious and spiritual practice whether ABRAHAMIC OR NOT that does not conform to the ROCK OR FOUNDATION OF JUSTICE AND RIGHTEOUSNESS is basically —- EVIL and is not serving THE MOST HIGH BUT SERVING THE HUMAN EVIL INCLINATION.

Therefore no SANCTUARY, TEMPLE, MOSQUE, CHURCH, RITUAL can make up and or replace the BASICS of ISSA- Y- YAH and so these become CANCELED in the EYES OF HEAVEN.

The book of ISSA- Y - YAH also contains messages for diverse NATIONS that are not Abrahamic. Why is that so? It is because the ROCK OF SI-ONNE THE JUST applies to ALL. It's a basic FOUNDATION of CREATION and SOCIETY that helps keep a relative ORDER IN A WORLD THAT WOULD OTHERWISE END UP

IN CHAOS. Can you see WHAT is happening all over the world with RELIGION, POLITICS, ECONOMICS, today? INSTITUTIONS are breaking down because of CORRUPTION and SOCIETY IN GENERAL IS FEELING THE PUNCH.

Therefore, although the message of ISSA-Y-YAH is in a JUDEO and XTIAN SACRED WRITING, the admonishment is UNNI-VERSAL since JUSTICE AND RIGHTEOUSNESS DO NOT belong to a particular religion or people but are basic tenets of HUMANITY since the beginning of this present world.

Therefore YAW-ISSA IS NOT IMPRESSED with sophisticated rituals and outward modes of worship because the real thing TAKES PLACE IN THE HEART and THE DIV-INNE CAN READ IT AND REALLY KNOW WHAT IS IN THERE HIDING AND READY TO COME OUT TO CAUSE EVIL AND MISCHIEF IN THE WORLD, DRESSED AS DEVOTION AND THE LIGHT.

It's time to TURN THE PAGE.

SINCERELY, "YAWISSA"

---

## 75.  ISSA-Y-YAH and the M-ONNO-DEISTIC TRADITION OF "JUSTICE"

A name or a title, just as a number and a word and a picture, are also symbols. And symbols can relate and connect to each other in a variety of ways. After all, WE ARE ALL DERIVING WISDOM and KNOWLEDGE from THE SAME ARCHETYPAL COSMIC MIND OF THE DIVINE MOTHER.

And so the name of the BOOK OF ISAIAH or ISSA-Y-YAH follows the same PROCESS. Let me explain myself better. The name ISAIAH can be spelled also as ISSA-Y-YAH as in ISSA -AND-YAH. What I'm trying to point out here is that THE BOOK OF ISSA-Y-YAH is not only the BOOK of ISAIAH the ancient Prophet of ISRAEL but also the PROPHET of THE NEW TESTAMENT who is YESHUA or YA-HUA or JESUS who is ...."ISSA" in the ISLAMIC TRADITION. ISSA son of YAH or DEITY!!!

So it seems that in the name of the book of ISAIAH we have an indication of YESHUA'S role in the future as a CHRIST PRINCIPLE. Showing up in HUMAN form and activating the GOD WITHIN while opening the PORTALS OF COMMUNION AND COMMUNICATION BETWEEN OUR MATERIAL WORLD AND THE SPIRITUAL REALMS behind the veil of MATTER and the UNI-VERSE. We can infer from this process that all traditions are united at the CENTER by WITHDRAWING WISDOM AND NOURISHMENT FROM THE SAME COSMIC SOURCE AND FOUNTAIN OF KNOWLEDGE aka THE TREE OF KNOWLEDGE OF GOOD AND EVIL. And YESHUA returns to fulfill the principle of JUSTICE in the Book of Isaiah.

In the tradition of ISAIAH we have the CONCEPT OF JUSTICE just as in the tradition of ISSA or YASHUA as well. Here in YESHUA we arrive at JUSTICE with what has been missing for a very long time which is what YESHUA is known for, —LOVE!!!" That is WHY ISSA-Y-YAH is referred to as the PRINCE OF JUSTICE WHO ALSO ADMONISHES US TO "LOVE ONE ANOTHER." JUSTICE WITHOUT LOVE BECOMES OPPRESSIVE, UNBEARABLE, ABUSIVE AND UNJUST. LOVE WITHOUT JUSTICE CAN ALSO BECOME WEAK AND DYSFUNCTIONAL. Remember that every POLE or DUALITY includes within itself the INCLINATION TO GO EXTREME AND BECOME ITS POLAR OPPOSITE WHICH IS WHAT THE YIN-YANG SYMBOL ALSO REPRESENTS. The YIN-YANG symbol BEING the ASIAN SYMBOL for EVERYTHING, THE UNI-VERSE, THE UNITY OF IT ALL, THE TAO, which are terms associated to the words THEO or DEO or DEA, which is DEITY in Western languages and myths and symbolism.

THE BOOK OF ISSA-Y-YAH is a CORNERSTONE BOOK AND FOUNDATION of the LINE OF THE M-ONNO-THEO-ISTIC TRADITIONS. M-ONNO as in THE GOSPEL OF THE "ONE" OR THE "UNI-TY OF ALL THINGS."

For instance in THE BOOK OF ISSA-Y-YAH you have the story of the BRILLIANT STAR THAT FALLS FROM GRACE which is the archetype of the ADAM-KAD-MON. story. Remember that not only GOODNESS FELL HERE BUT ALSO EVIL CAME ALONG WITH ITS POLAR OPPOSITE. 14 is another NUMBER or SYMBOL in numerology which represents the concept of "TEMPERANCE" which is about occupying THE MIDDLE PILLAR or CENTERING ONESELF BETWEEN TWO POLAR OPPOSITES without going into dangerous EXTREMES. The world today is in the DANGER ZONE because all over the world we have lost CENTERING or TEMPERANCE and have given into dangerous behaviors and emotions and actions that are LACKING BOTH IN "LOVE AND JUSTICE" towards planet, humans and all living beings.

SINCERELY, YESHUA aka YAWISSA aka YASHUA

---

## 76. ISSA-Y-YAH 29-32: YAW-ISSA, MA-AT and THE COSMIC SCALES OF JUSTICE

Do you recall one of those names given to DEITY by CHRISTIANS which is YAH-VE? Well, if you break the name in two it becomes TWO WORDS. The name YAH and the second part is the active verb "VE " which is the word VU,VE in Latin and Vi-dya in Sanskrit. All these —V—words related to the concept of VISION and TO SEE as in the MAYAN POPOL "VU." And so the NAME stands for YAH SEES or GOD or DEITY or HIGHER POWER OBSERVES. And this ALL SEEING EYE is not like a literal eye watching everything. It's deeper than that. REMEMBER THAT EVERYTHING IS LINKED AND SUSTAINED BY THE LIVING "QI."

Therefore, we are all DIRECTLY CONNECTED TO SOURCE which means that SOURCE IS CONSTANTLY WITH US "WATCHING" US, FOLLOWING US, SCRUTINIZING US since our DIVINE SPARK IS CONNECTED TO THE GREAT SPARK SOURCE OF LIFE AND CONSCIOUSNESS.

Everything we do is weighed in the BALANCE OF JUSTICE. That is what MA-AT signifies. MA-AT sounds a lot like DA-AT. And it stands like DA-AT in the MIDDLE OF THE TREE OF DUALITY and of LIFE. between CHOCHMA and BINAH or the SEFIROT that would represent the concepts of GOOD AND EVIL- EVIL AND GOOD. Therefore, THE TREE OF GOOD AND EVIL IS ALSO THE TREE OF SCALES, WEIGHTS AND BALANCES.

**Ma'at** was the goddess of truth, justice, balance, and most importantly - order. In paintings, she was depicted as a woman who is either sitting or standing with an ostrich feather on her head and, in some cases, she was depicted with wings. (egyptianmuseum.org).

Therefore, what we do DOES MATTER because the COSMIC ENERGY in the MATRIX is like an accounting system of debits and credits under THE LAW OF CAUSE AND EFFECT TO WHICH WE ARE ALL CONNECTED.

So, why are we talking about MA-AT and THE ALL SEEING EYE AND THE JUDGING AND WEIGHING EYES OF DIVINITY? Because that is what ISSA-Y-YAH is speaking about. Basically. ISAIAH or ISSA-Y-YAH is the CORNERSTONE OF THE TRADITION OF THE PROPHETS. WHAT HE SAYS does matter to ALL 3 MONOTHEISTIC TRADITIONS. And since the modern WESTERN WORLD was born of these traditions, modern day nations need to listen to ISSA and YAH.

To summarize the WORD OF THE L-OR-D in today's world, this DEC. 25th when supposedly people are observing the BIRTH OF THE NEW SUN, ISSA-Y-YAH 29 admonishes against GOING AFTER THE COUNSEL OF EVIL MEN AND SILENCING THE WISDOM OF THE MAN OF JUSTICE. ISSA-Y-YAH 29: 9 - 15 is admonishing against THOSE WHO RATHER LISTEN TO LIES AND DECEIT RATHER THAN TO THOSE WHO ARE SPEAKING AND EXPOSING TRUTH. Meanwhile ISSA-Y-YAH 32: 1-8 is once again admonishing that we should go after RIGHTEOUSNESS AND JUSTICE. When RIGHTEOUS behavior and JUSTICE are no longer important is when we have what we SEE happening today EVERYWHERE as in a world lacking in values and principles and embracing corruption which is a form of SELF-DESTRUCTION since a house built on sand rather than on the KEYSTONE VALUES AND PRINCIPLES OF ALL AGES SHALL NOT WITHSTAND THE WEIGHT OF CORRUPTION. 2 + 9 AS IN THE VERSE NUMBER 29 ADDS TO THE NUMBER "11" WHICH IN THE SACRED TAROT IS THE NUMBER FOR THE JUSTICE CARD.

SINCERELY, ISSA-Y-YAHWE

## 77. ISSA-Y-YAH and THE RETURN TO SI-ONNE: MEETING THE HOLY SHE-KI-"INNA"

SI-ONNE is another one of those MISUNDERSTOOD terms that religions love to use to describe so-called Holy places. However, as you have been able to see, all these terms are ARCHETYPAL and represent COSMIC concepts that make up the TAPESTRY OF THIS AND OTHER REALITIES.

Therefore SI-ONNE — IS NOT A LITERAL PLACE ON EARTH per se- or a GEOGRAPHICAL PLACE but is rather describing a STATE OF BEING AND OF CONSCIOUSNESS.

The term SI-ONNE in scripture is not only linked to the ancient word or name for the ANNU and its variations such as INNA or INNE or "ONNE" as in the UNNI-TY AND CENTER OF ALL THINGS. SI-ANNU also stands for the ROCK OR FOUNDATION or THE COSMIC PRINCIPLES that are described in ISSA-Y-YAH and in SCRIPTURE and found in ALL WORLD TRADITIONS. FOR THE CENTER OF ALL THINGS …IS ONE!!!

That FO-UNNE-DATION BEING "LOVE AND JUSTICE." This is WHAT "SI-ONNE" is pointing at. As you can see SI-ONNE is also S-INNA-I, another Holy Mountain SYMBOL. S-INNA-I as in THE HOLY SHE-KI-INNA in the story of MOSHE manifesting in all its GLORY AND GRACE to deliver THE BASIC COSMIC LAW OF JUSTICE AND ORDER TO PREVENT COSMIC CHAOS.

SI-ONNE is MOUNT MERU and GERIZIM and MOUNT PUTUO AND WUTAI as well as MOUNT SHASTA and HALEAKALA and POPOCATEPETL, etc. etc. etc. SACRED SYMBOLS that represent the LINK BETWEEN HEAVEN and EARTH AND PEOPLES. Each nation receives a SET OF COMMANDMENTS AND WISDOM from HIGH above through a PROPHET OR TEACHER OR SEER OR ELDER OR SHAMAN etc. etc. etc. who ensures that WE THE PEOPLE don't forget OUR "DIVINITY" AND THE COSMIC ORDER OF THINGS.

S-INNA-I OR "SION" IS EVERY MOUNTAIN ON EARTH that reminds people of the SACREDNESS AND UNITY OF THE WEB OF LIFE AND OUR RESPONSIBILITIES TOWARDS THESE WEB OF LIFE OR SACRED HOOP. THE PEAK OF THE MOUNTAIN POINTING UPWARDS AND LINKING DIVINE HIGHER WISDOM TO THE WORLD BELOW WHICH MAKES THE BASE OF THE HOLY MOUNT.

Go up a mountain and you will be CLOSER TO THE ORIGINS OF LIFE in a METAPHORICAL SENSE that points to the SPIRITUAL and UNSEEN WORLDS or THE SPIRITUAL COSMOS BEHIND THIS MATERIAL ONE. GOING UP A MOUNTAIN IS LIKE ASCENDING A "ROCK" where at THAT "PEAK" YOU ARE AT THE CENTER OF THE UNNI-VERSE and WHERE YOU CAN SEE ALL

THE FOUR DIRECTIONS PLUS ABOVE AND BELOW BEING ONE UNNI-TED "WHOLE."

ISSA-Y-YAH as the ROCK OF CHRIST in "ADAM KAD-M-ONNE" and YESHUA or "ISSA" SON OF MAN becomes the SACRIFICIAL LAMB who is immolated at AGE "33" as in ISSA-Y-YAH 33 —- 5 so that there be PEACE AND JUSTICE ON EARTH. 5 REPRESENTING THE DIVINE UNION OF THE 5 COSMIC PRINCIPLES SUCH AS KETER, BINNAH, CHOCMAH, and DA-AT or THE DIVINE TWINS. SI-ONNE IS "JUSTICE AND RIGHTEOUSNESS." WISDOM and KNOWLEDGE which the HOLY SHE-K-INNA IMPARTS TO HER CHILDREN.

Your spoil, O nations, is gathered as by locusts; like a swarm of locusts men sweep over it. [5]The LORD is exalted, for He dwells on high; He has filled Zion with justice and righteousness. [6]He will be the sure foundation for your times, a storehouse of salvation, wisdom, and knowledge. The fear of the LORD is Zion's treasure....

*Berean Standard Bible*

Therefore, THERE CANNOT BE A "REAL SI-ONNE" where EVIL, INJUSTICE, UNRIGHTEOUS BEHAVIOR ABIDES. WHERE EVIL AND INJUSTICE ABIDES, THE LINK BETWEEN THE SHE-KI-INNA LOGOS and THE PEOPLE has been BROKEN preventing humanity to access the WISDOM, KNOWLEDGE AND UNDERSTANDING that contributes to THE SI-ONNE "STATE OF MIND AND CONSCIOUSNESS which in turn TRANSLATES AS BLESSING TO THOSE LISTENING TO THE DIVINE WISDOM AND APPLYING IT." BUT, WOE TO THOSE THAT DO NOT!!!!

SINCERELY, "S-INNA SHE-KI-INNA"

---

## 78. "ISSA-I-YAH 6: 5 — THE "UNCLEAN LIPS" OF ISSA-Y-YAH 6:5—-- THE "LASHON HARA" AND THE BUDDHIST INJUNCTION OF "RIGHT SPEECH" —-THE LYING SNOWBALL EFFECT AND ITS TRAGIC AND DESTRUCTIVE EFFECTS ON PEOPLE, TRUST AND SOCIETY

..........SO FROM THE QURAN, WE ARE NOW MOVING ONTO THE JEWISH SCRIPTURES IN ISSA-Y-YAH. AS YOU WILL RECALL, ISSA IS ALSO THE ARABIC NAME FOR Y-ESH-UA. THE NAME Y-ESH-UA STANDS FOR "THE DIVINE FIRE NAILED TO THE CROSS WHICH IS THE TREE OF DUALITY." "THE DIVINE FIRE OR ENERGY IS LITERALLY NAILED TO THE TREE OF DUALITY WHICH IS THE REALM OF SPACE-TIME AND MATTER!!!

ISSA REPRESENTS "THE PRIMORDIAL MAN" SHATTERING INTO MANY PARTS LIKE A HOLOGRAM AND BEING ENCAPSULATED IN MATTER!!! THIS IS THE MATERIAL HUMAN EXPERIENCE AT ITS CORE. ENERGY HAVING

A HUMAN—MATERIAL LIFE IN ORDER TO EXPERIENCE THE WORLD OF DUALITY AND THAT WAY AND THROUGH IT ASCEND TO HIGHER STATES OF CONSCIOUSNESS WHICH IS THE BIRTHRIGHT OF EVERY HUMAN BEING. THE PRIMORDIAL MAN AND YAH REPRESENT ULTIMATE REALITY.

TODAY WE WILL DISCUSS ISSA - Y - YAH 6 :5!!! WHICH STATES:

"Woe to me!" I cried. "I am ruined! For I am a man of unclean lips, and I live among a people of unclean lips, and my eyes have seen the King, the LORD Almighty."

THIS BIBLE VERSE COMPLEMENTS AND ALIGNS PERFECTLY WELL WITH THE EIGHTFOLD NOBLE PRECEPT OF "RIGHT SPEECH" OF BUDDHISM AND THE PREVIOUS DIARY ON S-URA BAQA-ARA CONCERNING "RIGHT SPEECH AND TRUTH" IN THE QURAN.

THIS IS A HUGE "PROBLEM" RIGHT NOW AND THE MAIN REASON EVERYTHING IS A BIG MESS DUE TO THE DYSFUNCTIONAL HABIT OF "LYING" WHICH NOT ONLY HARMS THE PSYCHOLOGICAL STATE OF THE LIAR BUT ALSO CAUSES SO MUCH HARM TO OTHERS. HARM THAT ENDS UP SPREADING LIKE WILDFIRE. LYING IS THE BAD HABIT OF "SAYING ONE THING AND DOING THE OPPOSITE" AS IN NOT MEANING WHAT ONE SAYS AND OTHER FORMS OF "LASHON HARA" SUCH AS DOUBLE SPEAK.

IN ISSA-Y-YAH THIS "DISEASE OF THE SOUL OF MAN" IS DESCRIBED AS HAVING "UNCLEAN LIPS!!!"

WE AS A SOCIETY ARE FAILING AS A "WE THE PEOPLE" AND THE INSTITUTIONS THAT ARE MEANT TO SUPPORT THE ENTIRE STRUCTURE ARE WEAKENING DUE TO THIS DYSFUNCTIONAL AND DESTRUCTIVE HABIT OF "LASHON HARA" OR HAVING "UNCLEAN LIPS." MEN NO LONGER SPEAK "THE TRUTH" BUT SPEAK IN "DOUBLESPEAK" AND STRAIGHTFORWARDLY LIE IN ORDER TO GET WHAT THEY WANT WHICH IS MAINLY FOR POWER AND MONEY AT ALL COSTS; OR, TRYING TO GET SOMETHING BY ILLEGAL AND DISHONEST MEANS FROM OTHERS JUST LIKE IN THE STORY OF JEZEBEL IN THE BIBLE.

AT THE END, THIS CAUSES SO MUCH CONFUSION AND TURMOIL THAT NOTHING WORKS EFFECTIVELY AND NEITHER EFFICIENTLY AS IS SUPPOSED TO AND PEOPLE BEGIN TO NOTICE THIS TREND AND TO "LOSE TRUST IN THE WHOLE SYSTEM AND THE PEOPLE WHO ARE PART OF THAT SYSTEM."

LYING SPREADS LIKE DISEASE —BECAUSE WHEN ONE LIES, ONE NEEDS TO COVER AND DEFEND THAT LIE WITH MORE LIES AND THEN THOSE AROUND THE LIAR HAVE TO COVER THE LIARS TRACKS BY SUPPORTING THAT LIE AND ALL THE OTHER LIES AND FURTHERMORE CREATE MORE LIES TO COVER ALL THOSE OTHER LIES!!! IMAGINE THIS PROCESS OF CORRUPTION AND TOTAL CHAOS!!! HOW IS ANYTHING TO

FUNCTION PROPERLY AND AS IT IS SUPPOSED TO WITHOUT PROPER ACCOUNTABILITY AND "TRANSPARENCY" AND HONORABLE "TRUTH???"

THEREFORE IT IS TIME TO CLEAN OUR LIPS THROUGH THE USE OF METAPHORICAL FIERY CARBONS BY "HOLDING BACK ON LYING AND NOT MOVING OUR LIPS TO CAUSE HARM EVENTHOUGH IT MIGHT BE VERY DIFFICULT TO DO IN A WORLD WHERE LYING HAS BECOME NORMALIZED."

SINCERELY, THE "TONGUES OF FIRE" OF THE "PENTA" COST

---

## 79.  THE TONGUES OF FIRE: A TRUE STORY ABOUT THE Y-ESH-UA NAME AND THE SHAMANIC PROCESS OF PSYCHOTIC BREAKDOWN IN ORDER TO REACH INTEGRATION AND UNION WITHIN

AS YOU ALL KNOW BY NOW, I HAVE HAD MANY TESTIMONIES OF A SPIRITUAL NATURE THAT I HAVE HAD TO "LIVE TO TELL." FROM THE NATIVE AMERICAN TRADITION REVEALING TO ME SECRETS AND CONNECTING ME WITH MY ANCESTORS, TO THE GARIFUNA AND "PAGAN" TRADITIONS OF SPRITES AND GODDESSES AND THE APPEARANCE OF ASIAN "SAMMY" TO THE HEALING EXPERIENCES OF TAOISM THRU CHINESE HOLISTIC MEDICINE; AS WELL AS THE APPARITION OF THE HOLY SHEKINA and SOPHIA PRINCESS, ETC. BASICALLY, THERE IS TRUTH IN EACH EXPERIENCE. POINTING TO THE SPIRITUAL CONNECTION OF ALL THE TRADITIONS AND THEIR VALIDITY WHEN APPROACHED WITH TEMPERANCE, RESPECT AND MOST OF ALL WITH "LOVE AND KINDNESS."

FOR A WHILE I PUT MY HOLY BOOKS AWAY AND TURNED MY BACK ON THE BIBLE. BUT IT WAS UNTIL I HAD THIS VERY WEIRD EXPERIENCE JUST AS "A LA SAMMY" THAT I BEGAN TO WONDER MANY THINGS ABOUT JESUS AND WHY THIS WAS HAPPENING TO ME IN THE FIRST PLACE.

I AM NOT GONNA GET INTO DEFENDING OR TRYING TO CONFIRM WHETHER Y-ESH-UA WAS REAL OR NOT OR WHETHER THE MIRACLES ARE TRUE OR SIMPLY METAPHORS OR WHETHER THE GOSPEL IS A WORK OF FICTION OR BASED ON GREEK MYTHOLOGY. I AM SIMPLY GOING TO "EXPLAIN WHAT HAPPENED AS IT HAPPENED TO ME AND THE MYSTERY BEHIND IT ALL" JUST AS IN MY OTHER EXPERIENCES WITH THE OTHER TRADITIONS.

IT WAS BACK IN 2002 WHEN I WAS HAVING MY FIRST PSYCHOTIC BREAK BECAUSE OF PERSONAL TRAUMA. I WAS IN THE CONDITION OF MARY MAGDALENE AND THE 7 CHAKRAS THAT NEEDED PURIFICATION AND CLEARING. I WAS IN BAD SHAPE. BY THEN I HAD NO IDEA THAT IN THE SHAMANIC TRADITION, THE PROCESS OF AWAKENING AND RECONSTRUCTION HAPPENS AND BEGINS WITH "PSYCHOSIS."

THEREFORE, IT WAS UNTIL GOING THROUGH THIS LIFE-THREATENING EXPERIENCE THAT I BEGAN TO UNDERSTAND THAT THE "PSYCHOSIS" I HAD EXPERIENCED BY RELIVING MY PAINFUL PAST TRAUMA HAD BEEN "SPIRIT INDUCED" IN ORDER TO BE ABLE TO HEAL THAT PARTICULAR TRAUMA. AND SO I BEGAN A PROCESS OF SPIRITUAL AWAKENING, DEVELOPMENT AND TRANSFORMATION BY WHICH I WOULD RE-MEMBER MYSELF IN EVERY SENSE OF THE WORD.

AFTER MY BRIEF DEADLY PSYCHOTIC BREAK, I TRAVELED TO ANOTHER TOWN NAMED "ST PETER" .... I HOPE YOU NOTICE THE CONNECTION HERE AS IN "CEFAS-PETER" WHERE I STAYED WITH RELATIVES. AFTER A COUPLE OF DAYS WITH THEM I GOT STABLE ALTHOUGH I WAS BY THEN VERY PHYSICALLY SICK. ONE OF THOSE DAYS MY COUSIN WHO HAS THE NAME OF "JOHN THE BAPTIST AND JEHOVAH" IN ITALIAN, HAD ME OVER HER HOUSE TO PRAY FOR ME USING HER BIBLE AND IN THE NAME OF Y-ESH-UA AND WITH THE BOOK OF ISSA-Y-YAH OPEN SHE BEGAN TO PRAY FOR ME. AS SHE BEGAN PRAYING ALOUD AND CRYING AND BEGGING HEAVEN FOR HEALING, I IMMEDIATELY BEGAN TO HEAR '"VOICES WHISPERING IN BOTH MY EARS!!!" THESE WERE MALE VOICES IN AN ANGELIC LANGUAGE I COULD NOT UNDERSTAND. AND THESE VOICES WERE NOT INSIDE MY HEAD BUT OUTSIDE AS IF SEVERAL ENTITIES WERE WHISPERING IN BOTH MY EARS. I WAS IN SHOCK AND COULD NOT BELIEVE WHAT WAS HAPPENING. IMMEDIATELY, I SAT STRAIGHT ON THE CHAIR AND TOLD MY COUSIN THAT I WAS HEARING VOICES WHISPERING IN BOTH MY EARS CLEARLY AS SHE WAS DOING THE PRAYER OUT LOUD!!!

SHE WAS SKEPTICAL OR THOUGHT THESE TO BE DEMONIC. HOWEVER, AS YOU KNOW, RELIGIOUS PEOPLE CALL EVERYTHING THEY DO NOT KNOW AND UNDERSTAND TO BE DEMONIC ALTHOUGH THEY MIGHT NOT BE. PERHAPS THEY WERE, OR PERHAPS THEY WERE ANGELIC OR TRANSDIMENSIONAL. WHO KNOWS....

AFTER THIS EXPERIENCE I REALIZED THAT "THERE WAS SOMETHING WEIRD GOING ON WITH THE NAME OF Y-ESH-UA" BECAUSE OF THAT EXPERIENCE!!! AND SO IT CONFIRMED EVEN MORE MY HEBREW-CHRISTIAN PAST AS WELL AS THAT OF MY COUSIN WHO IS FROM CHRISTIAN BETHLEHEMITE ORIGINS IN PALESTINE. IN ADDITION TO HER NAME BEING AS "JOHN" AND "DEITY" HER LAST NAME IS AFTER THE "NAZARENES." WHICH IS EVEN MORE INTERESTING.

AND SO ALTHOUGH I MIGHT NOT AGREE WITH THE CHURCHES AND HOW THEY DO THEIR BUSINESS, AT LEAST SOME OF THEM, I KNOW THAT THAT NAME HAS SOMETHING MYSTICAL ABOUT IT. YEARS LATER I LEARNED THAT THE NAME Y-ESH-UA IS THE HOLY PENTAGRAMMATON AND THAT

IT REPRESENTS UNION AND INTEGRATION WHICH IS THE PROCESS THAT WAS BEGINNING TO TAKE PLACE THROUGH THE "SPIRIT INDUCED PSYCHOSIS" IN ME.

AND SO ALTHOUGH I COULD NOT UNDERSTAND WHAT THE VOICES SAID, I WENT TO THE GOSPEL AS SPIRIT MOVED ME AND TOLD ME TO DO SO AND AND READ WHAT THE DEITY SAID WHEN Y-ESH-UA WAS BEING BAPTIZED WITH WATER... IN MY CASE IT WAS WITH SPIRIT .... "THIS IS MY SON WHOM I HAVE APPROVED."

I DO NOT WISH RELIGIOUS EXTREMISTS TO USE THIS STORY OF MINE TO JUSTIFY AND SPREAD MORE RELIGIOUS OBSESSION AND INSANITY AND EXTREMISM. THAT NAME JESUS IS ABOUT TEMPERANCE AND EVENTUALLY RECOVERY. IT IS ABOUT LOVING- KINDNESS AND NOT INSANITY AND VIOLENCE. AS TO THIS EXPERIENCE, LET US NOT FORGET —-NOT FORGET — THAT THE OTHER SPIRITUAL EXPERIENCES I HAD WITH OTHER TRADITIONS ARE AS VALID AS THIS ONE. SUCH AS THE JUDAIC, THE NATIVE AMERICAN, THE SHAMANIC - PAGAN, THE AFRICAN, THE AUTOMATIC HEALING IN CHINESE TRADITION WHICH I WILL WRITE ABOUT LATER ON, ETC. ETC. ETC. AND I HAD SPIRITUAL EXPERIENCES EVEN DURING MY PERIOD OF DISBELIEF AND RELIGIOUS DISAPPOINTMENT WHICH MEANS THAT EVEN NON-BELIEVERS ARE CONNECTED TO SPIRIT AND ABLE TO HAVE AS WELL THESE TYPES OF SPIRITUAL EXPERIENCES THAT TRANSCEND RELIGION AND BELIEF.

SO HERE IS MY STORY. AND I KNOW IT WILL SHOCK SOME PEOPLE ESPECIALLY FROM THE JEWISH AND ISLAMIC TRADITIONS BUT IT IS AS IT HAPPENED TO ME BACK IN 2002. Y-ESH-UA WAS A POWERFUL SHAMAN IN THE JEWISH TRADITION!!! PERHAPS HE WAS .... MY ANCESTOR!!!!!!!!!!!!!!!!!!!!!!!!!!!!!!!!!!!!!!!!!

SINCERELY,
"TOUCHED BY AN ANGEL"

---

## 80. "MEHUE ALHIUN:" THE DRUM, THE TRANCE, THE LADY AND THE MESSAGE — "THE TREE OF LIFE" DECODED THROUGH THE NATIVE AMERICAN TRADITION!

THIS IS A "TRUE" STORY AND IT WILL CLARIFY MUCH ABOUT HOW "WE" CAME ABOUT THE "CODE" BEHIND "THE TREE OF LIFE" AS HAS BEEN SO FAR EXPLAINED HERE IN OUR INTERPRETATION.

IT HAPPENED AROUND 2012, AROUND THAT TIME. I HAD READ ABOUT THE "TREE OF LIFE" AND SEEN PICTURES OF IT BUT WAS UNABLE TO

UNDERSTAND WHAT IT WAS ALL ABOUT. TO ME IT WAS ALL A COMPLICATED DIAGRAM WITH THREE STICKS PARALLEL TO EACH OTHER AND CIRCLES ALL OVER IT. BEYOND THAT I DID NOT SEE ANYTHING USEFUL ABOUT IT. I WAS —CONFUSED AND IT BORED THE HELL OUT OF ME UNTIL.....! ONE EVENING WHEN I WAS DEEP IN MEDITATION RELAXING AND BEGAN TO DRUM MY NATIVE A-MARIE-KI-ANNE DRUM AND I FELL INTO A MILD TRANCE. THIS IS ONE OF THE FEW TIMES I HAVE BEEN ABLE TO ACCOMPLISH THIS, MUCH LESS NOW THAT I TAKE MEDS.

AS SOON AS I FELL INTO A LIGHT TRANCE STATE WHICH FELT LIKE BEING IN A STATE BETWEEN ASLEEP AND AWAKE OR "IN THE TWILIGHT ZONE," I HEARD CLEARLY A SOFT FEMALE VOICE THAT SAID TO ME "MEHUE ALHIUN." I COULD NOT UNDERSTAND WHAT THAT MEANT OR WHAT LANGUAGE IT WAS. PERHAPS SOME NATIVE AMERICAN LANGUAGE OR ANCIENT EGYPTIAN, (IF SOMEBODY KNOWS PLEASE, LET ME KNOW, THANKS).

AND AFTER THE LADY SAID "MEHUE ELHIUN" WHICH I REMEMBERED BECAUSE I HEARD IT VERY CLEARLY, I SAW A DIAGRAM BEFORE ME IN MY MIND LIKE IT WAS HAPPENING BEFORE MY EYES OF THE "TREE OF LIFE" WITH THE THREE PILLARS AND THE SEFIROT AND —DA-AT!!! AND WHAT AMAZED ME IS THAT AS SOON AS THE "DA-AT SEFIRA" APPEARED, IT BEGAN TO DESCEND AND TO DIVIDE IN TWO. AND WHEN I SAW THAT HAPPENING THE "TREE OF LIFE" DIAGRAM BECAME LIKE AN "OPEN BOOK" TO ME.

PERHAPS "ME-HUE AL-HE-UN" MEANS — "ME HAVA AND DEITY OR SH-E ARE ONE. "PERHAPS!

AND SO I WAS SHOCKED BY THIS "DIVINE REVELATION" BY MEANS OF THE INDIGENOUS DRUM AND NATIVE A-MARIE-KI-ANNE TRADITION. THE LADY OF THE DRUM MESSAGE WITH ITS DECODING OF THE TREE OF LIFE WHICH IS CENTERED ON THE POSITION THAT IS MOSTLY IGNORED, THE "DA-AT" POSITION WAS AN EPIPHANY FOR ME. THIS EXPERIENCE CONFIRMED TO ME THE SHAMANIC TRANCE STATES I HAD READ ABOUT AND HOW INFORMATION LIKE THIS IS DELIVERED FROM "THE TWILIGHT ZONE" INTO OUR WORLD. BY THE WAY, I DO NOT RECOMMEND PEOPLE DOING THIS TRANCE DRUMMING FOR OBVIOUS REASONS IF THEY ARE NOT IN TUNE WITHIN.

AND SO THIS INTERPRETATION OF THE "TREE OF LIFE" IS NOT FROM ME BUT FROM "THE TWILIGHT ZONE," REVEALING TO ME THE SECRETS BEHIND THE "TREE OF TREES." THIS EXPERIENCE ALSO SERVES TO CONFIRM, REAFFIRM AND AFFIRM THE VALIDITY AND IMPORTANCE OF THE INDIGENOUS TRADITIONS OF THE A-MARIE-KA'S AND THE WORLD THROUGH THE INDIGENOUS DRUM AND HOW ALL TRADITIONS COMPLEMENT ONE OTHER!

SINCERELY, "ME-HUE AL-HI-UN" THRU THE DRUMS AND BIPOLAR TRANCE STATES!

---

### 81.  A NIGHT WITH "GIANTS" AND THE "PEOPLE OF NATURE:" MY TESTIMONY REGARDING THE CELTIC AND OTHER TRADITIONS' "MYTHS" OF "THE RACE OF GIANTS," THE WATCHERS AND THE NEPHILIM

I know you will think I am losing my mind. Perhaps I have already lost it anyways or I HAVE REGAINED IT. But I will tell you this real life story which might be scary to some and magical to others.

Back in 2018 in the night when I saw the heavens open up and Kalki flying with his horse down to Earth, I also saw "other" THINGS :). I could not believe my eyes for I had only heard of these beings or "things" from the Bible and FAIRY TALES. And you know how fairy tales are mostly always connected or linked to NATURE.

Well, to get into the story, I was outside in the open in a large field lying on the ground. As it got dark I began to notice that I was not alone. I was like: "Am I seeing what I am seeing?" Perhaps I need a new glass prescription. Well, I was aware that I was not doing well but I was also wondering about what I was seeing or looking at. And THEY WERE LOOKING AT ME!!!!

I freaked out for a moment and my mind began to wonder if these beings were about to eat me alive. They looked so real. You might imagine that I was looking at something that did not react to my presence, but you are mistaken. They began to react to everything that I was doing as I was trying to get them distracted and entertained hoping that would keep them happy until sunrise. Something told me to keep them entertained til sunrise and they would leave as the sun rises. And so I began to sing and to talk to them and to act out little dramas and sketches. You will not believe it, and neither did I at the moment, but at least one of them was enjoying the program as HE WOULD SMILE back at me.

There were TWO GIANTS, one was by a huge TREE. And so something in my mind told me they were linked to NATURE. The other one was by an old abandoned building that was near that tree. One was WHITE and reminded me of IRISH FOLK TALES and the other one was BLACK with BRAIDS and looked like a Jamaican Rastafarian. And they just kept staring at me while I was lying on the field. Sadly, my interaction with them ended … and I say, sadly, because what interrupted my GIANT interaction was a very traumatic and evil experience as all of a sudden I was being KIDNAPPED by some bad boys who were brandishing a gun at me. Eventually, THANKS TO A HIGHER POWER, I made it away from the bad boys and into a gas station in the middle of nowhere. And guess what, right there I was able to see the trees moving and I realized that the GIANTS had found me and THEY WERE CALLING ME "by my name." It was only when the sun began to rise that the VOICES disappeared.

And so whether it was imaginary or real, who knows. To me the experience was very very real!!! And it confirmed to me the FAIRY TALES, JACK AND THE BEANSTALK and other stories from all nations, peoples and tribes that talk about GIANTS. Who can tell if what is considered imaginary is actually THE REAL THING. And so I was able to confirm the FAIRY TALES that night, A NIGHT spent WITH GIANTS! :0

OR..... PERHAPS THEY WERE THE "NEPHILIM." OR, BOTH!!!

SINCERELY "YAKOV OF THE HOS-ANNA AND THE BEANSTALK THAT CONNECTS HEAVEN TO EARTH."

---

## 82. I.N.R.I: Y-ESH-UA OVERCOMING THE "GOL" ATTITUDE THAT PERSECUTED "INRI"

THEY are nagging me to write this diary. And so I must. I know it will cause a lot of controversy and perhaps anger. But, it is just a SYMBOL OR SIGN that points to the MESSAGE and the PRESENCE.

The TERM I.N.R.I. is made up of 4 ROMAN LETTERS. Each one represents THE DIVINE PRESENCE or BASIC ENERGIES which manifest in EACH HUMAN. After all, humans are a complex combination of WATER, EARTH, FIRE AND AIR. The name represents the ACTIVE PRESENCE OF THESE ENERGIES in Y-ESH-UA and in SHA-M-ANNU.

The NAME is equivalent to the 4 FACES OF THE CHERUBIM. The OX, the EAGLE, the LION and THE HUMAN FACE.

The HUMAN FACE represents WISDOM. The LION represents the ARI FIRE. The OX represents BIPOLARITY having TWO HORNS. THE I.N.R.I. represents all these things as a UNIT. THE CHERUBIC ENERGY behind the FACE OF THE SHA-M-ANNE. As you will recall, the SHA-M-ANNE'S bird is THE EAGLE representing COMMUNICATION AND LINKING between THE COSMOS AND THE WORLD OF MAN.

SHA-M-ANNE or KUKUL-KI-ANNE appears at a certain time in order to help BALANCE THESE 4 ENERGIES or at least point to humanity its LACK OF BALANCE which is leading and contributing to the IMBALANCE TAKING OVER THE PLANET. Which is manifesting in the SOCIAL AND ENVIRONMENTAL as well as HEALTH CRISES we are facing right now.

These ENERGIES not only represent PHYSICAL ELEMENTS but also SPIRITUAL. There is a DIRECT CONNECTION between the SPIRITUAL "ELEMENTS" or ENERGIES AND THEIR PHYSICAL MANIFESTATIONS.

The INRI therefore is a SYMBOL for the UNITY OF COSMOS IN Y-ESH-UA who is the VETRUVIAN MAN who represents HARMONY in man that has to do with these diverse energies. As a human absorbs these ENERGIES from the EARTH HERSELF AND FOOD, the ingestion of UNHEALTHY SUBSTANCES does have an impact in the PHYSICAL AND SPIRITUAL health of that bodily system.

I-ESUS N-AZAR-ENNU-S R-EX I-UADERUM —-- THE SAVIOR or ESU THE NAZARENE JEW AND KING!!! REX is WHAT Y-ESH-UA was accused of being his main WRONGDOING, and MISCONDUCT because he was being accused of trying to become THE king and overthrow HEROD AND ROME. AZAR is linked to the SACRIFICE OFFERING as in N-AZAR. The NAZAR OF GOD ANNU. It's all SYMBOLIC. NASI means PRINCE in Hebrew. All pointing to the IDENTITY OF Y-ESH-UA and his eventual ENDING AT GOL-GOTHA. "GOL" GOTHA has the same root word as in GOL-EM AND GOL-IATH. Therefore, "GOL" stands for THOSE IN AN UNCONSCIOUS AND GOL-EM STATE who ACCUSED AND MURDERED Y-ESH-UA. Which is a UNIVERSAL CONCEPT or theme related to the 144,000 number code in the BOOK OF REVELATIONS or those like JESUS WHO BEAR THE MARK of HUMAN CONSCIOUSNESS and AWAKENED STATES who end up persecuted and murdered like JESUS.

GOTHA means APPEARANCE OR ATTITUDE. IN other words GOL-GOTHA stands for the ATTITUDE OF "GOL-EM" that eventually NAILS THE CHRIST TO THE CROSS.

As you remember, Y-ESH-UA was PERSECUTED, SLANDERED, MOCKED, SPAT AT, LIED TO, etc. which basically are GOL BEHAVIORS and BULLYING. THE DIVINE DOES NOT WANT THAT TO HAPPEN ANYMORE having the "GOL" ALWAYS PERSECUTE AND GET AWAY WITH YOU KNOW WHAT which is part of the TREND and which is what has brought about JUDGMENT DAY. Reason why the SHA-M-ANNE TRADITION is almost EXTINCT AND THE BALANCE BETWEEN THE WORLDS IN COLLAPSE.

The reason WHY the world is UPSIDE DOWN is not "BECAUSE OF GOD'S FAULT" but humankind's CHOICES. HUMAN keeps choosing DEMAGOGUES and "GOL" TYPES that end up bringing about CHAOS AFTER CHAOS. Rather than CHOOSING men and women of ETHICS AND INTEGRITY WHO ARE IN ALIGNMENT WITH "HIGH VALUES AND PRINCIPLES," PEOPLE go after the TOUGH AND ROUGH BULLY AND MACHO TYPES WITH LOADS OF MONEY AND MATTER WHO UNDERNEATH ALL THAT FACADE CARRY THE SPIRIT OF THE "GOL."

And so what they are nagging me to say is that INRI is the origin of the name HENRI or ENRIC or INRI-K. As in INNE-RIC or THE ANNU ARE RICH AND ALMIGHTY.

ERUM is PARADISE and so IUDA - ERUM refers to the JEWISH PARDES tradition that forms part of the belief systems of ISLAM AND CHRISTIANITY as well or THE KINGDOM OF HEAVEN. ARE YOU READY TO GET THE HECK OUT OF THIS GOL-IATHAN MESS?

SINCERELY, INRI FROM THE CROSS

---

## 83. THE "R-"ESU"-RECTION:" GOD SAVING THOSE WHO ARE "RIGHTEOUS AND ETHICAL" TO BE RECEIVED IN THE KINGDOM OF HEAVEN AND "NEVERLAND"---- G-ESU THE "GREEN MAN" IN THE EUROPEAN TRADITION

THE name "ESU" as in R-"ESU"-"RECT"- ION means in FINNISH:

GOD IS SALVATION!!!

The term RECT on the other hand stands for:

1. a written acknowledgment by a receiver of money, goods, etc, that payment or delivery has been made.
2. the act of receiving or fact of being received.(COLLINSDICTIONARY)

RECT is also the root word for the TERM —"RECT-ITUDE" which stands for: MORALLY CORRECT BEHAVIOR OR THINKING. "RIGHTEOUSNESS." (GOOGLE)

Therefore the word R-ESU-RECT- Y -ONE stands for —

GOD SAVES AND RECEIVES THOSE WHO ARE "RIGHTEOUS" AND "ETHICAL" as in the NOBLE 8 FOLD PATH etc. THE DIVINE "PAID THE PRICE" AND DELIVERY HAS BEEN MADE.

The NAME "J-ESU-S also has the root word ESU in it meaning that in J-ESU-S IS THE PRESENCE OF "GOD IS SALVATION." WHO "PAID THE PRICE" SO THAT THE RIGHTEOUS AND ETHICAL BE RECEIVED IN "NEVERLAND" KINGDOMS!!!

Which makes YOU wonder WHAT is the FATE of those WHO ARE NOT RIGHTEOUS AND ETHICAL and DO NOT REPENT OF THEIR EVIL DOINGS.

J-ESU-S therefore is the RIGHTEOUS AND ETHICAL – PRINCIPLE, and so those who erroneously have thought for 2000 years that they CAN BE EVIL AND SPREAD HATE AND VIOLENCE AND STILL ENTER THE "KINGDOM OF HEAVEN" are seriously MISTAKEN!!

That is WHY, in SCRIPTURE, J-ESU-S "YO-ESU-IS" or —I AM JESUS— ADMONISHES those who run after WRONGDOING, EVIL AND INJUSTICE; and, in REVELATIONS JESUS warns where EVIL DOERS who don't change because of PRIDE AND STUBBORNNESS AND LOVE OF EVIL — go. And it is NOT – to NEVERLANDS.

Therefore, what THIS R-ESU- and RECT-Y-ONNE EASTER, RAMA-DAN ... and, PASS-OVER teaches us is that NOT EVERYONE WHO CLAIMS TO KNOW THE L-OR-D or the TRUTH WILL "PASS- OVER TO THE NEW WORLD AND NEVERLANDS" BUT ONLY THOSE "LIKE CHILDREN" WHO DO "THE WILL OF THE FATHER OF LIGHT" WHICH IS THE SAME AS "RIGHTEOUSNESS and ETHICAL BEHAVIORS" which are the BASIS FOR "JUSTICE FOR ALL."

To those WHO DO NOT HAVE A "TICKET TO HEAVEN" YET, now is the time to LEAVE BEHIND THE PATH OF INJUSTICE AND EVIL and EMBRACE "ETHICS, JUSTICE FOR ALL, AND —-RIGHTEOUSNESS", THE NOBLE "8" FOLD PATH.

RIGHTEOUSNESS AND ETHICS AND JUSTICE ARE OF THE HOUSE OF "ANNU" AND THE "ANNU" UPHOLD THESE FOREVER.

SINCERELY,
ESU

---

## 84. R-"ESU"- "RECT"- I"ONNE:" THE ALCHEMICAL PROCESS OF AWAKENING AND BREAKING THE CYCLE OF REINCARNATION THRU AND BY —-RIGHT BEHAVIOR AND THOUGHT

THE name "ESU" as in R-"ESU"-"RECT"- ION means in FINNISH: GOD IS SALVATION!!!

The term RECT on the other hand stands for:

1. a written acknowledgment by a receiver of money, goods, etc, that payment or delivery has been made.

2. the act of receiving or fact of being received.(COLLINSDICTIONARY)

RECT is also the root word for the TERM —"RECT-ITUDE" OR "RECTO" IN CASTILIAN. which stands for: MORALLY/ETHICALLY CORRECT BEHAVIOR OR THINKING. "RIGHTEOUSNESS." (GOOGLE) ON or ONNE = ONENESS,

WHOLENESS, INTEGRATION OF THE MIND AND EMOTIONS INTO A HARMONIOUS WHOLE THRU THE "HIGHEST POWER" —LOVE!

THE R-ESU-RECTION HAS ANOTHER INTERPRETATION OF THIS ARCHETYPE OF COMING BACK TO LIFE FROM A STATE OF "DEATH" WHICH IS FOUND IN MANY TRADITIONS AND NOT JUST CHRISTIANITY.

AS WE EXPLAINED BEFORE, THE "DEATH" OF EASTER IS REFERRING TO A "CHANGE OR TRANSFORMATION." A PLACE OF "STILLNESS AND HIBERNATION" IN WHICH A PERSON IS CHANGING SKINS OR THE "OLD SELF" AND MOVING INTO THE "HIGHER SELF" THRU AND BY A PROCESS OF "SELF KNOWLEDGE." IT IS THIS PROCESS THAT LEADS TO THE ILLUMINATION OF THE SHADOW NECESSARY FOR THE PROCESS OF ALCHEMY TO TAKE PLACE.

THIS PROCESS EVENTUALLY LEADS TO —AWAKENING. WHEN YOU FINALLY ARE ABLE TO PERCEIVE LIFE FROM A PANORAMIC VANTAGE POINT AND SEE THRU THE VEIL OF MAYA OR ILLUSION.

THEREFORE, JUST AS THIS PROCESS HAPPENS IN ONE LIFETIME BY MEANS OF ONE'S OWN PERSONAL DISCOVERY AND GROWTH/EVOLUTION, IT ALSO REPRESENTS THE ONGOING PROCESS OF REINCARNATION OR LIVING LIFE AFTER LIFE WHICH IS LIKE POLISHING THE PHILOSOPHER'S STONE IN ONESELF THROUGHOUT LIFETIMES. FINALLY, HUMAN AWAKENS AND "AS IF BEING KISSED FROM A DEEP SLEEP," THE CYCLE OF REINCARNATION BREAKS OR ENDS AT LAST.

THIS ENDING OF THE CYCLE OF REINCARNATION AND POLISHING OF ONE'S SOUL THROUGHOUT LIFETIMES IS EQUIVALENT TO "EXPERIENCING A RESURRECTION." YOU ARE NO LONGER IN THE STATE YOU WERE BEFORE AND SO YOU "LOOK" DIFFERENT BECAUSE YOU MOVE AND ACT IN A DIFFERENT WAY AND AT A HIGHER FREQUENCY. THIS IS WHAT "AND THEY DIDN'T KNOW WHO HE WAS" IN THE EASTER STORY IS ABOUT.

"ESU" REFERS TO "SALVATION;" AND "RECTIO" REFERS TO BEING RIGHTEOUS AND BEING MINDFUL, BEHAVING ETHICALLY AND NURTURING LOVE. THESE STATES OF "RECTIO" CONSCIOUSNESS REPRESENT THE PATH THAT IS NARROW AND THAT ONLY FEW FIND IN THIS LIFETIME. THEREFORE, SALVATION FROM THE CYCLE OF REINCARNATION DEPENDS ON ONE'S OWN MORAL-ETHICAL STATE AND BEHAVIORS AND THE PURSUIT OF HIGHER CONSCIOUSNESS.

G-ESU OR YE-SH-UA IS AN ARCHETYPE WHO REPRESENTS THE JOURNEY THROUGH TIME AND SPACE AND MATTER OF THE DIVINE SPARKS OR HUMAN BEINGS. MEANING THAT PART OF THE REASON WE ARE HERE IS

TO LEARN THE DIFFERENCE BETWEEN RIGHT / WRONG WHICH IS ETHICS/ MORALS AND THE CONCEPT OF RIGHT-EOUSNESS. TO PRODUCE MORE LIGHT FROM OUR OWN DARKNESS AND THAT WAY WORK ON OUR INNER ALCHEMY AND PHILOSOPHER'S STONE.

THEREFORE, R-ESU-RECTI-ONNE IS EQUAL TO "RECTITUDE LEADS TO SALVATION THRU INTEGRATION!!!"

FORMS OF "RECTITUDE" ARE THE "EIGHTFOLD NOBLE PATH OF BUDDHISM" AND THE "LOVE ONE ANOTHER AS ESU LOVES YOU IN CHRISTIANITY." AS WELL AS THE "ETHICS IN JUDAISM AND IN ISLAM'S SUFISM OF LOVE AND UNION—AND OTHER TRADITIONS' SYSTEMS OF "KNOWING THYSELF" THAT HELP LEAD ONE FROM THE "UNREAL VEIL AND FORM OF MAYA TO THE —REAL" OR ONE'S OWN DIVINE SELF AND THE SACREDNESS OF THE ALL.

THUS BY LIVING AN UPRIGHT AND RIGHTEOUS LIFE WE CAN ACHIEVE —R-ESU-RECTION. SUCH AS NOT SPREADING LIES, VIOLENCE, ABUSIVE BEHAVIOR, HATE, DYSFUNCTION AND TRAUMA, ETC. ETC. ETC. THESE ARE CHARACTERISTICS OF A PERSON WHO IS IN A STATE OF IGNORANCE TO HIS/HER TRUE DIVINITY AND OF THE DIVINITY OF EVERYTHING AND EVERYONE AROUND. THE DARKNESS IS IN ITSELF THE "RAW MATERIALS" USED TO POLISH THE PHILOSOPHER'S STONE.

JUST LIKE THE "DAY OF ATONE-MENT," THE PROCESS OF R-ESU-RECTI-ON WON'T WORK BY CASTING ALL "SINS" ON JESUS CHRIST ON A CROSS AND "BEING FORGIVEN." TO ONLY END UP TAKING THAT ATONEMENT AS A GREEN LIGHT TO TURN AROUND AND "SPREAD MORE EVIL" THRU HATE AND VIOLENCE AND TRAUMA AND THEN SEEK FORGIVENESS IN JESUS ONCE AGAIN. ONLY TO CONTINUE WITH THE EVIL CYCLE OF DYSFUNCTION. AND TURNING THIS WORLD INTO A PERPETUAL LIVING HELL AS A RESULT.

IF WE WANT TO EVENTUALLY —R-ESU-RECT FROM THIS CYCLE OF SAMSARA, BEING KIND AND RIGHTEOUS IS NECESSARY.

SINCERELY, "ESU" THE "RIGHT"

---

## 85. "THE RESURRECTION" and THE SEPARATION OF ADAM(EVE) KADM-ONE

Resurrection = coming back to life after death.

And the serpent told Eve that if she ate from the forbidden fruit of the TREE OF DUALITY she would not die. But ELOHIM told Eve that she would indeed die. So here you have a very interesting episode where two opposite archetypes are telling Eve that she will die and that she won't die. However, at this point poor Eve has no idea what both God and the serpent mean by "TO DIE and NOT TO DIE." Eve has never experienced it. At this point her interest and curiosity has been piqued by BOTH Elohim and Serpent and CONFUSION enters the formula since both God and Serpent are toying with Eve's ignorance and innocence and so she is now CONFUSED.

So Eve ends up in a state of NO DEATH. But she still is not after the image and likeness of DEITY since she still cannot tell the difference between GOOD and EVIL. Eve is in a state of SUSPENSION as in the Tarot Card number 12, the Hanged Man. ADAM AND EVE ARE IN A TRANSITION PERIOD from being in a Golem like state where they are "human" but NOT CONSCIOUS YET OF THEIR INNER DIVINITY. They are not able to tell GOOD from EVIL or to notice differences and options and choices which are DIVINE traits.

And so Eve and Adam FALL for the first DIVINE KOAN on DUALITY. And so they metaphorically eat of the TREE OF DUALITY. Koan = a paradoxical anecdote or riddle, used in Zen Buddhism to demonstrate the inadequacy of logical reasoning and to provoke enlightenment.(GOOGLE) ISN'T REACHING ENLIGHTENMENT THE …GOAL OF EVERY SPIRITUAL PATH AFTER ALL?

What happens next is that HEAVENLY Eve and Adam "FALL" CREATING THE REALM OF MATTER and … DEATH. As people do not realize that the FIRST ADAM and EVE in the Genesis story is the HEAVENLY ADAM AND EVE or … DA'AT, who is the DIVINE CHILD or ANDROGYNE ADAM (EVE) KADMON whom are BOTH JOINED AS ONE. TWO HALVES FORMING ONE UNITED "BEING."

And so as they both "EAT" and FALL DOWN "INTO MATERIAL BONDAGE and GIVE BIRTH TO THE MATERIAL WORLDS", they BREAK UP AND SEPARATE INTO - and + or EVE and ADAM and so they begin to interact or have COSMIC "SEX" as in the interaction between TWO ATOMS and to multiply by creating a 3rd principle and further they both go as they fall down creating and giving birth to the entire MATERIAL REALM and COSMOS. This is the TZIMTZUM or BIG BANG. The DIVINE CHILD is the DIVINE ARCHITECT or Master Mason of the UNIverse. It is through HIM-HER that CHOKMAH and BINAH create the worlds.

Each human being and animal and other living beings everywhere are living sparks of that TZIM TZUM moment trapped in matter. And so going back to the story of DEATH AND NO DEATH, "BOTH" ELOHIM and the SERPENT are correct as HUMAN BEINGS would physically DIE over and over again over lifetimes in their quest for ENLIGHTENMENT. That A-HA moment would break the reincarnation curse which is PHYSICAL DEATH( or being trapped in a cycle of SAMSARA) and corruption in Earth. Eventually leading both ADAM and EVE who represent HUMANKIND NOT TO DIE ANYMORE. Both returning back up to SOURCE. When a soul has lived enough lives and reached Enlightenment, he or she has basically RESURRECTED from a state of death in the flesh through reincarnation to a state of no death in spirit.

Thus you WILL DIE OR PERISH IN MATTER but YOU WILL NOT DIE IN SPIRIT "ARE" BOTH CORRECT!

SINCERELY, "ADAMEVA"

---

## 86. "INDUS"-"TRIA:" THE RISE OF "INDUS"-"TRY" AND TECHNOLOGY IN THE VERY ANCIENT WORLD AND ITS DEMISE — THE INDUS VALLEY CIVILIZATION AS WARNING FOR POSTERITY!

IT'S VERY INTERESTING TO NOTICE HOW THE TERMS AND ROOT WORDS OF THE LANGUAGES OF THE WORLD INTERSECT AND CONNECT ALL OVER AND SO WE GET A VERY GOOD IDEA OF THE "NEVER ENDING STORY OF HUMANKIND" BEHIND THIS MODERN STORY. AS WE HAVE SEEN, TIME SEEMS TO BE MORE CYCLICAL THAN LINEAR AND IT TENDS TO REPEAT ITSELF. PERHAPS, TIME IS TRYING TO TELL US SOMETHING AS IN ... ARE WE GONNA FINALLY "UNDERSTAND THE MESSAGE?"

THE STORY BEHIND THE "STORIES" AND LEGENDS OF THE NATIONS OF THE WORLD POINT TO THE HISTORY OF MANKIND AND TO MAN'S MARK LEFT ON EARTH.

THE TERM "INDUS" AS IN THE "INDUS VALLEY" IN INDIA AND PAKISTAN POINTS TO THE "GREAT ANCIENT CIVILIZATION OF INDIA." THE TERM "INDUS" AS IN "INDUS-TRY" TELLS US OF A STORY THAT GOES BACK TO THE LAND OF THE SANKTA SKRIT-URA OR SANSKRIT AND —INDUSTRY; THE PLACE OF ATOMS OR OF THE ATOMIC TRIAD, OR ... "TRI" ...AS IN, PROTONS - NEUTRONS— AND ELECTRONS!!!

SO WE CAN SEE HERE THAT THIS CIVILIZATION WAS A PRECURSOR TO MODERN DAY CIVILIZATIONS IN WHICH TECHNOLOGY AND INDUSTRY FLOURISHED. IN THE ANCIENT VEDIC STORIES WE HAVE THE LEGENDS OF THE PANDAVAS AND THE WAR OF K-URUK-SHE-TRA AND AND OTHER WARS IN WHICH BALLS OF FIRE ARE DESCRIBED TO HAVE CONSUMED EVERYTHING. THESE STORIES ALSO SPEAK OF FLYING MACHINES!!!

THE FACT THAT THE LEGENDS SPEAK OF MONARCHIES AND FAMILIES FIGHTING EACH OTHER FOR POWER AND TO SAVE THE LAND AND NATION SOUNDS VERY MUCH LIKE THE POLARIZATION BETWEEN GROUPS TODAY VYING FOR POWER. SOME UPHOLDING RIGHTEOUSNESS WHILE OTHERS DOING IT FOR RAW POWER AND MATTER. THESE ANCIENT VEDIC — WARS— REMINDS US OF THE WORLD OF TODAY.

K-"URU"-K-SHE–TRA REMINDS US OF THE ANCIENT CITY OF "UR" OF THE CHALDEES OR "URUK." THE TERM "UR, ORO, URI, ARA, ARI, ETC, ETC, ETC. SHARE THE SAME MEANING IN MOST LANGUAGES POINTING TO A COMMON ORI-GIN. URU STANDS FOR—GOLD, LIGHT, FIRE, ELECTRICITY, QI, ENERGY, ETC. ETC. ETC. MEANING THAT THE WAR OF K-URU-K-SHE-TRA'S AND THE NAME OF THAT CITY-STATE IS FORMED OF THE WORDS THAT DESCRIBE MODERN CIVILIZATION. SUCH AS A CIVILIZATION THAT USED —GOLD, LIGHT, ELECTRICITY, AND WHICH PERHAPS ENDED IN UP CONSUMED BY FIRE. ISN'T IT INTERESTING THAT THE TERM K-URU-K-SHE-TRA ALSO HAS THE ROOT WORD FOR "THREE OR TRES" IN LATIN LANGUAGES SUCH AS —"TRA AND TRI"–AS IN INDUS–TRY!!! POINTING TO PERHAPS "NUCLEAR ENERGY BASED ON THE ATOMIC TRIAD" WHICH BROUGHT ITS EVENTUAL DEMISE AND THE INDUSTRIALIZATION OF THAT CIVILIZATION.

SO IT WOULD NOT BE SURPRISING THAT THE ANCIENT "INDUS" VALLEY INDUSTRY AND CIVILIZATION ENDED UP IN DECLINE DUE TO CORRUPTION, WAR AND POWER STRUGGLES AND WAS DECIMATED DUE TO THE —SAME ISSUES TROUBLING MANKIND TODAY SUCH AS — INDUSTRY AND ITS GOLD OR USE OF CURRENCY. AND THE WARS UPON WARS DUE TO CORRUPTION AND OBSESSION WITH GOLD IN HUMAN CIVILIZATION. IN THIS CASE THE NATION STATES OF THE INDUS VALLEY.

IT IS POSSIBLE THAT INDUS-TRY EVENTUALLY LED TO —ENVIRONMENTAL ISSUES OR COLLAPSE OR A MIX OF THE ABOVE.

I WAS VERY SHOCKED WHEN I READ THESE ANCIENT STORIES AND HOW THE "WORLD DESTROYED BY FIRE" SOUNDED MUCH LIKE NUCLEAR HOLOCAUST IN THE VEDAS. IT SEEMED THAT MAN'S ADVANCEMENTS IN TECHNOLOGY AND THE MANIPULATION OF MATTER COMES AT A HIGH COST AS IN THE DIMINISHMENT OF THE "SPIRITUAL- PSYCHO-EMOTIONAL" HEALTH AND BALANCE OF PEOPLES.

SINCERELY, "PAN-D-HAVA KALKI" IN THE 21ST CENTURY

---

## 87.  NAGAS-A-"KI" AND H-"IRO"-SHIMA: THE ENERGY OF THE FATHER AND THE FIERCE DESTRUCTION OF THE MOTHER ARCHETYPE — THE NAGA, DRAGON, THE SERPENT AND THE SALAMANDER OF FIRE

SO HERE WE CONTINUE WITH TODAY'S THEME OF THE "FIRE" IN THE CASE OF MAHA-BHARATA AND THE MODERN OPPENHEIMER AND —WORLD WAR II. AS WE HAVE STATED BEFORE, ALL THE NAMES AND WORDS HIDE A

"CODE" THAT ONCE PUT TOGETHER BECOMES A STORY BEHIND THE "HIS-STORY" OF MANKIND.

IN THIS CASE WE ARE MOVING FROM THE INDUS VALLEY MILLENIA AGO TO MODERN DAY JAPAN IN WORLD WAR II AND THE FIRST TIME AN ATOMIC BOMB WAS DROPPED ON THE CITIES OF.....

"H-IRO+SHI-IMA ....

AND ....... NAGAS-A-QI."

IF WE LOOK CLOSELY AT THE NAMES OF THESE TWIN CITIES YOU WILL REALIZE MUCH ABOUT THE EVENT ON THE YEAR OF 1945. 1 + 9 + 4 + 5 === 19 IS THE "SUN" CARD IN THE SACRED TAROT WHICH POINTS TO "HEAT AND FIRE" JUST AS THE SUN AND THE "AGNI or FIRE IN THE VEDIC TRADITION." FIRE THAT IS ALSO MANIFESTING IN TODAY'S CLIMATE AS "CLIMATE WARMING."

THE NAME "NAGAS-A - QI" HAS THE NAME FOR SERPENT IN THE HINDU TRADITION AND DRAGON IN JAPANESE. DRAGONS OF WATER OR —FIRE!!! NAGAS A KI or QI, AS IN DRAGONS OR SERPENTS OF QI OR ENERGY OR FIRE!!! WHICH IS THE ELEMENT THAT IS PRODUCED WITH THE FUSION OF THE ATOMIC NUCLEI AS ATOMIC BOMBS.

IN THE CASE OF H-IRO-SHI-IMA WE HAVE THE ANCIENT WORD GOING BACK TO THE GENESIS "UR" AND THE MESOPOTAMIAN URUK AS IN —THE CITY OF GOLD, LIGHT AND FIRE OR "URI." ARA, URI, IRA, ARI ETC. ARE ALL FORMS OF THE SAME CONCEPT USED IN MOST LANGUAGES AND TRADITIONS. IN THIS CASE IT IS THE "IRO" OF IRO-SHIMA. WE CAN ALSO NOTICE THAT THE "IMA" IS THE OLD TERM USED GLOBALLY IN DIVERSE FORMS FOR "MOTHER." THE CONCEPT OF MOTHER REPRESENTED IN THE TREE OF DUALITY AND UNION AS "BINAH" THE FIERCE ONE!!!

WE WILL RECALL THAT THE "FATHER CHOKMAH" IS THE SOURCE OF ENERGY AND OF FIRE AND LIGHT. BUT IN ITS EXTREME VERSION IT BECOMES "FIERCE AND DESTRUCTIVE" AS IN "BINAH THE FIERCE ONE." THEREFORE, THE MASCULINE AGNI or FIRE ENDS UP MANIFESTING THROUGH THE FIERCE MOTHER TO COME TO BE IN ITS DESTRUCTIVE ALL -CONSUMING FORM. AS IN —-ORI - IMMA!!!

THE BINAH MOTHER AND THE CHOKMAH FATHER BOTH —COMING TOGETHER —TO BRING ABOUT THE —-YIN-YANG— ENERGIES IN THEIR WRATHFUL FORMS AND SO YOU GET THE TRIAD OF PROTONS, NEUTRONS AND ELECTRONS. BINAH IS THE NEGATIVE CHARGE OR ELECTRON.

CHOKMA IS THE POSITIVE CHARGE OR PROTONS. NEUTRONS DON'T HAVE A CHARGE AND SO ARE IN THE MIDDLE.

AUGUST 6, 1945 — 8 + 6 =14 THE TEMPERANCE CARD OF THE SACRED TAROT WITH ST MIKAEL'S PICTURE BEARING THE "TRIANGLE" OR UPRIGHT PYRAMID REPRESENTING —FIRE ELEMENT. IN THE TEMPERANCE CARD WE HAVE AN "ISLAND" THEME AS IN THE ANGEL WITH ONE FOOT ON LAND AND THE OTHER ON WATER JUST LIKE JAPAN. WE CAN SEE A "FLASH OF FIRE / SUN" IN THE BACKGROUND. POINTING TO THE "DETONATION OR EXPLOSION OF THE ATOMIC BOMB." LACK OF TEMPERANCE IN THE AGNI OR INNER FIRE OF MAN LED TO THIS TRAGIC ENDING. 1 + 4= 5 THE 5 ELEMENTS IN A STATE OF DISSOLUTION AS A RESULT OF THE BOMB. THE VALUE OF THE DATE IS "15 THE DEVIL'S CARD" AS IN "MANKIND BEING CHAINED TO ITS OWN SHADOW AND DYSFUNCTION" THAT LED TO WWII. 6 LEADS TO THE LOVERS CARD AS IN —FREEDOM FROM THE SHACKLES OF THE DEVIL OR THE END OF WWII AS A RESULT OF THE BLOODBATH.

SINCERELY,
THE "NAGA OF ORI AND IMA"

---

## 88. BAQA- ARA: THE DIVINE BAQA OF FIRE AND WISDOM OF ALLAH ADMONISHING THE NATIONS TO "CHOOSE SATYA TRUTH AND PEACE" INSTEAD OF "FURTHER CORRUPTION OF MAN AND THE PLANET"

١٠ نَوُبدْكِيِ اوُنَاكَ اَمِبْمِيلاْ ببَاذَعْ مُهَلوْ ٱضَرَمَ ٱمُهَدازَفْ ضَرَمَّ مهبوُلْقَ ىف

١١ نَوُحِلصُمُ نْحَدَ اَمِذَا اوُلَاقِ ضرْ لاْ ىف اوُدِسفْتَ لاْ مُهَلَ لِيق اذإو

١٢ نَوُرُعْشَيِ لا نكُلو نوُدِسفُمْلاْ مُه مُهَذَا الاْ

مُه مُهذَا الاْ عآهفسُ لاْ نَماء اَمَكُ نْموُنَا اوُلَاقْ سانَّ لاْ نَماء اَمَكَ اوُنماء مُهَلَ لِيق اذإو

THE TERM "S-URA-H" in the COR-ANNE — IS —- related to the word for SUN,or S-URI-YAH IN SANSKRIT. Both point back to THE "DIVINE, URI" or "WISDOM AND LIGHT" or as being, "OF THE — DIVINE LIGHT" as an ADMONISHMENT THAT HELPS LIGHT THE WAY. Another interesting characteristic of the term S-URI-YA is the "SOUND" of the word S-URA-H and the ENGLISH word for SORRY!!! Therefore this BAQ-ARA SURAH is PLACING THE SPOTLIGHT ON THE SHADOW SELF IN ORDER TO BRING ABOUT —REPENTANCE —SO THAT MAN CHANGES HIS DESTRUCTIVE WAYS.

To remind YOU again, the term BAQA-ARA is related to the SPANISH word for COW which is "VACA" or BAQA IN ARABIC and in this case the BAQA OR COW OF "LIGHT AND FIRE" which is the DIVINE COW or BAQA of L-OR-D SHIVA in

THE VEDIC TRADITION. Therefore, this ADMONISHMENT is from the DIVINE represented in world tradition as THE SUN AND SHIVA and — AL-LA— who are THE MIGHTY ELOHIM, THE MANY WHO ARE ONE AND THE ONE WHO ARE MANY — THE ONE AND ONLY.

Here is the TRANSLATION of the BAQA- URI S-URA-H 1-286 and how it relates to the same ADMONISHMENTS found in JUDAISM, CHRISTIANITY, HINDUISM, etc. etc. etc. These pertain to the AGE OF KALI or CORRUPTION we are leaving behind and EXPLAINS THE WIDESPREAD ATTITUDE TODAY TOWARDS — CORRUPTION. Here is as FOLLOWS:

*There is sickness in their hearts and ALLAH only lets their sickness increase. They will suffer a painful punishment for their lies.*

*When they are told "do not spread corruption in the land,they reply, "we are only peacemakers" Indeed it is they who are the corruptors, but they fail to perceive it.*

THE BAQA OF FIRE AND THE "IRE" OF THE DIVINE admonishes HUMANS to move away from CORRUPTION. This SICKNESS OF THE HEART is to do with HATE and VIOLENCE, as WE have pointed out before. These HATE-FUL AND VIOLENT TENDENCIES HAVE SPREAD ALL OVER THE PLANET in many forms such as in RELIGIOUS, POLITICAL, ECONOMIC,

RACIAL, AND SOCIAL FORMS OF VIOLENCE ( just to mention a few examples). From violence in the streets to GENOCIDE AND PERSECUTION OF PEOPLES AND GROUPS to the DESTRUCTION OF MOTHER EARTH, this evil trend has crossed the point of NO RETURN.

Rather than to ACKNOWLEDGE THE VIOLENCE AND HATE WITHIN, MAN CHOOSES TO CONTINUE TO DEFLECT HIS RESPONSIBILITY AND CONTRIBUTION TO THE EVIL BY SCAPEGOATING PERSONAL DYSFUNCTION AND UNWISE CHOICES ON OTHERS OR — TO COVER THE TRANSGRESSIONS WITH "LIES." Therefore from the SANCTA-SCRIT-URA in BAQA-ARA we can see that LYING AND CORRUPTION GO HAND IN HAND!!!

This is the -6+6+6=18 THE MOON CARD IN THE SACRED TAROT RELATED TO THE FRONTAL LOBE "DYSFUNCTION"IN THE HU-MAN BRAIN in which MAN IS UNABLE TO FEEL EMPATHY FOR ANOTHER AND SORROW FOR HIS "MISTAKES." HE OR SHE IS UNABLE TO TELL THE DIFFERENCE BETWEEN GOOD AND EVIL AND SO — CALLS EVIL, GOOD AND CALLS GOOD, EVIL. This is the SAME AS MAKING THE CLAIM TO BE FOR "GOOD" WHILE CONCEALING "EVIL" PLANS WITHIN.

WE are CALLING, THEREFORE ON "HUMANKIND" TO EMBRACE "TRUE PEACE IN THY HEARTS AND MINDS" WHICH WILL TRANSLATE AS A PEACEFUL WORLD. BE TRUE TO YOUR WORD.

And he shall judge among the nations, and shall rebuke many people: and they shall beat their swords into plowshares, and their spears into pruninghooks: nation shall not lift up sword against nation, neither shall they learn war any more. (Isaiah 2:4).

SAY NO TO "TERROR!!!"

SINCERELY,
SIMPLY "ISSA"

---

### 89. "JINN-IE IN THE BOTTLE:" THE "J-INN SURAH" AND THE "MANIC STATES OF ECSTASY AND IN-SPIRIT-ATION" AS PROCESS OF HUMAN CREATIVITY THROUGHOUT THE AGES — TOUCHED BY AN ANGEL!!! PART I

وَ مَّبِحَصَ دَخذَّ أ أم انِبّر دُ ج ىلَعَت هذّ او

اططشّ أ ىلَع الهيفسد لوُقيَ ناك هذّ او اِدَلو لا

Now, we believe that our Lord —exalted is his majesty—- has neither taken a mate nor offspring.

And that the foolish of us -used to utter outrageous falsehoods about Allah. SURAH AL JINN.

AS YOU WILL RECALL, YEARS AGO I WENT THROUGH A PERIOD OF "COSMIC INFLUENCES" OR "CHANNELING" IN WHICH INTERPRETATIONS AND INFORMATION AND "UNDERSTANDING" ABOUT DIFFERENT THINGS WERE COMING MY WAY OR THROUGH ME. EVENTUALLY, IT ALL BEGAN TO TAKE FORM AS IN A "HOLY BOOK OR WRITING." I WAS IN A "MANIC" EPISODE WHICH LASTED YEARS AND IN OLDER TRADITIONS IT IS KNOWN AS "ECSTASY or BEING IN AN ECSTATIC STATE." ITS AKIN TO FEELING THAT YOU ARE "CONNECTED" TO A COSMIC "ELECTRIC CURRENT" OR SOURCE OF INFORMATION BY WHICH AND THROUGH WHICH ONE HAS ACCESS TO KNOWLEDGE AND UNDERSTANDING ABOUT WRITINGS AND PHILOSOPHIES AND ART AND MANY OTHER THINGS.

IN ANCIENT TIMES, THE "ECSTATIC STATES" OF CONSCIOUSNESS WERE NOT CATEGORIZED AS "DSM OR MENTAL ILLNESS OR SUCH OTHER DIAGNOSES" AS IT'S DONE TODAY. THIS PROCESS WAS CONSIDERED AS

BEING UNDER THE INFLUENCE OF SPIRIT OR IN A STATE OF "INSPIRATION." THE WORD "INSPIRATION" COMES FROM THE CONCEPT "TO BE UNDER THE SPIRIT, OR IN A STATE OF DIVINE INFLUENCE OR MADNESS." IT WAS NOT CONSIDERED A DISEASE BUT A "STATE OF CONSCIOUSNESS" AND PART OF THE "SPIRITUAL PROCESS OF AWAKENING."

AFTER THINKING MUCH ABOUT MY OWN EXPERIENCE WHICH LASTED FROM 2012 - 2017-18, AND HOW "IT FELT LIKE I WAS BRINGING THRU "DIVINE INFORMATION," ALTHOUGH IT MIGHT HAVE BEEN ONLY PART OF THE MANIC PROCESS WHICH MAKES ONE UNDERSTAND, PERCEIVE AND INTERPRET REALITY DIFFERENTLY; I HAVE COME TO THE CONCLUSION THAT THE ...BIBLE AND THE KORAN AND THE BOOK OF MORMON AND OTHER WRITINGS... CAME THRU BY THE SAME OR SIMILAR PROCESS OF "ECSTATIC STATES OF INSPIRATION" WHICH LEAD TO A HIGH CURRENT OF CREATIVITY AND IMAGINATION WHICH MAY HAVE A STRONG SPIRITUAL COMPONENT TO IT.

I WAS MOVED TO LOOK UP THE KORAN TODAY AND LOOK UP THE VERSE ABOVE ABOUT THE "MIGHTY JINN" OR "GENIES IN THE BOTTLE." WHICH WAS MY UNDERSTANDING OF WHAT WAS HAPPENING TO ME OR THRU ME BY THE "MIGHTY ELOHIM" OR COSMIC ENERGIES THAT BECOME ACTIVE DURING MANIC STATES AND BY WHICH THESE ENERGIES OF CREATIVITY MANIFEST. LIKE IT HAS BEEN SAID BEFORE, THE REALITY OF THIS UNIVERSE IS BOTH "YIN AND YANG!!!"

I HAVE BEEN MOVED TO LOOK FOR THE TWO VERSES ABOVE IN "THE JINN" SURAH IN ORDER TO CLARIFY SOME THINGS THAT NEED SOME EXPLANATION ABOUT THE PROCESS OF CHANNELING INFORMATION AND UNDERSTANDING BETTER HOW THAT WORKS AS HAS BEEN EXPLAINED HERE.

IN THE FIRST PLACE, AND AS IT WAS EXPLAINED TIME AGO, ALTHOUGH THE TERM "ALLAH" IS USED TO DESCRIBE ULTIMATE REALITY IN THE KORAN AND WHICH IS RENDERED AS "LORD" IN THE MASCULINE, THE TERM ITSELF IS "ANDROGYNOUS!!!" MEANING THAT IT IS BOTH "MALE AND FEMALE" AS ONE AS IN "YIN-YANG."

SINCERELY, J-INNIE IN THE BOTTLE

## 90. "JINN-IE IN THE BOTTLE:" THE "J-INN SURAH" AND THE "MANIC STATES OF ECSTASY AND IN-SPIRIT-ATION AND THE PROCESS OF HUMAN CREATIVITY THROUGHOUT THE AGES — TOUCHED BY AN ANGEL!!! PART II

AL-LA — "AL" IS THE MALE AND "LA" IS THE FEMALE!!!

"AL" STANDS FOR "THE" IN ARABIC. AND ITS RELATED TO THE "LATIN" LANGUAGE MASCULINE WORD "A EL" OR "AL" —"TO THE." "EL" POINTS TO "ULTIMATE REALITY" AND TO THE MALE PRINCIPLE. THE "LA" IS ALSO RELATED TO THE "LATIN" WORD FOR THE FEMALE." AS YOU CAN SEE, BOTH THE "AL AND THE LA" ARE THE INVERSE OF EACH OTHER WHICH POINTS TO THE CONCEPT OF "OPPOSITES THAT COMPLEMENT EACH OTHER." IN CASTILIAN "AL" IS MASCULINE AND "LA" IS FEMININE. AND BOTH ARE USED RESPECTIVELY TO DESCRIBE MASCULINE PLACES OR FEMALE THINGS. DO YOU NOTICE THE PATTERN HERE?

AS "YIN AND YANG" ENERGIES ARE BOTH ATTRIBUTED TO THE MALE AND FEMALE RESPECTIVELY, THE "AL AND LA" REPRESENT PERFECTLY THE NATURE OF ULTIMATE REALITY IN THE SENSE OF BEING ITSELF "BOTH" A "YIN-YANG" OR "AL-LA." MAKING IT NOT ONLY "ANDRO-GYNOUS" BUT ALSO "MASCULINE AND FEMININE" SIMULTANEOUSLY. AND, "GENDER NEUTRAL." WHICH TELL US THAT "ULTIMATE REALITY" IS "ALL OF THE ABOVE AND MUCH MORE" DEPENDING ON HOW "WE LOOK OR PERCEIVE....IT!!!!"

ISLAM MAKES THE SAME MISTAKE AS THE OTHER TRADITIONS OF PICTURING AND DESCRIBING THE DIVINE AS A "SOLE MASCULINE POWER." WHEN IN REALITY EVERYTHING COMES IN PAIRS AS IN DARK AND LIGHT, SUN AND MOON, YIN AND YANG, "AL" AND "LA." MASCULINE AND FEMININE, GIVER AND RECEIVER, THE CHALICE AND THE BLADE, ETC. AS HAS BEEN EXPLAINED BEFORE AND WHICH BECOMES MORE CLEAR IN THE COSMIC DIAGRAM OF THE "TREE OF DUALITY OR TREE OF LIFE." THE "YIN AND YANG" UNIT AS "ONE" —EMANATES AS TWIN ENERGIES THAT COMPLEMENT EACH OTHER IN ORDER TO BRING ABOUT THIS UNIVERSE. THE EMANATIONS ARE THE —TWIN ENERGIES INDEPENDENT OF EACH OTHER AS WELL AS INTERDEPENDENT TO EACH OTHER. THEY ARE THE "OFFSPRING" ENERGIES THAT INTERACT WITH EACH OTHER IN A COSMIC DANCE TO BRING ABOUT THE UNIVERSE AND EVERYTHING IN IT.

THE FACT THAT GENESIS STATES THAT "AND THEY MADE MAN MALE AND FEMALE AFTER THE IMAGE AND LIKENESS OF ULTIMATE REALITY" POINTS TO THE REALIZATION THAT IF THE DIVINE IS AN IMAGE AND LIKENESS OF THE MALE AND FEMALE MAN THEN IT IS —BOTH —YIN AND YANG!!! AND —

NOT— ONLY MASCULINE AS IT HAS BEEN THE POPULAR BELIEF FOR THE PAST THOUSANDS OF YEARS.

AND SO ...I GUESS ... I AM THE "DIVINE FOOL" OR "DIVINE MADMAN!!!" OR ONE OF MANY. FOOL AND MAD IN THE "GOOD SENSE OF THE WORD." AND SO I HAVE COME TO THE CONCLUSION THAT THE SO CALLED "HOLY BOOKS" ARE "INSPIRED" NOT IN THE SENSE THAT "GOD TOLD SOMEONE THIS AND THIS AND THIS..." BUT THAT THE PEOPLE WHO WROTE THESE WERE IN A STATE OF "DIVINE ECSTASY OR MADNESS" AND SO —"IN-SPIRITED!!!"

A DIVINE PROCESS WHICH IS NOT UNUSUAL SUCH AS MICHELANGELO AND DA VINCI AND ALL THE GREAT WRITERS AND THINKERS AND ARTISTS ETC. WHO HAVE GONE THROUGH THE SAME "CREATIVE PROCESS OF BEING UNDER THE INFLUENCE OF THE COSMIC FORCES" BY WHICH THEY CREATED AND WROTE "BIBLES, KORANS, BOOKS OF MORMONS, VEDAS, KABALAHS, THE MABINOGIONS, THE FAIRY TALES, THE GREAT NOVELS, THE PICASSOS AND FRIDA KAHLOS, THE MOZARTS AND AMADEUS, ETC. ETC. ETC.

THEREFORE, AS THE OLDER TRADITIONS AND ABORIGINAL PEOPLES HAVE ALWAYS SAID IN THEIR OWN ORAL TRADITIONS, THE "DIVINE MANIA" IS A SPIRITUAL PROCESS WHICH IS EQUIVALENT TO "BEING INSPIRED AND TOUCHED BY THE DIVINE."

SINCERELY, "JINN-Y IN THE BOTTLE"

---

## 91. "THE IMMA-CULATE CONCEPTION:" ANOTHER "CYPHER" AND METAPHOR THAT POINTS TO THE PROCESS OF ENLIGHTENMENT, ILLUMINATION AND AWAKENING

ايبِصَ مَكحْلاً هَتيْتاَعو طِّحُوّ قِدَ بـبَّكّلاً ِدُخ ىَّحْيـَ

'It was later said,' "O John! Hold firmly to the Scriptures." And We granted him wisdom while 'he was still' a child,

ايِغَدبُكَا مَلو رَّشَد ىِنَسَسِنمَدبِ مَلو مَـلْـّغ ىلُن وكُدِ ىَّدَا تَلاَق

She wondered, "How can I have a son when no man has ever touched me, nor am I unchaste?" (SURAH MARYAM)

And Jesus, when He had been baptized, went up straightway out of the water. And lo, the heavens were opened unto Him, and He saw the Spirit of God descending like a dove and lighting upon Him. (MATTHEW 3:16)

THE "IMMA-CULATE" CONCEPTION IS ANOTHER ONE OF THOSE MISUNDERSTOOD CONCEPTS JUST LIKE THE NAME OF Y-ESH-UA.

LET US START WITH THE CONCEPT OF "IMMA" WHICH STANDS FOR THE WORD FOR MOTHER IN MOST LANGUAGES.

"MACULATE" STANDS FOR "STAIN OR SPOT" IN LATIN.

"IM-MACULATE" STANDS FOR —- THE MOTHER WITHOUT "STAIN OR SPOTS."

THIS CONCEPT OF THE "IMMA-CULATE CONCEPTION" —-IS NOT —ABOUT A "LITERAL VIRGIN BIRTH!!!....." IN THE HUMAN SENSE OF THE WORD. THE IMMACULATE CONCEPTION IS BORN OF THE "SHE-KI-INNA" TRADITION WHICH IS TO DO WITH THE PROCESS OF "AWAKENING, ENLIGHTENMENT AND ILLUMINATION" JUST AS REPRESENTED BY THE SYMBOL AND ICON OF "LADY LIBERTY." IT - IS - NOT - ABOUT - RELIGION.!

AS YOU WILL RECALL, THE "BIRD" OF THE GOSPEL OR THE DOVE REPRESENTS "WISDOM AND LIGHT." IN MOST TRADITIONS "WISDOM" IS ATTRIBUTED TO THE "FEMININE" PRINCIPLE. IT IS REPRESENTED BY "BIRDS" SUCH AS THE QUETZAL BIRD OF THE MAYA AND THEIR PROPHET QUETZALCOATL. OR THE HEAD COVERING OF PAHANA IN NATIVE A-MARIE-KI-ANNE TRADITION WHICH IS MADE UP OF FEATHERS.

REMEMBER THAT "THE IDEAS AND ARCHETYPES OR CONCEPTS" ARE PART OF THE "BLUEPRINT OF CREATION" AND ARE ATTRIBUTED TO THE MOTHER OR BINAH THE CAULDRON OR WOMB OF CREATION. MOST ALL TRADITIONS DESCRIBE "WISDOM" IN THE FEMININE AND THAT SHE WAS WITH THE "DEITY" SINCE THE BEGINNING OF TIME. THIS "WISDOM" IS THE LIGHT BORN OF THE DARK. AS LIGHT IS ATTRIBUTED TO THE FATHER, IT ALSO MANIFESTS THROUGH THE MOTHER AS WISDOM AND KNOWLEDGE JUST AS THE SUN'S LIGHT IS REFLECTED ON THE MOON.

THAT THE "'DOVE" DESCENDS UPON "Y-ESH-UA" IS SIMILAR TO THE CONCEPT OF "THE DIVINE SPIRIT OR FIRE OR ELECTRICITY OR SOPHIA" DESCENDING UPON JESUS. IT IS THE "EUREKA" MOMENT IN WHICH — HUMAN WAKES UP AND REALIZES HIS HER OWN INNER DIVINITY AND HIGHER SELF!!!

IT HAS NOTHING TO DO WITH BEING A CERTAIN RELIGION OR DOGMA OR CREED.

THIS IS WHAT "BEING BORN AGAIN" AND "BEING BORN OF THE IMMACULATE CONCEPTION" MEANS. "WISDOM" IS A CONCEPT OF "THE LIGHT," THEREFORE IT IS "UNBLEMISHED AND IMMACULATE" IN THE SENSE THAT

IS NOT IN A STATE OF "CORRUPTION." CORRUPTION IS THE OPPOSITE OF —WISDOM!!!!

"WISDOM" WAKES UP IN THE PERSON OF Y-ESH-UA AND HE "TRANSFORMS WHILE ALIVE IN A THINKING AND CONSCIOUS MAN WITH THE DIVINE FIRE ACTIVE" IN HIM-HERSELF. THIS PROCESS OF "BEING BORN AGAIN" IS CALLED "IMMACULATE" BECAUSE IT IS NOT A LITERAL BIRTH BUT THE BIRTH OF A "HIGHER STATE OF CONSCIOUSNESS" THAT IS NOT BROUGHT ABOUT BY A WOMAN HAVING SEX WITH A MAN. "WISDOM AS THE DIVINE FEMALE PERSONIFICATION" GIVES "BIRTH TO Y-ESH-UA THE AWAKENED MAN, THE CHRIST" IN THE SENSE OF BEING ENLIGHTENED AND SO IT IS NOT A HUMAN SEXUAL PROCESS AND NEITHER THROUGH A WOMAN NAMED MARY WHO IS BORN WITH "THE NATURAL INCLINATION TO TRANSGRESS." IT IS THE "VIRGIN BIRTH OF THE CHRIST PRINCIPLE IN JESUS."

THE IMMA-CULATE IMMA OR MOTHER IS THE "PISTIS SOPHIA aka SHE-K-INNA."

SINCERELY, THE "DIVINE FEMININE" AS "PISTIS SOPHIA" THRU THE "BIPOLAR GATES"

---

## 92. "ISSA THE BEL'S" GREAT DISAPPOINTMENT: FROM EVANGELIZING HALF THE WORLD TO BEING PERSECUTED BY HALF THE WORLD — THE IRONY OF IRONIES IN THE CONCLUSION OF THE AGE OF KALI!!!

THE FOLLOWING STORY IS A TRAGI-COMEDY AND ITS ABOUT "ISSA THE BELLE'S" COMEBACK FROM 2000 YEARS AGO TO MODERN TIMES.

AS YOU WILL RECALL, ACCORDING TO THE DA VINCI CODE, THE BLOODLINE IS TIED TO THE KINGS OF THE EARTH. AND SO "ISSA-BELLITA" OF SPAIN IS ALSO PART OF THE MELTING POT OF JESUS BLOODLINE. BE AWARE THOUGH, THAT THIS IS JUST A STORY.

AND SO .... ISSA BELLE OR THE CHRISTIANIZED DAUGHTER OF TAMAR OF JUDAH 500 YEARS AGO WAS INFATUATED WITH BEING THE "LADY OF REVELATION" AND CONVERTING THE ENTIRE WORLD INTO A ONE WORLD CHRISTIAN RELIGION. IT WAS THE FAD BACK THEN. SHE WAS OBSESSED AND HAD BEEN BRAINWASHED HERSELF. MANY THINGS, BAD THINGS WERE DONE IN THE NAME OF THE CROWN AND CHRISTENDOM WHICH SET THE BASIS FOR THE CLIMAX OF THE MATERIALIZATION OF THE WORLD AND THE END OF THE AGE OF KALI. HOWEVER, ISSA-BELLITA OF SPAIN REALIZED AT THE END THAT ALTHOUGH SHE WAS A WOMAN, THE

CHURCH HEAD WAS A PATRIARCHY. SO THERE WAS ALWAYS A CONFLICT OF INTERESTS BETWEEN THE QUEEN AND THE CHURCH.

2000 YEARS LATER ISABELITA POPS UP AGAIN AND THIS TIME "SHE COMES BACK DRESSED AS A MAN." HAVING RE-INCARNATED OVER AND OVER AGAIN AND EVOLVING DURING EACH LIFETIME, SHE FINALLY "WAKES UP" FROM THE GREAT DREAM THAT IS REINCARNATION. OH GOSH ... SAYS ISSA THE BELLITA!!! WHAT AM I DOING HERE....AGAINNNNN????

AND NOW SHE HAPPENS TO BE ...VERY DIFFERENT...FROM HOW SHE WAS 500 YEARS AGO. AS YOU WILL RECALL, DURING EACH INCARNATION YOUR SOUL KEEPS CHANGING AND EVOLVING. AND SO .....BY NOW AS SHE WAKES UP, SHE IS NOW THE INNOCENT VICTIM OF THE PATRIARCHAL CHURCHES WHO NO LONGER ACCEPT HER FOR BEING "A GROWN WOMAN" IN THE SPIRITUAL SENSE. AT THIS POINT, ISSA THE BELLITA IS MORE LIKE "YENTL" TRAPPED IN A MAN'S BODY AND INTERESTED IN EVERYTHING THAT THE CHURCH CONDEMNS, VILIFIES AND DOES NOT ACCEPT. THE SAME CHURCH SHE HELPED SOLIDIFY AND EXPAND.

IS IT "ISSA THE BELLES'S" FAULT THAT "S-HE IS NOW A SHE IN A MAN'S BODY???" IT SEEMS THAT IT IS CLEARLY GOD'S WILL THAT SHE WAS "BORN THIS WAY." AND SO AS YOU CAN REALIZE, SHE FINALLY HAS TO CONTEND WITH ALL THESE CHALLENGES. "ISSA THE BELL" IS NO LONGER THE SAME AS 500 YEARS AGO WHEN SHE WAS UNDER THE CONTROL AND INFLUENCE OF THE CHURCH DOGMA AND NEITHER DOES SHE LOOK THE SAME. SHE HAS BECOME MORE INDEPENDENT AND REACHED SOME SORT OF WHAT PSYCHOLOGISTS CALL "INDIVIDUATION." IT WAS JUST THE WAY IT WAS MEANT TO BE FOR HER AND IS MEANT TO BE FOR EVERY SOUL THAT INCARNATES IN THE WORLD.

SO NOW WHAT IS "ISA THE BELLITA" TO DO WITH THE CHURCH THAT LOVED HER ONCE AND THAT NOW ....VILIFIES AND PERSECUTES HER?

SINCERELY, ISSA-BELLITA

---

### 93. QUALITIES OF THE MESSIAH (AND WHAT S-HE REPRESENTS) VS. THE EVIL QUALITIES OF THOSE DECEIVING THE DIVINE, THE PEOPLE AND THE MESSIAH

"He is described as an angelic being, who "was chosen and hidden with God before the world was created, and will remain in His presence forevermore." He is the embodiment of justice and Wisdom, seated on a throne in Heaven, who will be revealed to the world at the end of times, when he will judge all beings. (WIKIPEDIA)"

THE ABOVE IS AN EXCERPT FROM WIKIPEDIA. A DESCRIPTION OF "THE MESSIAH ACCORDING TO JUDAISM" AND THE BELIEF OF THE COMING OF THE MESSIAH AND HIS CHARACTER AND PERSONALITY. WHETHER YOU BELIEVE IN THIS OR NOT WE WILL NOT DELVE INTO THAT OR WHETHER S-HE IS AN ARCHETYPE. WE SAY S-HE CAUSE THE MESSIAH COULD BE A "SHE" OR A FULL ANDROGYNE HUMAN BEING.

THE POINT OF THIS DIARY IS TO "REMIND" THE RIGHT WINGERS FROM ALL OVER THE WORLD, CERTAIN FACTS ABOUT THE MESSIANIC FIGURE AND THAT UNFORTUNATELY DO NOT CORRESPOND TO THE "CHARACTER, ACTIONS, PERSONALITIES AND SPIRITUALITIES" OF THE SO CALLED "DEFENDERS OF THE FAITH" OR THOSE WHO CLAIM TO BE "REPRESENTATIVES OF THE MESSIAH." WHETHER IT IS A RABBI OR PASTOR OR IMAM OR POLITICO OR PRIME MINISTER OR WHATEVER IN THEIR RIGHT OR LEFT WING MIND….!!!

WE ARE RESPONDING TO THE CLAIM OF THE SO CALLED "DEFENDERS AND REPRESENTATIVES" OF THE FAITH WHO ARE CONDONING AND PERPETUATING AND CARRYING OUT ALL SORTS OF EVIL ACTIONS AND INDOCTRINATIONS AND PROMOTING—-HATE SPEECH, LIES AND DECEIT, COVERING UP THE TRUTH OF THE DIVINE WITH FALSEHOODS, PERPETRATING AND CONDONING VIOLENCE AND INJUSTICE AND MURDER, ETC. ETC. ETC.

OUR QUESTION TO "YOU" IS—- DO YOU THINK IN YOUR SICKEST MINDS THAT THE SO CALLED MESSIAH YOU ARE EXPECTING AND FOR WHOM YOU ARE CARRYING OUT ALL THESE EVILS IN PALESTINE AND JUSTIFYING THESE WITH ALL SORTS OF EVIL IDEOLOGIES, WILL BE HAPPY AND CONTENT AND GIVE YOU ALL AN AWARD FOR—-BRINGING HIM OUT OF THE HEAVENLY BURROW — BY CARRYING OUT EVIL AND HATE AND MURDER IN HIS - HER "NAMES?????"

THE ELOHIM STATE THAT YOU MUST BE VERY SICK OF THY MINDS AND HAVE FALLEN INTO THE DISEASE AND TRAP OF DELUSION BY THINKING THAT YOU CAN MANIPULATE THE SO CALLED MESSIAH TO DO YOUR BIDDING AND COME OUT OF HIS BURROW BY MEANS OF ALL THAT ….EVIL!!!!!!????????????????? AND ON TOP OF ALL THAT EXPECT HIM TO COME OUT WITH A HUGE SMILE AND OPEN ARMS "HAPPY AND GLAD" FOR ALL THE MISERY AND PAIN AND EVIL AND HURT AND DEATH THAT YOU HAVE INFLICTED UPON OTHERS IN HIS NAMES!!!!

YOU HAVE SOILED HIS NAME WITH INNOCENT BLOOD AS IN THE BOOK OF REVELATIONS!

THEREFORE, THE ELOHIM WISH TO LET THE "DECEIVERS" ON TOP AND IN POWER KNOW THAT CARRYING OUT SUCH EVILS IN THE NAME OF THE HOLY OF HOLIES IS EQUIVALENT TO "TARNISHING AND DESECRATING THE UTENSILS OF THE TEMPLE OF THE LADY AND THE LORD" WHICH ARE THE "COSMIC VALUES AND PRINCIPLES OF THE LIGHT, LOVE AND LIFE." !!!!

"THE ARK OF COMMUNICATION" OR OUR "BIPOLAR GATES" BY WHICH WE COMMUNICATE WITH YOU ABOUT YOUR EVIL CONCOCTIONS WOULD LIKE TO REMIND YOU THAT ALL YOU HAVE ACCOMPLISHED IS TO DEFILE AND BRING SADNESS TO THE "HEART OF THE OCEAN AND OF THE UNIVERSE."

SINCERELY, "THE ROSE OF SHA-R-ON AND ELIYAH THE JUST"

---

## 94. "THE PENAL COLONY" OF KAFKA: LEAVING BEHIND THE AGE OF KALI TO WELCOME THE AGE OF ILLUMINATION AND AQUARIUS

THE PENAL COLONY IS ANOTHER ONE OF THOSE MAGNIFICENT AND INTERESTING PSYCHOLOGICALLY CHARGED STORIES OF FRANZ KAFKA.

DOES NOT THE WORLD AT TIMES FEEL LIKE WE ARE LIVING AND ARE TRAPPED IN A PENAL COLONY OF SORTS FLOATING IN SPACE? THIS COULD BE PARADISE BUT FOR MANY TODAY IT FEELS FAR FROM THAT AND RATHER RESEMBLES A TRAP. LIKE BEING TRAPPED IN A PRISON CELL OF SORTS AS IN ... LIVING IN FEAR OF POLITICAL AND ECONOMIC AND SOCIAL UNREST AND DISEASE AND SO MANY MORE VARIABLES THAT WE INDIVIDUALLY DO NOT HAVE CONTROL OVER. BUT THAT COLLECTIVELY IF WE WANTED WE COULD CHANGE FOR BETTER AND MAKE THE PRISON INTO A BEAUTIFUL AND EXCITING "STATE OF PARADISE."

AND SO TO SUM UP KAFKA'S STORY, HERE IS A PENAL COLONY WHERE THIS STORY TAKES PLACE IN WHICH THOSE WHO "DISOBEY" AUTHORITY, EVEN IF IT'S FORGETTING TO PREPARE "BIG BROTHER'S COFFEE IN THE MORNING," ARE CONDEMNED TO —TORTURE AND DEATH. IT HAPPENS THAT ONE OF THE INMATES FAILS TO CARRY OUT ORDERS AS SPECIFIED AND IS SENT TO THE TORTURE/ DEATH CHAMBER TO BE EXECUTED. THE METHOD OF EXECUTION IS HORRENDOUS IN THAT LITTLE BY LITTLE BLOOD IS DRAINED FROM A PERSON AND LIFE IS SUCKED OUT AN INMATE'S SYSTEM.

IT HAPPENS THAT LATER IN THE NOVEL, A TOURIST FROM ANOTHER COUNTRY IS INVITED TO VIEW THE EXECUTION AND SO THE GUY IN

CHARGE OF THE EXECUTION EXPECTS THE TOURIST TO AGREE WITH THESE OUTDATED, INHUMANE, NONSENSICAL AND UNJUST TORTURE TACTICS AND PRACTICES. THE LAND WHERE THE TOURIST COMES FROM CARRIES OUT "JUSTICE AND PUNISHMENT" DIFFERENTLY IN A CIVILIZED AND HUMANE WAY AND AFTER THE "REHABILITATION MODEL." NOT THIS OUTDATED AND HORRIBLE WAY OF THE PENAL COLONY.

AND SO TO END THE DISCOURSE, THE TOURIST OBJECTS TO THESE METHODS AND THE INMATE IS SAVED. BUT THE OFFICER IN CHARGE OF THE EXECUTION TAKES THE PLACE OF THE INMATE AND HE ENDS UP ......

I WILL LEAVE THE REST TO YOUR IMAGINATION SO THAT YOU READ THIS STORY YOURSELF.

AND SO ONE OF THE MORALS OF THIS STORY IS ABOUT WHAT WE DISCUSSED EARLIER IN THE DIARY ABOUT THE "PSYCHO"-POMP LEADING THE SOULS TO A STATE OF PARADISE aka A PSYCHOLOGICAL AND CONSCIOUS STATE OF BEING. IN IN TODAY'S HUMANITY, IT WOULD BE LIKE COMING OUT OF THE "MINDSET OF THE AGE OF KALI AND CORRUPTION AND THE DYSFUNCTIONAL PAST" AND GETTING INTO THE" MINDSET OF LIFE, HEALTH AND COOPERATION!!" IN ORDER FOR THE WORLD AND HUMANITY TO CONTINUE ON THEIR HUMAN-DIVINE JOURNEY IN THIS PLANET.

AND SO, THE "OFFICER WITH HIS OUTDATED AND TERRIBLE WAYS OF EXECUTING AND JUDGING PEOPLE" REPRESENTS THE MINDSET THAT REFUSES TO CHANGE AND ADAPT AND EMBRACE BETTER WAYS — HOLISTIC WAYS— OF DOING THINGS, TREATING LIFE OVERALL, AND THE PLANET. HE IS SO SET IN HIS OLD DYSFUNCTIONAL WAYS, THAT HE RATHER DIE TO UPHOLD THESE WHEN THAT IS NOT EVEN NECESSARY BECAUSE HE CAN ALSO EMBRACE A BETTER WAY AND ENJOY THE BENEFITS ALONG WITH EVERYONE ELSE. THE TOURIST ON THE OTHER HAND, REPRESENTS THE AGE OF AQUARIUS AND THE NEW WAY OF TAKING CARE OF ONE ANOTHER, ALL LIFE AND THE PLANET ITSELF. WHICH ENSURES THAT THE "INMATE AND THE TOURIST" CONTINUE ON LIVING IN A BETTER AND MORE CONSCIENTIOUS AND HUMANE WAY.

EVENTUALLY THE TORTURE MACHINE MALFUNCTIONS WHICH REPRESENTS THE SYSTEM THAT MANKIND HAS SET UP AND WHICH IS NOT FUNCTIONING PROPERLY AS EXPECTED SINCE IT HAS STRUCTURAL AND SYSTEMIC PROBLEMS AND THE MAIN REASON THAT PEOPLE TODAY ARE SUFFERING AND STRUGGLING AND ARE UNHAPPY ALL OVER THE GLOBE.

SO WE HOPE YOU HAVE ENJOYED THIS BRIEF SYNOPSIS OF "THE PENAL COLONY" AND HOPE THAT JUST LIKE MOSES AND ANUBIS LEADING US AWAY FROM "THE DARK AND INTO THE LIGHT," WE CAN LEAVE BEHIND THE TORTURE CHAMBER WAYS OF DOING THINGS AND TAKING CARE

OF THE PLANET AND ONE ANOTHER AND EMBRACE THE —NEW AGE OF AQUARIUS' FEELING AND SPIRIT! A NEW DAY IS DAWNING, INDEED.

SINCERELY, "THE COSMIC TOURIST" PASSING BY THIS EARTH TO CHECK THINGS OUT

---

## 95. TO THE ZIONIST STATE OF —IS-RA-EL: LISTEN TO "THE CALL" OF MASHIAH AND REFUSE TO SERVE ANYMORE THE WILL OF "THE BEAST"

YOU HAVE POWER LIKE PHARAOH OVER THE PEOPLE OF PALESTINE. YOU INCITE "EVIL AND VIOLENCE" ON A PEOPLE THAT ARE UNDER YOUR YOKE!!!

YOU ARE INDEED VIOLATING THE "PASSOVER" STORY AND ITS SYMBOLS. FOR "WE" KNOW THAT "YOU" KNOW VERY WELL WHAT YOU ARE DOING IN ORDER TO INCITE VIOLENCE AND BLOODSHED ON ANOTHER. LIKE IN THE STORY OF THE "ANUSIM" THEMSELVES. YOU ARE FORCING THE "ISRAELI" PEOPLE TO GO AFTER EVIL AND VIOLENCE ON ANOTHER IN "OUR NAMES" WHICH IS EQUIVALENT TO "TAKING THE HOLY UTENSILS OF THE L-OR-D AND TARNISHING THEM" WITH YOUR EVIL AND UNJUST WAYS AND WITH THE BLOOD OF THE INNOCENT WHOM ARE "UNDER YOUR YOKE." WHICH MEANS THAT ALL ALONG YOU HAVE "HAD THE FULL ADVANTAGE OVER THEM" AND MEANWHILE "DRINKING OF THE WELL OF ANNU-$$$$$EE TO BENEFIT YOURSELF TO PERPETRATE INJUSTICE AND VIOLENCE OVER AND OVER AGAIN EXPECTING A DIFFERENT RESULT. YOUR ACTIONS FEED THE CRIES FOR RETALIATION AND JUSTICE FROM YOUR NEIGHBORS FOR YOUR OWN TRANSGRESSIONS AND INIQUITIES OVER THE PEOPLE UNDER YOUR OPPRESSION, TYRANNY AND YOKE. DOING ALL ON PURPOSE KNOWING WELL THE "RESULTS" OF YOUR ACTIONS IN ORDER TO JUSTIFY FURTHER EVIL AND BLOODSHED.

WE— DO NOT —DEAL NEITHER "CONSORT" WITH EVIL-DOERS AND THOSE THAT ENABLE IT IN OUR HOLY NAMES NO MATTER HOW MUCH THEY PRAY TO US ON THAT WALL. WE REFUSE TO LISTEN UNTIL YOU TURN AWAY FROM YOUR BLOODLINESS AND SET UP JUSTICE UPON MORIAH FOR "ALL PEOPLES INCLUDING THE PALESTINIAN.".

THEREFORE, AS YOU HAVE BENEFITED ALL ALONG AND DRANK YOUR FILL OF "OUR AMERICAN PIE" WE DEMAND THE RESTORATION OF PEACE AND THE ESTABLISHMENT OF JUSTICE AND OBSERVANCE OF "OUR HIGHER VALUES AND PRINCIPLES" LEAVING BEHIND THE "BEAST" ENERGY AND YOUR SERVICE TO IT BY YOUR TRANSGRESSIONS.

YOU TAKE "OUR" HOLY UTENSILS AND DEFILE THEM BY MANIPULATING EMOTIONS FOR THE SOLE PURPOSE OF GETTING AWAY WITH YOUR EVIL DEEDS UPON THE PEOPLE, AND IT WILL NO LONGER WORK. THERE ARE POWERS ABOVE YOU THAT YOU SHOULD FEAR AND LISTEN TO.

SHALL WE CONDEMN LEBANON AND THE PEOPLES NEED TO PROTECT THEMSELVES FROM YOUR EVIL ENCROACHMENT AND ABUSES UPON THE OTHER? YES, WE CONDEMN VIOLENCE BUT — WE CONDEMN FIRST AND FOREMOST THE CAUSE OF THE VIOLENCE WHICH STEMS FROM YOUR EVIL DOINGS AND LOVE OF BLOODSHED. BEING THE PRECURSOR TO ALL THAT VIOLENCE.

THEREFORE, "COME BACK TO US" AND "REFUSE TO SERVE THE BEAST" NO LONGER SO THAT WE CAN BEGIN TO HEAL AND MOVE ONTO SATYA. FOR ONLY JUSTICE WILL PREVAIL AND ONLY THOSE WHO UPHOLD THE "DIVINE VALUES AND PRINCIPLES" WILL PASS —OVER TO THE OTHER SIDE. YOU ARE "NOT" AN EXCEPTION. AND WE WILL—NOT— OVERLOOK YOUR EVIL AND TRANSGRESSION SUCH AS WE DID NOT 2000YEARS AGO. IS TIME FOR PEOPLE ISRAEL TO WAKE UP AND FOLLOW "THE PIPER OF THE MAY QUEEN" aka THE HOLY SHE-KI-INNA.

REMEMBER "2018" OF THE MIGHTY ELOHIM FOR YOU "KNOW" WHAT "WE" ARE REFERRING TO.

SINCERELY,
ELOHIM

---

## 96.  ZIONISM VS. DEMOCRACY:" THE INTEGRATION AND UNION OF A SOCIETY AS EXEMPLIFIED BY THE MOST DIVERSE CITY IN THE WORLD AS IS "THE BIG APPLE" NYC!

SO THE EXAMPLE OF A DEMOCRACY IS THE "UNITED STATES." AND SO "ISRAEL - PALESTINE" IF IT CALLS ITSELF A DEMOCRACY MUST AND SHOULD FOLLOW THE SAME EXAMPLE. THE ISSUE HERE IS THAT THE IDEOLOGY BEHIND ZIONISM IS INCOMPATIBLE WITH THAT OF A "TRUE FULL FLEDGED DEMOCRATIC SYSTEM."

AS WE EXPLAINED BEFORE IN THE MEANING BEHIND THE NAME Y-ERU-SHALEM, THAT THE NAME STANDS FOR "ERU" AS IN "INTEGRATION AND WHOLENESS." TO MAKE SOMETHING "WHOLE" IS FOR A SOCIETY TO BE RELATIVELY HEALTHY AND—INTEGRATED! AN EXAMPLE OF AN INTEGRATED AND "WHOLE" DEMOCRATIC SOCIETY IN WHICH DIVERSE

ELEMENTS CO-EXIST AND LIVE TOGETHER IN RELATIVE FUNCTIONING AND PEACE IS "NEW YORK CITY."

ZIONISM IS NOT COMPATIBLE WITH A DEMOCRATIC SYSTEM BECAUSE IT'S ALL ABOUT EXCLUSIVISM AND DENYING THOSE WHO ARE NOT OF A CERTAIN LABEL THEIR UNALIENABLE HUMAN AND CIVIL RIGHTS. SEPARATING PEOPLE ON PURPOSE ACCORDING TO A LABEL AND DENYING THE OTHERS THEIR HUMAN AND CIVIL RIGHTS ARE NOT QUALITIES OF A DEMOCRATIC SYSTEM. JUST AS EVERYONE IN THE UNITED STATES HAS THE RIGHT TO VOTE FOR REPRESENTATIVES AND EVERYONE BORN HERE IS A CITIZEN, SO IT SHOULD BE IN ISRAEL - PALESTINE THAT ISRAELI AND "PALESTINIAN" ALIKE SHOULD ENJOY THE SAME EQUAL HUMAN AND CIVIL RIGHTS AND EACH ONE HAVE A VOICE IN REGARDS TO GOVERNMENT AND BE A CITIZEN BY BIRTH IN THE LAND. THIS IS AN EXAMPLE OF AN INTEGRATED SYSTEM THAT PROMOTES PEACE AND MUTUAL UNDERSTANDING BETWEEN PEOPLES. THE "NEW YORK CITY" EXAMPLE SHOWS CLEARLY THAT IT WORKS.

AN APARTHEID SYSTEM AND A DEMOCRATIC SYSTEM ARE INCOMPATIBLE WITH EACH OTHER AND IS LIKE TRYING TO MIX OIL WITH WATER. CALLING AN APARTHEID SYSTEM A DEMOCRACY IS A "1984" PLAY OF WORDS IN ORDER TO COVER THE TRUTH OF A SYSTEM OF GOVERNMENT THAT IS NOT WHAT IT CLAIMS TO BE. AS ZIONISM'S GOAL IS TO "MAKE PALESTINE A SOLE JEWISH STATE" THE AIM OF THE IDEOLOGY AND ITS MOVEMENT IS TO FIND ANY WAY TO JUSTIFY WHAT IS UNDEMOCRATIC AT ANY COSTS IN ORDER TO CARRY OUT THE "FANTASY OF AN 100% JEWISH NATION." HOW ARE YOU GOING TO HAVE A FULL FLEDGED DEMOCRACY IN A LAND ALREADY INHABITED BY NON ZIONIST INDIGENOUS PEOPLES INCLUDING PALESTINIAN JEWS AND CHRISTIANS AND MUSLIMS AND ARMENIANS AND OTHER PEOPLES WHO ALREADY ARE "CITIZENS BY BIRTH" IN THAT LAND AND WHO ARE DENIED THAT CITIZENSHIP AND ALL RIGHTS AND PRIVILEGES THAT THEY DESERVE JUST BECAUSE THEY ARE NOT JEWISH BY RELIGION AND ZIONIST BY POLITICAL AFFILIATION?

IS THAT EVEN POSSIBLE? YES!!! IN THE UNITED STATES THROUGHOUT ITS HISTORY MANY PEOPLES WERE DENIED THE RIGHT TO VOTE INCLUDING WOMEN. BUT THROUGHOUT THE EVOLUTION AND DEVELOPMENT OF THE NATION INTO A DEMOCRACY, THOSE WHO WERE DENIED THOSE RIGHTS WERE GIVEN THOSE RIGHTS THANKS TO ACTIVISTS AND CIVIL RIGHTS MOVEMENTS ETC. AND SO JUST AS IT WAS WITH THE NATION, SO IT CAN BE WITH ISRAEL - PALESTINE IN WHICH PALESTINIANS CAN BE GIVEN THEIR CIVIL AND HUMAN RIGHTS AND —HEALING OF THE PEOPLE — CAN BEGIN ASAP. HEALING IS "WHOLENESS" AND IT CAN HAPPEN ONLY THROUGH INTEGRATION WHICH IS WHAT THE NAME Y-ERU-SHALEM

MEANS AND ALSO JUST AS IT WAS BEFORE 1948 WHEN PALESTINIAN JEW, CHRISTIAN AND MUSLIM LIVED IN RELATIVE PEACE AND COEXISTENCE.

THEREFORE, IF ISRAEL CALLS ITSELF A DEMOCRACY BUT DOES NOT "RESEMBLE" WHAT THE UNITED STATES IS ABOUT, IT'S REALLY NOT A FULL FLEDGED DEMOCRACY AND HAS A VERY LONG WAY TO GO TO BECOME A REAL ONE. THE QUESTION IS…WILL THE NATION CHOOSE TO CONTINUE ITS "ZIONIST PATH" WHICH IS UNSUSTAINABLE AND UNREALISTIC OR WILL IT CHOOSE THE "DEMOCRATIC PATH" WHICH IS POSSIBLE AS EXEMPLIFIED BY THE UNITED STATES AND "NEW YORK CITY'S LAZARUS POEM???" IT MUST CHOOSE ONE. SINCE BOTH CONCEPTS ARE NOT COMPATIBLE WITH EACH OTHER.

SINCERELY, "LADY LIBERT-US AND HER A-MARIE-KI-ANNE INTEGRATED AND WHOLE PIE"

---

## 97. THE HISTORICAL PATTERN OF "THE VIOLATION OF ETHICS AND HUMAN RIGHTS" IN THE "CHURCH/SYNAGOGUE/MOSQUE STATE" MODEL WHEN "THE INTERPRETATION OF THE RULE OF LAW IS TINGED BY THE "COMMANDS OF GOD" WHEN THESE ARE BASED ON "THE DARK SIDE" OF SCRIPTURE

DO YOU REMEMBER HOW THE HISTORICAL PERIOD OF "CHURCH AND STATE" BACK IN THE DAYS IN EUROPE WAS THE MAIN CAUSE OF SLAVERY AND "WITCH" BURNINGS AND JEWISH PERSECUTION AND PAGAN PERSECUTION AND NATIVE AMERICAN GENOCIDE AND FRATRICIDE BETWEEN CHRISTIAN DENOMINATIONS? JUST TO NAME A FEW OF THE TRAGIC EVENTS.

ONE OF THE REASONS WHY IT TURNED OUT TO BE THAT WAY IS BECAUSE THE "AUTHORITY" WHETHER IT WAS THE KING OR A GROUP WERE IN DIRECT CONSORT WITH THE CHURCH WHO AT THAT TIME WAS THE SOLE INTERPRETER OF THE SCRIPTURES. THEREFORE, AS THE GOVERNMENT WAS IN ASSOCIATION AND UNDER THE INFLUENCE OF THE "CHURCH," EVERY DECISION MADE WAS MADE ACCORDING TO THE OFFICIAL SCRIPTURAL INTERPRETATION "OF THE LAW." THIS REALLY BACKFIRED BECAUSE, FEW WERE WHO WOULD INTERPRET SCRIPTURE ACCORDING TO THE "TENETS OF JESUS' LOVE, MERCY AND FORGIVENESS," SADLY, THE MAJORITY IN POWER CHOSE TO INTERPRET SCRIPTURES ACCORDING TO THE CONCEPTS FOUND IN "THE MOSAIC LAW," "THE PAULINE LAW" AND "THE JESUS AS JUDGE AND DESTROYER" OF THE REVELATIONS OF JOHN.

AND SO THE "LAW OF THE LAND" WOULD BE TINGED AND OR REDACTED ACCORDING TO THE "INTERPRETATION AND VIEWS" OF WHOMEVER WAS IN CHARGE OF THE SCRIPTURAL INTERPRETATION AND WHO WOULD INTERPRET THE BIBLE ACCORDING TO HIS OWN MENTAL- EMOTIONAL-PSYCHOLOGICAL-RELIGIOUS AND —ETHICAL OR MORAL— STATES AND STANDARDS. THE RESULTS WERE OFTEN TO PASS AND SANCTION LAWS AND DECISIONS THAT WOULD END UP "CAUSING HARM" ONTO PEOPLE JUSTIFIED IN THAT IT HAD TO BE THAT WAY "BECAUSE GOD SAYS IT SOMEWHERE IN THE BIBLE" AND IF "GOD HARMS PEOPLE IN THE BIBLE STORY" THAT WOULD MEAN THAT "IT IS GOD'S WILL THAT WE HARM AS WELL OTHERS IN THE NAME OF GOD OR ON HIS BEHALF."

THE PROBLEM IS THAT — THE CHURCH— TOOK THE BIBLE AS BEING ALL "ONE BOOK" IN WHICH EACH INDIVIDUAL PART AGREES OR COMPLEMENTS THE OTHERS. THIS IS A MISTAKE BECAUSE THE "BOOKS OF THE BIBLE" ARE DIFFERENT WRITINGS CLUMPED TOGETHER AS ONE AND "EACH BOOK" CONTAINS A DIFFERENT MESSAGE OR THEME THAT IS UNIQUE TO THAT PARTICULAR WRITING AND WHICH MIGHT CONTRADICT THE OTHER WRITINGS. SUCH AS IN THE CASE OF "THE BOOK OF THE MOSAIC LAWS" THAT "JUDGE AND CONDEMN AND STONE TO DEATH" AND ON THE OTHER HAND, THE "BOOKS OF THE PROPHETS WHICH ARE ABOUT JUSTICE AND ETHICAL BEHAVIOR." WHEN YOU ADD THE "CHRISTIAN BOOKS" IT GETS MORE COMPLICATED BECAUSE "THE GOSPEL MESSAGE IS THE OPPOSITE OF THE MOSAIC MESSAGE" WHILE THE "PAULINE MESSAGE INTERPRETS THEOLOGY IN A MIXED BAG OF PHARISAICAL AND JESUS TRADITION." MEANWHILE, IN THE BOOK OF REVELATION" JESUS CEASES TO BE — THE FORGIVER OF SINS AND MERCY AND LOVE INCARNATE BUT THE DIVINE WARRIOR THAT JUDGES AND CONDEMNS TO DEATH AS IN THE MOSAIC TRADITION.:

THIS "MIX AND MATCH" OF IDEAS AND CONCEPTS AND THEMES THAT ARE DIFFERENT FROM EACH OTHER AND THAT CONTRADICT EACH OTHER — ENDS UP BECOMING THE BASIS FOR THE OFFICIAL INTERPRETER OF " "DIVINE LAW AND WORD" OF THE CHURCH-STATE TO PICK AND CHOOSE WHATEVER BIBLE VERSE AND THEME HE IS MORE IN CONSONANCE WITH AND TO USE THAT SCRIPTURE TO INTERPRET THE "RULE OF THE LAW" FROM THAT PARTICULAR VIEWPOINT. SINCE THERE ARE INJUNCTIONS OF BOTH "MERCY AND CONDEMNATION" IN THE BIBLE, WHATEVER THE INTERPRETER CHOOSES WILL ALSO DEPEND ON THE "ETHICAL AND MORAL—OR—UNETHICAL AND IMMORAL" UPBRINGING AND MINDSET OF THAT PERSON. INCLUDING HIS OR HER OWN "INCLINATION." MEANING THAT, IF THAT PERSON IS NATURALLY INCLINED TO "MURDER AND PUNISHMENT AND REVENGE" HE OR SHE WILL FIND MORE AFFINITY WITH THOSE VERSES IN THE BIBLE THAT CORRESPOND AND ALIGN WITH THAT

"ENERGY." ON THE OTHER HAND, IF THE INTERPRETER IS INCLINED MORE TO GOOD AND MERCY AND ETHICS, HE OR SHE WILL BE MORE INCLINED TO THOSE VERSES AND SCRIPTURAL TEACHINGS THAT ARE MORE IN CONSONANCE WITH THAT PARTICULAR ENERGY.

UNFORTUNATELY, AS THE CHURCH EVENTUALLY BECAME CLOSED OFF FROM ANY OTHER TYPE OF WISDOM AND SCIENCE AND PHILOSOPHY, THE INTERPRETATION AND APPLICATION OF THE THEOLOGY BECAME "EXCESSIVE OR EXTREME" AND NOT OPEN TO ANY OTHER FORM OF INTERPRETATION OR VIEWPOINT. EVENTUALLY, JUSTIFYING DEATH BY CLAIMING THAT "IT'S IN THE BIBLE" AND THAT "GOD'S WORD IS INFALLIBLE, INSPIRED AND HOLY AND THE ONLY RIGHT WAY OF THINKING AND VIEWING THE WORLD." IN ADDITION, THERE WERE THOSE AT THE TOP SUCH AS THE KING WHO WERE NOT RELIGIOUS BUT "SAW THE POWER AND INFLUENCE OF THE CHURCH ON THE PEOPLE VIA ITS OFFICIAL INTERPRETATION OF SCRIPTURE AND LAW" AS AN OPPORTUNITY FOR CONTROL AND INFLUENCE. THEREFORE, THESE INDIVIDUALS WOULD GO ALONG WITH THE CHURCH SUPPORTING AND PROMOTING SUCH INTERPRETATIONS IN ORDER TO ACCOMPLISH THEIR PERSONAL GOALS OF MONEY, POWER AND INFLUENCE. IN OTHER WORDS, SOMEONE WHO WAS INTERESTED IN TAKING THE LAND OF ANOTHER PERSON BY FORCE, WOULD CARRY OUT FAVORS OR PROVIDE BENEFITS TO THE CHURCH IN EXCHANGE FOR THE CHURCH'S HELP IN TAKING OVER THAT LAND. AND SO THE CHURCH WOULD COME IN WITH THE KING AND "IN THE NAME OF GOD AND ACCORDING TO WHAT THE BIBLE STATES IN THE STORY OF CANAAN AGAINST THE HEATHEN INFIDELS," AND THE WHOLE OPERATION WOULD BE JUSTIFIED AND BOTH WOULD BENEFIT FROM THE PLUNDER.

AND SO THE SAME PROCESS HAS HAPPENED IN THE CASE OF THE "KORAN" WHICH IS OPEN TO INTERPRETATION AND VERSE CHOOSING ACCORDING TO THE "MORAL AND ETHICAL – OR —IMMORAL AND UNETHICAL" MINDSET AND INCLINATION OF THAT PARTICULAR IMAM. HERE WE HAVE THE BASIS FOR THE "MUSLIM EXTREMISTS" SYNDROME.

ON THE OTHER HAND, WE HAVE THE CASE OF THE "SYNAGOGUE-STATE" COMBINATION TODAY IN THE ZIONIST STATE, WHERE THE SAME THING IS HAPPENING. THE "LAW OF THE LAND" IS BEING INTERPRETED ON THE BASIS OF THE "MOSAIC LAWS" AND OTHER CONCEPTS FOUND THERE THAT ARE NOT COMPATIBLE WITH THE "TEACHINGS OF THE PROPHETS." AS THE GOVERNMENT IS A COMBINATION OF "MOSAIC RELIGION AND THE LAW" THERE IS A HUGE –MORAL AND ETHICAL—BLUNDER TAKING PLACE THERE IN WHICH THE "LAW OF THE LAND" IS BEING TINGED AND INTERPRETED ACCORDING TO THOSE PARTS OF THE BIBLE THAT CONDONE "UNETHICAL AND UNJUST BEHAVIORS." AND SO THE "RULE OF LAW" IS

BEING APPLIED AND INTERPRETED ACCORDING TO THAT LENS. AND SO THE RESULTS ARE THE SAME AS THOSE OF THE "CHURCH-STATE" ABOVE, IN WHICH "THOSE EXERTING RELIGIOUS INFLUENCE ON GOVERNMENT" ARE INTERPRETING THE BIBLE ACCORDING TO THEIR "UNETHICAL AND IMMORAL" INCLINATION AND SO THAT IS THE WAY THE "RULE OF THE LAW" ENDS UP BEING APPLIED ON EVERYONE. PICKING AND CHOOSING THOSE PARTS OF SCRIPTURE THAT ALIGN WITH THEIR OWN WAY OF THINKING AND "PARTICULAR GOALS AND PLANS." AT THE END YOU HAVE A "COMBINATION OF POLITICAL AND RELIGIOUS IDEOLOGY" THAT WORKS TOGETHER "ACCORDING TO THE INTERPRETATION OF SCRIPTURES SUCH AS — THE CHOSEN PEOPLE, THE LAND OF CANAAN, THE HEATHEN NATIONS, GOD PUNISHING AND REJECTING THE SURROUNDING NATIONS, ETC. ETC. ETC. FOUND IN BIBLICAL WRITING WHICH INFLUENCES BOTH "RELIGION, LAW, AND ZIONISM" AND THE HISTORICAL TRAGEDIES BORN OF THIS ADULTEROUS RELIGIO-POLITICAL AFFAIR."

ON THE OTHER HAND, WE HAVE THE EVANGELICAL CHURCHES FACING THE SAME PROCESS UNABLE TO MAKE THEIR MINDS WHETHER TO "EMBRACE LOVE AS JESUS" OR "WHETHER TO PUNISH AND MURDER THE SINNER AS IN LEVITICUS." AND SO THERE IS A "CONFLICT BETWEEN ONE THING AND THE OTHER." SUPPORTING AND ENABLING AND CONDONING AS "GODS WILL" WHAT IS TRANSPIRING IN "PALESTINE" BASED ON THE SAME "FLAW" AS EVERYONE ELSE IN THE MONOTHEISTIC TRADITIONS. JUSTIFYING THE UNJUSTIFIABLE AS TO BE "THE WILL AND WORD OF GOD BECAUSE GOD TOLD THE ISRAELITES TO WIPE THE CANAANITES AND TAKE THE LAND BY FORCE." WHICH IN TURN CONTRADICTS THE "GOSPEL" MESSAGE AND ALSO THE "CODES OF ETHICS AND MORALS OF THE PROPHETICAL BOOKS" AND THE "GLOBAL CODES OF HUMAN AND CIVIL RIGHTS" THAT THEY CLAIM TO UPHOLD. "THE DO UNTO OTHERS WHAT YOU WOULD LIKE TO BE DONE UNTO YOU" OF JESUS IS IGNORED AND THE "EXECUTE THE EVIL HEATHENS WHO DON'T BELIEVE IN GOD" IS CHOSEN. YOU SEE HERE THE SAME "PICK AND CHOOSE" WHATEVER VERSE OR PART OF THE BIBLE FITS AND ALIGNS WITH YOUR PARTICULAR "INCLINATION WHETHER "GOOD OR EVIL" –"ETHICAL OR UNETHICAL." IF YOUR NATURE IS MORE INCLINED TO "VIOLENCE" YOU WILL CHOOSE "THE VIOLENCE IN THE BIBLE" TO CONFIRM AND APPLY YOUR BELIEFS AND MAKE YOUR DECISIONS. AND ON THE OTHER HAND, IF YOU ARE MORE INCLINED TO "GOOD" AND TO "ETHICAL BEHAVIORS" THAT IS WHAT YOU WILL CHOOSE FROM THE BIBLE AND WILL APPLY ON YOUR DECISIONS AND WORLD.

THEREFORE, WHAT WE HAVE TODAY IS A "CRISIS AND COLLAPSE OF BASIC ETHICS AND VALUES" IN RELIGION AND LAW AND IDEOLOGY, ETC.

ETC. ETC. AND SO — CAUSING PHYSICAL AND PSYCHO EMOTIONAL HARM ON EVERYBODY.

SINCERELY, THOTH, THE INTERPRETER OF SCRIPTURE

---

## 98.  "PRO-PALESTINE JEWS ARE NOT AN —--ANTI-SEMITIC HATE GROUP" —--!!!! A PHILOSOPHICAL COMMENTARY

THIS IS A TACTIC BORN OUT OF "FEAR!!!!" FEAR IN THE SENSE THAT "THE TIDE IS TURNING AND THE NARRATIVE IS NO LONGER WORKING!!! THEREFORE, THE ORGANIZATIONS USE THE "DISCREDITING" STRATEGY IN ORDER TO HARM PRO-PALESTINIAN JEWS.

WHY ARE "PRO-PALESTINIAN JEWS" NOW CALLED AN "ANTI-SEMITIC HATE GROUP" IF THEY ARE SUPPOSEDLY SEMITES THEMSELVES? THE LABELING ALSO WORKS THE OTHER WAY AROUND, IN THE SENSE THAT —-- "PRO- ZIONIST JEWS" ARE NOT CALLED AN "ANTI-SEMITIC HATE GROUP" WHEN THEY PERSECUTE AND MURDER PALESTINIANS WHO ARE ALSO "SEMITES AND WHO SPEAK ARABIC WHICH IS A SEMITIC LANGUAGE." REASON HEBREW AND ARABIC HAVE MANY WORDS IN COMMON OR THAT ARE SIMILAR AND EVEN SOUND ALMOST THE SAME.

PRO-PALESTINIAN GROUPS ARE A "PEACE MOVEMENT BASED ON JUST AND EQUAL TREATMENT" OF PEOPLES. WE ARE CLARIFYING THIS SINCE THE NARRATIVE FOR TOO LONG HAS BEEN TO VILIFY AND DEHUMANIZE PALESTINIANS IN ORDER TO SUSTAIN AND MAINTAIN THE OFFICIAL NARRATIVE THAT "PALESTINIANS ARE TERRIBLE PEOPLE UNABLE TO LIVE IN PEACE" WHICH HELPS FEED THE "ZIONIST EXTREME RIGHT MESSAGE" AND "SQUASH THE VOICE OF THE PALESTINIAN PEOPLE AND PRO- PEACE JEWISH MOVEMENTS."

PRO-PALESTINIAN JEWS ARE EQUIVALENT TO PRO-JEW PALESTINIANS. BOTH ARE FOR PEACE AND JUSTICE AND EQUALITY AND ARE THE "KEY" TO SOLVING AND RESOLVING THE ENTIRE CONFLICT SINCE BOTH ARE SIMPLY, LIKE WE STATED BEFORE, "PUTTING EACH OTHER IN EACH OTHERS SHOES AND GAINING EMPATHY AND UNDERSTANDING OF EACH OTHERS PAIN AND SUFFERING AND COMMON HUMANITY!!!

THAT IS THE WAY IT SHOULD BE!!! DON'T YOU THINK!!!??? WE ...THINK.... SO!!!!!

HOW DIFFERENT EVERYTHING WOULD BE AND HOW PEACEFUL EARTH WOULD BE IF PEOPLE WOULD CELEBRATE EACH OTHER'S HUMANITY RATHER THAN USING THE MIND AND THE MOUTH TO SPREAD AND

SUSTAIN HATRED AND DIVISION IN ORDER TO MAINTAIN THE ILLUSION OF "SECURITY." WHEN IN REALITY REAL SECURITY CAN ONLY COME ABOUT BY — LOOKING AFTER EACH OTHER AND MAKING SURE THAT JUSTICE IS APPLIED BY THOSE IN CHARGE EQUALLY ALL ACROSS THE BOARD." IF AND WHEN THAT IS NOT THE CASE, AS WE HAVE SEEN IN THE "FASCIST ZIONIST GOVERNMENT TODAY" — THE GOVERNMENT IS NOT ONLY UNJUST AND VIOLENT TOWARDS THE "ENEMY" BUT ALSO HAS TURNED AGAINST "THE SAME PEOPLE IT CLAIMS TO REPRESENT." BOTH THE "SECURITY AND JUSTICE FOR JEWS AND ISRAELIS AND PALESTINIANS ALIKE ARE INTERTWINED AND ARE DEPENDENT ON EACH OTHER." AND IT MAKES SENSE SINCE SOMEONE WHO LACKS A STRONG ETHICAL / MORAL BACKBONE AND TRUE VALUES AND PRINCIPLES OF THE LIGHT WILL EVENTUALLY TURN AGAINST EVERYONE BECAUSE "THE TRUTH AND JUSTICE ARE NON-EXISTENT IN THAT PERSON OR GROUP OR IDEOLOGY" EXCEPT WHEN USED TO MANIPULATE PEOPLE TO CARRY OUT THEIR UNETHICAL/IMMORAL AIMS AND SELFISH AGENDAS.

THEREFORE THE ONES DOING THE "HATE" ARE NOT THE "PRO-PALESTINIAN JEWS!!!" BUT RATHER PRO-PALESTINIAN JEWS ARE "LOVING THEIR BRETHREN" AND IS NOT THAT "WHAT YESHUA STATED WE SHOULD DO???" –LOL— AND SO, THOSE WHO ARE USING THEIR POWER AND INFLUENCE AND POSITION TO PUSH THE NARRATIVE OF HATE AND DIVISION AND PERPETUAL WAR AND MURDER BETWEEN PEOPLES ARE THE ACTUAL "HATE GROUPS" WE SHOULD ALL BEWARE OF. THINK ABOUT IT …..

THINK ABOUT IT ….

IF A GROUP SUCH AS "PRO-PALESTINE JEW GROUPS" ARE PROMOTING "LOVE AND UNDERSTANDING AND PEACE BETWEEN JEWS AND PALESTINIANS" …WOULD YOU CALL THAT "HATE???" OH PLEASE, LET'S CALL THINGS AS THEY REALLY ARE AND STOP MISUSING AND CONFUSING LANGUAGE AND TERMS AND WORDS ON PURPOSE. THOSE WHO "PROMOTE THE NARRATIVE OF PERPETUAL HATE AND MURDER BETWEEN THE JEW AND PALESTINIAN" ARE ACTUALLY THE ONES PROMOTING "HATE" WHICH IS EXACTLY —WHAT—HATE IS DEFINED AS WHICH IS ABOUT "HATING AND MURDERING EACH OTHER" AND NOT ABOUT "PEACE, LOVE AND UNDERSTANDING!"

THEREFORE, WHO IS THE REAL ….."HATE GROUP" PROMOTING "BAD???"

SINCERELY, PHILO—"SOPHIA" AND THE LIGHT OF THE COSMIC CHRIST

### 99. Y-"ERU"-SHALEM: THE "ERA OF PEACE" AND THE STATE OF "INTEGRATION AND WHOLENESS" —- FROM REPRESENTING A DEAD EMPTY IDOL —TOWARDS — BECOMING THE CITY OF PEACE AND INTEGRATION FOR ALL PEOPLES

Eru (ಎರು):—[verb] to become an integrated whole. Eru (ಎರು):—[noun] = ಎರುಗು [erugu]. 1) [verb] to go to a higher level, position or place; to rise; to ascend; to mount; to climb up. 2) [verb] to advance in social status, rank, importance. (WISDOM LIBRARY).

FROM THE SACRED LANGUAGE OF "SAN-SKRIT" OR "SANCTA SCRITURA" THE HOLY WRITING AND ALPHABET, THE TERM "ERU" REFERS TO "INTEGRATION AND WHOLENESS!!!" TO RISE AND TO ASCEND AND TO CLIMB UP THE REEEALLLL MOUNT SION!!!!

THE TERM "ERU" ALSO SHARES THE LATIN LETTERS FOR "ERA" OR AGE. ON THE OTHER HAND, "SHALEM" REFERS TO THE ARAMAIC TERM FOR "PEACE" AND BEING "WHOLE." IN OTHER WORDS, THE NAME OF THE CITY STANDS FOR THE …

"ERA OF PEACE AND WHOLENESS" WHICH CAN ONLY BE ACCOMPLISHED BY "INTEGRATION AND UNION" OF ALL PEOPLES ON EARTH; RISING UP TO A HIGHER LEVEL IN OUR HUMANITY OR "HIGHER CONSCIOUSNESS" WHICH IS THE ONLY WAY THAT "ERA OF PEACE" CAN HAPPEN.

THEREFORE, THE DIVISION OF PEOPLE AND SEPARATION THAT IS TAKING PLACE THERE RIGHT NOW AND THE ENSUING HATRED, DISTRUST AND VIOLENCE AMONGST PEOPLES IS AGAINST THE "SPIRIT BEHIND THE CONCEPT AND NAME OF Y-ERU-SHALEM AND THE TRUE SION." LOGICALLY, THERE CAN BE NO PEACE OR ERA OF PEACE WHEN PEOPLE ARE ENCOURAGED BY THE POWERS THAT BE TO HATE EACH OTHER AND LIVE IN PERPETUAL HATE AND DISTRUST OF EACH OTHER CAUSING WAR AND EVIL AND MURDER!!!

AS THE NAME Y-"ERU-SHALEM" STATES, THE ONLY WAY UP AND OUT OF THE TERRIBLE CONDITIONS IN THE LAND OF PALESTINE IS TO EMBRACE AND TEACH PEOPLE "THE PRINCIPLES OF PEACE AND COEXISTENCE" AND "INTEGRATION THAT LEADS TO WHOLENESS" JUST AS IT WAS BEFORE 1948 WHEN "PALESTINIAN JEWS AND CHRISTIANS AND MUSLIMS" USED TO LIVE IN RELATIVE PEACE AND UNDERSTANDING. AS WE EXPLAINED YESTERDAY, THIS CAN ONLY HAPPEN WHEN PEOPLE STOP BUILDING ALL TYPES OF RELIGIOUS AND PSYCHOLOGICAL AND EMOTIONAL AND PHYSICAL WALLS AND START REACHING OUT TO EACH OTHER IN

GOOD WILL AND IN THE NAME OF THEIR COMMON HUMANITY. THOSE ENCOURAGING FRAGMENTATION POSSESS A FRAGMENTED AND NOT AN INTEGRATED OR WHOLY (HOLY) MIND. REASON THESE FRAGMENTED MINDS ARE FAR AWAY FROM BEING HOLY AND ARE RATHER IN A VERY UNHOLY STATE.

THE REASON "Y-ERU-SHALEM" OR "ERA OF PEACE AND UNDERSTANDING" IS NOT TAKING PLACE IS MAINLY BECAUSE THE "MEN IN CHARGE IN BOTH THE RELIGIOUS AND THE POLITICAL ARENAS" ARE EXACERBATING THE HATE AND VIOLENCE AND LACK OF TRUST BETWEEN PEOPLES. WERE YOU TO REPLACE THE "WARMONGERS AND HATE FILLED LEADERS" THAT ONLY FEED MORE OF THE SAME INTO THEIR OWN GROUPS AND PEOPLES, WITH "MEN AND WOMEN OF GOODWILL" WE WOULD BE SEEING A VERY DIFFERENT STORY IN THE LAND. HOWEVER, THE "ROLE MODELS" IN CONTROL OF THE NARRATIVE AND MENTAL-EMOTIONAL INFLUENCE OF THE PEOPLE ARE NOT THE TYPE OF MEN AND WOMEN WHO CAN BRING PEOPLE TOGETHER AND SPREAD GOODWILL.

WHEN YOU HAVE "LEADERS" SPREADING LIES AND HATEFUL SPEECH ABOUT OTHERS, THAT IS THE SPIRIT THAT WILL MULTIPLY IN THE PEOPLE. PEOPLE LOOK UP TO THEIR LEADERS. BEING IN A POSITION OF INFLUENCE AND POWER CARRIES GREAT RESPONSIBILITY THAT SHALL NOT BE PLAYED WITH BECAUSE WE ARE DEALING HERE WITH "LIFE AND DEATH" AND THE "FATES AND LIVES OF PEOPLE EVERYWHERE."

"ERU" ALSO SHARES THE ROOT WORD OF "ARA OR ARI OR ORO" WHICH STANDS FOR "LIGHT, GOLD, ELECTRICITY, ETC. ETC. ETC. IN ANCIENT ARAMAIC. AND SO "Y-URI-SHALEM' ALSO STANDS FOR "THE LIGHT AND FIRE OF PEACE." THE FACT THAT THERE HAS BEEN NO PEACE FOR THE PAST 75 YEARS AND THE SITUATION KEEPS GETTING WORSE BY THE DAY MAKES IT CLEAR THAT "SOMETHING VERY WRONG AND OUTRIGHT EVIL" HAS TAKEN HOLD OF THE "CITY OF PEACE" AND THAT THE OPPOSITE OF "INTEGRATION, WHOLENESS AND LIGHT AND PEACE" IS HAPPENING THERE.

THAT JEWS AND ISRAELIS AND PALESTINIANS AND ARABS AND EVERYONE ELSE CANNOT GET ALONG AND LIVE TOGETHER IS NOT BECAUSE OF THE CLICHE THAT "THEY HAVE BEEN FIGHTING EACH OTHER FOR CENTURIES" BUT BECAUSE "THE POWERS THAT HOLD THE LAND TODAY DO NOT WISH THAT TO BE THE CASE." SIMPLE AS THAT.

AS WE EXPLAINED BEFORE, WHEN SOMETHING DOES NOT LIVE UP TO ITS SIGNIFICANCE OR MEANING OR REPRESENTATION IT BECOMES A MERE "IDOL!!" THE FACT THAT Y-ERU-SHALEM HAS BECOME A CITY OF CONFLICT AND DIVISION AND HATE AND WAR AND STRIFE MAKES IT CLEAR THAT "THE CITY OF PEACE" NO LONGER REPRESENTS THAT AND THAT INSTEAD

IT HAS BECOME AN EMPTY IDOL BECAUSE IT IS NOT WHAT IT WAS MEANT TO BE ANYMORE, "AN EXAMPLE OF PEACE AND COEXISTENCE AND INTEGRATION....WHOLENESS." IT MAKES NO SENSE FOR IT TO BE CALLED "CITY OF PEACE" WHILE THE PEOPLE IN THAT CITY ARE HATING AND CURSING AND TREATING EACH OTHER BADLY."

UNTIL JEWS AND ISRAELIS AND PALESTINIANS ARE ABLE TO LIVE TOGETHER IN PEACE AND UNDER LEADERSHIP THAT IS "WISE AND AFTER THE SUBLIME AIMS OF PEACE AND COEXISTENCE OF PEOPLES" THE CITY OF SHALEM RATHER THAN "RISING HIGHER LIKE A LIGHT UPON THE MOUNT" WILL BE SINKING FURTHER DOWN TO THE LEVEL OF HELLISH STATES AND WORLDS AND WILL EVENTUALLY LEAD TO GREATER PAIN AND SUFFERING, MORE THAN TODAY, FOR THE PEOPLE AND FOR THE ENTIRE WORLD.

SINCERELY, "Y-ESHU-SHALIM"

---

### 100. "NO ONE CAN COME TO THE FATHER BUT THROUGH ME:" CLARIFYING THE MYSTICAL MEANING BEHIND THIS VERSE AND THE PLAY BETWEEN "THE DARK AND THE LIGHT" (A PSYCHO-SPIRITUAL INTERPRETATION) —-"I AND THE FATHER CHOKMAH ARE ...ONE"

IT WOULD BE VERY ARROGANT FOR ANYONE TO CLAIM THAT HE OR SHE IS THE ONLY WAY THAT ANYONE CAN GET TO THE FATHER. CAN YOU IMAGINE ALL THE PROBLEMS THIS CLAIM HAS CAUSED AND THAT CERTAIN CHRISTIAN SECTS TAKE LITERALLY AND APPLY IT IN A WAY THAT DISPARAGES AND VILIFIES ALL OTHER TRADITIONS. ACTUALLY IT IS BECAUSE OF THE MISUNDERSTANDING AND MIS-APPLICATION OF THIS VERSE THAT MUCH PERSECUTION, FORCED CONVERSION AND GENOCIDE HAS BEEN CARRIED OUT AND IN THE NAME OF GOD OR, THE LIGHT.

JOHN 14:6

No one comes to the Father except through me." Jesus told him, "I am the way, the truth, and the life. No one can come to the Father except through me."

AS WE HAVE CLARIFIED BEFORE, THE FATHER REPRESENTS "THE LIGHT." AS IN "CHOKMAH" THE FATHER IN THE TREE OF LIFE. REASON WHY THE TERM "LIGHT" AND "LIGHT OF THE WORLD" IS SO PREVALENT IN THE GOSPEL LITERATURE. AS WE HAVE STATED, "LIGHT" IS REFERRING TO "WISDOM" AND THE ONLY WAY TO GET TO WISDOM (THE FEMALE FACE MANIFESTING THROUGH THE FATHER AS THE SHE-KI-INNA) IS THROUGH THE MOTHER PRINCIPLE OR BINAH OR THE DARK SIDE OF REALITY!!!

THEREFORE, WHEN Y-ESH-UA IN THE GOSPEL AND IN THIS VERSE IN PARTICULAR IS SPEAKING, HE IS SPEAKING FROM THE POINT OF VIEW AND VOICE OF THE SOPHIA OR WISDOM HERSELF. REMEMBER THAT TO GET TO THE LIGHT OR STATE OF ILLUMINATION, THE LIGHT OF THE FATHER SHINES UPON THE FEMININE SUBCONSCIOUS CONTENTS OF THE SHADOW OF THE MOTHER PRINCIPLE AND SO ONE REACHES THRU THIS PROCESS "UNDERSTANDING" OF THE PSYCHO-EMOTIONAL PROCESSES IN ONESELF AND THE UNDERSTANDING OF WHAT IS BEHIND ONE'S OWN ACTIONS.

THEREFORE, "KNOWLEDGE" WHICH IS WHAT THE TREE OF LIFE AND OF GOOD AND EVIL REPRESENTS, IS THE "WAY, THE TRUTH AND THE LIFE." AND THAT KNOWLEDGE IS PERSONIFIED AS THE MYSTIC SOPHIA OR THE SHE-KI-INNA PRESENCE BY WHICH A WO-MAN BECOMES A CHRIST OR ENLIGHTENED ONE.

THEREFORE, WHEN YESHUA STATED THE ABOVE, THE FEMALE ACTIVE PRINCIPLE IN HIM WAS STATING THAT WISDOM HERSELF IS THE WAY TO THE FATHER OR THE LIGHT. VIA "KNOWLEDGE AND THE MOTHER" ONE GETS TO THE FATHER OR THE LIGHT, ILLUMINATION AND ENLIGHTENMENT. IT IS "VIA THE INNER KNOWLEDGE OF ONESELF THAT A HUMAN FINALLY ARRIVES AT THE FATHER'S LIGHT" ALIGNING BOTH "WISDOM WITH UNDERSTANDING" WHICH MAKES ONE AWARE OF ONE'S OWN HUMANITY AND DIVINITY. AND IF WE CAN FINALLY NOTICE THIS IN OURSELVES, WE CAN ALSO NOTICE IT IN OTHERS. UNTIL WE DO NOT FACE OUR OWN SHADOW, WE CANNOT FREE OURSELVES OF OUR UNCONSCIOUS IMPULSES AND REACTIONS AND SO WE ARE UNABLE TO REACH THE COMPLEMENTARY POLE OF THE SHADOW/ DARKNESS WHICH IS CHOKMAH THE FATHER OF LIGHT.

SO WHEN Y-ESH-UA STATES EVENTUALLY THAT "I AND THE FATHER CHOKMA ARE ONE" HE IS REFERRING TO "I AM IN ALIGNMENT OR AT - ONENESS WITH THE LIGHT." Y-ESH-UA WAS IN THE LIGHT OR A BUDDHA!!!

Y-ESH-UA SPOKE IN SYMBOLS, METAPHORS AND STORIES TO MAKE SENSE OF METAPHYSICAL CONCEPTS AND SUBJECTS.

SINCERELY, "BINAH AND HER SHE-KI-INNA"

---

## 101. "AUTOMATIC" HEALING: THE CHINESE MEDICINE TESTIMONY AND THE RAVAGES OF STRESS AND TRAUMA ON THE HUMAN BODY AND THE HUMAN BODY CAPACITY TO HEAL

BESIDES "SAMMY," MY HUMONGOUS TIBETAN MONK "FRIEND" WHO LINKS ME TO ASIA, THERE IS MY OTHER ASIAN TESTIMONY AS IN THE

MIRACULOUS CAPABILITY OF THE BODY TO HEAL ITSELF AND THIS TIME THROUGH CHINESE MEDICINE AND ACUPUNCTURE.

THE TIME FRAME OF THIS TESTIMONY WAS AFTER 2002 WHEN I CAME BACK TO THE USA IN PRETTY BAD SHAPE BECAUSE OF MY FIRST SPIRITUALLY INDUCED PSYCHOTIC EPISODE AND WHEN I HAD "THE NAME OF Y-ESH-UA EXPERIENCE" WHICH I DESCRIBED BEFORE IN ANOTHER ESSAY. THIS TIME I WAS IN THE PROCESS OF LITERALLY "DYING" AS MY HAIR WAS FALLING OFF, MY STOMACH WAS SWOLLEN AND DISTENDED, I WAS YELLOW AND PALE AND MY STOMACH HAD STOPPED WORKING. I WAS —-DYING!!!! I HAD GONE FROM DOCTOR AND HOSPITAL TO DOCTOR AND HOSPITAL WITHOUT ANY LUCK AS TO WHAT WAS REALLY GOING ON, UNTIL—--ONE DAY I WAS HAVING BAD CHEST PAINS DUE TO MY STOMACH NOT WORKING FOR AN ENTIRE MONTH. I DID GO TO THE "E.R." AT THE LOCAL PUBLIC HOSPITAL THIS TIME BACK IN THE USA WHERE FINALLY A VERY YOUNG DOCTOR WHO HAD JUST GRADUATED FROM MED SCHOOL FOUND OUT WHAT WAS WRONG WITH ME. AFTER YEARS OF RECEIVING A WRONG DIAGNOSIS OF "STRESS." HE FOUND OUT THAT IT WAS MY "THYROID." I GIVE CREDIT TO THIS PUBLIC HOSPITAL AND TO THIS YOUNG DOCTOR AND IN THIS CASE, WESTERN MEDICINE FOR SAVING MY LIFE.

HOWEVER, THE SYMPTOMS WOULD CONTINUE IN A LESS LIFE - THREATENING WAY NOT AS SEVERE AS THEY WERE BEFORE, BUT MY STOMACH WAS STILL IN BAD SHAPE. SOMEHOW I FOUND OUT ABOUT THE CHINESE CLINIC AND ACUPUNCTURE AND DECIDED TO GIVE IT A TRY. IT IS SO INTERESTING AND MIRACULOUS HOW THESE THINGS WORK. HOW IN TIMES OF NEED LIFE-SAVING INFORMATION COMES ONE'S WAY WHICH LEADS TO RELIEF AND A WAY OUT OF DANGER.

AND SO I WENT TO THE CHINESE DOCTOR AND EXPLAINED WHAT WAS GOING ON IN REGARDS TO MY STOMACH AND OTHER SYMPTOMS THAT WERE STILL LINGERING AND MAKING MY LIFE MISERABLE. AND A VERY WISE AND KNOWLEDGEABLE CHINESE DOCTOR FROM CHINA GIVES ME A BRIEF SPEECH ABOUT "HEALING" LOOKING AT ME STRAIGHT INTO MY EYES WITH KINDNESS AND TELLS ME THE WORDS I REMEMBER TO THIS DAY AND WHICH REMIND ME OF THE GOSPEL MESSAGE OF Y-ESH-UA. WHAT SHE TOLD ME WITH FAITH AND CONVICTION WAS THE FOLLOWING DECREE:

"YOUR BODY CAN HEAL ITSELF.... OF ANYTHING"

THOSE WORDS "YOU CAN HEAL" OR "YOUR BODY CAN HEAL ITSELF" WERE SIMPLE BUT PROFOUND AND THEY HAD SUCH AN IMPACT IMMEDIATELY IN MY PERSON THAT I "BELIEVED HER AND HER WORDS GAVE ME HOPE" AND THAT IS WHAT HAPPENED. I DID WHAT SHE TOLD ME TO DO FOR A WHILE

THROUGH ACUPUNCTURE AND CHINESE HERBS AND "DIET!!!" AFTER A WHILE I WAS BROKE AND HAD TO STOP THE HERBS AND ACUPUNCTURE BUT "FOLLOWED HER DIETARY PRESCRIPTIONS" AND AS "IF BY MAGIC" I BEGAN TO FEEL BETTER AND AT LAST MY THYROID ISSUE WHICH I WAS TOLD WAS GOING TO BE FOR LIFE BY WESTERN HEALTH-SCARE, DISAPPEARED.

FOR YEARS I WOULD HAVE THE THYROID EXAMS DONE AND THEY WOULD COME NORMAL AND NEGATIVE WITHOUT TAKING WESTERN MEDICATIONS AND JUST BY FOLLOWING THE CHINESE DOCTOR'S DIETARY RECOMMENDATIONS.

I COULD NOT BELIEVE IT!!!!

IT WAS UNTIL 2018 THAT MY THYROID MESSED UP ONCE MORE TO THIS DAY AND NOW I HAVE TO TAKE MEDS. BUT THIS EXPERIENCE OF GETTING SICK AGAIN HAS A POWERFUL LESSON TO TEACH AS WELL. IT WAS AFTER A MOMENT OF OVERWHELMING TRAUMA AND PHYSICAL "DI-STRESS" THAT THE SYMPTOMS CAME BACK!!! THEREFORE, THIS EXPERIENCE TAUGHT ME THAT — TRAUMA AND OVERWHELMING "STRESS" RAVAGES THE MIND AND THE BODY. MUCH OF TODAY'S HEALTH CRISIS IS DUE FOR THE MOST PART TO ALL TYPES OF STRESSORS AND TRAUMATIC EXPERIENCES THAT PEOPLE GO THROUGH. THEREFORE, ONE'S HEALTH IS LINKED TO ONE'S MENTAL STATES AND EMOTIONAL STATES TO THE POINT WHERE REGULATING ONE'S PSYCHO-EMOTIONAL STRESSORS WILL ALLOW THE BODY TO HEAL ITSELF NATURALLY AND AT TIMES "AS IF BY MAGIC, AUTOMATICALLY."

SINCERELY, "DR. MAYQUEEN, MEDICINE WOMAN"

---

## 102. "SUCCESS" AS A STATE OF BEING RATHER THAN "THE PRESSURE TO—BE —- SOMEBODY!"

I WAS BORN SOMEBODY - THE DIVINE GAVE ME A NAME!

FOR YEARS I WAS IN A STATE OF PERPETUAL MANIA AND SOMETHING INTERESTING THAT HAPPENED TO ME DURING THAT TIME WAS THAT I FELT "SUCCESSFUL" WITHOUT BEING "SUCCESSFUL AS HOW PEOPLE DEFINE IT IN THIS WORLD TODAY." I AM NOT SAYING THAT "MAKING IT IN SOME FIELD" IS BAD. NOT AT ALL. WE WERE ALL GIVEN INTERESTS AND ABILITIES AND SKILLS THAT WE CAN HONE AND BECOME GOOD AT AND FEEL GOOD ABOUT. THAT'S WHY WE HAVE THEM IN THE FIRST PLACE. HOWEVER, AFTER THAT EXPERIENCE, I LEARNED THAT A FEELING OR

STATE OF BEING "SUCCESSFUL " IS INDEPENDENT OF "DOING AND ACCOMPLISHING" ANYTHING AS IT IS DEFINED TODAY.

ONE OF THE THINGS THAT EXACERBATED MY CONDITION OF DEPRESSION FOR YEARS WAS THE "SOCIETAL PRESSURE TO BE …SUCCESSFUL!!!" I REMEMBER I WANTED TO DO SO MUCH BECAUSE IN MY MIND AT THE TIME THE MORE I ACCOMPLISHED AND HOARDED, THE MORE I FELT I WAS GONNA BE AND LOOK "SUCCESSFUL" IN THIS WORLD. I WAS SELF VALIDATING MYSELF THROUGH THE OUTSIDE. HOWEVER, KARMA — OR DISEASE SET IN AND I WAS UNABLE TO COPE AMONGST OTHER THINGS WITH THE PRESSURE EVERYWHERE TO BE A CERTAIN TYPE OF PERSON AND TO HAVE A CERTAIN MUCH. AT THAT TIME I FELT THAT MY "SELF WORTH WAS DEPENDENT ON HOW SUCCESSFUL I WAS IN THE EYES OF SOCIETY AND ON HOW MUCH I HAD ACCOMPLISHED IN WORLDLY TERMS."

I FEEL THAT WE HAVE BECOME SO FOCUSED ON "ACCOMPLISHING AND DOING" THAT WE HAVE FORGOTTEN TO NOTICE AND ENJOY THE SIMPLE THINGS IN LIFE THAT MAKE LIFE, LIFE. I FEEL THAT THERE MUST BE A BALANCE BETWEEN "DOING AND…BEING." AND THAT WE HAVE PLACED SO MUCH EMPHASIS ON "MAKING IT" THAT WE END UP "LOOKING DOWN ON THOSE WHO DON'T" ACCORDING TO HOW PEOPLE ARE MEASURED TODAY.

WELL, I WAS UNABLE TO BE LIKE OTHERS BECAUSE OF WHATEVER IS THAT I HAVE.I DO NOT MEAN IT IN A BAD WAY BUT DUE TO MY CONDITION IT IS VERY CHALLENGING TO JUST BE ALIVE AND BE LIKE PEOPLE ARE "SUPPOSED TO BE" ACCORDING TO THE DICTATES OF THIS WORLD. BUT I DISCOVERED ALONG THE WAY THAT MY TRUE PATH IS ONE OF CREATIVITY AND MOST IMPORTANTLY —NOT FORCING IT —BUT GOING WITH THE CREATIVE FLOW AND "ENJOYING IT" BECAUSE THAT IS THE PURPOSE AND MEANING OF MY LIFE. I JUST LOVE WRITING AND PAINTING AND EXPRESSING MYSELF CREATIVELY BECAUSE IT GIVES ME JOY AND MEANING AND PURPOSE. IT IS NOT ABOUT MONEY, BUT ABOUT SOMETHING DEEPER WHICH AN EXCLUSIVE FOCUS ON MAKING MONEY WOULD END UP KILLING, KILLING THE MAGIC AWAY. I MEAN THE…FEELING.

IS IT NOT ABOUT …"WHAT A …FEELING!?" AFTER ALL??????

THAT'S THE WAY I FELT WHEN I WAS MANIC AND THROUGH THAT CONDITION I ENDED UP EXPRESSING MYSELF CREATIVELY AND FEELING SUCCESSFUL. I DISCOVERED THAT THERE ARE VARIOUS AND DIVERSE WAYS OF BEING AND FEELING SUCCESSFUL THAT ARE NOT LIMITED TO EARNING LOTS OF MONEY, HOARDING LOTS OF THINGS AND ACCLAMATION. I HAVE MET "EXCELLENT PARENTS" OF ECONOMICALLY POOR FAMILIES WHO ARE INDEED SUCCESSFUL PARENTS. I HAVE MET

CREATIVES THAT ARE IN THE STREETS OR STRUGGLING TO MAKE ENDS MEET WHO ARE SUCCESSFUL ARTISTS IN WHAT THEY DO. I HAVE MET "OVERCOMERS" OF ADDICTION AND TRAUMA THAT IN ITSELF IS A MAJOR .....SUCCESS! I HAVE MET PEOPLE WHO ARE VERY GOOD AT THEIR HUMBLE JOBS AND SIMPLE LIVES AND ARE SUCCESSFUL IN THEIR OWN WAY. THEY ARE CONTENT AND OR HAPPY. ISN'T THAT THE POINT OF ... LIVING!? TO BE CONTENT AND HAPPY?

I FEEL THAT AS A SOCIETY WE NEED TO RE-DEFINE WHAT "SUCCESSFUL" MEANS. AND ENCOURAGE AND SUPPORT ALL TYPES OF SUCCESS. IT IS VERY STRESSFUL AND TEDIOUS TO BE TOLD EVERYDAY THAT I AM NOT GOOD ENOUGH AND THAT TO BE I HAVE TO BE RICH AND ACCOMPLISH MUCH AND HOARD THINGS, ETC. THAT TO HAVE A VOICE AND BE TAKEN SERIOUSLY I HAVE TO BE "SUCCESSFUL IN THE SENSE THAT WORD IS DEFINED FOR THE MOST PART TODAY."

BEING HUMAN IS TOUGH ENOUGH...AND IT IS A SUCCESS ALREADY MAKING IT THROUGH THE DAY AND THROUGH ANOTHER ...DAY.

SINCERELY, THE SCAPEGOAT "WHO IS NO LONGER CARRYING THE KARMIC BAGGAGE" OF THE WORLD

---

## 103. KAL-"QI" CHALISA: THE KAL-QI AND THE NUMBER "40" AS G-ANNY-MEDE AND "HIS/HER AGE OF AQU-"ARI" US

40 IS A VERY IMPORTANT NUMBER THAT KEEPS REPEATING ITSELF IN MOST TRADITIONS. OF COURSE THE NUMBER IS A SYMBOL THAT REPRESENTS THE FOLLOWING:

40 In Numerology

The number 40 is a very special number in numerology. It is often associated with change, new beginnings, and fresh starts. If you are experiencing a lot of changes in your life, it is likely that the number 40 is playing a role in those events.(SARAH SCOOP NUMEROLOGY)

THE NAME OR TITLE "CHALISA" MEANS "40." AND THE NUMBER 40 IS SYMBOLIC OF "CHANGE, NEW BEGINNINGS AND FRESH STARTS!!!" OF TRANSITION AND TRANSFORMATION!!! THE FACT THAT THE WORLD IS EXPERIENCING MANY CHANGES TODAY IS A "SIGN" THAT THE PRESENCE OF THE KAL-KI CHALISA ENERGIES ARE USHERING THE END OF KALI AND THE BEGINNING OF A NEW WORLD.

JUST AS IN THE 40 DAYS OF THE FLOOD STORY, AND THE 40 YEARS IN THE DESERT AND THE 40 DAYS OF Y-ESH-UA'S FASTING AND REFLECTION. THESE STORIES POINT TO THE SAME CONCEPT OF —CHANGES AND NEW BEGINNINGS —IN A GLOBAL AS WELL AS INDIVIDUAL LEVEL.

AS "SARAH SCOOP" CLARIFIES ABOVE— THE NUMBER "40" MOMENT WE ARE GOING THROUGH RIGHT NOW REMINDS US OF THE FOLLOWING:

1.   CHANGE IS INEVITABLE.

2.   IT POINTS TO NEW BEGINNINGS

3.   WE ARE ALWAYS GROWING AND EVOLVING

THE NUMBER 40 IS TWO TIMES "20" WHICH IS THE "JUDGMENT CARD" BUT IF YOU NOTICE IN THE JUDGMENT CARD SYMBOLISM, IT'S ABOUT THE PROCESS OF "REBIRTH." AND WATER IS AN ELEMENT IN THAT CARD OF REBIRTH WHICH STANDS FOR "RESURRECTION" AS IN "R-ESU-RECT-ION OR RECTITUDE OR JUSTICE. WHICH IS WHAT THE MIKVAH IMMERSION AND THE BAPTISM POINT TO AS IN –A NEW BEGINNING AND A SPIRITUAL REBIRTH (NOT IN RELIGIOUS TERMS BUT IN HUMAN CONSCIOUSNESS TERMS) AS TO LIVE A LIFE OF RIGHTEOUSNESS.

CHALISA TERM SOUNDS MUCH LIKE "CHALICE AND CALIZ (IN CASTILIAN)" WHICH IS THE SYMBOL ATTRIBUTED TO GANYMEDE WHO IS THE "ANDROGYNOUS" ENERGY THAT IS ASSOCIATED TO THE AGE OF AQUARIUS AND THE CHALICE THAT HOLDS THE WATERS AND THE ELEMENTS.

THEREFORE, AS WE PASS THROUGH "THE WATERS" IN A SYMBOLIC SENSE TO CROSS TO THE OTHER SIDE, THE WORLD WILL BE IN COMMOTION AS NEVER BEFORE REMINDING US ALONG THE WAY THAT WE ARE EXPERIENCING A NEW START AND THAT THIS CHANGE IS NECESSARY FOR OUR SURVIVAL. IT IS AN "INEVITABLE" PROCESS OF GROWTH AND EVOLUTION AS NEVER BEFORE. LOOKING BACK TO THE MISTAKES IN OUR HISTORIES AND THE DECISION TO LEARN AND MOVE FORWARD IN A DIFFERENT PATH IS THE WAY OF KAL-QI CHALISA, THE ONE WHO DISPELS IGNORANCE AND FEAR.

SINCERELY, "GANYMEDE AND THE HOLY GRAIL"

## 104. NAMASTE, LEADS US AWAY FROM IGNORANCE TO THE LIGHT— MOSES (MOUSSA) THE HERMIT WITH THE GUIDING LIGHT LEADING THE PEOPLE TOWARDS THE NEW AGE OF AQU–ARI—US OR THE AGE OF LIGHT (PART I)

الٓرۚ كِتَٰبٌ أَنزَلۡنَٰهُ إِلَيۡكَ لِتُخۡرِجَ ٱلنَّاسَ مِنَ ٱلظُّلُمَٰتِ إِلَى ٱلنُّورِ بِإِذۡنِ رَبِّهِمۡ إِلَىٰ صِرَٰطِ ٱلۡعَزِيزِ ٱلۡحَمِيدِ

ٱللَّهِ ٱلَّذِى لَهُۥ مَا فِى ٱلسَّمَٰوَٰتِ وَمَا فِى ٱلۡأَرۡضِۗ وَوَيۡلٌ لِّلۡكَٰفِرِينَ مِنۡ عَذَابٍ شَدِيدٍ

ٱلَّذِينَ يَسۡتَحِبُّونَ ٱلۡحَيَوٰةَ ٱلدُّنۡيَا عَلَى ٱلۡءَاخِرَةِ وَيَصُدُّونَ عَن سَبِيلِ ٱللَّهِ وَيَبۡغُونَهَا عِوَجًاۚ أُو۟لَٰٓئِكَ فِى ضَلَٰلٍۭ بَعِيدٍ

وَمَآ أَرۡسَلۡنَا مِن رَّسُولٍ إِلَّا بِلِسَانِ قَوۡمِهِۦ لِيُبَيِّنَ لَهُمۡۖ فَيُضِلُّ ٱللَّهُ مَن يَشَآءُ وَيَهۡدِى مَن يَشَآءُۚ وَهُوَ ٱلۡعَزِيزُ ٱلۡحَكِيمُ

وَلَقَدۡ أَرۡسَلۡنَا مُوسَىٰ بِـَٔايَٰتِنَآ أَنۡ أَخۡرِجۡ قَوۡمَكَ مِنَ ٱلظُّلُمَٰتِ إِلَى ٱلنُّورِ وَذَكِّرۡهُم بِأَيَّىٰمِ ٱللَّهِۚ إِنَّ فِى ذَٰلِكَ لَءَايَٰتٍ لِّكُلِّ صَبَّارٍ شَكُورٍ

وَإِذۡ قَالَ مُوسَىٰ لِقَوۡمِهِ ٱذۡكُرُوا۟ نِعۡمَةَ ٱللَّهِ عَلَيۡكُمۡ إِذۡ أَنجَىٰكُم مِّنۡ ءَالِ فِرۡعَوۡنَ يَسُومُونَكُمۡ سُوٓءَ ٱلۡعَذَابِ وَيُذَبِّحُونَ أَبۡنَآءَكُمۡ وَيَسۡتَحۡيُونَ نِسَآءَكُمۡۚ وَفِى ذَٰلِكُم بَلَآءٌ مِّن رَّبِّكُمۡ عَظِيمٌ

*""ALIF LAM RA. THIS IS A BOOK WHICH WE HAVE REVEALED TO YOU O' PROPHET SO THAT YOU MAY LEAD PEOPLE OUT OF DARKNESS AND INTO THE LIGHT, BY THE WILL OF THEIR LORD, TO THE PATH OF THE ALMIGHTY, THE PRAISEWORTHY...*

*ALLAH, TO WHOM BELONGS WHATEVER IS IN THE HEAVENS AND WHATEVER IS ON THE EARTH. AND WOE TO THE DISBELIEVERS BECAUSE OF A SEVERE TORMENT!*

*THEY ARE THE ONES WHO FAVOR THE LIFE OF THIS WORLD OVER THE HEREAFTER AND HINDER OTHERS FROM THE WAY OF ALLAH, STRIVING TO MAKE IT APPEAR CROOKED. IT IS THEM WHO HAVE GONE FAR ASTRAY.*

*WE HAVE NOT SENT A MESSENGER EXCEPT IN THE LANGUAGE OF HIS PEOPLE TO CLARIFY THE MESSAGE FOR THEM. THEN ALLAH LEAVES WHOEVER HE WILLS TO STRAY AND GUIDES WHOEVER HE WILLS. AND HE IS THE ALMIGHTY ALL WISE.*

*INDEED, WE SENT MOSES WITH OUR SIGNS, ORDERING HIM, LEAD YOUR PEOPLE OUT OF DARKNESS AND INTO LIGHT, AND REMIND THEM OF ALLAH'S DAYS OF FAVOR. SURELY IN THIS ARE SIGNS FOR WHOEVER IS STEADFAST, GRATEFUL.*

*CONSIDER WHEN MOSES SAID TO HIS PEOPLE, "REMEMBER ALLAH'S FAVOR UPON YOU WHEN HE RESCUED YOU FROM THE PEOPLE OF PHARAOH, WHO AFFLICTED YOU WITH DREADFUL TORMENT — SLAUGHTERING YOUR SONS AND KEEPING YOUR WOMEN. THAT WAS A SEVERE TEST FROM YOUR LORD. "" SURAH IBRAHIM 1 - 6 (QORAN.COM)*

AL-AMRA — MEANS "THE CROWN" AS IN "AMR" PRINCESS OR NOBLEWOMAN. THE ALIF HAS THE NUMERICAL VALUE OF "1" AND "ALIF" STANDS FOR "ONENESS, STRENGTH, AND WISDOM." "AMRA" IS "AMR" WHICH IS THE ROOT WORD FOR "LOVE" IN LATIN AS IN "AMAR." THE CROWN CHAKRA IS A SIGN OF ILLUMINATED AND ENLIGHTENED STATES OF CONSCIOUSNESS. IT CONNECTS TO THE "MULADHARA" CHAKRA WHOSE SOUND IS "LAM." SO HERE WE HAVE A CONNECTION BETWEEN YESOD WHICH CORRESPONDS TO MULADHARA AND THE KETER OR CROWN CHAKRA. THE MOON IS ABOUT LEARNING OR THE PROCESS OF ILLUMINATION AND LAM REPRESENTS LEARNING IN THE HEBREW LANGUAGE. ESPECIALLY LEARNING FROM THE HEART AND NOT JUST THE MIND. USUALLY LEARNING FROM THE HEART HAPPENS THROUGH LIFE EXPERIENCE AND GAINING EMPATHY TOWARDS OTHERS. "WISDOM" IS OF THE HOLY "SHE-KI-INNA" WHO IS CONSIDERED "HOLY" BECAUSE SHE IS "WHOLE" OR REPRESENTS "A STATE OF UNION AND INTEGRATION" IN A PERSON AND IN THE UNIVERSE.

AND SO LIKE THE FIRST VERSE STATES, THE STORIES POINT TO A UNIVERSAL PROCESS OF "AWAKENING" AS IN "MOVING FROM A STATE OF IGNORANCE TOWARDS A STATE OF ILLUMINATION OR TO THE LIGHT. THE ABILITY TO DISCERN AND TO SEE FROM AN INTELLECTUAL AND EMOTIONAL STANDPOINT.

THE "DISBELIEVERS" ARE NOT THOSE WHO DO NOT BELIEVE IN THE KORAN SINCE BOTH JEWS AND CHRISTIANS ARE CONSIDERED "PEOPLE OF THE BOOK." IT IS NECESSARY TO CLARIFY HERE THAT SINCE THE JEWS AND MUSLIMS ARE CALLED OR REFERRED TO AS "PEOPLE OF THE BOOK," THIS ASSERTION CLARIFIES THAT MOHAMMAD DERIVED MOST OF HIS EXEGESIS AND "REVELATIONS" FROM THE PROCESS OF "INSPIRATION THRU THE MANIC STATES" AS WELL AS FROM READING AND STUDYING AND BECOMING EXPOSED TO "THE BOOK" WHICH IS THE TORAH AND THE GOSPELS INCLUDING GNOSTIC GOSPELS GOING AROUND AT THAT TIME IN THE OASIS TRIBES OF MEDINA.

THE "DISBELIEVERS" REFERS IN GENERAL TO THOSE WHO REJECT THE LIGHT " OR THE SEEKING OF ILLUMINATION AND ENLIGHTENMENT" AND RUN AFTER IGNORANCE AND EVIL. THEY SUFFER "SEVERE TORMENT" BECAUSE THAT IS THE KIND OF LIFE THAT "LIVING IN IGNORANCE" BRINGS ABOUT SUCH AS CHAOS AND STRIFE AND VIOLENCE AND THE FEAR TO BE DISCOVERED IN REGARDS TO EVIL ACTIONS. IT MAKES FOR A VERY HELLISH LIFE, WORLD AND SOCIETY RIGHT HERE, RIGHT NOW. INITIALLY, MOHAMMAD WAS TRYING IN HIS VISION TO BRING ABOUT THIS KIND OF ILLUMINATED AND ENLIGHTENED SOCIETY THROUGH ISLAM.

*"THEY ARE THE ONES "WHO FAVOR THE LIFE OF THIS WORLD OVER THE HEREAFTER AND HINDER OTHERS FROM THE WAY OF ALLAH, STRIVING TO MAKE IT APPEAR CROOKED. IT IS THEM WHO HAVE GONE FAR ASTRAY."*

FAVORING THE "LIFE OF THIS WORLD" DOES NOT REFER SPECIFICALLY TO NORMAL LIFE BUT TO "THOSE WHO PLACE THE —VALUE —OF THE "THINGS" OF THIS WORLD OVER AND ABOVE THE VALUE OF LIFE ITSELF AS WELL AS THE HUMAN RIGHT TO SEEK AND FIND AND ACHIEVE ILLUMINATED AND ENLIGHTENED STATES OF BEING. PEOPLE WHO ARE ALWAYS PLACING OBSTACLES ALONG THE WAY TO PREVENT HUMANKIND FROM REACHING AWAKENING AND ILLUMINATION.

SINCERELY,
 ISA SON OF MOHAMA-D-INNA

---

## 105. NAMASTE, LEAD US FROM IGNORANCE TO THE LIGHT— MOSES THE HERMIT WITH THE GUIDING LIGHT LEADING THE PEOPLE TOWARDS THE NEW AGE OF AQU—ARI—US OR THE AGE OF THE ARI (PART II)

FOR THE MOST PART, THOSE WHO SACRIFICE THE PROCESS OF ILLUMINATION AND TRAMPLE UPON HUMAN DIGNITY AND LIFE ON EARTH ARE IN A STATE OF "IGNORANCE." IN THEIR CROOKEDNESS, THEY USE CROOKED WAYS AND CROOKED LAWS TO DECEIVE OTHERS AND TO LEAD THEM ASTRAY. THE "HEREAFTER" DOES NOT REFER ONLY TO THE AFTERLIFE BUT TO THE "PROCESS OF REINCARNATION." SINCE THE KARMIC LESSONS CARRY OVER TO FUTURE LIVES. THEREFORE, WHAT WE DO TODAY DOES MATTER AND THE PROCESS OF ILLUMINATION IS "THE EXIT" FROM THE CONSTANT REINCARNATION PROCESS.

*"WE HAVE NOT SENT A MESSENGER EXCEPT IN THE LANGUAGE OF HIS PEOPLE TO CLARIFY THE MESSAGE FOR THEM. THEN ALLAH LEAVES WHOEVER HE WILLS TO STRAY AND GUIDES WHOEVER HE WILLS. AND HE IS THE ALMIGHTY ALL WISE."*

THE "WE" HERE FOLLOWS THE LITERARY TRADITION OF GENESIS AND THOSE WHO ARE "MANY AS ONE AND ONE AS MANY." REFERRED IN GENESIS AS THE "ELOHIM" OR THE MANY DEITIES OR VOICES OR MANIFESTATIONS OF DEITY OR ULTIMATE REALITY. THAT ALLAH WILLS PEOPLE TO GO ASTRAY AND OTHERS TO BE GUIDED IS NOT AN ACCURATE INTERPRETATION BECAUSE IT WOULD MAKE NO SENSE FOR ULTIMATE REALITY TO CHOOSE WHO IS IN AND WHO IS NOT, THAT WOULD ALSO CONTRADICT THE NOTION OF "FREE WILL." ULTIMATE REALITY "ALLOWS" PEOPLE IN THIS SPACE-TIME AND MATTER CONTINUUM TO MAKE THEIR OWN MISTAKES AND DECISIONS AND TO LEARN FROM THEM; OR, NOT LEARN FROM THEM BUT ALLOWS HUMANS TO KEEP FALLING UNTIL THEY FINALLY "GET IT" OR TO SOMEDAY WAKE UP. IN THIS SENSE "IT" WILLS THOSE WHO CHOOSE TO GO ASTRAY FROM THOSE WHO ARE GUIDED BY THEIR OWN LEARNING EXPERIENCE WHICH ACTIVATES INNATE WISDOM AND HUMAN GROWTH.

*"INDEED, WE SENT MOSES WITH OUR SIGNS, ORDERING HIM, LEAD YOUR PEOPLE OUT OF DARKNESS AND INTO LIGHT, AND REMIND THEM OF ALLAH'S DAYS OF FAVOR. SURELY IN THIS ARE SIGNS FOR WHOEVER IS STEADFAST, GRATEFUL"*

HERE WE HAVE MOSES AGAIN OR MOSHE OR MOUSSA AS THE "GUIDING PRINCIPLE" WHO REPRESENTS THE "ILLUMINATED MAN OR THE HERMIT CARRYING THE LAMP OF KNOWLEDGE" LEADING THE PEOPLE FROM IGNORANCE INTO THE LIGHT! HERE IT IS MOSTLY REFERRING TO "STATES OF CONSCIOUSNESS." BEING IN A STATE OF ILLUMINATION FOR A PERSON AND A SOCIETY IS A BLESSING BECAUSE IN SUCH STATES THERE IS RELATIVE ORDER THAT ALLOWS FOR RELATIVE HEALTH, WELL BEING AND STABILITY FOR THE PEOPLE AND SOCIETY ENABLING ALL TO THRIVE AND REACH ENLIGHTENED STATES AND "EUREKA" MOMENTS.

*"CONSIDER WHEN MOSES SAID TO HIS PEOPLE, "REMEMBER ALLAH'S FAVOR UPON YOU WHEN HE RESCUED YOU FROM THE PEOPLE OF PHARAOH, WHO AFFLICTED YOU WITH DREADFUL TORMENT — SLAUGHTERING YOUR SONS AND KEEPING YOUR WOMEN. THAT WAS A SEVERE TEST FROM YOUR LORD. ""*

EVERYTHING IN LIFE IS A LEARNING EXPERIENCE!!! EVERY CHALLENGE AND EVERY OPPORTUNITY BECAUSE THAT IS THE WAY THIS TIME-SPACE-MATTER CONTINUUM AND PLANE OF EXISTENCE WORKS. THEREFORE THE WAY WE APPROACH EVERYTHING HAS MUCH TO DO WITH HOW THAT EXPERIENCE MAKES US OR BREAKS US WHICH ARE BOTH NECESSARY TO MOVE FORWARD UNTIL WE REACH "THE LIGHT OF WISDOM AND DISCERNMENT OF THE TREE OF GOOD AND EVIL AND OF KNOWLEDGE."

THIS LAST POINT IS —-VERY IMPORTANT—FOR ISLAM AND THE OTHER TRADITIONS TO REMEMBER, LET US REPEAT...

*",WHO AFFLICTED YOU WITH DREADFUL TORMENT —SLAUGHTERING YOUR SONS AND KEEPING YOUR WOMEN."*

SLAUGHTER OR MURDER/ KILLING IS AN ACT OF IGNORANCE AS IT SPREADS TRAUMA TO A COMMUNITY AND INTERRUPTS THE LEARNING PATH OF THE SOUL INCARNATED AS THE PERSON WHO IS BEING AFFLICTED AND CUT SHORT. THEREFORE TWO IMPORTANT POINTS NEED TO BE KEPT IN MIND HERE AND ARE NECESSARY TO REMEMBER AND THESE ARE THAT:

MURDER AND KILLING—-VIOLENCE—- IS NOT HALLAL / KOSHER!!! BUT ARE ACTS OF IGNORANCE AND THOSE IN THE LIGHT UPHOLD THE RIGHT TO LIFE AND LIVING. AND... THAT WOMEN HAVE AS MUCH RIGHT TO BE TREATED EQUALLY AND FAIRLY AS THE MALE. BOTH MALE AND FEMALE MUST BE TREATED WITH DIGNITY AND RESPECT AND CONSIDERATION. THEREFORE, LET US STAY AWAY FROM —VIOLENCE AND INEQUALITY, SO THAT UNLIKE THAT PHARAOH, WE REMAIN UNDER THE LIGHT'S ILLUMINATION!!!! AND NOT TRAPPED UNDER THE GRIP OF IGNORANCE AND PAIN!!!

SINCERELY,
BINAH THE SHADOW AND CHOKMAH THE ILLUMINATOR OF MUSSA"

---

## 106. THE EMPATH EFFECT: THE KEY TO WISE GOVERNANCE AND HEALING AND THE STRENGTH THAT IS CARRIED WITHIN

Remember how the BULLY TYPE or -6+6+6= "NEGATIVE 18" is unable to MAKE GOOD AND WISE DECISIONS for EVERYBODY because HIS BRAIN'S FUNCTIONING has been stunted, included the ABILITY TO FEEL emotions?

On the other hand, you have the OPPOSITE of the BULLY in the person of the EMPATH. THE EMPATH is the SENSITIVE ONE or the ONE WHO FEELS THE PAIN AND SUFFERING OF THE WORLD AND WHO WILL LOOK FOR WAYS, SOLUTIONS AND IDEAS TO BRING EASE TO THAT PAIN AND SUFFERING.

EMPATHS "ARE NOT WEAK" as many believe. Instead, EMPATHS are strong like WATER and like ANNE-TENAE are able to LINK TO COSMIC ENERGIES in a much easier and direct way than any other people.

EMPATHS belong to every nation, people and culture. BEING AN EMPATH has nothing to do with being RELIGIOUS as EMPATHS ARE ALREADY "SPIRITUAL"

BY THE WAY THEY ARE WIRED TO SEE THE WORLD THROUGH THE EYES OF THE DIVINE WHICH REPRESENTS THE ARCHETYPE of the "TENDER HEART OF Y-ESH-UA."

It takes a lot of STRENGTH to be able to go through the HELLS OF THIS WORLD and witness the EVIL AND INJUSTICE and still come back to THE HEART OF -Y-ESH-UA and EMPATHY FOR THE WORLD.

In the OLDEN DAYS OF THE WISE, the EMPATH was held in GREAT ESTEEM and CONSIDERATION by the TRIBE. Just as in the FAIRY TALES, the WISE ONES OF THE TRIBE WOULD COME TOGETHER TO FORM THE COUNCIL OF ELDERS and NOT according to leadership appointments based on status or clout or material wealth. These appointments would be based mostly on THE EMPATHIC MAKEUP AND CHARACTER OF THOSE APPLYING FOR THESE POSITIONS OF RESPONSIBILITY. THEY WOULD BE EMPATHS of diverse skills and abilities having the EYE AND THE HEART TO NOTICE THE PAIN AND SUFFERING OF THE PEOPLE AND COME UP WITH THE NECESSARY AND NEEDED ... SOLUTIONS AND LAWS AND PRESCRIPTIONS.

The NON -EMPATH who were able to tame their FIRE especially those of a very TOUGH AND ROUGH CHARACTER AND DISPOSITION, were NOT placed in positions of RESPONSIBILITY in the TRIBE since they lacked the ability to FEEL AND DISCERN THE NEEDS AND CONDITIONS OF THE PEOPLE. Instead, this type of leader served in the LOWER LEVELS of governance of the TRIBE especially in the areas of THE MILITARY AS WARRIORS SERVING IN THE PROTECTION OF THE TRIBE or NATION.

Today, the functions seem to be in REVERSE and THE BULLY TYPE OF MAN seems to be the IDEALIZED TYPE CHOSEN TO HEAD THE NATION AND ORGANIZATIONS. Meanwhile the EMPATH TYPES AND SENSITIVES are rendered as WEAK, SICK, IRRELEVANT AND TOTALLY IGNORED. THE EMPATH has been persecuted by the -666 for a very long time because the -666 fears the EMPATH STRENGTH, SKILLS AND ABILITIES and SENSE OF JUSTICE.

And now the EARTH is plagued with VIOLENCE-EVIL-TRAUMA all over because for the most part THE BULLY TYPE has been placed in positions of leadership and power and GOVERNANCE of the TRIBE.

THEREFORE, it would be in the best interest for mankind and the PLANET to bring back to the ROUND TABLE the ELDER AND THE WISE WOMAN AND THE EMPATHS, etc.. etc.. etc. for they hold THE KEY to the HEALING AND THE PROPER MANAGEMENT OF THE WORLD.

SINCERELY, ANNE–ATENNA (DIVINE ANTENAE) GUARDIAN OF WISDOM"

## 107. THE AGE OF AQUARIUS: THE WATERBEARER, THE CHALICE, THE PHRYGIAN CAP AND THE AGE OF HUMAN TRANSCENDENCE

The symbol of the AGE OF AQUARIUS is "NOT" JUDAS as some claim but actually GANYMEDE or G-ANNIE-MEDE. He is the WATER BEARER and the reason why there has been issues with the WATER ELEMENT lately.

G-ANNIE-MEDE as in:

From Ancient Greek Γανυμήδης (*Ganumḗdēs*, "meant to please"), from γάνυμαι (*gánumai*, "I rejoice, I am glad") + μήδεα (*mḗdea*, "thought, intention"). Doublet of *catamite*.WIKIPEDIA

The elements of THE CUP OR CHALICE OF G-ANNY-MEDE are WATER as in EMOTIONS and AIR as in THOUGHT AND INTENTION. HUMAN MIND IS AFTER THE UNIVERSAL MIND.

And the intention of man to build a NEW WORLD based on RIGHT THINKING AND RIGHT INTENTION is explained in the NOBLE EIGHTFOLD PATH of BUDDHISM. G-ANNU-MEDE IS AFTER THE "ANNU" ENERGIES OF CREATION AND RENEWAL.

The AGE OF AQUARIUS is about REJOICING IN THE MIRACLE OF LIVING AND BEING GLAD TO BE ALIVE. It is not about more of the same KALI YUGA patterns of man creating a world of PAIN AND SUFFERING based on DYSFUNCTIONAL THOUGHT AND EVIL OR SELFISH INTENTION.

WATER represents EMOTIONS and it is defined in TAOISM as follows:

Ancient Chinese philosopher Lao Tzu also highlighted the characteristics of water in the "Tao Te Ching" stating, "Water is fluid, soft and yielding. But water will wear away rock, which is rigid and cannot yield. As a rule, whatever is fluid, soft and yielding will overcome whatever is rigid and hard. (CAMPUSRECMAGAZINE)

THOSE WHO CANNOT YIELD such as RIGID STRUCTURES and SYSTEMS and IDEOLOGIES and WAYS OF TREATING ONE ANOTHER and who refuse to COMPROMISE AND DIALOGUE —FOLLOW— the ways of KALI YUGA and THESE ENERGIES as WE speak are BEING TRANSFORMED INTO THE WAYS OF AQUARIUS. FLUID, SOFT AND YIELDING WILL OVERCOME WHAT IS RIGID AND HARD. Much of the wars and strife today is because of the RIGIDITY OF THESE IDEOLOGIES, RELIGIONS, AND INSTITUTIONS that refuse to sacrifice EGO AND PRIDE FOR THE SAKE OF THE WORLD AND PEOPLE'S WELL BEING. RIGIDITY WILL NO LONGER PAY. This RIGIDITY is what Y-ESH-UA and the NAZARENES were critical about as this RIGIDITY had become a BURDEN UPON THE PEOPLE rather than a source of JOY AND GLADNESS

AND FREEDOM. You can find clues and bits and pieces of this in the story behind the GOSPEL account.

The symbol of THE AQUARIAN GANYMEDE is the GRAIL OR CUP. The GRAIL is what links the MEDIEVAL EUROPEAN TRADITION OF THE GRAIL TO THE AGE OF AQUARIUS. Even the BOOK of REVELATIONS mentions the GRAILS or CUPS OF JUDGEMENT AND RENEWAL and so it all points to the END OF AN AGE AND THE BEGINNING OF A NEW CYCLE known as the PRECESSION OF THE AGES. The GRAIL represents:

The Holy Grail is a dish, plate or cup said to have been used by Jesus at the Last Supper and is an important symbol in the Arthurian myth. The Holy Grail represents the unattainable perfection that Arthur's knights must strive towards. (LITCHARTS)

Basically, the GRAIL represents the ALCHEMICAL PROCESS IN THE VIRTUOUS MAN and WOMAN. The "knights" on the other hand represent the archetype of LEADERSHIP that is ETHICAL AND THAT UPHOLDS HIGHER VALUES AND PRINCIPLES. These GRAIL qualities are necessary to cultivate and develop today and MUST BE REQUIRED for LEADERSHIP roles and positions if man wishes not to repeat more of the same evils of the past. No form of government can ever succeed when and if there are NO ETHICS AND HIGHER SPIRITUAL VALUES AND PRINCIPLES. BY SPIRITUAL "WE" are NOT referring to RELIGION but to TRUE AND REAL SPIRITUAL VALUES AND PRINCIPLES such as KINDNESS, MERCY, LOVE, FORGIVENESS, TRUTH), GOOD WILL, etc. etc. etc.

G-ANNY-MEDE is a PHRYGIAN and his PHRYGIAN CAP represents all democracies who share in common this symbol and the DEMOCRATIC IDEALS of "LIBERTE, FRATERNITE AND EGALITE" which are the 3 main pillars that depict modern DEMOCRATIC SYSTEMS. FRENCH MARI-ANNE is linked to these IDEALS which are all based on SYMBOLS REPRESENTING COSMIC ENERGIES that are manifesting at this time to complete the OLD CYCLE AND BEGIN THE NEW ONE. The phrygian cap represents the following as well:

*Although Phrygian caps did not originally function as liberty caps, they came to signify freedom and the pursuit of liberty first in the American Revolution and then in the French Revolution,[2] particularly as a symbol of jacobinism it has been also called a **jacobin cap**. The original cap of liberty was the Roman pileus, the felt cap of emancipated slaves of ancient Rome, which was an attribute of Libertas, the Roman goddess of liberty. (WIKIPEDIA)*

AQUA-ARI-US IS ABOUT THE E-MAN-CIPATION OF MAN from a state of CONSTRICTION to one of LIBERTY which begins with the MIND. Most of humankind has been ENSLAVED IDEOLOGICALLY, acting out centuries of CONDITIONING ; thus, spreading WAR AND MORE OF THE SAME DISEASE ALL OVER THE WORLD. THE WORD "MAN" IS RELATED TO THE WORD "MENES" WHICH IS LATIN - SANSKRIT FOR "MIND."

G-ANNU--MEDE is linked to the return of the ANNU to the MEDE or MIDDLE WORLD which is the material realm. The name also shares similar root words with the name of the God GANESHA who is the REMOVER OF OBSTACLES and who removes these obstacles for the REGENERATION OF THE NEW AGE. GANYMEDE IS ZEUS "FAVORITE" human who in myth takes the form of the EAGLE AND TAKES GANYMEDE WITH HIM TO HEAVEN. This is similar to ELOHIM TAKING Y-ESH-UA BACK TO HEAVEN in the GOSPEL story and in other similar stories worldwide. EAGLE IS LINKED TO "SHAMAN" and therefore to THE LINK BETWEEN HEAVEN AND EARTH.

ORI-GINAL "MAN" is BOTH MALE-FEMALE or the DIVINE ANDROGYNE WHOM IS A SCIENTIFIC REALITY IN ATOMIC PRINCIPLES such as PROTON, ELECTRON AND—NEUTRON. As in GENDER "NEUTRAL." And so the AGE OF AQUARIUS moves away from the total MATRIARCHY, the total PATRIARCHY into the AGE OF "BOTH AS ONE UNIT" as it was before THE FALL OR SEPARATION OR FRAGMENTATION BETWEEN THE "MALE" AND "FEMALE" ENERGIES. Now all is being RECONCILED IN CHRIST CONSCIOUSNESS AND HIS SHE-KI-INNA WHO ARE "ONE!!!" And so the G-ANNY-MEDE SYMBOL is ANDROGYNOUS AND "QUEER" just as —ZEUS falls in LOVE with G-ANNY-MEDE who takes him up to heaven to serve as his cupbearer in Greek myth.

THEREFORE THE SYMBOL OF THIS NEW AGE IS THE "DIVINE CHILD" OR "DIVINE "ANDRO"-GENESIS!!!"

WELCOME TO "OUR" NEW AGE AS WE ARE NOT LIMITED AND NEITHER GO BY MALE FEMALE ANATOMY DESCRIPTIONS. WE ARE BOTH AND NEITHER AT ONCE AND — GLORIOUSLY, TRANS-CENDENT!!! —SAY THE MIGHTY ELOHIM.

SINCERELY, "G-ANNE- Y- MEDE"

---

## 108. "USELESS" PRAYERS: A PSYCHOLOGICAL AND SPIRITUAL PERSPECTIVE ON PRAYING FOR THE SALVATION OF ONE AND THE DEATH OF THE OTHER

WE HAVE NOTICED FROM "UP HERE" AND FROM OUR PANORAMIC VIEWPOINT, UNLIKE YOURSELVES AND YOUR CLEARLY LIMITED VISION AND UNDERSTANDINGS, THAT — SOME OF YOU ARE PRAYING FOR ISRAEL'S SALVATION WHILE PRAYING FOR THE DEATH OF PALESTINIANS. ON THE OTHER HAND, THE OTHER PART IS PRAYING FOR THE SALVATION OF PALESTINE AND FOR THE DEATH OF ISRAELIS.

WE HAVE A PROBLEM WITH THIS!!!!

YOU SEE, BOTH ARE "PRAYING TO THE SAME —- DEITY— SINCE THESE TRADITIONS REVERE THE SAME DEITY ALTHOUGH BOTH CALL IT BY A DIFFERENT "TITLE." OUR QUESTION IS.....

IF "BOTH ARE SUPPOSEDLY WORSHIPING AND PRAYING TO THE SAME DEITY," WHO IS THE "BLOODY IDOL" GOING TO LISTEN TO AND CHOOSE FROM??? YOU SEE NOW WHAT THE MAIN PROBLEM IS?

WE DO NOT CONDONE "HATE AND VIOLENCE" WHICH IS THE REASON YOU HAVE BEEN CAST OUT OF THE CONFEDERATION OF GALAXIES DOWN TO EARTH FOR YOUR REFUSAL TO ABIDE BY THE TENETS OF THE HIGHER PLANES; AND, REGARDLESS OF GOD OR TRADITION YOU HAVE ALL MADE A PROMISE TO US JUST AS ALL THE OTHER "NATIONS" THAT YOU WILL" "COMPLY AND UPHOLD" YOUR PARTICULAR "LIFE /SOUL CONTRACTS" IN ORDER TO COME BACK TO US. YET, YOU ARE VIOLATING OUR "PLEDGE OF ALLEGIANCE TO THE CONFEDERATION OF GALAXIES" THROUGH YOUR HYPOCRISY BY CLAIMING TO UPHOLD "OUR VALUES OF LIFE AND PEACE AND BROTHERHOOD PRINCIPLES" AND INSTEAD ARE TURNING AWAY FROM Y-OUR PROMISSORY NOTE TO DO THE OPPOSITE.

SO LET US SUMMARIZE ... YOU ARE (—-ARE, INCLUDES THE SO CALLED "CHRISTIAN" NATIONS AS WELL —-) SUPPORTING AND CONDONING THE CARNAGE ONE WAY OR ANOTHER AND VIOLATING YOUR PLEDGES OF ALLEGIANCE TO THE CONFEDERATION. WHILE CLAIMING TO STAND FOR "LOVE AND JUSTICE AND ALL THESE LOFTY IDEALS" BUT ONLY ON PAPER AND BY MOUTH AND VIOLATING OUR TERMS AND CONDITIONS OF YOUR "PROMISSORY CONTRACTS." THAT YOU ARE WORSHIPING A "BLOODY IDOL" MEANS THAT —-NO ONE IS TAKING HEED OF ALL YOUR EMPTY AND FOUL PRAYERS SINCE YOU ARE NOT IN ALIGNMENT WITH OUR "LOVE AND PEACE VIBRATIONS." WE CAN ONLY HEAR THAT WHICH IS IN ALIGNMENT WITH THE HIGHER PLANES AND SINCE WE ARE UP HERE WE CAN SEE THE WHOLE PICTURE INCLUDING THOSE WHO PRAY BELIEVING THAT NO ONE IS "SEEING" WHAT EVIL THEY ARE DOING AND CONCOCTING IN THE PRIVACY OF THEIR HEARTS AND HOMES.

THEREFORE, THY PRAYERS ARE "OBSOLETE" TO US FOR WE ARE NOT IMPRESSED WITH PRAYERS BASED ON HATE AND MURDEROUS INTENT AND EMOTIONS.

THEREFORE, WE DO NOT GO BY WORDS ONLY JUST AS YOU DECEIVE YOURSELVES WITH THE EMPTY WORDS OF YOUR CORRUPT "SO CALLED LEADERS" BUT WE "SEE AND NOTICE" WHETHER THAT WHICH YOU ARE UTTERING WITH YOUR LIPS IS IN ALIGNMENT WITH YOUR ACTIONS TOWARDS EACH OTHER AND EVERYBODY ELSE AND WITH THE "VALUES AND PRINCIPLES" OF THE "CONFEDERATION OF STAR NATIONS."

SINCERELY, "THE COUNCIL OF THE MOTHER CONSTELLATION 13 THROUGH OUR DIVINE BIPOLAR GATES"

---

## 109. "HEAVEN" AND "EARTH:" THE DIVISION OF THE SO CALLED "PAGAN" OR EARTH BASED AND "SKY" BASED TRADITIONS—--- ALL TRADITIONS ARE A COMBINATION OF SKY AND EARTH BASED PRACTICES, BELIEFS AND TRADITIONS.

THERE HAS BEEN A TERRIBLE AND HORRIBLE CONFUSION AND MISUNDERSTANDING AND AS A RESULT MUCH TRAUMA AND KARMA THAT HAS BEEN PASSED DOWN FROM GENERATION TO GENERATION BECAUSE OF THE VILIFICATION OF SOME TRADITIONS AND THE MAGNIFICATION OF OTHERS.

AS WE HAVE STATED BEFORE, ALL TRADITIONS SHARE MUCH IN COMMON IN MANY WAYS. FROM THE USE OF SONG AND DANCE AND RITUAL TO THE USE OF "SYMBOLS" TO REPRESENT AND GIVE MEANING TO COSMIC CONCEPTS THAT ARE DIFFICULT TO UNDERSTAND. ALL THESE TRADITIONS ARE NOT SO —UNLIKE TO EACH OTHER—AS MANY WOULD LIKE TO BELIEVE. AFTER ALL, THE CORE AND FIRST "TRADITION" WAS THE "NATURE BASED" TRADITION BECAUSE IT IS THE CLOSEST WE HAVE TO THE DIVINE LAWS AND POWERS WHICH GIVE US AN IDEA OF HOW THE COSMOS (—AND OUR BODIES—) WORKS AND RULES ITSELF BY THESE SAME NATURAL LAWS.

THE BASIC IDEA THAT WE HAVE MENTIONED BEFORE IS THAT OF THE "DIVINE TRIAD" OR THE THREE COSMIC PRINCIPLES WHICH ARE THE "NEGATIVE", "POSITIVE" AND "NEUTRAL OR BINOMIAL." THE NEGATIVE IS ATTRIBUTED TO THE MOTHER YIN, THE POSITIVE TO THE FATHER YANG AND THE NEUTRAL OR BINOMIAL TO THE "IN BETWEEN" PRINCIPLE OR THE "CHILD" OF YIN AND YANG WHO OCCUPIES —THE DA-AT —POSITION IN THE TREE OF LIFE. THESE THREE PLUS KETER FORM THE BASIC BUILDING BLOCKS OF EXISTENCE AND SO THIS IS ANOTHER REASON THAT ITS CALLED THE "TREE OF LIFE AND OF DUALITY."

THEREFORE, THE TREE OF LIFE IS SHOWING US THAT THERE IS A MASCULINE POSITIVE ASPECT TO REALITY WHICH SOME ATTRIBUTE TO THE "HEAVENS." HERE IS WHERE THE "SO CALLED MONO-THEISTIC" TRADITIONS ARE BORN. THE SYMBOL FOR THE MASCULINE PRINCIPLE IS THE SUN SHINING IN THE SKY. THE SUN WAS THE FIRST SYMBOL FOR "GOD" THE FATHER. DESCRIBED AS THE GIVER OF LIFE BECAUSE IT GIVES LIGHT AND ENERGY FOR THINGS TO BE BORN AND LIVE. THE SUN REPRESENTS THE "CREATOR" PRINCIPLE. HE IS THE IMPREGNATOR.

HOWEVER, WE ARE —INCOMPLETE—WITHOUT THE OTHER HALF OF THE DUALITY WHICH IS THE MOTHER PRINCIPLE OR YIN. SHE IS GIVEN THE NEGATIVE POLARITY AND HER SYMBOL IS THE MOON. THE SKY CANNOT BE SEEN CLEARLY IN THE NEW MOON, THEREFORE SHE WAS ASSOCIATED TO THE WORLDS THAT ARE NOT SEEN. OR NETHERWORLDS. SHE "RECEIVES" THE LIGHT OF THE SUN IN THE FULL MOON POINTING TO THE PROCESS OF "GROWTH AND REBIRTH OF THINGS." SHE REPRESENTS THE "EARTH ELEMENT" THAT RECEIVES THE "LIGHT OF THE FATHER SUN" WHICH MAKES LIFE SPROUT FROM THE DARK EARTH AND —- GROW WITH THE HELP OF THE CYCLES OF THE MOON. SHE IS THE RECEIVER AND THE BIRTHER.

IT'S ALL ABOUT —SCIENCE —DESCRIBED IN RELIGIOUS, SYMBOLIC AND SPIRITUAL GARB UNDERNEATH THE STORIES AND SYMBOLS. SO BASICALLY, THE MOON IS "IMPREGNATED" BY THE LIGHT OF THE FATHER AND BECAUSE OF IT THE IDEAS OF THE MOTHER OR COSMIC TEMPLATE COME TO REALITY BY MEANS OF THE CREATIVE ENERGY OF THE FATHER. BASICALLY, EACH "SEED" HAS THE "INFORMATION INSIDE"

THAT MAKES IT BECOME WHAT IT BECOMES. LIKEWISE, JUST AS A SEED, THE EARTH IS A "HUGE" SEED FLOATING IN SPACE IMPREGNATED BY THE SUN TO SPROUT LIVING AND INANIMATE BEINGS AND THINGS AND MADE TO GROW BY THE CYCLES OF THE MOON AND WATER. WATER IS ATTRIBUTED TO THE WOMB OF THE MOTHER AND HER DIVINE FEMININE.

TODAY'S SO CALLED "PAGAN OR EARTH BASED TRADITIONS" ARE OF THE MOTHER PRINCIPLE WHILE THE SO CALLED MONO-THEISTIC TRADITIONS ARE ATTRIBUTED TO THE FATHER PRINCIPLE. SO WHAT HAPPENS TO THE "THIRD PRINCIPLE" OR THE—-NEUTRAL - BINOMIAL—ASPECT? WELL, IN THE MIDDLE IS THE "CONFLUENCE OR COMBINATION OF BOTH THE SO CALLED EARTH BASED AND SKY BASED TRADITIONS OR A HYBRID "SKY-EARTH" WHICH TRIES TO BALANCE BOTH ASPECTS OF THIS REALITY INTO "OUR WORLD AS ONE."

MEANING THAT THE SO CALLED MONOTHEISTIC TRADITIONS ARE NOT COMPLETELY "MONO" AND NEITHER ARE THE SO CALLED "PAGAN" COMPLETELY POLY AND EARTH BASED. THE FACT THAT THE JEWISH AND ISLAMIC TRADITIONS FOLLOW A "LUNAR" CALENDAR POINTS TO THE EARLY EARTH BASED "FEMININE" BELIEFS AND PRACTICES OF THESE "GOD" BASED TRADITIONS. AS WE HAVE ALREADY MENTIONED, THE MOON / LUNA IS OF THE MOTHER PRINCIPLE AND IS LINKED TO THE HARVEST AND GROWING OF THINGS SUCH AS HER "CRESCENT MOON" LUNAR PRINCIPLE OF "GROWTH." THE POLYTHEISTIC TRADITIONS WITH THEIR PANTHEONS IN THE SKY ALSO SHARE MUCH WITH THE MONOTHEISTIC

AND THE EARTH BASED SINCE THESE SKY DEITIES ARE LINKED TO EARTH ELEMENTS AND CONCEPTS IN THESE TRADITIONS.

ON THE OTHER HAND WE HAVE THE SO CALLED PAGAN IN WHICH SOME WORSHIP THE DIVINE MOTHER PRINCIPLE INCLUDING HER "SON." ..... ALTHOUGH WORSHIPPERS MIGHT BE MAINLY FOCUSED ON THE MOTHER AND HER ELEMENT EARTH, THE —SON— REPRESENTS THE MASCULINE AND SO HE IS LINKED TO THE SUN AS WE HAVE SEEN PREVIOUSLY AND TO THE "GIVER OF LIFE OR LIGHT" PRINCIPLE.

SO TO SUM UP THIS DIARY, THE SO CALLED MONOTHEISTIC TRADITIONS FOCUS ON THE "GOD", THE "SUN" OR "CHOKMAH" FATHER PRINCIPLE. MEANWHILE, THE EARTH BASED TRADITIONS FOCUS MAINLY ON "THE MOTHER PRINCIPLE" "THE MOON" "THE EARTH" "THE DARK" "BINAH" ETC. HOWEVER, SINCE WE ALL LIVE IN A DUAL WORLD WHERE WE ALL ARE MADE UP OF BOTH MALE AND FEMALE PRINCIPLES AND HAVE THE CAPACITY TO VIEW AND LIVE LIFE AND EXPERIENCE THE WORLD FROM BOTH MALE AND FEMALE VIEWPOINTS, OUR HUMAN TRADITIONS, WHEN YOU DISSECT THEM CAREFULLY AND IN DETAIL, ARE AN AMALGAMATION AND COMBINATION OF BOTH "SOLAR AND LUNAR" PRINCIPLES AND VALUES.

WHICH MEANS THAT THERE IS NO TOTALLY AND COMPLETE MONOTHEISTIC OR POLYTHEISTIC OR MOTHER BASED OR FATHER BASED TRADITIONS. IN A HEALTHY AND BALANCED WORLD BOTH "ASPECTS OF REALITY" LIVE ONE NEXT TO THE OTHER IN EQUALITY AND HEALTH. BRINGING ABOUT HARMONY AND DOING AWAY WITH "THE BURNING TIMES AND THE PERSECUTION TIMES."

SINCERELY, "ARA-DIA AND DI-ANNA AND LUZ-Y-FERO"

---

## 110. THE ANNU AND THE NAKI: THE NAKI OR NAGAS OF ANNU — AND THE HOUSE OF BEIT-ANNU

THE "ANNU" - "NAKI" NAME IS FORMED BY TWO WORDS DESCRIBING WHO THEY ARE. THE "NAKI" IS THE PLURAL FORM WORD FOR "NAGA.""THEREFORE, "NAKI" AND "NAGA" ARE POINTING TO THE SAME BEINGS OR COSMIC PRINCIPLES.

THE "ANNU" IS THE ADAME OF "SOURCE" AS IN "DEITY" WHICH COMBINED WITH THE WORD "NAKI" BECOMES THE —-NAGAS OF ANNU.

"NAKI" CAN BE UNSCRAMBLED AND PUT BACK TOGETHER TO FORM THE NAME "ANKI" WHICH IS ANOTHER NAME OR FORM FOR THE "CHILD OR

SON OF ANNU" NAMED "ENKI OR ANKI." ANNE-KI OR ANNU-KI-DU. ANNU-NAKI THEREFORE ALSO STANDS FOR "ANKI CHILD OF ANNU. ANNE-KI THE ANNU WHO COMES TO EARTH IN THE BEGINNING OF TIME TO TEACH CIVILIZATION AND THE ARTS AND ADMINISTRATION AND CULTURE ETC. ETC. ETC. TO HUMANS.

ANNE-KI ARRIVES WITH OTHERS AND SETS UP "THE HOUSE OF ANNU" OR "ANNE-KI" OR "ANNA." A HOUSE OR LINE THAT HAS ORIGINS —"SOMEWHERE OUT THERE WHERE DREAMS COME TRUE"!!!

THE ANNU-"KI" TITLE CARRIES THE "KI" OR "KEY" OR "HOLY QI!!!!"WORD and ENERGY. THEY ARE THE BEINGS OF FIRE AS IN NAGAS AND ARE THE GUARDIANS OF THE HOLY —KI— OR —"QI" AND SO THEY ARE THE SACRED LINEAGE OF HEALERS WORLDWIDE.

THE HOUSE OF "BETH-ANNI" IS POPULAR IN THE GOSPEL ACCOUNT AND LINKED TO "THE HEALING STORIES" BECAUSE IT HAILS FROM ENKI AND THE LINE OF HEALERS AND TEACHERS OF HUMANKIND. THE BEIT OR THE HOUSE OF ANNA!!!!! THERE ARE BRANCHES OF THE ANNU ALL OVER THE EARTH AND THEY ARE NOT WORLDLY ROYAL LINES PER SE BUT ARE "THE WISE PEOPLE WHO HEAL AND KEEP THE WORLD IN BALANCE" SUCH AS THE NATIVE AMERICAN "PAH-ANNA" WHO IS THE "BIRD OR FEATHERED ONE OF THE HOUSE OF ANNU IN THE NATIVE AMERICAN CONTINENT.

THE LINE OF ANNU IS LINKED TO BOTH HEAVEN AND THE UNDERWORLDS AND SO THEY ARE THE ORIGINAL "SHAMANIC LINES" OF THE WORLD.

THE GOSPEL STORY THEREFORE IS A METAPHOR POINTING OUT TO THE "ANNU-KI" LINE OF HEALERS AND TEACHERS AND THEIR ORIGINS "SOMEWHERE OUT THERE WHERE DREAMS COME TRUE." THEY ARE THE BEINGS OF HOLY FIRE AND SO THEY HELP IGNITE AND ACTIVATE THE "SACRED FIRE" IN HUMANS AND BRING BALANCE TO IT.

SINCERELY, "ENKI-DU "

---

## 111. KAABA: THE CIRCUMAMBULATION OF THE CUBE and the HOLY MANDALA I

"The cube is a three-dimensional SQUARE; it is **a symbol of stability and permanence, of geometric perfection**. It represents the final stage of a cycle of immobility, it can be seen as the truth, because it looks the same from any perspective, it is commonly thought of as the counterpart of the sphere." GOOGLE

The circle is a universal symbol with extensive meaning. It represents the notions of **totality, wholeness, original perfection, the Self, the infinite, eternity, timelessness, all cyclic movement, God** ('God is a circle whose centre is everywhere and whose circumference is nowhere' (Hermes Trismegistus)). GOOGLE

M-ANNE-D-ALLA (MANDALA) :

1.  a geometric figure representing the universe in Hindu and Buddhist symbolism.

2.  a symbol in a dream, representing the dreamer's search for completeness and SELF-UNITY. (GOOGLE)

MULADH-ARA is the ROOT CHAKRA and it's about GROUNDING and the EARTH.

How does the CIRCUMAMBULATION at KAABA (or CUBO, in SPANISH) have to do with BUDDHISM and THE EASTERN TRADITIONS? It would seem ridiculous to associate a MONOTHEISTIC tradition of the WEST with a TRADITION such as BUDDHISM. Some will say "YE CRAZY, DUDE." But in reality, all traditions have been observing THE SAME ARCHETYPES. After all, THE SOURCE IS "ONE" and so despite the differences in tradition and cultures WE ARE ALL DRAWING INFORMATION AND INSIGHT FROM THE SAME UNI-VERSAL SOURCE. Only that we are seeing the SAME UNI-VERSAL DIAMOND from our particular perspective and vision but still the DIAMOND IS THE SAME ONE.

And so what WE are trying to point here is that the CIRCUMAMBULATION of the KAABA at MAKKAH is basically a MANDALA seen from up above and following similar meanings as in the BUDDHIST TRADITIONS even if Muslims are not aware of that, yet.

And so as you can see above, THE MANDALA is also a SQUARE SURROUNDED BY A CIRCLE. It also represents or stands for the MULADHARA CHAKRA in the Hindu yoga tradition. It represents an ENERGY WHEEL, A REPRESENTATION OF INFINITY AND THE CYCLICAL NATURE OF ENERGY. (GOOGLE)

SINCERELY, FAT-IMA OF MOHAMADINA THROUGH OUR UNIVERSAL BIPOLAR SON

---

## 112. THE CIRCUMAMBULATION OF THE CUBE and the HOLY MANDALA II

Basically the CIRCUMAMBULATION or WIDDERSHINS which is the COUNTER CLOCKWISE movement is AFFIRMING the "UNITY" OF ALL THE UNI-VERSE IN TERMS OF BOTH THE MATERIAL REALM as well as ETERNAL OR SPIRITUAL. IT BECOMES AN AFFIRMATION OF THE "CIRCLE OR WEB OF LIFE." It is

AFFIRMING THE "QI" IN ALL LIVING THINGS AND INANIMATE THINGS. The ritual going counterclockwise affirms the DIVINE PRESENCE OR DIVINE FEMININE and HER LUNAR CYCLE. While going clockwise belongs to the FATHER, SUN.

"Lift up the rock and there you will find QI, split the wood and there I AM." ( JESUS, GOSPEL OF THOMAS)

THE CIRCUMAMBULATION is intending to AFFIRM the SPIRITUAL WITHIN THE MATERIAL as in the DIVINE SPARK OR FIRE TRAPPED IN THE KLIPPOT or shards. THE UNI-TY of it all. It is reminding us that we are living in a multi-dimensional world in which we are TRAPPED BETWEEN "DOS MUNDOS" or TWO WORLDS, the material and the spiritual. Therefore, you and I are BOTH spiritual beings experiencing a material existence.

As THE SQUARE OR CUBE AND THE CIRCLE FORM THE "ROOT MANDALA".... it also stands for the BEGINNING OF OUR EARTHLY - COSMIC journey. We are here and about to begin a HUMAN EXPERIENCE that takes us from THE FALL to this plane of existence moving up the TREE OF LIFE going back upwards.

The mandala also stands for "MOTION as in the CIRCLE" and "GROUNDEDNESS OR IMMOBILITY as in the SQUARE." SPIRIT particles moving at diverse speeds in order to bring about this material world although everything in the eye seems to be fixed or not moving or stationary. Do you see the OPPOSITES working here?

WE are not as different as we might think we are or mutually exclusive as we think we might be since we are all drawing wisdom and meaning from the SAME ARCHETYPICAL SOURCE.

M-ANNE-D-ALLAH as in THE MAN OF ALLAH (THE EL-OHEEM or GOD). M-ONNE-D-ALLA is also similar to the LATIN - SPANISH M-ONNE-D or MUNDO which is WORLD or ONE WORLD of EL or ALLAH who REPRESENTS THE FORCES AND POWERS OR ENERGIES OF THE UNIVERSE THAT MAKE BOTH SPIRIT AND MATTER POSSIBLE.

It's a small world after all.

SINCERELY, ME "ANNA" OF GOD

---

## 113. THE SACRED CIRCLE OF LIFE (THE SHEEP EVENT) and THE NEW AEON OF AQUARIUS 11/4/2022

11 JUSTICE CARD, 4 EMPEROR, 20 JUDGMENT of 4, 10 WHEEL OF FORTUNE, 16 THE TOWER.

This diary is about the SHEEP going in circles like the pilgrims worshiping DEITY around the KAABA event in 2022.

John 21:16:

"Again Jesus said, "Simon son of John, do you love me?" He answered, "Yes Lord, you know that I love you." Jesus said "take care of my sheep."

In other words, take care of MY PEOPLE, especially those who like sheep are clueless about the reality of this material realm. (JESUS)

21 is THE WORLD CARD and the CIRCLE is the orb of the Earth planet. The CUBE or SQUARE as in QAABA or QUBO (in Spanish) represents the MATERIAL PLANE / WORLD. 16 is the TOWER CARD as in UNAVOIDABLE CHANGES or changes that must be made if we want the nations and the globe to keep on living. The 3 EMPRESS QI-KI-INNA is back in the world to help the CHARIOT 7 Earth keep on moving. THE CHARIOT is also about MOTION AND WHEELS which are circular in shape.

As was explained years ago, the circling of the QAABA is after the DIVINE FEMININE. It's related to the other global dances of tribes and peoples everywhere that go in a circle. Imagine it as a MANDALA or M-ANNE-D-ALLAH or DIVINE SQUARE WITHIN A CIRCLE as in the Buddhist mandala representing the DIVINE, the UNIVERSE and MAN. IT REPRESENTS THE "UNION OF OPPOSITES or of THE SPIRITUAL AND MATERIALrealms.

From Crystal Clear Intuition:

**A circle represents evolution as a process of transformation from death to birth, ending, and beginning, as a circle has no beginning and no end. In this sense, a circle represents eternity. In many customs and spiritual beliefs, a circle represents the Divine life-force or Spirit that keeps our reality in motion. It is symbolic of vitality, wholeness, completion, and perfection.** (Crystal Clear Intuition)

The circle as you can see also represents QI as in QI-KI-INNA and RUACH ELOHEEM.

**Spiritually, the circle represents a supernatural motion that keeps things moving continuously. A circle represents the heavens, whereas the earth and human form are seen as the square. One a larger scale, a circle represents the Divine that keeps everything moving through spiritual law and order. On a smaller scale, a circle represents our own individual spiritual force that keeps us evolving.(Crystal Clear Intuition)**

Sheep are for the most part WHITE so that circle becomes a WHITE CIRCLE:

**A white circle represents the beginning of a new cycle and opportunities for spiritual growth. It represents purity, perfection, and new life. In a positive context, a white circle represents spiritual evolution and beginning a new cycle with a higher perspective. In a negative context, a white circle can represent someone stuck in spiritual growth and expressing abandonment of the physical reality for solely spiritual pursuits. (Crystal Clear intuition)**

13 is DEATH AND TRANSFORMATION- death of an old Aeon and beginning of a new one or the Age of Aquarius. The symbolism on this card seems to be based on the BOOK OF REVELATION or at least coincides with the PALE HORSE ARCHETYPE. Revelation 6:7 which numbers add up to "13." 1 + 3 = 4 THE EMPEROR. The MASCULINE PRINCIPLE is not in TEMPERANCE and thus JUDGMENT and JUSTICE are being passed. KARMIC CYCLES are activated in order to balance the karmic accounting books. READ AGE OF AQUARIUS diary. Atomic bombs, violence, aggression, male extremism, destruction of life and ecosystems, etc. etc. etc. It will be a tough and rough road ahead but DO NOT DESPAIR.

As the CIRCLE is movement. So it is a call for ACTION. REPAIRING rather than destroying, for destroying the Earth is destroying OURSELVES. (So called) WORLD LEADERS are accountable to HIGHER POWERS for tending WISELY AND JUSTLY over the PEOPLE or CHILDREN OF THE MOST HIGH.

SINCERELY, M-ANNE-D-ALLAH

---

## 114. BREAK IT TO ME GENTLY: NO PHYSICAL TEMPLE ANYWHERE ON EARTH CAN SAVE THE EARTH AND PEOPLE!!! TIME TO START PROTECTING AND CARING FOR THE "REAL TEMPLE OF THE DIVINE" AS IN —"GAIA AND HER LIVING AND INANIMATE BEINGS!!!"

BASICALLY, THE "TEMPLE" WAS OR IS AN ARCHETYPAL REPRESENTATION OF SOMETHING GREATER. THE TEMPLE ARCHETYPE OR SYMBOL IS NOT THE ANSWER OR THE GOAL BUT JUST A SYMBOL THAT POINTS BACK AT SOME UNIVERSAL OR COSMIC PRINCIPLE AND VALUE.

THAT COSMIC PRINCIPLE AND VALUE THAT IT POINTS TO IS THE "SACRED PRINCIPLE OF LIFE ITSELF."

THIS BELIEF IN THE "LIVING WALKING TEMPLE" OF THE DIVINE IS AT THE CORE OF ALL WORLD TRADITIONS AND SO IT IS NOT JUST A JUDEO-CHRISTIAN-ISLAMIC CONCEPT. IT IS FOUND CLEARLY IN THE EASTERN SALUTATION OF "NAMASTE" AS IN—I UPHOLD, ACKNOWLEDGE AND SALUTE THE—DIVINE IN YOU —AS IT IS IN ME."

SO THE LESSON FROM THE TANAKH AND GOSPEL IS THAT "PHYSICAL TEMPLES MADE OF MATTER" AND BY HUMAN HANDS ARE PRONE TO CORRUPTION, AND JUST AS EVERYTHING ELSE IN THIS MATERIAL PLANE, IT FOLLOWS THE LAWS OF "IMPERMANENCE. " EVENTUALLY THE TEMPLE COLLAPSES AND BECOMES PAST HISTORY. AND SO IF THERE WAS ANOTHER TEMPLE TO BE BUILT ON THE BELIEF THAT SOMEHOW IT WOULD SAVE THE EARTH, IT WOULD BE ANOTHER HUGE MISTAKE AND MISUNDERSTANDING FOR THE "FORCES OF NATURE" DO NOT RESIDE IN TEMPLES MADE BY MEN ESPECIALLY WHEN THE HANDS BUILDING THESE TEMPLES ALSO DO EVIL OR ARE BLOODY.

THE TEMPLE OF Y-ERU-SHALEM AND ANY OTHER TEMPLES IN ALL TRADITIONS ALL OVER THE EARTH ARE REPRESENTATIONS OF THE SACRED AS IN SACRED "PLACES" THAT REPRESENT THE CONGRESS OF THE DIVINE FORCES OF NATURE THAT COME TOGETHER TO BRING ABOUT ALL COMPLEX AND SIMPLE LIVING AND INANIMATE THINGS AND BEINGS IN THIS BEAUTIFUL PLANET.

THEREFORE THE "TEMPLE" REPRESENTS THE "PLACE WHERE THE DIVINE FORCES OF NATURE MANIFEST OR COME TOGETHER TO BRING ABOUT LIFE!!!" IN OTHER WORDS, THE TEMPLES MADE BY MEN ARE POINTING TO THE "GREAT TEMPLE OF THE DIVINE" AS IN "....-----THE EARTH HERSELF— AND THE —LIFE BEINGS WHICH ARE ANIMATED WITH THE HOLY "QI" OR DIVINE FIRE WHICH MAKES LIVING BEINGS INCLUDING HUMANS "LIVING TEMPLES MANIFESTING AS HUMAN BEINGS IN WHICH THE SACRED NAMASTE OR HOLY FIRE RESIDES."

THE POINT IS THAT —-IF HUMANS DO NOT RESPECT AND ACKNOWLEDGE THE INNATE AND INHERENT DIVINITY IN EVERYONE AND IN NATURE ITSELF AND IF HUMANS DO NOT RESPECT AND TAKE CARE OF THE SACRED TEMPLE OF EARTH .... DO YOU THINK THAT WORSHIPING SOME PIECE OF HUMAN MADE MASONRY WOULD MAKE ANY DIFFERENCE???

NOPE!!!!

TIME TO LET GO OF THE IDOLS AND EDIFICES AND MOVE BEYOND THAT TO "THE GREATER MEANING IT ALL WAS POINTING TO AFTER ALL — AT THE EARTH ITSELF AND AT THE INNATE DIVINITY IN HUMAN AND NATURE." NO HUMAN MADE BUILDING CAN REPLACE THE ACTUAL "DIVINE FIRE" MANIFESTING AS LIFE AND NEITHER CAN A BUILDING CREATED THROUGH DEATH AND VIOLENCE AND EVIL AND INJUSTICE MAKEUP FOR THE "SANCTITY OF ALL LIFE AND THE HOLINESS OF HUMAN LIFE AND LIFE IN GENERAL IN THIS TEMPLE OF THE COSMOS CALLED PLANET —-EARTH!!!"

SINCERELY, "GAIA SPEAKING THROUGH THE BIPOLAR GATES OF COMMUNICATION"

---

## 115. AL MA-D-INNA AL M-UNNA-W-"ARA" – THE HOUSE OF D-INNA IN IS-EL-AM

The second holiest city in Islam is MEDINA which is AL MA-D-INNA and whose former name was YATHRIB or YATRIB. YA-TRIB as in the TRIBE OF YAH around the oasis in MA-D-INNA. As you will recall, it was around YATHRIB OASIS that for a while the diverse tribes co-existed with one another.

AL stands for "THE," MA for "UM-MA" and DE for "IS OF" and "INNA" . As in THE MOTHER OF INNA, ME INNA THE LIGHT, FIRE AND GOLD or ARA who is born of the WOMB OF THE DARK MOTHER B-INNA. THE HOLY SHE-QI-INNA. The HOLY SHE-QI-INNA is the DIVINE PRESENCE in the world and in each human being. N-AMAS-TE!

THE HOLY SHE-QI-INNA is linked to THE ANNU or ELOHIM. Whose energies were represented by the P-ANNE-THEO-ANNU of 365 DEITIES at KAABA before it all was COMPRESSED back to ONE DIVINE PRINCIPLE WHO IS "EL" who is AL-LAH.

As you will recall, the HOSANNA or BEIT-ANNI is to do with the ANNU and the 13th HOUSE OF D-INNA. It seems MOHA-MAD was of the house of INNA himself and a reason why he went through the PSYCHO-SPIRITUAL schizo experience too which led to the COR-ANNE or the BOOK OF THE HEART OF ANNU.

So do you see his name, or rather NEW NAME or title after undergoing the process and REALIZATION OF THE UNITY OF ALL THINGS? and receiving a new name. MOHAS is a Sanskrit name and MA is after the MOTHER or "MA." He named himself or was named after the MOTHER PRINCIPLE after the name of the city of MA-DINNA. As in MOHA-MAD-INNA! Mohammad of the INNA or ANNU and of "D-INNA."

AND "WISDOM AND REVELATION" IS ATTRIBUTED TO THE FEMININE PRINCIPLE.

He knew about the HOLY SHE-QI-INNA MOTHER and the whole JUDEO AND CHRISTIAN traditions having lived with the tribes at YA-TRIB where the TRIBES OF YA-WEH and JESUS lived.

Moha's name then became MOHA-MAD-INNA AL M-UNNA-W-ARA. MOHAMMAD OF D-INNA THE ONE AND THE LIGHT. MUNA means in Arabic WISHES AND DESIRES. WARA means PIETY. MOHAMMAD OF D-INNA THE PIOUS ONE WHO

GRANTS WISHES AND FULFILLS DESIRES just like in the HOS-ANNA tradition. MEDINA the latinized version of AL MADINA also shares the latin root word for MEDIC or MEDICINE as in HEALING. Linking it to the HOUSE OF HEALING. Therefore just like JUDAISM AND CHRISTIANITY before ISLAM, the movement started as a REFORM MOVEMENT born of the previous two and with the intention to TIKKUN OLAM. That is WHY in THE GOLDEN AGE OF ISLAMIC SPAIN they had some of the best doctors in the world when the rest of EUROPE was in a state of superstition and ignorance. Unfortunately, that is no longer the case with Islam as it has veered away from the TIKKUN OLAM tradition of the beginning and embraced DOGMA AND BELIEFS just like the other two. The closest version of ISLAM to the original is SUFISM.

ME-D-INNA, named after the SHE-QI-INNA being herself the COSMIC MEDIC that heals and the HOUSE OF BEIT-ANNI in AL-MA-DINNA. Some members of the HOUSE OF ANNA went west while others went east after the fall of Jerusalem and the death of ISSA and ensuing persecutions.

The ARA also comes from the ARA-MAIC tongue which is shared by the 3 traditions and which forms the basis for both HEBREW AND ARA-BIC.

SINCERELY,
SIMPLY "DINNA"

---

## 116. NATURE BASED TRADITION IS NOT "WITCHCRAFT AS RELIGIOUS FUNDAMENTALISTS AND EXTREMISTS DEFINE IT TO BE !!!" THE "WICCE TRADITION" IS OF AND IS ABOUT THE "WISE ONES!!!" PART I

JUST AS THERE ARE DIVERSE MONOTHEISTIC TRADITIONS OR "SKY BASED" TRADITIONS SO THE SAME IS WITH THE "EARTH BASED" TRADITIONS.

IT'S MOSTLY ABOUT "WISDOM" DRAWN BY OBSERVING NATURE JUST AS IN TAOISM.

NATURE IS LINKED TO "GAIA OR MOTHER EARTH" AND LIKE WE SAID BEFORE, THE WORKS AND FUNCTIONS OF NATURE ARE MAGICAL IN THE SENSE THAT WONDERFUL TRANSFORMATIONS TAKE PLACE SUCH AS A CATERPILLAR BECOMING A BUTTERFLY OR IN THE CASE OF VENOMOUS HERB WITH MEDICINAL AND HEALING PROPERTIES.

"QI," THE LIVING SUBSTANCE AND WHAT NIETZSCHE DESCRIBED AS THE "WILL TO POWER" IS THAT MAGICAL —AND —SCIENTIFIC— FORCE THAT PROPELS "QI" TO MANIFEST AS MANY AND DIVERSE LIVING BEINGS AND FORMS. WE AS HUMANS ARE NOT SEPARATE BUT —PART —OF NATURE ITSELF AND ITS NATURAL PROCESSES. WITHOUT NATURE WE ARE —

DEAD!!! OUR BODIES ARE MADE UP OF "THE BODY OF MOTHER EARTH AND HER ELEMENTS" WHICH WE ABSORB FROM THE PLANTS AND ANIMALS WHICH IN TURN ARE MANIFESTATIONS OF THE EARTH ELEMENTS AS WELL. AS WE CAN SEE HERE, WE ARE ALL A BIG INTERCONNECTED —CIRCLE OR WEB OF LIFE—IN WHICH EVERYTHING DEPENDS ON EVERYTHING ELSE.

REASON WHY THE "CIRCLE" IS A SACRED SYMBOL IN NATURE BASED TRADITIONS. BUT WE NEED TO CLARIFY HERE THAT NATURE BASED TRADITION IS NOT WHAT MONOTHEISTIC TRADITIONS LABEL AS — WITCHCRAFT OR DEVIL WORSHIP AND OTHER NONSENSE!

AS YOU CAN SEE EVEN THE "PAGAN" SYMBOLS HAVE A NATURAL SCIENTIFIC BASIS BEHIND THEIR USE AND PURPOSE. SUCH AS IN THE CASE OF THE SACRED CIRCLE REPRESENTING THE ONGOING CYCLE OF LIFE OR THE RECYCLING OF "QI / LIFE FORCE ENERGY" ACCORDING TO THE NATURAL "WILL TO POWER." OR, NATURE'S IMPULSE TO EXPRESS ITSELF IN DIVERSE LIFE FORMS. THIS SOUNDS NATURALLY MAGICAL TO ME.

JUST AS WE EXPLAINED BEFORE, NATURE IS A MANIFESTATION OF "THE ALL." THE SUN SUSTAINS AND PRESERVES THE NATURAL WORLD WITH ITS LIGHT ENERGY AND AND IN MANY TRADITIONS THE SUN REPRESENTS THE "LIGHT OF CHOKMAH" THE FATHER PRINCIPLE. REASON THIS MANIFESTATION OF ENERGY IN MOST TRADITIONS IS CONSIDERED MASCULINE. AND SO IN THIS CASE, NATURE IS THE "CHILD OF THE FATHER —SUN" AND SO "HUMANS ARE AS WELL.". THE MOON ON THE OTHER HAND SERVES ITS NATURAL PURPOSES TOO AND REPRESENTS THE BINAH MOTHER.

THEREFORE MAKING US CHILDREN SUSTAINED BY THE WISDOM OR ILLUMINATING PROCESS OF THE MOTHER.

THE ABOVE ARE JUST EXAMPLES OF THE — REASONING AND THINKING— BEHIND THE NATURE BASED TRADITIONS. YOU CAN SEE THIS HAS NOTHING TO DO WITH EVIL OR SATAN WORSHIP AS IS SO COMMONLY CLAIMED BY MONOTHEISTIC TRADITIONS TO VILIFY AND DESTROY THESE BEAUTIFUL NATURE BASED TRADITIONS. AFTER ALL, THE DIVINE MANIFESTS FIRST AND FOREMOST IN AND THROUGH THE NATURAL WORLD.

SINCERELY, GAIA AND HER WICCE CRAFT AND TRADITIONS

## 117. NATURE BASED TRADITION IS NOT "WITCHCRAFT AS RELIGIOUS FUNDAMENTALISTS AND EXTREMISTS DEFINE IT TO BE !!!" THE "WICCE TRADITION" IS OF AND ABOUT THE "WISE ONES!!!" PART II

ONE OF THE MAIN BRANCHES OF NATURE BASED TRADITIONS IS ...."ECOLOGY" AS IN — "ADAM AND EVE TAKE CARE OF THE GARDEN OF EDEN!!!" THAT SOUNDS A LOT LIKE "NATURE BASED TRADITIONS IN THE BIBLICAL CONTEXT." AND ALSO THE BRANCHES OF "HEALING" WHICH FORM THE BASIS FOR HOLISTIC MEDICINES IN ALL TRADITIONS. AND, DO NOT WE BENEFIT GREATLY FROM THE ORIGINAL MODALITIES OF HEALING INCLUDING CHINESE HERBAL AND ENERGY MEDICINE WHEN WESTERN MEDICINE NO LONGER WORKS?

SOMETHING REALLY BEAUTIFUL AND MAGICAL ABOUT NATURE ARE THE ELEMENTAL BEINGS AND FAMILY THAT GUARD NATURE. THESE BEINGS LIVE WITHIN EACH PLANT AS IN "CONSCIOUS QI ENERGY!!!" IT IS CONSCIOUS BECAUSE IT HAS TO KNOW WHAT TO DO IN ORDER TO BRING ABOUT THAT PLANT AND MAKE THAT PLANT THE WAY IT IS. THE SHAMANS CONNECT TO THE "QI BASED ELEMENTAL" OF SUCH PLANT AND THE PLANT ITSELF OR THE "QI SPIRIT" TELLS THE SHAMAN OR MEDICINE DOCTOR WHAT THAT PLANT IS GOOD FOR AND NOT GOOD FOR AND HOW IT IS TO BE USED IN REGARDS TO MEDICINAL AND HEALING PURPOSES. THIS IS GOOD MAGIC!!! AND THE BASIS FOR MODERN PHARMACEUTICALS!!!

THEREFORE, NEXT TIME YOU TAKE A PILL THAT GIVES YOU SOME SORT OF RELIEF AND THAT IS OF NATURAL SOURCES, GIVE THANKS TO THE —NATURE BASED TRADITIONS OF THE AMAZON AND OTHER INDIGENOUS PEOPLES—FOR THEY HAVE SAVED YOUR LIFE WITH THEIR MAGICAL KNOWLEDGE BASED ON THE "QI SPIRIT OF THAT PLANT." STOP VILIFYING AND PERSECUTING THAT WHICH HAS SAVED YOUR LIFE AND GIVEN YOU HOPE IN THE FACE OF DISEASE AND DEATH. IT IS NOT EVIL PER SE BUT DEPENDS ON HOW YOU USE IT. AT THE END WE AS PEOPLE MAKE THINGS GOOD OR EVIL OR NEUTRAL BY THE WAY WE USE THINGS. THEREFORE, LET US CHOOSE WISELY.

THE CURANDERA/O OR TRADITIONAL HEALERS OR MEDICINE WO-MEN (NOT THE CHARLATANS BUT THE REAL ONES WHO TODAY ARE HARD TO FIND) WHO ARE ETHICAL IN THEIR KNOWLEDGE AND APPLICATION ARE THE 'WICCE' OF OLD OR THE WISE ONES. REGARDED AS WISE BECAUSE OF THEIR SECRET KNOWLEDGE AND HEALING ABILITIES AND THEIR HIGH LEVEL OF INTUITION AND CONNECTION TO NATURE. THESE TYPES, JUST LIKE KING SOLOMON IN THE BIBLE, ARE ABLE TO UNDERSTAND

THE "LANGUAGE OF NATURE AND COMMUNICATE WITH IT." THE WHOLE UNIVERSE AND PLANET EARTH IS A LIVING CONSCIOUS BEING!!!

WE WILL DELVE MORE ON THIS TOPIC IN THE FUTURE.

SINCERELY, EVA THE FIRST "MEDICINE WOMAN" AND ADAM THE FIRST TO "CULTIVATE THE SACRED HERBS"

---

## 118. THE COMPLEMENTING AND SYNCHRONIZATION OF BOTH THE EARTH BASED AND SKY BASED SCIENCES AND TRADITIONS - OPPOSITES ATTRACT AND BECOME AS "ONE"

SO THE "EARTH BASED" TRADITION BELONGS TO EARTH AND IS THE ORIGINAL TRADITION. GUESS WHAT HAPPENS AFTER THE ARRIVAL OF THE ANNU? THEY CAME FROM "SOMEWHERE OUT THERE WHERE DREAMS COME TRUE" AND HUMANKIND AS IT WAS THEN REALIZED THAT THERE ARE "PEOPLE FROM THE SKY" AND THAT THEIR "FATHER" IS CALLED "ANNU" WHO MUST BE THEIR "FATHER SKY."

IN THE BEGINNING, THE FOCUS WAS ON NATURE AND ITS LAWS AND THE WORKINGS OF THE HUMAN BODY. AFTER THE ARRIVAL OF THE ANNU, AND WITH THEM THE CONCEPT OF "HEAVEN AND SKY BEINGS AND HEAVENLY FATHER" WAS ADOPTED.

THE NAME "ENNO-KI" IS A VERSION OF THE NAME "ENKI OR ANNE-KI." AS IN "ENOCH." AS WE HAVE EXPLAINED BEFORE, THAT NAME IS INCLUDED IN THE NAME OF THE "TEL" OR MOUND OR HILL IN THE MIDDLE OF TEX-COCO LAKE AS IN THE CITY OF "T-ENNOK-T-TEL-ANNU. THAT ENNOK "WENT TO HEAVEN" JUST POINTS OUT TO THE COSMIC CONNECTION BETWEEN THE "ANNU-KI AND THE HEAVENS." ENNO-KI WHO ARRIVES WITH THE COSMIC LAWS THAT REMIND HUMANS TO BE "KIND WITH ONE ANOTHER" SO THAT THE WORLD CAN CONTINUE AND DOES NOT FALL INTO CORRUPTION, DESTRUCTION AND ANNIHILATION BY HUMANS THEMSELVES.

THEREFORE WE HAVE HERE THE "NATURAL LAWS" OF THE EARTH BASED TRADITIONS WITH THE "COSMIC LAWS" OF THE SKY BASED TRADITIONS. BOTH ARE VALID AND MIRRORS TO EACH OTHER. SINCE THE NATURAL LAWS FOLLOW COSMIC LAWS AND COSMIC LAWS ARE THE FOUNDATION OF NATURAL LAW. "AS ABOVE SO IS BELOW AND AS BELOW SO IS ABOVE."

WHEN BOTH "EARTH AND COSMIC" LAWS ARE IN SYNCHRONICITY WITH ONE ANOTHER, EVERYTHING RUNS SMOOTHLY AND HUMANS RELATE BETTER WITH EACH OTHER AND WITH THE ECOLOGY OF THE PLANET. THIS GETTING ALONG WELL IS THE BASIS OF THE WORD CIVILIZATION

OR TO TREAT EACH OTHER IN A CIVILIZED MANNER. HUMANKIND IS IN TURMOIL TODAY BECAUSE IT HAS FOR A VERY LONG TIME "EXILED THE DIVINE FEMININE AND HER QUALITIES AND SCIENCES" WHILE MAGNIFYING THE DIVINE MASCULINE TO THE POINT WHERE IT ECLIPSES THE DIVINE FEMININE WHILE CORRUPTING THE MASCULINE SINCE BOTH NEED AND DEPEND ON EACH OTHER TO COMPLEMENT AND BALANCE ONE ANOTHER.

THEREFORE, THE SO CALLED "MONOTHEISTIC MALE-GOD" BASED TRADITIONS FOCUSED SOLELY ON THE SKY TO THE POINT WHERE THEY BEGAN NEGLECTING THE EARTH AS IT IS HAPPENING TODAY WITH THE DESTRUCTION OF THE ECOLOGY. IN OTHER WORDS, THE DIVINE FEMININE AND HER SCIENCES WERE VILIFIED AND FORGOTTEN IN THE RECESSES OF THE UNCONSCIOUS. AND AS WE HAVE SAID BEFORE, WHAT ONE DENIES AND REPRESSES COMES OUT DYSFUNCTIONALLY AND STRONGER. AND SO IT WAS THE END OF THE "GODDESS" ASPECT OF THE MALE DEITY ALTHOUGH IT SURVIVES TODAY SOMEHOW AS IN THE CONCEPT OF THE HOLY SHE-KI-INNA AND THE VIRGIN MARY DEVOTIONS IN JUDEO-CHRISTIAN-ISLAMIC TRADITIONS.

BASICALLY, TO UNDERSTAND THE "SCIENCES" AND TRADITIONS WELL AND FOR THESE TO BE BALANCED AND NOT MOVE TO EXTREMES AND BECOME DANGEROUSLY DYSFUNCTIONAL, —-NATURAL EARTH BASED LAW AND SCIENCE AS WELL AS COSMIC UNIVERSAL OR SKY BASED SCIENCE AND LAW —-MUST BE TAKEN INTO ACCOUNT TOGETHER AS COMPLEMENTS TO ONE ANOTHER AND NOT AS ENEMIES WITH UNRECONCILABLE DIFFERENCES. IN REALITY, BOTH MIRROR AND COMPLEMENT EACH OTHER. FOR NOW, EACH ONE PER SE IS "IN INCOMPLETE MODE" TAKING INTO ACCOUNT OR MAGNIFYING JUST ONE SIDE OF REALITY WHILE DENYING THE OTHER.

WE ARE ALL CHILDREN OF THE "EARTH AND OF THE —SKY" THEREFORE IS IN OUR BENEFIT TO EXPAND OUR KNOWLEDGE OF BOTH EARTH BASED AND SKY BASED SCIENCES AND INTEGRATE THEM TOGETHER.

THE EARTH-BASED TRADITION OF THE MOTHER, GODDESS OR BINAH, AND THE SKY BASED TRADITION OF THE FATHER, GOD OR CHOKMAH NEED TO COME TOGETHER AT LAST IN THE MIDDLE OF THE TREE OF LIFE IN ORDER TO BE IN A STATE OF RELATIVE PEACE, BALANCE AND HARMONY FOR THE BENEFIT OF HUMANKIND.

SINCERELY, "ENNO-KI"

## 119. AIN'T NOBODY MORE SPECIAL THAN ANOTHER: WE ALL FALL AND RISE TOGETHER—- WE ARE ALL THE SAME UNDERNEATH IT ALL

IT WAS NOT LONG AGO THAT THE COVID PANDEMIC WAS RAGING. IT WAS A SAD BUT VERY REALISTIC REMINDER OF HOW FRAGILE AND TRANSIENT HUMAN LIFE IS. HOWEVER, THIS TERRIBLE EVENT ALSO BROUGHT TO THE FORE OUR INNATE COMMON HUMANITY.

IF THERE WAS EVER A "BELIEF" ON A "SUPERIOR RACE" OR "CHOSEN PEOPLE" OR WHATEVER, IT BECAME MORE THAN CLEAR DURING THE PANDEMIC THAT "WE ARE ALL THE SAME." WE ALL FALL TOGETHER AND ... RISE TOGETHER AS WELL.

REGARDLESS OF NATIONAL ORIGIN OR ETHNICITY OR RELIGION WE ALL GOT SICK TOGETHER AND WERE SWEPT BY FEAR TOGETHER AND ... ALSO GOT TOGETHER TO BRING ABOUT A SOLUTION TO THE CHALLENGES BEING FACED FROM THE PANDEMIC.

IS IT POSSIBLE TO "REMEMBER THAT CHALLENGING TIME?" TO REMEMBER "HOW HUMANITY WAS CONCERNED FOR THE MOST PART" FOR EACH OTHER WHEN FACED BY A COMMON ENEMY AS THE "PANDEMIC?"

SADLY, WE KEEP MOVING FROM TRAGEDY INTO FORGETFULNESS. FORGETTING HOW WE WOULD COME TOGETHER IN TIMES OF DESPAIR AND CHOOSE TO FORGET OUR PETTY DIFFERENCES AND COME TOGETHER IN OUR COMMON HUMANITY IN ORDER TO OVERCOME "DEATH" ITSELF.

NOW THAT THE PANDEMIC HAS MOSTLY PASSED BY, WE FALL BACK AGAIN INTO FORGETFULNESS AND COMPLACENCY AND AGAIN BRING OUT THE WORST PARTS OF OUR HUMANITY IN ORDER TO HURT ONE ANOTHER BECAUSE OF "MISPERCEIVED DIFFERENCES" THAT HAVE NOTHING TO DO WITH REALITY BUT ARE FOR THE MOST PART "CREATIONS OF ONE'S OWN IMAGINATION."

AFTER ALL, AND AS IT HAS BEEN EXPLAINED BEFORE ... WHAT PEOPLE CONSIDER "HUMAN DIFFERENCES" ARE PART OF THE MATRIX' "MAYA" OR ...ILLUSION... BECAUSE THESE SO CALLED DIFFERENCES ARE PART OF THE FRAGMENTED MIND'S OBSESSION WITH CATEGORIZING AND PLACING THINGS AND PEOPLE INTO BOXES. BUT IN REALITY, IT IS JUST AN ILLUSION. IT IS AN INTRINSIC CHARACTERISTIC OF THE WORLD OF "MATTER" WHICH IS SPIRIT ENERGY MANIFESTING IN "DIVERSE FORMS." AND IF YOU LOOK BEYOND THE "APPEARANCES" OR THE "OUTER SHELL" YOU WILL NOTICE THAT IT IS ALL THE SAME. THAT THE CATEGORIES AND BOXES ARE JUST DESCRIPTIONS THAT HUMANITY USES TO "DESCRIBE

THE OUTER MATERIAL COVER" BUT THAT UNDERNEATH IT ALL …IT IS ALL …THE SAME LIGHT!

AND THIS IS WHAT THE PANDEMIC IN A WAY CAME TO REMIND US ALL… AS IT DID NOT DIFFERENTIATE OR EXCLUDED ONE PERSON OVER ANOTHER. WE ALL GOT SICK AND EVEN DIED REGARDLESS OF RACE, NATION, RELIGION, BELIEFS AND TRADITIONS, ETHNICITY, HEALTH, SOCIAL STATUS, ETC. MAKING IT CLEAR THAT "WE ARE ALL THE SAME" UNDERNEATH IT ALL.

SINCERELY, "L'CHAIM"

---

## 120.I AM THAT I AM, PLAIN AND SIMPLE

I think that the name Y-ESH-UA is too BIG for me. Honestly, I AM no better than anybody else as I have messed up big time along the way. I have learned from it THANKS DEITY so that I can deliver a DIVINE MESSAGE. And THE DIVINE has shown me MERCY AND FORGIVENESS. And has taught me through TRIALS AND TRIBULATIONS many important things that otherwise I would be unable to understand about life in general and about myself.

WHAT is happening with me is that I AM CHANNELING DIVINE MESSAGE AND ADMONISHMENT from DIVINE SOURCE AND ENERGIES. IT'S ALL COMING FROM "THEM."

Therefore, THEY take ALL THE CREDIT. If someone was to come to me asking me for a grandiose speech I would probably not be able to do anything or express myself well just like MOSES. I sit down when ELOHIM moves me to and begin to transcribe THE MESSAGES.

Perhaps some things I'M REMEMBERING from past lives. While other messages I am just channeling from the AKASHIC RECORDS with the HELP OF THE GRAND LIBR-ARY OF ALEXANDRIA DOWN HERE. I need to GET TO WORK because THEY HAVE TOLD ME I NEED TO.

THE POWERS are BEYOND AND ABOVE ME and so I DO NOT "IDENTIFY" myself as THEM as THEY ARE THE ARCHETYPAL ENERGIES AND LIGHT OF CREATION. I AM ONLY THAT WHO I AM– PLAIN AND SIMPLE. I had to LEARN THAT LESSON THE HARD WAY.

HOWEVER, "THEY" do want me to post the following AS DIVINE PROOF FROM THEIR PART THAT THERE IS DIVINE INTERVENTION AND MANIFESTATION HAPPENING HERE SO THAT PEOPLE WILL LISTEN AND CEASE TO WALK ON A PATH OF IGNORANCE AND EVIL.

THEY took me to this JEWISH NAMES website YEARS AGO when all this began to HAPPEN back in — 2012.

This SERVITOR'S NAME OF THE DIVINE is associated to the names AHARON, ELIYAHU, CHAIM (SALVADOR), ISAAC, REBECCA, YAAKOV, YEHOSHUA (VIA —SALVADOR L CHAIM), etc. Therefore, these energies are associated with this servitor's name which is very interesting and kind of weird that the EXACT BIRTH NAME IS EQUIVALENT TO ALL THESE NAMES AND IS ALL OVER THAT LIST IN ITS ITALIAN FORM.

AGAIN...THE DIVINE POWERS ARE ABOVE AND BEYOND AND ON TOP OF ME AND EVERYONE. I AM JUST A —"SERVANT" AND SCRIBE OF THE ALMIGHTY ELOHIM. I SUFFER LIKE EVERYONE ELSE AND GET SICK WITH REALLY BAD COLDS TO THE POINT WHERE I THINK I AM GOING TO FLY AWAY.

SINCERELY, "MORIM THOTH"

---

**121.=THE ANTI-CHRIST**

IN ORDER TO DEFINE WHAT THE ANTI-CHRIST REPRESENTS, ONE MUST FIRST DEFINE WHAT THE CHRIST IS. THE CHRIST REPRESENTS SPIRIT. SPIRIT AS IN A STATE OF HEALING, WHOLENESS, INTEGRATION AND HEALTH. A REASON JESUS IS NAMED THE CHRIST IS BECAUSE HE REPRESENTED AND EXEMPLIFIED AND INCARNATED THE HEALING SPIRIT OF RESTORATION AND MAKING WHOLE. THE CHRIST IS NOT ONLY ABOUT REDEMPTION AS IN REDEEMING THE FALLEN SPARKS BUT IS ALSO ABOUT THE RESTORATION BACK TO WHOLENESS. AS A REPRESENTATION AND HUMAN VEHICLE OF THE CHRIST SPIRIT, JESUS WAS ABLE TO HEAL AND BRING CORRUPTION BACK TO HEALTH. THAT IS WHY HIS MESSAGE AND MOVEMENT WAS ONE OF HEALING HUMANKIND FROM THE INSIDE OUT NOT ONLY PHYSICALLY BUT ALSO PSYCHO-EMOTIONALLY, MORALLY AND SPIRITUALLY AND THAT WAY HELP RESTORE HUMAN SOCIETY AND CIVILIZATION FROM RAMPANT STATES OF CORRUPTION AT THE TIME.

THIS PROCESS OF RESTORATION OF JESUS AS THE CHRIST WAS AN ACTIVE PRINCIPLE OF HEALING. IT WAS NOT WELCOME BY THE POWERS THAT BE OF THE TIME SINCE THESE WORLDLY POWERS BENEFITED THEMSELVES FROM THE SUFFERING AND EXPLOITATION OF THE PEOPLE BELOW AND THE CORROSIVE STATE AND PROCESS OF THE ENTIRE SYSTEM OF GOVERNMENT AND RELIGION WHICH LED TO JESUS BEING SLANDERED AND PERSECUTED AND EVENTUALLY SOLD TO CORRUPT MEN. THIS IS A CLEAR EXAMPLE OF HOW CORRUPT WAS THE ROMAN-

JEWISH SYSTEM OF JESUS TIME. THIS ANTI-CHRIST SPIRIT OPERATING IN MEN AND HIS INSTITUTIONS AT THE TIME IS DECRIBED ALL OVER THE GOSPEL ACCOUNT STORIES AS A REMINDER FOR HUMANKIND THAT THERE IS A PROCESS OF DESTRUCTION AND CORRUPTION EVER PRESENT THAT MEN MUST GUARD THEMSELVES FROM BY TENDING THE LIGHT WITHIN. THAT DIVINE LIGHT IS THE CHRIST SPIRIT WHOM IS CHARACTERIZED AS STATES OF INTEGRATION, HEALING, PEACE, LOVE, UNION, ETC. THE QUALITIES OF THE CHRIST SPIRIT ARE THE FRUITS OF THE SPIRIT DESCRIBED IN SCRIPTURES AND ITS LIGHT IS EXEMPLIFIED AS THE STATE OF ENLIGHTENMENT OR ILLUMINATION IN HUMAN.

THE CHRIST SPIRIT THEREFORE IS THE LIGHT THAT SHINES A SPOTLIGHT AT CORRUPTIVE FORCES SO THAT MAN BE ABLE TO CORRECT THESE DEFICIENCIES ON TIME BEFORE THE ENTIRE BODY OF CHRIST OR HUMAN SOCIETY CORRUPTS AND FALLS APART. THE CHRIST SPIRIT IS NOT PASSIVE BUT AN ACTIVE PRINCIPLE THAT MANIFESTS ITSELF BY ITS FRUITS WHICH ARE JOY, HAPPINESS AND HEALTH, COMPASSION, KINDNESS AND LOVE. ANYTHING OR ANYONE CLAIMING TO EMBODY THE CHRIST SPIRIT WHILE DOING, AND EMBODYING AND SPREADING EVIL, DISEASE, INJUSTICE, DEATH, CORRUPTION, ENMITY, ETC. IS NOT OF THE CHRIST SPIRIT BUT OF THE ANTI-CHRIST.

THE ANTI- CHRIST THEREFORE IS OPPOSED TO AND THE OPPOSITE OF THE CHRIST SPIRIT. ANYTHING OR ANYONE THAT CLAIMS TO BE OF THE CHRIST SPIRIT BUT CARRIES OUT THE OPPOSITE OF THE CHRIST SPIRIT IS A LIAR. AND THIS IS WHAT THE ANTI-CHRIST IS KNOWN FOR TO BE A LIAR AND DECEIVER WHO TAKES ON A VENEER OF LIGHT IN ORDER TO DECEIVE PEOPLE AND WHOLE SOCIETIES PRETENDING TO BE THE CHRIST ITSELF BUT RATHER SPREADING DEATH AND CORRUPTION.

THE CHRIST PRINCIPLE AS A LIVING ACTIVE PRINCIPLE IS NOT PASSIVE. IT CANNOT FULFILL ITSELF BY WORD ONLY. MEANING THAT PROFESSING BELIEF IN A HOLY SCRIPTURE AND KNOWING DOGMA DOES NOT CONSTITUTE BEING A CHANNEL OF THE CHRIST. MANY TODAY PROFESS TO BE OF THE CHRIST BUT BY THEIR ACTIONS TOWARDS OTHERS AND LIFE ON THIS PLANET ARE ACTUALLY ACTING IN THE OPPOSITE SPIRIT OF THE ANTI-CHRIST. THEIR BELIEF SYSTEM DOES NOT SYNCHRONIZE OR IS IN SYNC WITH THEIR ACTIONS. THE ANTI- CHRIST CLAIMS TO BE FOR HEALTH AND HEALING WHILE SPREADING MORE PSYCHO-EMOTIONAL DYSFUNCTION AND DISEASE - TRAUMA, CHAOS AND WAR. THE CHRIST SPIRIT CANNOT BE DECEIVED. BY ONE'S OWN FRUITS OR ACTIONS, THE SPIRIT THAT INHABITS ONE'S TEMPLE BECOMES MANIFEST. EITHER WE EMBODY A SPIRIT OF LIGHT INHABITING OUR FLESHY TEMPLE OR A SPIRIT OF EVIL AND DYSFUNCTION.

THEREFORE LOOK AND SEE WHAT COMES OUT OF A MAN, WHETHER GOOD FRUIT OR A CORRUPT ONE AS HIS OWN ACTIONS, WORDS AND DEEDS POINT TO EITHER THE CHRIST SPIRIT OR THE ANTI-CHRIST SPIRIT.

THE UNIVERSAL VALUES AND PRINCIPLES OF ALL TRADITIONS ARE THERE TO HELP MAINTAIN RELATIVELY HEALTHY AND WHOLESOME HUMAN SOCIETIES. THESE LAWS AND PRINCIPLES AND VALUES SERVE AS GATES THAT HELP KEEP CORRUPTIVE INFLUENCES FROM DEVELOPING TO THE POINT OF OVERTAKING HUMANS AND THEIR SOCIETIES. THESE UNIVERSAL VALUES AND PRINCIPLES ARE OF THE CHRIST SPIRIT AND THE HEALTHY JUSTICE SYSTEMS ARE IN PLACE TO ENSURE THAT A NATION AND PEOPLE REMAIN RELATIVELY HEALTHY AND WHOLE.

THE FACT THAT TODAY MOST HUMAN SYSTEMS ARE DYSFUNCTIONAL AND UNDERGOING MASSIVE CORRUPTION IS BECAUSE THE ANTI-CHRIST SPIRIT HAS TAKEN OVER AS HUMANS SEEM TO NO LONGER RESPECT AND OBSERVE AND BLUNTLY IGNORE THESE UNIVERSAL VALUES AND PRINCIPLES. CONSEQUENTLY, NOW MORE THAN EVER, HUMANITY IS IN A STATE OF DISEASE AND MORAL AND ETHICAL DECAY. IT IS CLEAR BY THE STATE AND CONDITION OF THE WORLD TODAY AND THE CONDITION OF THE PLANET'S ECOSYSTEM THAT THE ANTI-CHRIST HAS ARRIVED AND HAS OVERTAKEN THE ENTIRE EARTH. ANYONE AND ANY INSTITUTION SERVING THE SELFISH INTERESTS OF DYSFUNCTION AND INJUSTICE ARE PART OF THIS ANTI-CHRIST SPIRIT WHO HAS NO HEALTHY BOUNDARIES BUT WHOSE AIM IS TO DISRUPT, CONFUSE, DISEASE, RENDER DYSFUNCTIONAL AND USELESS AND UNHEALTHY AND ...DESTROY ENTIRE ORGANIC SYSTEMS.

THE ENTIRE SYSTEM HAS GIVEN WAY TO THE ANTI-CHRIST SPIRIT. PEOPLE TODAY ARE IN STATES OF DISEASE BECAUSE OF CORRUPT GOVERNMENTS AND INSURANCE SYSTEMS THAT PLACE MONEY AND PROFIT OVER AND ABOVE THE HEALTH AND WELL BEING OF PEOPLE AND PLANET. RELIGIOUS SYSTEMS ARE COLLAPSING DUE TO THE RAMPANT CORRUPTION IN ITS RANKS IN WHICH PREACHERS AND LEADERS OF THESE CHURCHES AND RELIGIOUS SYSTEMS PLACE MONEY AND FAME AND CORRUPT POLITICS IN FIRST PLACE UNLIKE JESUS THE CHRIST WHO PLACED THE HEALING AND WELL BEING OF THE COMMUNITY IN FIRST PLACE. THE ANTI-CHRIST SPIRIT IS WILLING TO SACRIFICE THE UNIVERSAL VALUES AND PRINCIPLES IN ORDER TO ADVANCE SELFISH AND ANTI-CHRIST AGENDAS. POWER-HUNGRY DYSFUNCTIONAL COMPANIES PLACE PROFIT FIRST AND FOREMOST WILLING TO SACRIFICE EARTH AND ITS LIVING BEINGS TO THE god MAMMON POLLUTING BODY AND SOUL AND EARTH AS WELL.

THE ABOVE ARE JUST A FEW EXAMPLES OF THE CURRENT DYSFUNCTIONAL STATE OF THE WORLD. IT'S REALLY A VERY SAD STATE. WHEN "LEADERS" AND HUMAN INSTITUTIONS NO LONGER SERVE THE CHRIST SPIRIT BUT THE ANTI CHRIST. THEIR BAD EXAMPLE JUST SERVES TO FOSTER THIS EVIL SPIRIT AND TO FURTHER CORRUPT THE STATE OF HUMANITY. EVENTUALLY EVERYTHING COMES TOPPLING DOWN AND CHAOS ENSUES. IT'S TIME TO RETURN TO THE NOBLE TRUTHS AND THE ETERNAL UNIVERSAL VALUES AND PRINCIPLES OF BASIC ETHICS, CIVILITY AND MORALITY.

THE CHRIST SPIRIT IS NOT LIMITED TO A RELIGION AND IS NOT A RELIGION. RELIGION IS A VEHICLE AMONGST MANY OTHERS THAT SERVES AS GUARDIAN AND CARETAKERS OF THESE SUBLIME HEALING TRUTHS OF THE PRINCIPLE OF LIGHT. THE CHRIST PRINCIPLE IS TRANSCENDENT AND CAN INHABIT AND MANIFEST ITSELF BEYOND RELIGION AND APART FROM RELIGIOUS SYSTEMS. IT CAN MANIFEST IN A SOCIETY'S HEALTH AND SPIRITUAL AND CULTURAL SYSTEMS JUST AS LIGHT CAN PERMEATE AND LIVE IN EVERYTHING IF WE ALLOW IT TO. SADLY, MANY A RELIGION AND RELIGIOUS LEADER TODAY CLAIMS TO BE OF THE CHRIST BUT ACTUALLY PROMOTES IN HIS ACTIONS, WORDS AND EXAMPLE THE SPIRIT OF THIS WORLD WHICH IS THE ANTI-CHRIST. IT'S OUR JOB AS SEEKERS OF THE LIGHT, FOLLOWERS OF THE LIGHT AND CHANNELS OF THE LIGHT TO BRING DOWN TO THIS EARTH THE CHRIST SPIRIT IN ORDER TO BRING HEALING, BALANCE, HEALTH, GOODNESS ALONG WITH WISDOM BACK TO HUMANKIND, SOCIETY, INSTITUTIONS AND THE EARTH AS A WHOLE.

AND BEWARE OF THE MANY DECEIVERS WHO HIDE THEIR TRUE ANTI-CHRIST SPIRIT BEHIND A VENEER OF HONORABILITY ACCORDING TO THIS WORLD, CLAIMING TO BE THE PRINCE OF PEACE BUT INSTEAD PROMOTE WAR AND DISEASE AND INJUSTICE AND ALL SORTS OF EVIL JUST TO GARNER POWER, MONEY AND INFLUENCE. BEWARE OF THE ANTI-CHRIST SPIRIT.

SINCERELY, "THE CHRIST IN ME"

---

**122. THE "PENTAGRAM OF BAFO-OMET" VS. THE "MARK OF THE BEAST;" THE "CYPHER" OF THE BOOK OF REVELATIONS — CHRIST CONSCIOUSNESS VS. THE ANTICHRIST UN-CONSCIOUSNESS (Y-ODA VS. DARTH SIDIUS)**

AS WE EXPLAINED BEFORE, THE SCRIPTURES AND ALL SACRED BOOKS OF ALL TRADITIONS INCLUDING THE VEDAS AND THE HOLY GRAIL STORIES, ETC. SPEAK IN SYMBOLS AND CODES. THE BOOK OF REVELATIONS

HAS BEEN MISINTERPRETED IN SUCH A WAY THAT IT HAS BROUGHT ABOUT MUCH PAIN AND SUFFERING TO MANY INNOCENTS THROUGHOUT THE CENTURIES. HOWEVER, THE MOST IMPORTANT CONCEPT OF THAT BOOK IS THE DIFFERENCE BETWEEN THE "ENLIGHTENED OR ILLUMINATED SELF" AND THE "UNCONSCIOUS OR IGNORANT SELF."

CHRIST CONSCIOUSNESS IS NOT ABOUT "RELIGION" OR RELIGIOUS AFFILIATION. IT IS ABOUT THE CONCEPT OF THE "AWAKENED MIND AND THE HIGHER SELF" IN EACH AND EVERY PERSON. ON THE OTHER HAND, THE "ANTICHRIST" SPIRIT IS THE OPPOSITE OF "CHRIST CONSCIOUSNESS" AND IT IS ABOUT BEING IN A "GOLEM" STATE.

Empathy is associated with dynamic change in prefrontal brain electrical activity during positive emotion in children. ( NATIONAL LIBRARY OF MEDICINE)

AS YOU WILL RECALL AND AS WE STATED BEFORE, THE INTEGRATED HUMAN BEING "FEELS EMPATHY" AND SO HIS MIND AND BRAIN ARE CONNECTED AND IN SYNC WITH EACH OTHER AND BOTH WORK AS THEY ARE MEANT TO IN A SYMBIOTIC WAY. EMPATHY — IS A KIND OF REGULATORY MECHANISM IN A HUMAN THAT ENABLES A PERSON TO FEEL THE PAIN OF ANOTHER AND THAT WAY "CAUSE NO HARM." EMPATHY —IS REGULATED BY THE —PREFRONTAL BRAIN — WHICH IS CONNECTED TO THE EMOTIONAL HEART CENTER. AS YOU CAN OBSERVE FROM THIS BRAIN-HEART CONNECTION, "EMPATHY" RESIDES IN THE "FOREHEAD" AREA!!!!

THEREFORE, IF YOU HAVE "EMPATHY" YOU ARE A VERY LUCKY AND BLESSED PERSON!!!

WHEN THE PREFRONTAL CORTEX IS DAMAGED OR NUMB OR ASLEEP, — A HUMAN BEING HAS NO INNER REGULATION OR COMPASS IN THE FORM OF FEELINGS THAT WILL TELL A PERSON THRU EMOTION THAT WHAT HE OR SHE IS DOING IS WRONG!!! AND SO THE PERSON WILL GO ON CARRYING OUT EVIL DEEDS AND VIOLENCE BECAUSE HE/SHE IS DISCONNECTED FROM HIS HEART CENTER AND PREFRONTAL CORTEX.

A PERSON WHO HAS A HEALTHY PREFRONTAL CORTEX AND WHO AS A RESULT HAS AN INNER COMPASS AND A HEALTHY SEAT OF CONSCIENCE AND CONSCIOUSNESS IS IN A "CHRIST CONSCIOUS" STATE. IF YOU FEEL THAT THIS RESONATES WITH YOUR OWN PERSONAL EXPERIENCE AND STATE, YOU ARE ALSO LUCKY AND BLESSED AND YOU ARE IN A STATE OF "CHRIST CONSCIOUSNESS."

THE PENTAGRAM IS THE SYMBOL THAT REPRESENTS CHRIST - CONSCIOUSNESS IN A HUMAN.

THE OPPOSITE OF CHRIST CONSCIOUSNESS IS THE "MARK OF THE BEAST!!!" THIS MARK —IS NOT THE PENTAGRAM!!! BUT IS ACTUALLY — NOTHING! THERE IS—NOTHING THERE YET BECAUSE THAT PART OF THE BRAIN IS NOT FUNCTIONING AS IT SHOULD. IT'S IN A STATE OF NON-ACTIVITY AND IS NUMB OR DORMANT OR DAMAGED. THIS –NOTHING— IS REPRESENTED BY AN EMPTY CIRCLE SYMBOL.

IN THE STORY OF DAVID AND GOLIATH, DAVID REPRESENTS "CHRIST CONSCIOUSNESS" AND A REASON THAT THE PENTAGRAM IS ATTRIBUTED TO KING SOLOMON, HIS SON. MEANWHILE, GOLIATH, ON THE OTHER HAND — IS IN A GOLEM STATE LACKING IN EMPATHY WHO JUST FOLLOWS ORDERS TO CAUSE HARM TO OTHERS WITHOUT FEELING ANY REMORSE WHATSOEVER OR LACKING THE ABILITY TO "REASON" ABOUT WHAT HE OR SHE IS ACTUALLY DOING. HE IS THE ARCHETYPE OF A MONSTER IN HUMAN FORM. AND SO THE KEY OR CYPHER TO THE STORY IS ABOUT THE "PEBBLE THAT CRASHES THE SKULL OF GOL-IATH ON HIS "FOREHEAD."

THE "ANTICHRIST" SPIRIT PRETENDS TO BE "THE CHRIST" BUT LACKS "EMPATHY AND REASONING SKILLS AND TURNS TO VIOLENCE!!!

ANOTHER SYMBOL FOR "CHRIST CONSCIOUSNESS" IS THE EASTERN AND NATIVE AMERICAN —CROSS WITHIN A CIRCLE. THE CROSS WITH ITS CENTER REPRESENTS THE INTEGRATION OF THE "FIVE." ON THE OTHER HAND, THE EMPTY CIRCLE WITHOUT THE CROSS REPRESENTS — NOTHING, NADA!!! NO CONSCIENCE AND NEITHER CONSCIOUSNESS AND INTEGRATION. BY THE WAY, THE "ANTI - CONSCIOUSNESS OR ANTI –CHRIST" FOR LACK OF EMPATHY AND WISDOM, BABBLES WHAT YOU TODAY REFER TO AS "B.S."

SINCERELY, Y–ODA

Y==== "I"

ODA === AN ASSISTER OF THE TRADITION AND TEACHING

---

## 123. BAPHO-OMET: THE "DIVINE ANDROGYNE" IN THE TEMPLAR TRADITION — THE "BREATH AND THE BODY OF LIGHT" DIVINE

SO "WHO" IS BAPHOMET IN THE TEMPLAR TRADITION? THIS IS ANOTHER TRAGIC STORY WITH TRAGIC HISTORICAL ENDINGS. MANY PEOPLE HAVE BEEN BURNT AT THE STAKE BECAUSE OF THIS "SYMBOL."

THE NAME CAN BE DIVIDED AS IN "BAFO-OMET" OR:

BAFO === BREATH (OCCITAN) OMET === LIGHT (HEBREW)

THE —----LIGHT AND BREATH —--OR "RUACH ELOHIM," THE LIVING "PRANA OR QI." THE BREATH OF LIGHT!

DOESN'T THAT ABOVE SOUNDS LIKE "THE BODY OF LIGHT AND THE CHAKRA SYSTEM" AND THE "PLEASE FOCUS ON YOUR BREATH! PLEASE."

IT'S POINTING TO THE SAME CONCEPTS AS IN THE MEN-ORA AND THE CHAKRA SYSTEM.

S-HE IS A REPRESENTATION OF "ADAM KAD-M-ONNE" —- THE "KAD- MAN" AS IN THE "FALLEN STAR." THIS FALLEN STAR REPRESENTS "HUMANITY" AS IN THE "KLIPPOT THAT DESCEND AND BECOME MATERIALIZED OR TRAPPED IN MATTER. THIS IS WHAT THE "PENTAGRAM" IN BAFO-OMET'S FOREHEAD REPRESENTS!

IT REPRESENTS THE "FIVE ELEMENTS" BUT POINTING DOWNWARDS TOWARDS THE EARTH OR DESCENDING OR FALLING INTO THIS MATERIAL REALM AND FORMING IT.

THE TWIN HORNS REPRESENT THE "YIN AND YANG" ENERGIES. THE WORLD OF DUALITY OR POLARITY, OPPOSITES AND COMPLEMENTS. THE BEING IS "ANDROGYNOUS" LIKE "ADAM KADM-ONE." THERE IS THE SUN AND THE MOON WHO REPRESENT BINAH AND CHOKMAH AND THE COSMIC ENERGIES THAT INFLUENCE THE CHAKRA SYSTEM OR BODY OF LIGHT. THE WINGS REPRESENT "AIR" ELEMENT AND THE FACULTY OF THOUGHT AND "THE DIVINE IN HUMAN."

THE PENTAGRAM IS NOT ABOUT DEVILS OR DEMONS OR SATAN AS YOU CLAIM TO ERRONEOUSLY BELIEVE. IT REFERS TO "CHRIST CONSCIOUSNESS" OR TO "WISE MIND!!"

I KNOW THE REPRESENTATION IS SCARY AND KINDA WEIRD BUT LET US FOCUS ON THE SYMBOLISM. THE PENTAGRAM IS BETWEEN THE YIN AND THE YANG WHICH STANDS FOR THE —--PISTIS SOPHIA— !!! AS IN THE "ARK OF THE COVENANT" ICON AND SYMBOL.

BASICALLY, THIS IS A—PICTURE OF EVERY HUMAN BEING'S INNER DIVINITY AND THE WORKING OF THE BODY OF LIGHT THAT LEADS TO LIBERATION AND BREAKS THE PROCESS OF REINCARNATION AND OF DISEASE!!!

"OMET" HAS ALSO THE SAME ROOT AS THE WORD "EMET" OR "TRUTH" IN HEBREW, THEREFORE THE TERM IS POINTING TO "COSMIC AND SCIENTIFIC AND PHYSICAL TRUTHS" AND CONCEPTS THAT THE TEMPLARS HID WITHIN THE DESIGN OF BAFO-EMET.

THE CHURCH ENDED UP PERSECUTING AND BURNING THE TEMPLARS BACK IN HISTORY, AS THEY BELIEVED ERRONEOUSLY BAFO-OMET TO BE "SATAN OR LUCIFER, AND BOTH TO BE CONCEPTS OF EVIL, ETC." BAFO-EMET IS A SYMBOL OF "ENLIGHTENMENT AND ILLUMINATION." THE PENTAGRAM ALSO REPRESENTS "STARS" AS IN "LIGHT!!!" SOPHIA OR KNOWLEDGE IS "LIGHT" AND SO —THE LOVE OF SOPHIA—-IS WHAT THE SYMBOL REPRESENTS AND HER MANIFESTATION IN HUMAN. BAPH-OMET IS POINTING TO THE "PHILOSOPHER'S STONE!!!"

THERE IS MORE TO THE GRAPHIC AND PICTURE BUT THAT WILL BE FOR ANOTHER—DIARY!!!

SINCERELY, BAFO- OMET "THE SCAPEGOAT"

---

## 124. THE CREATIVE BI-POLAR PROCESS: THE PROCESS AND ENERGY OF "CREATION" OF THE "PRIMORDIAL WO-MAN" THRU THE PERSON OF THE "SH-AM-ANNE-KI"

AS WE EXPLAINED BEFORE, "THE ARK OF COMMUNICATION" REPRESENTS THE "HOLY SEER OR DIVINE SHAMAN" AND S-HE IS CALLED LIKE THAT BECAUSE THESE INDIVIDUALS CAN LINK TO THE COSMOS AND UNITE WITH THE DIVINE.

THEY WILL EXPERIENCE "THE DIVINE MADNESS OF PSYCHOSIS" THAT LEADS TO THE "WAKING UP" STATE AND TO THE ACTIVATION OF THE "TWIN YIN AND YANG POLES" TO THE POINT IN WHICH THE "DIVINE GATES" OPEN IN BETWEEN AND THE "PROCESS AND ACT OF CREATION" COMMUNICATION AND INSPIRATION AND SPEECH MANIFESTS.

THIS IS A REASON "WHY" THE SO CALLED "BI-POLAR TYPES" FOR THE MOST PART HAVE ACCESS TO "CREATIVITY" SUCH AS —MUSIC AND POETRY AND STORYTELLING AND CREATIVE WRITING AND HEALING ETC. ETC. ETC. AND SO MANY OTHER "FRUITS OF THE SPIRIT."

THE "SHAMAN" IS A PERSONIFICATION OF THESE BIPOLAR ENERGIES OF THE UNIVERSE AND THE TWIN REALMS OF BINAH AND CHOKMAH OR — THE LOWER UNCONSCIOUS AND THE SUPERCONSCIOUS. SYNCHRONIZING BOTH AND REACHING A SORT OF "EQUILIBRIUM" BY WHICH "BOTH WORLDS CAN BE ACCESSED BY THE SHAMAN."

SHA-M-"ANNA!"

THE "BIPOLAR TYPE" PERSONIFIES THE "PRIMORDIAL WO-MAN" WHO IS DEPICTED AS THE COSMIC VETRUVIAN MAN IN RENAISSANCE DIAGRAMS.

AND THIS VETRUVIAN WO-MAN IS THE "PERSONIFICATION" OF THE TWIN ENERGIES OF "YIN AND YANG" UNITED AS ONE WHO COME TOGETHER AND SEPARATE AND COME TOGETHER AGAIN IN A COSMIC COITUS AND INTERPLAY OF POLARITIES TO BRING ABOUT CREATION. IT'S PURE CREATIVE AND CONSCIOUS ENERGY.

AND SO THE "SHA-M-ANNU" IS THE ORIGINAL "GUIDE" OF THE TRIBE WHO WOULD HELP WITH THE "CREATION" AND WISE ADMINISTRATION OF A RELATIVELY HEALTHY AND BALANCED SOCIETY AND COMMUNITY PROVIDING KNOWLEDGE AND SKILLS AND OTHER SORTS OF GUIDANCE. SHA-M-ANNU REPRESENTS THE "BIPOLAR PRIMORDIAL UNIT IN THE COSMOS."

SADLY, THIS TYPE OF INDIVIDUALS HAVE BEEN VILIFIED AND OSTRACIZED AND PERSECUTED AND MURDERED THROUGHOUT HISTORY FOR BEING WHO THEY ARE AND FOR STRIVING TO KEEP THE COMMUNITY HEALTHY AND THE WORLD IN BALANCE. PERSECUTED BY THE "POWERS OF THIS WORLD WHO ARE DISCONNECTED FROM DIVINE WISDOM AND HAVE BEEN OVERTAKEN BY MATERIAL GREED AND POWER."

SINCERELY, "SH-AM-ANNE-KI"

---

## 125. MARY MAGDALENE AND THE "7 CHAKRAS:" THE —CLEANSING AND STABILIZATION OF THE CHAKRA SYSTEM AND THE RETURN TO RELATIVE BALANCE AND HEALTH

YOU WILL RECALL THAT THE STORIES IN THE BIBLE ARE ALLEGORICAL AND METAPHORICAL AND METAPHYSICAL. AS WE STATED BEFORE, HUMANKIND POSSESSES "UNDERNEATH THE MATERIAL BODY" AN ENERGY- ELECTRICAL BODY OR SYSTEM THAT MANIFESTS WITHIN AND AS THE MATERIAL BODY.

IF YOU WILL RECALL, IN HEALING TRADITIONS WORLDWIDE THE ENERGY BODY IS KNOWN TO BE THE HUMAN "BODY" IN WHICH DISEASE MANIFESTS FIRST. WHEN THE ENERGY BODY WHICH IS CONNECTED TO THOUGHT ENERGY AND EMOTIONAL ENERGY GETS CLOGGED AND SICK (KNOWN IN EASTERN TRADITION AS "STAGNATION) DISEASE ENSUES AND BEGINS TO MANIFEST SOON AFTER IN THE PHYSICAL BODY. THEREFORE, DISEASE FOR THE MOST PART BEGINS IN THE ENERGY "BODY OF LIGHT" AND THEN IN THE MATERIAL BODY.

AS YOU MIGHT KNOW, THE ORGANS OF THE BODY STORE DIVERSE EMOTIONS WHICH ARE ENERGY AND SO WHEN WE GET "CLOGGED" IN AN EMOTIONAL SENSE AND WE FEED THAT EMOTIONAL CLOGGING WITH

UNHEALTHY THOUGHT PATTERNS, THAT "NEGATIVE EMOTION" ENDS UP BEING FED PRODUCING MORE "NEGATIVE ENERGY," THEN, THE ORGAN AND ORGAN SYSTEM THAT IS THE SEAT OF THAT EMOTIONAL ENERGY BEGINS TO DETERIORATE AND STAGNATE AND SO THE BODY BEGINS TO MANIFEST THAT STAGNATION AS PHYSICAL DISEASE.

NOT ALL DISEASE IS EMOTIONAL ESPECIALLY TODAY WHEN THERE IS MUCH POLLUTION AND ADDITIVES IN WHAT WE EAT PLUS, OTHER EXTERNAL STRESSORS THAT CONTRIBUTE TO DISEASE. BUT IN GENERAL, STRESSORS END UP AFFECTING OUR MIND TO SUCH AN EXTENT THAT EVENTUALLY OUR EMOTIONS FOLLOW SUIT AND DISEASE BEGINS TO MANIFEST THROUGHOUT THE BODY.

WHEN WE ARE IN A STATE OF IMBALANCE AND THE FLOW OF ENERGY IS STAGNANT, THAT NEGATIVE ENERGY BEGINS TO COLLECT AND TO BECOME GREATER AND GREATER UNTIL IT BEGINS AFFECTING OUR MINDS AND OUR EMOTIONS AND EVENTUALLY OUR BODY ORGANS AND BODY PARTS. WE END UP BECOMING LIKE TICKING BOMBS THAT CAUSE AN INTERNAL IMPLOSION AND AN EXTERNAL EXPLOSION IN THE FORM OF PHYSICAL DISEASE. AT THIS POINT THE HUMAN BODY HAS REACHED SUCH AS STATE OF IMBALANCE THAT OUR CHAKRAS AND ENERGY CHANNELS BEGIN TO MALFUNCTION AND BECOME THE OPPOSITE OF "LIGHT" WHICH IS DISEASE.

THEREFORE, HEALING MODALITIES THAT HELP BALANCE THE BODY OF LIGHT AND TO BRING IT BACK TO HEALTH, BELONG TO THE SHAMANIC TRADITIONS WHICH INCLUDE TAOISM, THE EARTH BASED TRADITIONS, AND THE MIDDLE EASTERN "THERAPEUTAE" TRADITIONS OF THE DAYS OF JESUS. AND SO, ANOTHER WAY TO INTERPRET THE "CASTING OUT THE 7 DEMONS" FROM MARY MAGDALENE IS NOT IN A SUPERNATURAL WAY BUT IN A MORE HUMAN AND ORDINARY WAY. AS IN THE "CHAKRAS OR VORTEXES OF LIFE AND ENERGY" THAT FUNCTION TO DISTRIBUTE COSMIC ENERGY IN THE BODY. THESE MAIN CHAKRAS OR WHEELS OF LIGHT ARE 7 IN NUMBER AND DO BECOME CLOGGED AND ILL. WHEN THIS HAPPENS, THE AFFECTED PERSON GETS OUT OF BALANCE IN THE PSYCHE AND MIND, EMOTIONS, AND IN THE BODY. WHICH WOULD RESEMBLE AS IF THE PERSON WAS "POSSESSED AS IN "STATES OF EXORCISMS." BUT IN REALITY, HIS OR HER CHAKRAS ARE NOT FUNCTIONING PROPERLY AND OR ALIGNED WITH ONE ANOTHER.

THEREFORE, THERE ARE "7 MAIN" WHEELS OF LIFE OR CHAKRAS!!! AND SO, IN THE STORY OF MARY MAGDALENE, THESE ARE CLEANSED AND REBALANCED AND RECALIBRATED NATURALLY WITH THE HELP OF YESHUA. TODAY PEOPLE CAN DO THIS WITH QI GONG EXERCISES AND

HEALTHY EATING AND LIVING AND SO — THE "DEMONS" ARE CASTED OUT IN A METAPHORICAL, ALLEGORICAL AND METAPHYSICAL SENSE.

MARY MAGDALENE CEASES TO BE IN A STATE OF GREAT PAIN AND SUFFERING.

MORE WILL BE DISCUSSED ABOUT THE "ENERGY BODY" IN FUTURE DIARIES. FOR NOW IT SHALL SUFFICE.

SINCERELY, MARY MAGDALENE (22 = 4) AND HER "MONTH OF JULY (7)!!!

---

**126. YOU HAVE BEEN HERE THOUSANDS OF YEARS AGO, IT IS JUST NOW THAT "I AM" REMEMBERING!: THE ETERNAL LIGHT, THE MORTAL BODY AND....THE EVER CHANGING "IDENTITIES AND LABELS THAT HAPPEN "TIME AFTER TIME"**

YOU KNOW HOW WE CARRY OVER OUR SOUL'S SPIRITUAL LESSONS "TIME AFTER TIME" AS IN "LIFE AFTER LIFETIMES." THE FACT WE ARE HERE FROM A LONG LINE OF ANCESTORS THAT CRISS CROSS THE GLOBE AT THIS POINT IN TIME IS AMAZING. IT MEANS THAT WE HAVE BEEN HERE SINCE THE BEGINNING, SINCE WE ARE A CONTINUATION OF ALL THESE PEOPLES.

THE FACT THAT YOU AND I ARE HERE MAKES IT CLEAR THAT —-WE HAVE BEEN MANY DIFFERENT PEOPLES THROUGHOUT ALL THESE LIFETIMES. THAT "ADAMAS" IS HERE AFTER THE ROSELINE CRISS CROSSING THE ENTIRE GLOBE FOR MILLENNIA MEANS THAT S-HE CARRIES WITH HIM-HER THE "IDENTITIES OF ALL PEOPLES." ESPECIALLY AFTER FACING MUCH PERSECUTION FOR MILLENNIA HAVING TO RUN FROM PLACE TO PLACE.

THE FACT THAT EVERYONE HAS BEEN HERE SINCE THE BEGINNING OF HUMANITY MEANS THAT YOU AND I ARE NOT JUST WHAT WE ARE TODAY AND WHAT YOU SEE TODAY. WE ARE MUCH MORE HIDING BEHIND THAT "FLESH AND BLOOD AND —LABEL" WE USE TO IDENTIFY OURSELVES WITH. IN ALL THESE PAST LIVES YOU AND I HAVE BEEN BLACK AND WHITE AND YELLOW AND RED AND MIXED AS WELL AS MALE AND FEMALE AND TRANS AND ....... CHRISTIAN AND JEW AND MUSLIM AND TAOIST AND SO AND SO AND SO ON.

SO WHEN "ADAMAS" WOKE UP FROM HIS HER SLUMBER, S-HE REALIZED THAT S-HE WAS ALL THOSE PEOPLES BACK THEN WHICH IS KNOWN AS "GENETIC MEMORY." AND SO YES, S-HE CAN IDENTIFY WITH EVERYONE AND SO IS NOT JUST THIS OR THAT BUT HAS EVERYONE IN S-HE.

DO NOT TAKE YOUR CURRENT "LABEL" TOO SERIOUSLY FOR IT IS TEMPORARY AND HAS BEEN TEMPORARY ALL ALONG SINCE IN A PAST LIFE YOU AND I HAVE IDENTIFIED WITH HUNDREDS OF THEM. MANY OF THESE LABELS HAVE BEEN RENDERED "MUTUALLY EXCLUSIVE" BY THE STANDARDS OF SOCIETY BUT IN REALITY THEY ARE NOT. THE "SOUL" REMAINS THE SAME BUT THE COVERING AND ITS MATERIAL ATTRIBUTES AND IDENTITIES CHANGE OVER TIME AND LIFETIMES JUST AS IN CHANGING OUTERWEAR EACH DAY.

SO WHO "AM I????" ..... "I AM" EVERYONE. BECAUSE I HAVE BEEN HERE FOR A VERY LONG TIME AND CARRY WITH ME A LOT AND LOTS OF PEOPLES FROM ALL OVER THE GLOBE. DO NOT GET CAUGHT UP IN "LABELS" THAT HAPPEN TO BE TRANSITIONAL AND DEPENDENT ON THE PLACE AND FAMILY AND CULTURE AND RELIGION YOU WERE BORN INTO IN A PARTICULAR LIFETIME.

SOUL CAME HERE TO EXPERIENCE THE "TOTAL LIFE EXPERIENCE" WHICH INCLUDES – BEING ALL SORTS OF PEOPLES AND IDENTITIES AND EXPERIENCES — WHICH CAN ONLY BE POSSIBLE THROUGH REINCARNATING AS DIFFERENT PEOPLE AND IN DIFFERENT NATIONS AND IDENTITIES THROUGHOUT TIME. THEREFORE, THE HUMAN SOUL THROUGH EXPERIENCE AND LEARNING CAN EVENTUALLY REACH MATURITY AND "AWAKEN" AND RETURN TO "SOMEWHERE OUT THERE WHERE DREAMS DO COME TRUE."

THEREFORE, THE "CORE" OF EACH HUMAN IS" THE SPARK OF LIFE WHICH IS LIGHT WHICH IS ETERNAL. THE LIGHT IS ENCASED IN THE BODY WHICH IS TEMPORAL AND CHANGES ACCORDING TO KARMA AND REINCARNATION AND LIFE LESSONS THAT THE SOUL NEEDS TO EXPERIENCE IN ORDER TO LEARN SPIRITUAL AND MORAL LESSONS. THE BODY BECOMES IDENTIFIED WITH "THE LABELS AND IDENTITIES" OF EACH LIFETIME BUT THESE ARE NOT REAL ETERNAL IDENTITIES SINCE THEY ARE ONLY HUMAN CONSTRUCTS OF THE MIND AND ITS PROCESSES OF CATEGORIZING THE ENVIRONMENT.

AFTER ALL, HUMANS HAVE BEEN MOVING AND MIGRATING AND IMMIGRATING AND EMIGRATING FOREVER FOR MILLENNIA SINCE THE BEGINNING OF TIME. DO YOU THINK YOU REMAINED "THE SAME" SINCE THE BEGINNING OF YOUR ARRIVAL MILLIONS OF YEARS AGO?

PHYSICALLY NOBODY IS "ONE THING" AND THE SAME. HOWEVER, IN "SPIRIT OR LIGHT " WE ARE ALL THE SAME.

SINCERELY, "ADAMAS"

**127. THE "EARTHMAN" OR "ADAM:" THE EARTHMAN "ADAM" AND THE "EARTH" ARE ONE!!! THE BASIS BEHIND THE CONCEPT OF "THE WEB OR CIRCLE OF LIFE" —-ALL EARTH IS CREATED EQUAL!!!!**

WHY DO PEOPLE "LABEL" EVERYTHING AND EVERYONE???? I HAVE SEEN THIS THROUGHOUT MY LIFE. IT'S LIKE THAT SAYING THAT STATES THAT "ONCE YOU NAME SOMETHING IT LOSES ITS MAGIC." THERE IS ONLY "ONE" EARTH ELEMENT FOR GOSH'S SAKE!!! IT MIGHT CHANGE COLOR AND TEXTURE FROM PLACE TO PLACE BUT IT'S STILL THE SAME, THE EXACT SAME "ELEMENTS" COMING TOGETHER TO MAKE THE EARTH ELEMENT. ALL "EARTH" IS CREATED EQUAL!!!

IF "ALL EARTH IS CREATED EQUAL" THAT MEANS THAT "ALL WO-MEN OR ADAM ARE CREATED EQUAL!!!!" SINCE, ALL MEN BODIES ARE MADE OF THE SAME EARTH. IN OTHER WORDS, ALL BODIES REGARDLESS OF FORM AND COLOR AND SHAPES ARE FORMED OF THE SAME ELEMENTS OF THE EARTH WHICH ARE "THE SAME ALL OVER THE GLOBE."

THAT'S WHY A WHITE, BLACK, ASIAN, LATINO, ETC. ETC. ETC. CAN GO TO AFRICA OR ASIA OR LATIN AMERICA OR THE MIDDLE EAST AND "EAT OF THE FOODS GROWN AND HARVESTED IN THAT PLACE" AND — THE ELEMENTS IN THOSE "FOREIGN FOODS" DO THE SAME THING AS IN SUSTAINING THE BODIES ALL THE SAME. THEREFORE, ALL BODIES ARE "EQUAL." THE "ILLUSION" OR THE "PLAY OF MAYA" IS TO MAKE US BELIEVE THAT "BECAUSE IT LOOKS DIFFERENT AS IN FORM, SHAPE OR COLOR IT MUST BE DIFFERENT AND MUTUALLY EXCLUSIVE TO THE WHOLE" BUT IT IS ....NOT!!!!

THE EXAMPLE IS IN THE AMERICAN EXPERIMENT IN WHICH "ALL PEOPLES OF ALL CORNERS OF THE GLOBE AND WHO CARRY ALL SORTS OF LABELS THAT HUMANS LIKE TO AFFIX TO THEMSELVES" LIVE IN A PARTICULAR AND DEFINED GEOGRAPHIC LOCATION NAMED "THE UNITED STATES." AS SUCH ALL THESE DIVERSE PEOPLES WHO ARE "AMERICAN" —-FOR THE MOST PART EAT THE SAME PRODUCE AND PRODUCTS REGARDLESS OF THE RACE, COLOR, LANGUAGE, RELIGION, ORIGIN,

SEX, SOCIAL STATUS, ETC. ETC. ETC. DO YOU SEE THE POINT HERE? ALL THESE DIVERSE AMERICAN PEOPLES ARE SUSTAINED BY THE SAME "EARTH" DESPITE THEIR EXTERNAL DIFFERENCES. SHOWING US THAT "ALL MEN ARE CREATED EQUAL AND THAT ALL EARTH IS CREATED EQUAL" AND BOTH CONCEPTS GO HAND IN HAND.

THEREFORE, THE BELIEF OF "BEING DIFFERENT ONE FROM ANOTHER" IS PART OF THE "ILLUSION OR WHAT THE HINDU CALL —MAYA." IT DECEIVES AND CONFUSES ONE TO BELIEVE THAT "WE ARE DIFFERENT FROM EACH OTHER" BUT WHEN YOU GO TO "THE SCIENCE" BEHIND LIFE WE FINALLY REALIZE THAT "WE ARE ALL THE SAME MATERIALS ONLY THAT MANIFESTING IN DIVERSE WAYS" JUST AS THESE SAME ELEMENTS COMBINE IN DIVERSE FORMS TO BRING ABOUT OR CREATE ANIMALS AND PLANTS AND INSECTS ETC. ETC. ETC. OF ALL KINDS AND TYPES AND YET IT IS ALL "THE SAME" ENERGY MANIFESTING AS ELEMENTS MANIFESTING AS ONE WORLD, ONE "LIFE."

THE ABOVE IS THE BASIS FOR THE CONCEPT OF THE "WEB OR CIRCLE OF LIFE AND THE FRATERNITY OF HU-MANITY."

SINCERELY, ADAM 2024

---

## 128. BEING "WIDE AWA-KE:" AND "AWA"/ "AVA" ATE OF THE FORBIDDEN FRUIT OF WISDOM AND GUESS WHAT? SHE "WOKE UP" AND SAW THE TRUTH BEHIND MAYA OR ILLUSION

IS NOT IT INTERESTING THAT THE ENGLISH WORD "AWA-KE" HAS IN IT THE NAME OF EVE IN HEBREW AS IN "H-AWA" OR AVA, WHO ACCORDING TO THE STORY OF THE FALL IN GENESIS, EXPERIENCED "AWA-RENESS" AFTER THAT FALL!!! ABLE TO NOTICE AND TO SEE THE "DUALITY" OF THIS REALITY WHICH SHE WASN'T ABLE TO SEE AND NOTICE BEFORE?

THE PROCESS OF "AWA-KENING" IS ATTRIBUTED THEREFORE TO "H-AWA" OR TO THE DIVINE FEMININE PRINCIPLE. MEANING THAT SHE TOOK THE "INITIATIVE AND CURIOSITY AND ACTION" TO TAKE THE FRUIT AND TAKE A BITE AND "BECOME AS GODS ABLE TO TELL THE DIFFERENCE BETWEEN WHAT WAS GOOD AND WHAT WAS EVIL" WHICH SHE COULD NOT DO BEFORE.

WE ARE SPEAKING HERE OF A PROCESS OF "EVOLUTION" AS IN "EVO" WHICH IS THE MASCULINE RENDERING OF THE NAME "EVA OR EVE OR H-AWA." THUS, THE PROCESS OF HUMAN PROGRESS IN THE PSYCHOLOGICAL SENSE AND OF EVOLUTION IS LINKED TO THAT OF "AWA-KENING" AND ..... THE SO CALLED "FALL FROM GRACE."

SO THE QUESTION IS, "IF THE FALL WAS SO SO BAD" WHY IS IT THAT IT INITIATED A PROCESS OF "AWAKENING AND EVOLUTION THAT WOULD GIVE HUMANS THE OPPORTUNITY TO BE AS GODS ABLE TO TELL THE DIFFERENCE BETWEEN DUALITIES? WAS IT THAT ADAM AND AWA WERE

NOT ABLE TO DISTINGUISH DIFFERENCES BEFORE? WERE THEY LIKE "ROBOTIKA" IN NEED OF SOMEONE LIKE A FATHER FIGURE TELLING THEM WHAT TO DO, WHERE TO GO, WHAT TO SPEAK, WHEN TO SLEEP, WHAT TO SEE OR NOT SEE, ETC. ETC. ETC????

THE ORIGINAL ADAM AND EVE IN THE GENE-SIS STORY IS REFERRING TO "THE BEGINNING OF THE BEGINNING" WHICH IS NOT HERE ON EARTH. EARTH IS NOT THE BEGINNING BUT THE "RESULT" OF THE BEGINNING. MEANING THAT THE ADAM AND AWA IN GENESIS IS REFERRING TO THE "DIVINE YIN AND YANG" ENERGIES IN HEAVEN OR "BINAH AND CHOCKMA." WHO —BOTH TOGETHER FORM "THE NEXT ADAM AND AWA" AS IN PUTTING TOGETHER ONE ANDROGENOUS ENERGY BEING AND LATER "SPLITTING THIS ONE BINOMIAL ATOM INTO TWO/ (SEPARATE) TWINS" AND THERE WE HAVE THE LESSER ADAM AND H-AWA. THE WORD "ADAM" ALSO MEANS "RED MAN" AND RED IS ATTRIBUTED TO THE ELEMENT OF FIRE. AND H-AWA HAS IN IT THE WORD FOR "AWA-TER or AGUA (AWA) IN LATIN/ SPANISH AND ITS COLOR IS BLUE. HERE WE HAVE THE "RED AND THE BLUE." THE YIN AND THE YANG.

THEREFORE, ONE OF THE TEACHINGS OF THE G-ENNE-SIS STORY IS ABOUT — THE NECESSITY FOR "THE FALL" OR THE "SPLITTING OR FRAGMENTATION" TO HAPPEN IN ORDER FOR FIRE AND WATER AND ALL THE OTHER ELEMENTS TO EXIST AND COME TOGETHER TO FORM THIS INTERESTING AND YET CHALLENGING DUAL AND POLAR REALITY WHICH IS THE MATERIAL WORLD. AND SO FOR OUR "SOULS" IT IS NECESSARY TO PASS THROUGH THIS REALM OF DUALITY IN ORDER TO AWA-KEN AND EVO-LVE AND BECOME AS THE FORCES OF CONSCIOUSNESS WHO KNOW THE DIFFERENCE BETWEEN ONE THING AND ANOTHER BECAUSE THESE FORCES OF CONSCIOUSNESS ARE THE POLARITIES THEMSELVES.

SO WHEN WE MAKE MISTAKES WE ARE JUST FOLLOWING THE NATURE OF THIS REALM WHICH WAS DESIGNED TO BE THIS WAY AND EACH MISTAKE IS A MINI FALL THAT HELPS US LEARN TO DISTINGUISH BETWEEN GOOD AND EVIL AND JOY AND PAIN AND SO HELP US BE MORE "CONSCIOUS OF OUR OWN ACTIONS AND THE REPERCUSSIONS AND CONSEQUENCES OF THESE ACTIONS ON OTHERS AND ON OUR OWN SELVES."

IF WE MAKE MISTAKES OR "FALL" AND WE REFUSE TO "LEARN FROM THAT MISTAKE AND KEEP REPEATING IT OVER AND OVER AGAIN" WE ARE STUCK IN A GOLEM STATE JUST AS BEFORE "ADAM AND H-AWA" "FELL FROM GRACE." BECAUSE OF "FEAR" WE REMAIN TRAPPED IN UNHEALTHY CYCLES AND SO WE END UP INTERRUPTING OUR OWN PROCESS OF AWA-RENESS (AWA-KENING) AND EVO-LUTION.

SINCERELY, ADAMAS AND H-AWA NAGILA (THE ONE WHO REJOICED TO BE AWA-KE)

---

## 129. H-ANNU-KA IS ABOUT "UPHOLDING AND RE-AFFIRMING THE DIVINE FIRE AND LIGHT:" THE BODY OF M-ANNU

AS WE HAVE STATED BEFORE, THE "M-ENNE-ORA" OR CANDELABRA OF 7 - 9 LIGHTS IN H-ANNU-KA REPRESENTS THE "PRIMORDIAL M-ANNE."

**Manu (Sanskrit: मनु) is a term found with various meanings in Hinduism. In early texts, it refers to the archetypal man, or to the first man (progenitor of humanity). The Sanskrit term for 'human', मनुष्य (IAST: manuṣya) or मानव (IAST: mānava) means 'of Manu' or 'children of Manu'.(WIKIPEDIA)**

THE PRIMORDIAL MAN IS THE "FIRST MAN" OR "THE COSMIC ANDROGYNE COMPOSED OF BOTH THE YIN AND YANG ENERGIES " THAT EVENTUALLY SPLITS IN HALF TO BRING ABOUT THE INTERACTION OF DUALITIES AND FROM THAT INTERACTION BEGIN THE CREATIVE PROCESS. THE PRIMORDIAL M-ANNE aka "MANNU" WHICH IS THE SANSKRIT WORD FROM WHICH THE ENGLISH WORD "MAN" COMES FROM. M-ANNU, AS IN "M-ANNU-ORA" THE PRIMORDIAL WO-MAN OF FIRE AND LIGHT WHO IS COSMIC MIND OR MENES.

REMEMBER THAT LIGHT HAS ITS OPPOSITE AS THE DARK ONE OR THE SHADOW. JUST LIKE WHEN YOU PUT A LIGHTED MENORAH IN A DARK ROOM AND YOU CAN SEE ITS SHADOW ON THE WALL. M-ANNU HAS ITS OWN SHADOW SELF AS WELL.

HUMANS AND OTHER LIVING BEINGS ARE IN A STATE OF ANIMATION THANKS TO THIS "SACRED BODY OF LIGHT." WHICH IS AFTER —- M-ANNU'S OR THE "PRIMORDIAL MAN" COSMIC BODY—DEPICTED IN THE DIAGRAM OF THE TREE OF LIFE AND DUALITIES AND UNITIES.

THE H-ANNU-KA "M-ANNU-ORA" IS A REPRESENTATION OF THE TREE OF LIGHTS OR EMANATIONS OR SEFIROT AND THE DIVISION OF POWERS.

THEREFORE, THIS "M-ANNU-ORA" IS UNIVERSAL AND IS IN EVERY HU-MAN. THE "MAN OF LIGHT AND FIRE" IS "THE CHAKRA SYSTEM IN THE HINDU TRADITION. AND THE —-PAGAN-CHRISTIAN CHRISTMAS TREE WITH ITS MYRIAD —LIGHTS— REACHING UP TO THE "STAR" AT THE TOP OF THE TREE IS ALSO A REPRESENTATION OF THE SAME CONCEPT.

THEREFORE, THE "BODY OR M-ANNU OF LIGHT" IS THE TEMPLATE IN MINIATURE OF THE COSMIC M-ANNU OR THE "DIVINE ANDROG-ENNE.

WE MUST TURN ON OUR INNER LIGHT BEFORE WE ARE OVERTAKEN BY OUR OWN "SHADOW" SO THAT THIS "DIVINE LIGHT IN US" ILLUMINATES THE "SHADOW" AND AT LAST WE CAN REACH "AWA-RENESS OF OUR OWN SHADOW SELF SO THAT AWA-KENING WHICH IS....CONSCIOUSNESS" CAN BEGIN.

LEAVE THE GUNS AND AMMUNITION AND BOMBS —BEHIND— BECAUSE ALL THAT IS BORNE OF THE UN-ILLUMINATED SHADOW AND NOT FROM THE LIGHT. EACH MURDER IS EQUIVALENT TO THE "SACRED M-ANNU-ORA" BEING EXTINGUISHED AND DESTROYED. IT IS EQUIVALENT TO THE DESTRUCTION OF "M-ANNU!!!!!" AS S-HE MANIFESTS IN EVERY M-ANNE ON EARTH.

THE HOUSE OF "ANNA" AFFIRMS AND UPHOLDS THE LIGHT IN ALL.

SINCERELY, M-ANNU, THE PRIMORDIAL MAN THRU THE BIPOLAR GATES OF COMMUNICATION

---

## 130. IMMA-ANNU-EL: AN INTERPRETATION OF THE DIVINE TRIAD AND THE ACTIVATION OF THE "GOD OR DIVINE IN US."

YOU WILL NOTICE THAT WHEN YOU BREAK THE WORD IMMANUEL INTO PARTS IT BECOMES —"IMMA" - "ANNU" - "EL."

THE NAME "IMMANUEL" IS FOUND IN THE BOOK OF ISSA-Y-YAH 7: 14 AS FOLLOWS:

Therefore the Lord himself will give you[a] a sign: The maiden or virgin[b] will conceive and give birth to a son, and[c] will call him Immanuel. (BIBLEGATEWAY)

THE NAME "IMMANUEL" ITSELF HAS IN IT THE "THREE CREATIVE PRINCIPLES." AS IN "THE MOTHER (OR VIRGIN) AND THE "M-ANNU" OR THE "PRIMORDIAL CHILD" AND THE FATHER "EL." FROM THE HOUSE OF "ANNU."

IF YOU FOLLOW THE CASTILIAN FORMATION OF SENTENCES YOU CAN WRITE "EL-IMMA-ANNU" WHICH SOUNDS MUCH LIKE "EL HUMANO" WHICH IS THE WORD FOR "HUMAN" IN CASTILIAN. THAT IMMA-ANNU-EL —IS RENDERED AS "GOD IS WITH US" ALONG WITH THE ABOVE EXPLANATION WE CAN INFER THAT:

IMMA or MOTHER IS A "VIRGIN" OR MAIDEN. M-ANNU IS MAN AND CHILD. "EL" IS THE FORM FOR THE MASCULINE DEITY. AND THE HOUSE OF "ANNU." THEREFORE, "ANNU-EL" IS THE NAME OF THE MALE DEITY AS IN "EL-ANNU" OR "EL IS ANNU, ANNU IS EL." HERE WE HAVE THE HOLY FAMILY CONCEPT

AND THE TRIAD IN THE TREE OF LIFE OR OF UNION AND DUALITIES. EL -ANNU IS TRANSLATED IN CASTILIAN AS "THE ANNU", "HE THE ANNU" OR "HE IS ANNU OR OF THE MESOPOTAMIAN TRADITION OF THE ANNU-NAGA DEITIES.

SO WHEN DELVE INTO THIS VERSE WE SEE CLEARLY THE PARALLELS WITH THE CHURCH'S INTERPRETATION AND THE TREE OF LIFE IN QABALAH AND ITS TRIAD OF UPPER SEFIROT. "EL IS CHOKMAH" AND "BINAH IS IMMA" AND "M-ANNU IS —THE DIVINE ANDROGYNE DA-AT." THE DIVINE TRIAD BY WHICH EVERYTHING IN THE WILL AND MIND OF "KETER" COMES TO FRUITION AND CREATION.

WE CAN SAY THAT "EVERYONE" IS AN "IMMA-ANNU-EL" SINCE EVERYONE IS A MINIATURE "BODY OF LIGHT" COVERED IN FLESH. WHEN A PERSON AWA-KENS AND REALIZES HiS HER INNER DIVINITY, IS LIKE BEING RE-BORN AND BEING ANOINTED BY THE "DIVINE SOPHIA" WHO IS "THE VIRGIN" AND BY "THE EL" THE FATHER WHO REPRESENT RESPECTIVELY THE DARKNESS AND THE LIGHT BECOMING MANIFEST AND CLEAR AS WATER IN THE HUMAN'S OWN "DIVINE SELF AND BODY OF LIGHT."

SINCERELY,
"EL-UMMA- ANNO" FROM THE HOUSE OF ANNA

---

**131. DO NOT FIGHT THE MOON-LITE = NO MORE!!!! CAN'T FIGHT THE MOONLIGHT …. SURRENDER …TO THE POWER OF LOVE AND ILLUMINATION!**

REMEMBER HOW WE STATED LONG TIME AGO THAT THE "MOON" IS THE MOTHER'S SPHERE AND HOW SHE REPRESENTS THE ACTIVE PRINCIPLE OF "GROWING UP???" HOW IS IT THAT WE GROW UP? WE GROW UP BY LEARNING FROM OTHER'S "NOBLE AND PRINCIPLED" EXAMPLES AND ALSO …. AND MOST IMPORTANTLY, WE LEARN FROM EXPERIENCING…. THE UPS AND DOWNS OF LIFE ITSELF SUCH AS WAR, HATE AND VIOLENCE.

WHAT DO WE LEARN FROM WAR, HATE AND VIOLENCE? WE LEARN FIRST OF ALL HOW BAD THE THREE ARE AND THAT NOTHING GOOD COMES FROM THEM AS THESE REPRESENT DESTRUCTION OF MAN'S HUMANITY AND THE HUMANITY IN OTHERS. WHEN THE SACRED LIGHT WITHIN ANOTHER IS RENDERED CHEAP, EVERYTHING AND EVERYONE BECOMES CHEAP AND DISPOSABLE.

HATE, WAR AND VIOLENCE PRODUCE "EVIL" AS IN PAIN, SUFFERING AND MORE TRAUMA THAT CREATES MORE OF THE SAME PERPETUATING AND PRODUCING MORE CYCLES OF VIOLENCE, PAIN AND SUFFERING.

EVERYONE HAS UNDERGONE SOME KIND OF PAIN AND SUFFERING AND VIOLENT INCIDENT IN THEIR LIVES THEREFORE WE ALL KNOW HOW BAD IT FEELS. THAT FEELING BASED ON PERSONAL EXPERIENCE TEACHES US AND MAKES US REALIZE THAT …. WAR, HATE AND VIOLENCE …ARE NO GOOD BECAUSE THEY PRODUCE THE SAME PAIN AND EVIL IN OTHERS AND THE WORLD. EVERYONE KNOWS HOW BAD IT FEELS. SURE IF YOU FEEL BAD EXPERIENCING SUCH THINGS, YOU WOULD NOT WANT TO CAUSE SUCH EVIL UPON OTHERS. WHEN YOU ARE AT LAST CONSCIOUS OF YOUR OWN PAIN, YOU BECOME CONSCIOUS OF EVERYONE ELSE'S PAIN.

SUFFERING SHOULD MAKE US MORE EMPATHIC AND NOT — BRING US CLOSER TO THE DEMONIC SIDE OF REALITY.

AND …. WAR, VIOLENCE AND HATE …SERVE AS "INDICATORS", JUST AS "BODILY PAIN SERVES TO POINT TO THE SOURCE OF THE HEALTH PROBLEM IN OUR BODIES", THAT —THERE IS SOMETHING VERY WRONG GOING ON WITH US SPIRITUALLY, PSYCHICALLY AND MENTALLY-EMOTIONALLY — THAT WE NEED TO TACKLE AS SOON AS POSSIBLE BEFORE WE CROSS THE POINT OF NO RETURN AND BECOME "VERITABLE DEMONS INCARNATED IN FLESH."

THEREFORE, THE PROCESS OF "ILLUMINATION" AND "AWA-KENING TAKING PLACE RIGHT NOW IS BECAUSE THE FORCES OF THE FATHER PRINCIPLE ARE SHINING LIGHT ON THE MOTHER "SHADOW" PRINCIPLE MAKING US AWARE OF THE CONTENTS OF OUR MINDS — MOVING US FROM IGNORANCE AND EVIL TOWARDS CRESCENDO OR THE PROCESS OF GROWTH IN THE FORM OF GAINING MORE AWA-RENESS UNTIL WE REACH "FULL MOON" STATUS AND CAN RECLAIM OUR "HALO" AS WE HAVE BEEN FREED FROM ALL THAT EVIL POWER AND IGNORANCE OVER US.

THEREFORE, FIGHTING THE PROCESS OF AWA-RENESS AND AWA-KENING TAKING PLACE IS EQUIVALENT TO "FIGHTING THE MOON-LITE" WHICH IS A MAJOR TRANSGRESSION SINCE "THE MOON IS THE SUN'S SWEETHEART" AND THE PROCESS OF ILLUMINATION AND ENLIGHTENMENT IS "SACRED AND HOLY TO THE FATHER AND MOTHER PRINCIPLES WHO BOTH REPRESENT IT!!!"

MAY TRUTH, JUSTICE, PEACE AND LOVE PERSEVERE NOW THAT KALI IS GIVING BIRTH TO THE LIGHT OF REASON AND GOOD WILL BY MEANS OF THE FATHER LIGHT AND THE MOTHER'S DARK WOMB!

SINCERELY,
"L-UNNA"

## 132. OH, CHRIST-MAS TREE: THE GERM-ANNE-IC "TREE OF GOOD AND EVIL AND OF LIFE"

The CHRISTMAS TREE is a GERM-ANNE-IC TRADITION. And not many in the CHRISTIAN TRADITION know that it is ALSO a JEWISH symbol. Well, to be more accurate … IT IS "BOTH!!!"

Let me clarify.

Although the CHRIST-MAS TREE is of GERM-ANNE- IC "PAGAN" tradition, THE CONCEPT is the same as that of the QABALISTIC TREE OF LIFE. Both are pointing to the SAME concepts and message and MEANING.

You can appreciate here what has been taking place ever since the beginning of time. The migrations of peoples from place to place taking their symbols and customs and cultures and traditions all over the world and leaving their indelible mark creating a rich SYNCRETISM of traditions. The interesting development here is that basically these SYMBOLS fit pretty well into the "new religion" or predominant tradition because the SYMBOL IS UNI-VERSAL and has the same meaning as that of the other TREE in the other tradition. Do you understand?

The GERM-ANNE-IC CHRIST-MAS TREE, although considered "PAGAN" is the same TREE as THE QABALAH TREE OF LIFE and THE TREE OF CRUCIFIXION IN CHRISTIANITY.

Let me explain, THE TREE OF LIFE is a UNI-VERSAL ARCHETYPE and so BOTH the CHRIST-MAS TREE and the TREE OF LIFE are the same ARCHETYPE. THE CHRISTMAS TREE is an EVER-GREEN representing EVERLASTING LIFE!!! Do you see what WE see? THE EVERGREEN points upwards and it represents ETERNAL LIFE. And so IS NOT THE TREE OF CRUCIFIXION representing RESURRECTION AND ETERNAL LIFE!!!

And so the EVERLASTING EVERGREEN CHRISTMAS TREE reminds us of the PARADISE concept up in heaven WHERE NOBODY HAS TO EXPERIENCE DEATH EVER AGAIN. And its pointing UPWARDS up towards ORI-GENES or to HEAVEN. Pointing up to the STAR from which all come from. The LIGHTS in the TREE OF LIFE represent ALL OF US THE SPIRIT ENERGIES WHO DESCEND TO THIS MALKUTA REALM. HUMANKIND are the FALLEN STARS OF HEAVEN represented by the CHRISTMAS LIGHTS.

THE STARS DESCEND to MALKUTA or to the EARTHLY KINGDOM represented by the LITTLE TOWN OF BETHLEHEM decorations placed underneath the Tree with THE MANGER, the animals and the DIVINE FAMILY. ALL these archetypes represent THE HUMAN FAMILY and NATURE and HUMAN SOCIETY. YESHUA is incarnated in this realm from above in MALKUTA. The Holy family represents ALL THE FAMILIES ON EARTH.

As THE CHRISTMAS TREE DESCENDS from the STAR AT THE TOP ALL THE WAY TO THE BOTTOM, it becomes the TREE OF GOOD AND EVIL or MATTER AND DUALITY. And when YESHUA ascends eventually and all the STARS OR LIGHTS as well, looking at the TREE from below and going upwards towards THE STAR OF BETHLEHEM, IT BECOMES THE TREE OF ETERNAL LIFE.

Do you understand?

WE are IN A STATE OF BEING CRUCIFIED TO THIS WORLD in the hopes of being RELEASED INTO ETERNAL LIFE back to SOURCE since WE ARE ALL FRAGMENTS OF DIVINE LIGHT, QI, CONSCIOUSNESS WHO BELONG TO THE BODY OF LIGHT OF ADAM KAD-M-ONNE.

So when someone begins to disparage the CHRIST-MAS TREE as being PAGAN as if PAGAN was equivalent to evil, remember that THE CHRIST-MAS TREE IS THE SAME AS THE TREE OF KNOWLEDGE OF GOOD AND EVIL AND THE TREE OF LIFE.

TO end this diary, let me mention that it is interesting that SPHERES are used to adorn the CHRIST-MAS TREE which resembles the concept of the SEFIROT which are the SPHERES that run down and up THE TREE OF DUALITY AND OF LIFE in the Qabalah.

Let's save EARTH'S TREES as they are an integral part of life on Earth.

SINCERELY,
Y-ESH-UA KAD-M-ONNE

---

## 133. THE PSYCHOTIC BREAKDOWN and the PATH TO SELF-REALIZATION and DIVINE SERVICE

Years ago in my desperate search for answers about PSYCHOSIS, I was shocked to find in ancient stories and documents and myths that THE ANCIENT PEOPLES REGARDED THE PSYCHOSIS "BREAKDOWN" AS A SPIRITUAL INITIATION OF SORTS.

When I read the above it made perfect sense to me since I was not only hearing voices and seeing things and noticing what I had not noticed before, including a new way of seeing the landscape. I realized that THIS BREAKDOWN was a literal breaking down of the WALLS that separate this world with other worlds.

Then I investigated further into this and found out that PSYCHOSIS in these older traditions is called or regarded as THE CALL OF THE SPIRITS or GOD!!!

And so after undergoing many weird things since 1991, everything started to add up and I began to realize that what my intuition or SPIRIT had told me years ago about everything that has been happening to me since my 20's and perhaps my entire life was basically a SPIRITUAL INITIATION.

Later I read in some Qabalistic book about some JEWISH stories of MOSHE and was shocked to read and find out that MOSES WAS CHASED TO DEATH BY ELOHIM AND STRUCK by something similar to PSYCHOSIS. It's the same concept in the global SHAMANIC traditions of the EAST AND WEST. Basically the entire spiritual process begins with a DEPRESSIVE PSYCHOTIC break at about 20 years of age or teen years and so the PERSON OR "INITIATE" is taken to the TRIBE'S ELDER and to be trained and prepared to take the role of SHA-M-INNA or LEADER or STORY TELLER or ARTIST etc.. for the TRIBE. Remember that all the above activities were part of the SPIRITUAL ACTIVITIES AND CULTURE OF THE TRIBE and OF THE SHAMANS SET OF SPIRITUAL SKILLS.

Therefore I began to understand that many times the PSYCHOTIC breakdown can actually represent a SPIRITUAL INITIATION OF SOME SORTS.

When you are called by SPIRIT or GOD "you are called" just as in the near death experience of MOSES before becoming the leader of ISRAEL. so the same story repeats itself in the other world traditions where the CALL FROM HEAVEN INVOLVES A NEAR-DEATH EXPERIENCE INDUCED BY THE COSMIC FORCES.

In the case of YESHUA and other SHA-M-INNA types, their lives do not mean that are going to be EASY like the rest of the people since they are being STRUCK BY HEAVEN ITSELF and so carry with them the ABILITIES that GOD bestows upon them thru SPIRIT but also a sort of DIVINE CURSE THAT THEY WILL HAVE TO BEAR FOR THE REST OF THEIR LIVES ON BEHALF OF THE PEOPLE. THEY HAVE BEEN CHOSEN TO HELP AND SERVE THE PEOPLE. Therefore this group of people are some of the most misunderstood peoples in the entire Earth especially today when the HOLY BREAKDOWN cannot complete its cycle of development because it is rendered as a DISEASE rather than a SPIRITUAL BREAKDOWN AND PROCESS OF COSMIC PROPORTIONS.

And so the HOLY SHA-M-INNA go through the biblical description below which became manifest and made PERFECT IN THE PERSON OF YESHUA:

ISSA- Y- YAH 53: 5

*BUT HE WAS PIERCED FOR OUR TRANSGRESSIONS. HE WAS CRUSHED FOR OUR INIQUITIES. UPON HIM WAS THE CHASTISEMENT THAT BROUGHT US PEACE AND WITH HIS WOUNDS WE ARE —--HEALED.*

*Surely He took on our infirmities and carried our sorrows; yet we considered Him stricken by God, struck down and afflicted. 5 But He was pierced for our transgressions, He was crushed for our iniquities; the punishment that brought us peace was upon Him, and by His stripes we are healed. 6We all like sheep have gone astray, each one has turned to his own way; and the LORD has laid upon Him the iniquity of us.*

SINCERELY, THE WOUNDED "HEALER"

---

## 134. MANY LANGUAGES OUT OF "ONNE"--- THE LANGUAGE OF "DIVINE LIGHT"

So as we saw earlier the ROOT WORD "UR" and its many variations such as OR is ANCIENT. And, what the story of Abraham from "UR" of CHALDEES is trying to convey is that all languages have a COMMON ANCESTRY.

The story of the TOWER OF BAB- EL implies this COMMONALITY. And so just as there has been MANY PEOPLE OUT OF ONE, so there is also a MANY LANGUAGES OUT OF "ONE" process.

BAB-EL stands for WHEN "EL" or THE ONE WHO IS MANY AND THE MANY WHO ARE ONE or I AM spoke for the first time to WE THE PEOPLE.

Therefore, the CONFUSION of the languages was simply A DIVINE INTERVENTION PROCESS in which the ONE language was SCRAMBLED into many versions or ways of placing the letters or vowels or SYLLABLES such as prefixes, suffixes, root words, sounds, in diverse ways and combinations, etc. That's what CONFUSION stands for. For instance, each word became many words by changing the placement of the sounds, letters, syllables into diverse combinations. Therefore the root syllables and words remained the same but the wording and meaning changed. And so we get the first family of languages from where all modern and ancient languages come from. Each one evolving in diverse ways.

UR or OR means "LIGHT or FIRE" or GOLD and even the word F-IRE has the root word for LIGHT and FIRE or IRE. "UR" is an Aramaic or CHALDEAN word from Mesopotamia, the cradle of Civilization. From there the word passed onto the MORE MODERN LANGUAGES. In Arabic N-UR is the female name for DIVINE LIGHT!!! And so the root word "UR, OR" exists even before Hebrew, Arabic, English, Spanish and other languages appeared. It's ANNE-CIENT!!!

And so we have the word ORI-GINAL as in "present and existing since the beginning." The word itself is pointing back to BAB-EL and UR or that area of Mesopotamia where it all began and spread everywhere. ORI-GINAL as a word DESCRIBES ITS ORIGIN AT "UR" or the area of the CITY OF LIGHTS or UR OF CHALDEES in the cradle of civilization and home of the ORI-GENE-AL TOWER and GENEALOGY. Or the PLACE WHERE THE "GENES OF LIGHT OF HUMANITY" began to spread everywhere and to form civilization!!! You see, basically we are beings of LIGHT or ENERGY dressed in MATTER.

The TOWER card number 16 in the Tarot represents UNEXPECTED, UNFORESEEN and UNAVOIDABLE CHANGES which is what the story is trying to convey as something UNFORESEEN happening all of a sudden that led to the ONE TRIBE TO FLEE AND BECOME MANY ALL OVER THE EARTH.

Basically, we are all speaking the same language and sounds which have been SCRAMBLED FROM THE FIRST "ONE" in many diverse ways and combinations.

SINCERELY,
THE DIVINE BABBLER

---

## 135. THE ARCHETYPAL ENERGIES: THE ONE AND A MILLION FACES of THE ARK OF THE COV-INNA-NT

So everything "is" a FRAGMENT or PARTICLE of a GREATER WHOLE. That GREATER WHOLE can be regarded as THE CENTER or the DIVINE MIND manifesting as FORMS AND SHAPES AND CONCEPTS or ARCHETYPES.

DEFINITION OF ARCH-ETYPES:

*a very typical example of a certain person or thing.*

*an original that has been imitated.*

*a recurrent symbol or motif in literature, art, or mythology.*

*Ie, "mythological archetypes of good and evil" (GOOGLE)*

As you can infer from the above excerpt, EACH ARCHETYPE IS A "CONCEPT" OF THE ORIGINAL MIND OF GOD-DESS THRU ADAM KAD-M-ONNE WHO MULTIPLIED ITSELF INTO MANY FRAGMENTS. Each CONCEPT is describing or giving us a NOTION of the NATURE OF ULTIMATE REALITY. That is what each ARCHETYPE represents or stands for. A FORM OF MENTAL ENERGY.

The ORI-GINAL ADAM KAD-M-ONNE has become US. WE are archetypes in MATERIAL FORM after the original DIVINE TEMPLATE or MODEL such as the TREE OF GOOD AND EVIL or DUALITIES. As our minds are a MINI MIND OF

THE DIVINE, the ARCHETYPAL FORMS AND ENERGIES ARE ALSO PART OF OUR MAKE UP AND PSYCHE.

And so THE ARCHETYPAL ENERGIES AND SYMBOLS repeat themselves in every NATION AND CULTURE because WE ARE ALL LINKED OR CONNECTED TO THE DIVINE MIND. Therefore, we are all individual beings separated by time and space; however, MENTALLY we are all LINKED TO SOURCE AND SO ARE ABLE TO DRAW INSPIRATION AND MEANING FROM IT. This is WHY the myths and stories and symbols repeat over and over again all over the world. WE ARE "ONE MIND" MANIFESTING AS MANY.

Have you noticed WHAT is hidden in the word "ARCHETYPE?" Yep, there is the word ARCH as in ARK of the COVENANT or COMMUNICATION. That ARK OF THE COVENANT SYMBOL stands for the SOURCE OF ALL ARCHETYPAL ENERGIES and so if you look at it face to face YOU GET FRIED!!! IT'S OVERWHELMING!!! And so YOU need to cut the WHOLE INTO PARTS so that you can make sense of and get a NOTION of what ULTIMATE REALITY IS LIKE without getting burned in the process..

And so just as SI-ONNE is an an ARCHETYPE for the MOUNTAIN OF GOD OR ALL MOUNTAIN SYMBOLS which in turn stand for or represent some FUNCTION OR ASPECT OF THE WHOLE, so is the ARCHETYPE OF THE "HOLY LAND" REPRESENTING ALL "HOLY LANDS" WHICH IS THE ENTIRE EARTH and the EARTH element. And so is the same concept with the MESSIAH!!!! It represents the ARCHETYPE OF ADAM KADM-ONNE FALLING DOWN TO SAVE HUMANITY which in turn represents PEOPLE throughout history who have drawn from that ENERGY.

Each ARCHETYPE represents a form of DIVINE ENERGY OR ESSENCE represented as a SYMBOL.

EACH ARCHETYPE is like a SEED WITHIN and it lives in every human being. Including the MESSIAH archetype. Basically there is a SAVIOR ARCHETYPAL ENERGY in every one of us such as in the example of ADAMAS where he is SAVED FROM BEING HOMELESS AND DYING IN THE STREETS BY A FEMALE MESSIAH ARCHETYPE . Each person has a part of him-herself that has empathy for the human condition and so does something about it which is what the YESHUA STORY IS POINTING to YESHUA himself being an ARCHETYPE FIGURE AFTER ADAM KAD-M-ONNE. And humankind being human archetypes of both in material form.

MLK, GANDHI, CESAR CHAVEZ, THE REVEREND OG, etc etc etc. and many other men and women known and unknown are those who draw from the MESSIAH ARCHETYPE ENERGY consciously or unconsciously in order to TIK-UNNE OLAM or REPAIR THE WORLD OF BROKEN SHARDS AND KLIPPOT.

HUMAN is a MULTI-FACETED BEING like a DIAMOND IN THE SKY. EACH FACE BEING AN ARCHETYPE. ENERGIES that one can access at any time and work with in order to learn more about OUR HUMAN NATURE.

WARNING though— BE CAREFUL YOU DO NOT GET BURNT.

SINCERELY, THE ARK OF ANNA

---

## 136. THE CRESCENT AND THE STAR OF "IS-EL-AM" BELONGS TO THE MOTHER: THROUGH THE MOTHER'S WISDOM WE CONNECT AND REACH THE "STAR OF BETHLEHEM"

THE STAR — THE STAR REPRESENTS "HOPE!!!" WHICH IS WHAT THE GOSPEL STORY IS ABOUT. TEACHING US THAT IT IS THROUGH OUR OWN ILLUMINATION AND ENLIGHTENMENT THAT WE AS HUMANS BRING HOPE AND GOOD WILL TO THE WORLD. AND LIBERATE OURSELVES FROM THE CHAINS OF SAMSARA AND REINCARNATION.

WISDOM WAS WITH THE FATHER PRINCIPLE SINCE THE BEGINNING. BOTH WORKING TOGETHER TO BRING ABOUT THE WHOLE ECO-COSMIC-SYSTEM IN WHICH WE LIVE IN AND MANY OTHERS AND OTHER PLANETS AS WELL. THIS WISDOM IS INHERENT IN US ALL BECAUSE WE WERE DESIGNED THROUGH AND BY IT. IT IS CALLED COSMIC "CONSCIOUSNESS."

THE STAR OF BETHLEHEM IN THE STORY REPRESENTS MANY THINGS AMONGST THEM "AWA-RENESS AND AWA-KENING!!! IT ALSO REPRESENTS THE HUMAN AIM TO "GROW IN WISDOM AND UNDERSTANDING" WHICH IN THE TREE OF LIFE ARE REPRESENTED BY BOTH BINAH THE MOTHER AND CHOKMAH THE FATHER PRINCIPLES. SO THAT WE CAN RETURN BACK TO OUR "ONCE UPON A STAR, HOME!"

AND SO THE ISLAMIC SYMBOL OF THE "CRESCENT MOON AND THE STAR" BELONGS TO THE "MOTHER PRINCIPLE!!! AND ISLAM LINKED TO THE OTHER TWO TRADITIONS — JUDAISM AND CHRISTIANITY — BY THE SAME SYMBOLS WHICH ARE POINTING TO THE "MOVING FROM UNCONSCIOUSNESS TO SEMI-CONSCIOUSNESS TOWARDS THE LIGHT AND FULL- CONSCIOUSNESS - AWA-RENESS AND UNDERSTANDING!!!" OF OUR ACTIONS, WORDS. MOTIVES, THOUGHTS, EMOTIONS.... AND .... THEIR CONSEQUENCES!!!

THE STAR ALSO REPRESENTS A "HALO" AND THE SPIRITUAL ANOINTMENT THAT TAKES PLACE WHEN A HUMAN BEING IS ABLE TO UNDERSTAND HIM / HER SELF AND TO PARTAKE OF THE GOOD OF THE TREE OF KNOWLEDGE WHILE LEARNING FROM THE EVIL SIDE OF LIFE FOR GOODNESS SAKE.

THE CRESCENT MOON STANDS IN THE MIDDLE OF THE FEMALE LUNAR TRIAD, THEREFORE IN THE POSITION OF THE "DIVINE CHILD" WHO IS EVERY HUMAN BEING FORMED AFTER "ADAM KADMONE" THE PRIMORDIAL MAN. THEREFORE, EVERYONE HAS THE POTENTIAL TO REACH "THE HALO" AND "THE STAR." EACH ONE US IS IN A "SEMI- CONSCIOUS STATE." BUT, LIKE EVE, ONE MUST LEAVE THE COMFORT ZONE OF CONDITIONING AND PROGRAMMING AND TAKE THE RISK OF "EXPERIENCING LIFE" AND "EXPERIENCING EACH OTHER'S HUMANITY." AND THROUGH "LIFE ITSELF AND FROM LIVING LIFE" MOVE FROM A STATE OF SEMI-CONSCIOUSNESS TOWARDS —-ILLUMINATION.

IT IS THROUGH THE CRESCENT MOON AND HER WISDOM THAT WE GET TO THE "STAR." WE MUST REMEMBER THAT.

SINCERELY, "MARIANNE OF THE CRESCENT MOON AND THE STAR BY, THE HARB-OR"

---

## 137. CHRIST-MA'S 2023 —-- 12 + 25 + 20 + 23 THE STAR OF BETHLEHEM'S CALL TO THE WORLD

3 + 7 + 2 + 5 === 17 "THE STAR" OF BETHLEHEM AND OF HOPE!!! And 21 "THE WORLD" CARD.

WE ARE IN THE 21st CENTURY AND GOING THRU THE TRANSITION FROM THE AGE OF PISCES TO THE AGE OF AQUARIUS. THE LAST OF THE KALI YUGA AND INTO THE SAT-YA. HAVE YOU NOTICED HOW "THE TRUTH" IS COMING OUT IN SO MANY LEVELS AND HOW THE WIDESPREAD LYING IS COMING TO THE FORE AND PEOPLE ARE FINALLY RECOGNIZING THAT MANY A THING TODAY HAS BEEN BUILT UPON LIES?

JOHN 14:yjnk6 —

"I am the way and the truth and the life. No one comes to the Father except through me.

AS WE HAVE EXPLAINED BEFORE, THE ABOVE VERSE IS SPOKEN "THROUGH" Y-ESH-UA AS A CHANNEL OF THE DIVINE PRESENCE MANIFESTING THROUGH HIS BIPOLAR SELF. THAT DIVINE PRESENCE IS THE "IMMACULATE CONCEPTION" OR THE "MOTHER" OR BINAH MOTHER THROUGH "THE HOLY SHE-KI-INNA." SHE IS WISDOM AND HAS BEEN WITH THE ACTIVE PRINCIPLE OF CREATION SINCE THE BEGINNING. SHE IS "TRUTH" AND THE MOTHER PRINCIPLE NAMED ALSO SOPHIA, SHE-KI-INNA, WHO POSES "LIKE A WHITE DOVE" METAPHORICALLY OVER A HUMAN AT

THE TIME WHEN A HUMAN REACHES LIBERATION FROM SAMSARA OR ILLUMINATION/ ENLIGHTENMENT.

"I AM THE TRUTH" — THE AGE OF SAT-YA!!!! AND THIS IS WHY THERE SEEMS TO BE A BATTLE RAGING BETWEEN "LIES VS. TRUTH." ESPECIALLY IN POLITICS AND RELIGION.

AS WAS EXPLAINED BEFORE, THE FATHER REPRESENTS THE SUN. 25 DECEMBER REPRESENTS THE BIRTH OF THE "NEW SUN." THE SUN IS "LIFE" AND "LIGHT" WHICH SHINES UPON THE DARKNESS, EXPOSING THE REAL, THE TRUTH. BUT TO GET TO THE SUN OR THE FATHER AND ENJOY THAT LIGHT, WE MUST GO THROUGH THE MOTHER'S MOONLIGHT AS IN — FROM THE DARK OR NEW MOON TO THE CRESCENT MOON OR SEMI-CONSCIOUSNESS TOWARDS THE FULL MOON OR "ILLUMINATION." THE "HALO"OF THE SAINTS IS A REPRESENTATION OF THE LIGHT OF THE MOON AND THE SUN AS "ONE."

THEREFORE, AS THE EARTH IS IN TURMOIL, THIS CHRIST-"MA'S" or SEASON OF THE "MA"(THER) OF THE CHRIST PRINCIPLE, BOTH ARE CALLING HUMANKIND TO EMBRACE "THE WAY, THE TRUTH AND THE LIFE" WHICH IS NOT FOLLOWING A CERTAIN RELIGION OR DOGMA BUT IS MORE ABOUT "FACING THE HUMAN EXPERIENCE WITH COURAGE WITH ALL ITS UPS AND DOWNS AND LEARNING AND ACQUIRING COMPASSION, EMPATHY AND WISDOM" THROUGH THIS DIVINE HUMAN JOURNEY.

THE HATE AND WARS AND EXACERBATIONS OF THESE IS EQUIVALENT TO "FEEDING THE DEMONS" WITHIN AND WITHOUT. STOP "IN THE NAME OF LOVE" FEEDING DEMONS WITH WAR AND HATRED AND LYING AND MURDER, ETC. THIS BAD ENERGY ONLY SERVES TO MULTIPLY ITS INFLUENCE AND HOLD OVER THE WORLD. DEMON IS SIMPLY — THE DESTRUCTIVE ENERGY IN THE TRIMURTI, WHICH BELONGS TO THE MOTHER PRINCIPLE. IT RECYCLES AND EATS WHAT IS NO LONGER NEEDED IN THE UNIVERSE AND PROPELS US TO MOVE TOWARDS HIGHER ENERGIES AND SPHERES OF INFLUENCE. IT'S TIME TO EMPATHIZE, RATHER THAN POLARIZE, WITH OTHERS AND MAKE PEACE.

17 IS THE STAR OF BETHLEHEM CARD WHICH REPRESENTS "GLAD TIDINGS AND PEACE TO MEN OF GOOD WILL." ARE YOU EMBRACING PEACE AND SPREADING GOOD WILL AMONGST MEN OR .... ARE YOU VIOLATING THE STAR OF BETHLEHEM PROMISE TO THE WORLD? THE WAY IS — TRUTH!!! IF ONE EMBRACES LIES ONE IS NOT IN THE TRUTH AND SO FAR AWAY FROM THE —WAY—- BACK TO THE FATHER "SUN."

SINCERELY, 12/25 = 25/12 AKA 3/7 = 7/3

## 138. Y-ESH-UA: THE DIVINE FIRE OR SERPENTINE ENERGY NAILED TO THE TREE OF GOOD AND EVIL

Y- I, THE DIVINE POINT OF ENERGY
ESH - FIRE
UA - NAIL, MESSIAH

THE "Y" IS LIKE AN "I" AND IN MANY CULTURES IT IS USED FOR THE DESCRIPTIVE WORD "I" AS IN "I AM."

THE DIVINE POINT OR THE ORIGINAL "I" OF ENERGY WHICH IS THE DIVINE FIRE NAILED TO THE "TREE OF GOOD AND EVIL" WHO IS THE MESSIAH.

In the Jewish mystical tradition, Yod represents a mere dot, a divine point of energy. Since Yod is used to form all the other letters, and since God uses the letters as the building blocks of creation, Yod indicates God's omnipresence. (HEBREWFORCHRISTIANS)

ISA OR ....IS - "A" ....THE FIRST LETTER OF THE LATIN ALPHABET. OR THE "FIRST CAUSE" THAT LED TO THE EFFECTS AS IN THE MATERIAL UNIVERSES. "ISA" AS IN "ISA-IAH" MEANS ....SALVATION!!!!

IT IS A GREAT EVIL AND TRANSGRESSION TO USE "FIRE" FOR EVIL AND DESTRUCTION WHICH WAS GIVEN BY THE WATCHERS FOR THE EVOLUTION OF HUMANKIND AND NOT FOR WAR AND ANNIHILATION. FIRE ...IS "ESH" AS IN DIVINE FIRE OR LIFE FORCE, "QI", ELECTRICITY.

USING "DEADLY FIRE" VIOLATES THE NATIVITAS OR CHRISTMAS IDEAL AND PROMISE OF "PEACE AMONGST MEN OF GOOD WILL." Y-ESH-UA IS THE ARK OF COMMUNICATION OR THE COVENANT IN THE PERSONHOOD OF A HUMAN. REPRESENTING THE ACTIVE "QI" ENERGY IN "ALL LIVING SOULS."

SAY GOOD-BYE TO WAR AND GENOCIDAL IMPULSES AND PUT A REIN TO HUMAN EVIL FIRE (F - IRE) OR ANGER, HATRED AND PASSION TO DESTROY. EMBRACE AND PROTECT THE "ETERNAL FLAME" IN EACH ONE OF THY BRETHREN AND SELVES.

SINCERELY, "NO LONGER THE SCAPEGOAT OF CAPRICORN"

## 139. THE HEXAGRAM: THE COSMIC UNION OF YIN AND YANG AND THE DIVINE ANDRO-GENIE

I'M WATCHING THE "DA VINCI CODE" AND HAD NOT REALIZED BEFORE THAT THE HEXAGRAM OR "STAR OF DAVID" IS MADE UP OF BOTH THE "CHALICE AND THE SWORD."

BASICALLY, THE HEXAGRAM REPRESENTS AS WELL THE "UNION" BETWEEN THE DIVINE MASCULINE AND THE DIVINE FEMININE SIMILAR TO THE HINDU "LINGAM".

WHICH IS A SYMBOL OF FERTILITY. THE LINGAM IS MADE UP BY THE UNION OF THE MALE AND FEMALE.

THIS "UNION" IS POINTING AT THE — UNION OR HARMONIZING OF THE —YIN AND YANG — PRINCIPLES IN HUMANITY AND IN CREATION. IT IS ALL ABOUT "ALCHEMICAL PROCESSES" TAKING PLACE IN A HUMAN BEING AND NATURE.

THE HEXAGRAM IS A REPRESENTATION OF THE "WORLD TREE" IN ALL TRADITIONS. IN WHICH THE BRANCHES TOUCH THE HEAVENS AND THE ROOTS TOUCH THE UNDERWORLDS. SO IS WITH THE "HEXAGRAM" IN WHICH ONE "TRIANGLE" POINTS UP TO HEAVEN OR THE MASCULINE AND THE OTHER TRIANGLE POINTS DOWNWARDS TO THE UNDERWORLDS OR THE FEMININE. THE UPPER TRIANGLE REPRESENTS CHOKMAH AND THE LOWER TRIANGLE REPRESENTS B-INNAH.

THE CENTER OF THE HEXAGRAM OR POINT OF INTERSECTION BETWEEN BOTH "EQUAL TRIANGLES" REPRESENTS "THE HUMAN OR THE VETRUVIAN WO-MAN." THE CENTER OR MIDDLE IS THE POSITION OF "DA-AT." DA-AT IS THE PLACE OF THE "PRIMORDIAL MAN ARCHETYPAL ENERGY" OR THE "FIRST BORN" OF BOTH CHOKMAH AND B-INNA-H WHO IS "ANDRO-GENOUS."

IN CHRISTIAN LORE "HEAVEN" OR DEITY REPRESENTS THE UPPER TRIANGLE AND "MARY" REPRESENTS THE LOWER TRIANGLE. FIRE COMES DOWN TO WATER, AIR COMES DOWN TO MATTER. AND GIVES BIRTH TO "Y-ESH-UA." YESHUA WOULD TAKE THE POSITION OF THE "PRIMORDIAL MAN." IN REALITY, THE MIDDLE REPRESENTS EVERY HUMAN SINCE WE ARE THE CHILDREN OF BOTH THE "YIN AND YANG" PRINCIPLES.

THE HEXAGRAM OR "STAR OF DAVID" IS A SYMBOL THAT BELONGS TO THE "HOLY SHAMAN!!!" THE ONE WHO CAN CONNECT AND LINK TO THE UPPER AND LOWER REALMS IN ALL WORLD TRADITIONS. DRAWING DOWN

WISDOM FROM ABOVE AND BELOW, FROM BOTH THE GOD AND THE GODDESS ARCHETYPAL ENERGIES IN ORDER TO BRING HARMONY AND RESTORE BALANCE TO THE WORLD AND HUMANKIND REPRESENTED BY THE MIDDLE.

UNWISE WAYS AND LACK OF HARMONY AND TEMPERANCE IN HUMAN DEALINGS WITH EACH OTHER AND EVERYONE ELSE VIOLATES THE "HEXAGRAM" AS SACRED SYMBOL.

SINCERELY, "MARIA MAGDALENE THRU THE BIPOLAR GATES"

---

## 140.SOPHIE: THE HOLY GRAIL ----------THE ROSE—- THE "WORD" AND THE "TRUTH" OR KNOWLEDGE WILL SET US ----FREE!!!!!!!!

AND SO CONTINUING WITH THE "DA VINCI CODE," THE HOLY GRAIL IN THE MOVIE IS "SOPHIE" HERSELF!!!!

SOFIA AS IN "FILO-SOFIA" OR THE "LOVE OF WISDOM AND KNOWLEDGE." THE "SOPHIA" OR "WISDOM" HERSELF WHO WAS WITH THE LIGHT SINCE THE BEGINNING OF THE TZIM TZOOOM.

THE "ROSS-LYN" CHAPEL IS THE CHAPEL OF THE "ROSE OR THE MYSTIC ROSE." THE BEAUTIFUL ROSE OR THE "ROSA LINDA."

Long a symbol of love and passion, the ancient Greeks and Romans associated roses with Aphrodite and Venus, goddess of love. Used for hundreds of years to convey messages without words, they also represent confidentiality.(TELEFLORA)

THEREFORE, THE SOPHIA IS LINKED TO THE HOLY SPIRIT AND TO THE HOLY SHE-KI-INNA. ONCE THE "GATES" OPEN, THE "SOPHIA OR KNOWLEDGE" MANIFESTS. BASICALLY, ALL HUMAN KNOWLEDGE IS "SOPHIA" AND A REASON WHY THE "ARA-GO" SYMBOL IN THE MOVIE "DA VINCI CODE" IS SO SIMILAR TO THE "AG-ORA" MOVIE NAME. "HYPATHIA" FROM ANCIENT ALEXANDRIA WHO EMBODIES THE "WISDOM OF THE DIVINE FEMININE" AND THE SACRED "LIBRARY."

THE SAME THEME IS WITH MARY MAGDALENE AS BEING AN ENLIGHTENED FEMALE TEACHER WHO WAS ENTRUSTED WITH "THE KNOWLEDGE" THAT WAS KEPT AWAY FROM THE OTHER MALE DISCIPLES. AS IN "CONFIDENTIALITY" BETWEEN YESHUA AND THE MAGDALENE WHICH IS A QUALITY OF THE ROSE.

ALL THESE FEMALE ARCHETYPES ALONG WITH THE GODDESSES "VENUS AND APHRODITE" ARE FACES OR ENERGIES OF THE DIVINE FEMININE AND "THE ROSE" IS THEIR TRADITIONAL FLOWER.

THIS IS THE REASON MEDIEVAL PAINTERS WERE IN LOVE WITH THE FEMALE IMAGE IN MOST OF THEIR PAINTINGS. THEY WERE PAINTING THE "DIVINE MYSTIC SOPHIA" IN THE FORM OF MARY, MARY MAGDALENE, VENUS, DIANA, APHRODITE, ETC. ETC. ETC. IT WAS THROUGH HER DIVINE ENERGY AND INSPIRATION THAT THEY CREATED MARVELOUS WORKS OF ART AND LITERATURE AND POETRY.

BASICALLY, "HU-MAN CANNOT REACH ILLUMINATION/ ENLIGHTENMENT WITHOUT THE DIVINE FEMININE PRINCIPLE!!!" WE ARE NOT REFERRING HERE TO SEX BUT TO — INNER WORK— !!!!

SOPHIA —THEREFORE IS NECESSARY FOR THE ALCHEMICAL PROCESS AND THE BIRTH OF WISDOM.

THEREFORE, LET US WELCOME THE DIVINE "SOPHIA:"

**JOHN 8: 31** So Jesus said to the Jews who had believed him, "If you abide in SOPHIA, you are truly my disciples, **32** and you will know SOPHIA, and SOPHIA will set you free."

WORD, TRUTH— OR —KNOWLEDGE AND SOPHIA — THE ORIGINAL "LOGOS OR WORD" WILL SET US FREE!!! FREEDOM STARTS WITH WISDOM JUST LIKE "FRENCH LADY LIBERTY aka MARIAMNE."

SINCERELY, "ROSE LINDA"

---

## 141. ASH-ER AND A-SH-ERAH: THE BLESSED AND HAPPY ONE AND WHO TREADS ON THE SEA

ASHER – I AM/ WILL BE —-ASHER. THE NAME ASH-ER IS INTERPRETED AS MEANING "HAPPY AND BLESSED" AND IS CONSIDERED A MASCULINE NAME. INTERESTINGLY IT APPEARS DURING THE B-UR-NING B-USH STORY AND THE DIVINE MANIFESTING AS FIRE. HAVE YOU NOTICED THE NAME "ASH-ER" OR "ASH-URI??" IT HAS IN IT THE ROOT WORD "ASH" WHICH IS A COMPOUND OF FIRE AS IN CARBON. AND ..URI... WHICH IS RELATED TO THE CONCEPT OF FIRE AND LIGHT.

ASH-URI THEREFORE IS A MASCULINE NAME AND IS RELATED TO THE ELEMENT OF FIRE.

EHEYE - ASHER- EHEYE, IS TRANSLATED AS "I AM WHO I WILL BE" OR SOMETHING SIMILAR. BUT IT CAN ALSO BE TRANSLATED AS: I AM ASH-URI I AM, OR — I AM THE FIRE AND ASH I AM (THE DIVINE FIRE OR LIVING FLAME) ; OR, I AM THE HAPPY AND BLESSED ONE I AM!!!!

ON THE OTHER HAND, WE HAVE THE MUCH VILIFIED AND PERSECUTED FEMININE "ASH-ERAH" WHO IS THE FEMININE VERSION OF ASH-URI. ALTHOUGH THE NAME HAS IN IT BOTH THE "ASH AND THE FIRE OR LIGHT," HER NAME IS INTERPRETED AS BEING "SHE WHO TREADS ON THE SEA." IN THE STORY OF THE LIBERATION OF THE ISRAELITES FROM EGYPT, MOSES STAFF IS USED TO OPEN THE SEA OF REEDS. DO YOU SEE THE —--LINKS HERE— AS IN —-ASH-ERAH OF THE SEAS, OPENING THE WATERS?

"ASH-ERAH OF THE SEAS" IS A FACE AND QUALITY OF THE DIVINE FEMININE WHO IN THE TREE OF LIFE IS B-INNA-H THE DARK ONE AND THE ONE WHO IS "FIERCE ABOUT JUSTICE." AND AS YOU WILL RECALL, IN MOST WORLD TRADITIONS THE WATER ELEMENT IS ATTRIBUTED TO THE FEMININE. WE COULD REPLACE HER NAME ASH-ARA WITH YORUBA YEMANYA AND OTHER WATER GODDESSES WHO REPRESENT THE ONE MOTHER OR FEMALE PRINCIPLE.

A-SHERAH HAS AS WELL IN IT THE HEBREW FOR "BRIGHTNESS" WHICH IS A QUALITY OF FIRE AND LIGHT AS IN "ERA, URI, ARI." I AM THE BRIGHT ONE I AM.

SO HERE WE HAVE BOTH THE "MALE AND THE FEMALE." THE MALE MANIFESTS AS IN THE BURNING BUSH BUT THE FEMALE MANIFESTS AS IN THE PARTING OF THE WATERS.

BASICALLY, WE NEED TO HAVE "TWO" TO MAKE THINGS "ALRIGHT." BOTH THE GOD AND THE GODDESS WORKING TOGETHER FOR A COMMON PURPOSE.

THEREFORE, AN INTERPRETATION OF THE EXODUS STORY IS THAT "I AM THE HAPPY BLESSED I AM" BRINGS ABOUT LIBERATION THRU AND WITH THE MOTHER ASHERAH FEMALE PRINCIPLE AND HER WATER ELEMENT IN ORDER FOR THE PEOPLE TO BE "HAPPY AND BLESSED" AT LAST.

THE STORY IS ALSO POINTING TO THE "4 BASIC ELEMENTS." THE MALE FIRE AND AIR BECOME ACTIVE IN THE CASE OF THE "PILLAR OF FIRE" KEPT ALIVE AND BURNING LIKE A FLAME THANKS TO THE ELEMENT OF AIR. MEANWHILE, THE FEMALE WATER AND EARTH ELEMENTS BECOME ACTIVE IN THE PASSAGE THRU THE PARTED WATERS AS TWO WALLS OF WATER AND GROUND- EARTH TO WALK ON.

SINCERELY, "ASH-URI AND HIS ASH-ARAH"

## 142. YE-MAYA: A-SHERA OF THE SEAS IN ALL TRADITIONS AND HER "MAYIM"

FOR THOSE WHO STILL THINK THAT ALL TRADITIONS ARE MUTUALLY EXCLUSIVE. NOPE. ACTUALLY THEY ARE ALL INTERSECTED AND INTERRELATED. SUCH AS IN THE NAME FOR —YE-MAYA!!!

YE- —-MAYA!!!!

YE, YO, IO, Y ==== I

"MAYA" RELATED TO THE ARABIC AND HEBREW WORD FOR WATER "MAYIM"

SHE COULD AS WELL BE CALLED "YE-MAYIM" OR "I THE WATER!!!" DOES THAT MEAN THAT THE ELEMENT WATER IS ALIVE? WHAT DO YOU THINK? WATER ANIMATES LIFE AND ALLOWS LIFE TO GROW AND LIVE. IF IT HAD NO CONSCIOUSNESS AND ACTIVE PRINCIPLES IN IT, IT WOULD NOT DO ANY OF THESE THINGS. BUT IT DOES MAINTAIN LIFE AND MAKES THINGS GROW BECAUSE THE WATER ELEMENT IS HERSELF "ALIVE."

SO "YE-MAYIM" IS A VERSION OF ASH-ERA OF THE WATERS IN THE AFRICAN TRADITION. THE ONE WHO TREADS THE WATERS AND WHO IS WATER HERSELF. AN ARCHETYPE OR PERSONIFICATION OF THE WATER ELEMENT JUST AS THE UNDINES AND MERMAIDS AND APHRODITE.

AND THE NAME YE-MAYIM IS RELATED TO THE NAME MAR-YAM OR MIRYAM WHICH BOTH HAVE THE WORDS FOR MARIS OR OCEANS AND YAM FOR BEACH.

SINCERELY, "I THE WATER AND THE SEA, MAR-YAM"

## 143. ORI-ISHA: THE FIRE AND LIGHT BEINGS OF THE Y-ORU-UBA AFRICAN PANTHEON— THE AFRICAN "E PLURIBUS"

"Isha is a gender-neutral name of Hindu origin, meaning "one who protects". This name comes from a Sanskrit word that means "the ruling Goddess" or "the ruler". (THEBUMP.COM)"

THE AFRICAN WORD "ORI-ISHA" IS MADE UP OF TWO ANCIENT WORDS FOUND IN MANY LANGUAGES AND TRADITIONS OF THE WORLD. ON ONE HAND WE GET THE MESOPOTAMIAN WORD FOR "FIRE, GOLD, QI, LIGHT" OR —URI; AND, ON THE OTHER WE GET THE NAME OR WORD "ISHA" WHICH MEANS IN THE SACRED LANGUAGE OR SAN-SKRIT, "THE RULER,

RULING GODDESS, ONE WHO PROTECTS." THEREFORE, THE "ORI-ISHAS" IS THE TITLE OR NAME FOR A COLLECTIVE OF "DIVINE BEINGS OF FIRE OR LIGHT WHO RULE AND PROTECT."

THERE ARE 7 MAIN ORI-ISHAS BUT MANY IN THE TRADITION CLAIM THERE ARE MANY MORE AND THAT THEY ARE INNUMERABLE. WHAT THEY ARE REFERRING TO IS TO THE "COSMIC FORCES" FOUND IN ALL TRADITIONS BUT CALLED BY DIFFERENT NAMES. SUCH AS IN THE JUDEO-CHRISTIAN-ISLAMIC TRADITION WHERE WE HAVE THE "ELOHIM." AND JUST AS IN THE ANCIENT GREEK AND ROMAN PANTHEONS WHERE THESE ENERGIES ARE REPRESENTED BY THE GODS AND GODDESSES OR POWERS OF OLYMPUS. ETC. ETC. ETC.

ISHA IN HEBREW IS ANOTHER NAME FOR "EVE." HERE WE HAVE THE DIVINE FEMININE LINKED TO THE "ISHA" AND TO THE "RULING GODDESS" BOTH POINTING TO THE ARCHETYPAL FEMALE ENERGIES.

TO CLARIFY THIS A LITTLE BIT MORE....

IN THE KAABA OF MAKKA IN SAUDI ARABIA IN THE DAYS OF MOHAMMAD BEFORE THE BIRTH OF ISLAM, THE ARAB PANTHEON CONTAINED AT LEAST 365 DEITIES OF WHICH —VENUS — WAS THE MAIN GODDESS. MANY OF THESE DEITIES WERE BASED ON THE INFLUENCE OF THE PLANETS AND ASTROLOGY. AS YOU WILL RECALL, THE ANCIENTS STUDIED THE STARS. AFTER MOHAMMAD'S ISLAM, THE "E PLURIBUS" OF DEITIES WAS CONDENSED INTO "ONE DEITY" WHICH TODAY GOES BY THE TITLE "ALLAH." SO THE "E PLURIBUS OF COSMIC ENERGIES" BECAME AN "UNUM" OR "ONE." AND SO THE AFRICAN Y-ORU-UBA PANTHEON WITH ITS MYRIAD ORI-ISHAS FOLLOWS A SIMILAR PATTERN.

AS WE EXPLAINED BEFORE, THE WORD Y-ORU-UBA HAS IN IT THE ROOT WORD FOR "LIGHT AND FIRE" AS IN "ORU" WHICH IS A FORM OF THE ANCIENT TERM "URI" OR LIGHT. AND THE NAME CONTAINS AS WELL THE WORD "UBA" WHICH IS AN AFRICAN NAME FOR DEITY WHICH MEANS "L-OR-D." THE NAME MEANS "FATHER, LORD" AS IN THE HEBREW AND ARABIC AND ARAMAIC WORD FOR "FATHER" WHICH IS "ABA, ABU, ABBA."

JUST AS EVERYTHING IS DUAL AND COMES IN "TWINS" OR "TWO'S" THERE ARE MASCULINE AND FEMININE ORI-ISHAS, AND EACH CLASS OF ENERGIES FOLLOW THE TRIMURTI DIVISION OF POWERS OF THE HINDU TRADITION AS IN THE "DESTRUCTIVE ORI-ISHAS" AND THE "CONSTRUCTIVE OR BENEVOLENT ORI-ISHAS" AND IN THE MIDDLE WE HAVE THOSE WHO ARE "NEITHER AS WELL AS BOTH DESTRUCTIVE/MALEVOLENT AND / OR NEUTRAL"

ALL THE PANTHEONS ARE BASED ON —-- THE NATURAL AND COSMIC WORLDS AND ENERGIES— AND IT IS A WAY FOR THE INDIGENOUS AFRICAN PEOPLES TO GET MEANING OF AND MORE UNDERSTANDING OF THE NATURAL AND COSMIC WORLD AND ORDER WE ARE A PART OF. JUST AS IN THE "NAMES OF GOD" TRADITION OF JUDAISM AND ISLAM, EACH ORI-ISHA REPRESENTS A CHARACTER AND QUALITY ATTRIBUTED TO THE —SOURCE OF ALL—-ONLY THAT IN THE CASE OF THIS MULTI-PANTHEON, "THE WHOLE" IS DIVIDED INTO PARTS WHICH BECOME THE "ORI-ISHAS."

SINCERELY, "K-ARI-V-UNA KID (GARIF-UNA KID)"

---

## 144. EMBRACING "THE ONE AND THE MANY, THE MANY AND THE ONE;" IT'S ALL AN ILLUSION — UNION AND FRAGMENTATION, FRAGMENTATION AND UNION: IT'S ALL THE SAME

ALL WORLD CULTURE IS RICH AND BEAUTIFUL. NO CULTURE OR TRADITION IS BETTER THAN ANOTHER. AND THAT IS THE POINT OF IT ALL!!! AND ONE OF THE MAIN ISSUES WITH THE SO- CALLED MONO-THEISTIC TRADITIONS WHICH IRONICALLY BEGAN WITH "PANTHEONS," IS THAT LATER THEY CONDENSED THESE INTO "ONE UNION." WHICH MAKES SENSE SINCE EVERYTHING IS "ONE" ENERGY MANIFESTING IN DIVERSE FORMS AND WAYS.

THE OTHER CULTURES VIEW THE ONE INTO MANY DIVERSE PARTS WHICH IS THE ORIGIN OF THE DEITIES. WHICH ARE THE LESSER DEITIES OR — ENERGIES— THAT BRANCH OUT OR EMANATE AND ARE FACETS OF "THE ALL." DO YOU SEE WHAT WE SEE?

BASICALLY, THE MONO-THEISTIC TREAT "THE MANY AS ONE UNION" MEANWHILE THE POLI-THEISTIC VIEW "THE ONE AS MANY."

THE IRONY IS THAT EVERYONE IS LOOKING AT THE SAME "THE ALL" OR "SOURCE" AS IT IS. ONLY THAT SOME ARE LOOKING AT "THE ALL" AS ONE MONOLITH WHILE THE OTHERS ARE LOOKING AT THE ALL AS MANY PARTS.

THE E PLURIB-US UNUM —WORKS BOTH WAYS AS IN, "THE ONE IS MANY, AND THE MANY IS ...ONE."

THIS HAS BEEN A VERY PROBLEMATIC SOURCE OF MISUNDERSTANDING AND ALSO -PERSECUTION AND DESTRUCTION AND MURDER IN HUMAN HISTORY WITH THE MONO-THEISTS CLAIMING FOR THE MOST PART THAT THEIR INTERPRETATION AND VIEW OF DEITY IS THE ONLY RIGHT WAY OF VIEWING REALITY. BUT REALITY IS MUCH MORE COMPLICATED THAN THAT. AND BEHIND THE UNION AND ONE IS THE MULTIPLICITY AND

VICE VERSA. JUST AS HUMAN LOOKS LIKE "ONE UNITED BEING," WHEN YOU SEE BEHIND AND BEYOND A HUMAN YOU WILL FIND THAT A HUMAN IS A COMPOSITE OF DIVERSE PARTS AND ENERGIES AND ELEMENTS THAT COME TOGETHER TO FORM "YOU." HERE WE HAVE THE UNION OF ELEMENTS AND PARTS THAT COME TOGETHER TO FORM "YOU." THE ONE OUT OF MANY. THE MANY AS....ONE.

THE DISPARAGEMENT OF OTHER WORLD TRADITIONS IS BASED ON "FEAR" OF THE UNKNOWN. FEAR OF WHAT IS DIFFERENT. BUT IN REALITY, EVERYTHING IS SUSTAINED AND ANIMATED BY THE "SAME ENERGIES AND POWERS" THAT IN TURN ARE EMANATIONS OF THE "ONE SOURCE MADE UP OF TWO EQUAL PARTS IN UNION WITH EACH OTHER."

SINCERELY, "THE UNNO WHO IS M-ANNIE"

---

## 145. THE POLI-THEISM WITHIN THE MONO-THEISM: THE FEMALE ELOAH BECOMING THE MANY MASCULINE ELOHIM (THE DANCE OF YIN AND YANG)

IF DEITY WAS ONLY "ONE MONOLITH," HOW COME IT MANIFESTS AS "MANY THINGS, BEINGS, ELEMENTS, PLANETS, STARS, ANIMALS, PLANTS, PEOPLES, ETC. ETC. ETC. IF "THE ALL" WAS JUST "ONE THING" IT WOULD BE UNABLE TO MULTIPLY INTO SO MANY FACES AND FORMS AND WAYS AS DESCRIBED ABOVE.

STARTING WITH THE "NAME" GIVEN TO THE MONOTHEISTIC DEITY AS IN "YHVH." ITS NAME IS FORMED OF MULTIPLE LETTERS WHICH REPRESENT THE ELEMENTS. THE NAME IS "ONE NAME" BUT FORMED OF "MANY LETTERS EACH REPRESENTING AN ELEMENT AND THE DIVINE MASCULINE AND THE DIVINE FEMININE." HERE WE CAN SEE THAT —THE MONO-THEISTIC DEITY —IS NOT "ONE" BUT RATHER A "UNION THAT BECOMES ONE." WHICH CORRESPONDS AS WELL TO THE FIRST NAME FOR DEITY OR COSMIC ENERGIES IN THE TANAKH WHICH IS "ELOHIM."

ELOHIM DERIVES FROM THE FEMALE "ELOAH" AND ITS PLURAL FORM IS MASCULINE "ELOHIM." YOU MIGHT BE TELLING YOURSELF THAT THIS IS WEIRD BECAUSE THE PLURAL IS MASCULINE WHILE THE SINGULAR IS FEMININE. THE KEY IS IN THE TAOIST "YIN - YANG" SYMBOL. AS YOU KNOW ALREADY THE "DIVINE TWINS YIN AND YANG BELONG TO EACH OTHER." IN OTHER WORDS, THE MASCULINE BECOMES FEMININE AFTER A CERTAIN POINT AND THE FEMININE BECOMES MASCULINE AFTER A CERTAIN POINT. THE MASCULINE IS IN THE FEMININE AND THE FEMININE IS IN THE MASCULINE.

THEREFORE, THE "FEMALE" YIN MULTIPLIES AND BECOMES MANY "MASCULINE ENERGIES." THE ELOHIM ARE THE CLOSEST TO THIS REALM THEREFORE ARE "ANDROGYNOUS" BOTH YIN AND YANG. THEREFORE WE CAN INFER THAT ELOHIM CAN MANIFEST AS MALE AND FEMALE. "LET US CREATE MAN AFTER OUR IMAGE AND LIKENESS" —-WHICH "IMAGE AND LIKENESS???" —- THE YIN AND THE YANG AND THE IN - BETWEEN. 3 VALUES AND PRINCIPLES AS - ONE UNION. LET'S MAKE THEM —MALE AND FEMALE MEN!!! DO YOU SEE THE POINT HERE?

THE SAME HAPPENS WITH THE TITLE "ALLAH" WHICH IS MADE UP OF SEVERAL LETTERS THAT COME TOGETHER TO BECOME "ONE."

THEREFORE, THE ORIGINS OF THE MONO-THEISTIC TRADITIONS IS JUST LIKE THE ORIGINS OF THE "POLI-THEISTIC" TRADITIONS.

TO CONCLUDE THIS DIARY, BOTH JUDAISM AND ISLAM HAVE THE "72 AND 99 NAMES OF DEITY" RESPECTIVELY. THE FACT THAT THE "ONE NAME" CAN BE DIVIDED AND MULTIPLIED TO 72 AND 99 NAMES CONFIRMS THE "MANY OUT OF ONE AND ONE OUT OF MANY." THESE NAMES ARE FURTHER DIVIDED INTO MALE AND FEMALE QUALITIES. THEREFORE, WE SEE HERE THE MULTIPLICITY MANIFESTING AS BOTH YIN THE FEMALE AND YANG THE MALE.

SINCERELY, "THE DIVINE ANDROGYNE"

---

## 146. THE WISE SERPENT AND THE DIVINE FEMININE VS. THE AUTHORITARIAN FATHER AND THE PATRIARCHY (ACCORDING TO THE STORY OF GENESIS)

AIN'T IT FUNNY! HOW MANY INTERPRETATIONS AND STORIES THERE ARE ABOUT THE GENESIS ACCOUNT WHICH IS SYMBOLIC AND METAPHYSICAL AND METAPHORICAL. AIN'T IT FUNNY ....THAT PEOPLE ACTUALLY BELIEVE THAT IT IS REFERRING TO A REAL SERPENT LIKE THE ONES WE HAVE HERE ON EARTH AND THAT IT SPEAKS AND SO AND SO AND SO.

THE SERPENT AS ANIMAL IS PART OF THE ECOSYSTEM JUST AS EVERY OTHER CREATURE AND SERVES A VITAL ROLE IN THE NATURAL BALANCE AND HARMONY OF EVERY ECOSYSTEM.

WE DO HAVE TO GIVE CREDIT TO THOSE INTERPRETING GENESIS FOR THEIR GREAT IMAGINATION AND CREATIVITY.

HAS ANYONE SEEN A SERPENT THAT TALKS? OH PLEASE...... THERE IS A SERPENT THAT TALKS THOUGH BUT IT IS NOT WHOM PEOPLE THINK AND IT IS NOT WHOM IS CALLED SATAN BY THE MONOTHEIST.

DO YOU REMEMBER GILLIAN IN THE MOVIE "PRACTICAL MAGIC" WHO WEARS A SERPENT TATTOO? JUST LIKE MOSES, AND THE SERPENT COILED AROUND HIS STAFF? IS IT THAT BOTH OF THEM ARE "SERPENTINES?" ----AND THE SERPENT WAS "WISER" THAN THE REST OF THE ANIMALS OF THE GARDEN. AND THE "WISE" SERPENT IS COILED AROUND THE "TRUNK" OF THE TREE OF "GOOD AND EVIL."

SO IT SEEMS THAT THOSE WHO ARE "SERPENTINE - LIKE" ARE "WISE AND KNOW THE DIFFERENCE BETWEEN GOOD AND EVIL." ON TOP OF THAT, THE SERPENT STATED THAT — IN THE DAY YOU EAT OF THE TREE YOU WILL "KNOW" THE DIFFERENCE BETWEEN GOOD AND EVIL JUST LIKE ELOHIM. WAS THE SERPENT LYING? NOPE. BECAUSE "CONSCIOUS HUMANS" CAN TELL THE DIFFERENCE BETWEEN GOOD AND EVIL OR DUALITY.

SO HERE WE HAVE "WISDOM, KNOWLEDGE, REASON" WHICH ARE VILIFIED. ISN'T THAT WHAT RELIGIOUS FUNDAMENTALISTS AND FASCISTS DO AS IN PERSECUTE AND DESTROY WISDOM AND KNOWLEDGE AND THE EXERCISE OF CHOICE. FOR THE "PATRIARCHY" IT IS ALL ABOUT BLIND OBEDIENCE AND FOLLOWING RULES WITHOUT THINKING AND REASONING WHY I HAVE TO FOLLOW THOSE RULES. ON THE OTHER HAND, WISDOM AND KNOWLEDGE ARE ATTRIBUTED TO "SOPHIA THE SERPENTINE ENERGY" AND THE DIVINE FEMININE WHICH AT THE CORE HAVE TO DO WITH ACQUIRING KNOWLEDGE AND WISDOM THROUGH LIVED EXPERIENCE.

SO WE CAN SEE CLEARLY HERE THAT SINCE THE BEGINNING OF GENESIS THE STORY HAS BEEN POINTING OUT TO THE ENMITY AND CLASH BETWEEN THE "PATRIARCHY IN EXTREMIS WHICH BECOMES FASCIST" AND ON THE OTHER HAND WE HAVE THE "MATRIARCHY WHICH IS MORE OPEN AND ALLOWS FOR KNOWLEDGE AND WISDOM AND REASON." REASON FOR THE WORSHIP OF "REASON AS MARIAMNE" AFTER THE FRENCH REVOLUTION.

THE MASCULINE IS THE EAGLE AND THE FEMININE IS THE SERPENT AS IN THE SYMBOL OF ENNOK IN TEXCOCO T-ENNOCK-TI-TEL-ANNU. BASICALLY, THE IDEAL OF THE SHAMAN IS TO RECONCILE AND BLEND BOTH ASPECTS — THE SERPENT AND THE DOVE — IN HARMONY AND BALANCE.

SINCERELY, THE "SERPENT-EAGLE OF TEX-COCO"

## 147. THE CLAIM THAT Y-ESH-UA "WAS NOT MOSHIAH" BECAUSE HE WAS "CURSED" IS INCOMPATIBLE WITH THE DESCRIPTION OF THE MOSHIAH IN "ISAIAH 53!!!!!!!!!!!!"

*"For he shall grow up before him as a tender plant, and as a root out of a dry ground: he hath no form nor comeliness; and when we shall see him, there is no beauty that we should desire him. 3 He is despised and rejected of men; a man of sorrows, and acquainted with grief: and we hid as it were our faces from him; he was despised, and we esteemed him not. 4 Surely he hath borne our griefs, and carried our sorrows: yet we did esteem him stricken, smitten of God, and afflicted.5 But he was wounded for our transgressions, he was bruised for our iniquities: the chastisement of our peace was upon him; and with his stripes we are healed.6 All we like sheep have gone astray; we have turned every one to his own way; and the LORD hath laid on him the iniquity of us all.7 He was oppressed, and he was afflicted, yet he opened not his mouth: he is brought as a lamb to the slaughter, and as a sheep before her shearers is dumb, so he openeth not his mouth.8 He was taken from prison and from judgment: and who shall declare his generation? for he was cut off out of the land of the living: for the transgression of my people was he stricken.9 And he made his grave with the wicked, and with the rich in his death; because he had done no violence, neither was any deceit in his mouth. (BIBLE, GOOGLE)"*

ISAIAH 53...... IS ABOUT A CURSED MOSHIACH OR A CURSE PLACED UPON MOSHIACH ON BEHALF OF THE PEOPLE AS A COLLECTIVE. IT IS THE ARCHETYPAL "GOAT OR SHEEP OR RAM OF AZAZEL" WHO CARRIES RED RIBBONS ATTACHED TO IT WHICH REPRESENT THE "BLOODY TRANSGRESSIONS OF THE PEOPLE." IT IS A CURSE THAT BELONGS TO THE PEOPLE THEMSELVES FOR THEY HAVE PERPETRATED GREAT EVILS AND PASSED ONTO THE "SCAPEGOAT" TO CARRY FOR THEM.

SO THE RABBI IS ABSOLUTELY "RIGHT" IN THAT Y-ESH-UA WAS CURSED BUT NOT BECAUSE OF HIS OWN DOING BUT BECAUSE OF THE TRANSGRESSIONS OF THE PEOPLE. Y-ESH-UA WAS A "HEALER AND A SHAMAN WITHIN THE JEWISH TRADITION." AND AS WE HAVE EXPLAINED BEFORE, A SHAMAN IS "TOUCHED BY THE POWERS OF HEAVEN AND HELL" WHICH IS THE "CALL OF SPIRIT" AND BY WHICH S-HE CAN CARRY OUT THE HEALING OF PEOPLE AND DIVINE WILL.

ON WHAT THE RABBI IS NOT CORRECT IS IN THE BELIEF THAT Y-ESH-UA COULD NOT BE THE MESSIAH BECAUSE HE WAS CURSED. ACTUALLY, "--- HE WAS THE RIGHT MOSHIACH EXACTLY BECAUSE OF THE CURSE THAT FELL UPON HIM ON BEHALF OF THE PEOPLE." AND IT IS CONFIRMED AND RE-AFFIRMED THAT HE WOULD SUFFER MUCH AND CARRY A HEAVY LOAD

IN ISAIAH 53. THAT HEAVY LOAD ALSO SERVED THE PURPOSE OF MAKING Y-ESH-UA A VERY COMPASSIONATE, EMPATHIC AND JUST PERSON. WHEN YOU FEEL THE PAIN OF THE WORLD, YOU WILL UNDERSTAND THE PAIN OF THE WORLD IN YOURSELF AND IN YOUR COMMUNITY.

ANYWAYS, I AM NOT A RELIGIOUS FANATIC BUT AS YOU WILL RECALL I HAD THE EXPERIENCE YEARS AGO BACK IN 2010 OF "THE TONGUES OF FIRE" THAT APPEARED AT THE MENTIONING OF THE NAME "JESUS" IN CASTILIAN. THEREFORE, THERE "IS SOMETHING" WITH THAT NAME THAT IS NOT OF THIS WORLD — AND THAT CONFIRMED TO ME THAT THERE MUST BE SOME TRUTH TO THE GOSPEL STORY. OTHERWISE, THE "VOICES" WOULD NOT HAVE APPEARED AT THE MENTIONING OF THE NAME.

SINCERELY, "RABB-ONNI, Y-ESH-IVA OF THE WORLD TRADITIONS"

---

## 148. THE NAME "IS-RA-EL:" THE "ONE WHO PREVAILS WITH GOD" AND WHO IS "INNOCENT AS A LAMB" AND IN "UNION" WITH HIM OR HERSELF

IS -" RAEL" — IS "INNOCENT" AS A LAMB!

YAKOV IS NOT ONLY THE ONE WHO PREVAILS WITH GOD BUT ALSO THE ONE WHO IS INNOCENT AS A LAMB. THE FACT THAT THE NAME "IS—RAEL" HAS THE ANCIENT ROOT WORD FOR "IS, ES, S" AND THE NAME "RAEL" TRANSLATES AS "FEMALE LAMB AND PURITY" SUCH AS IN "YAKOBUS IS THE ONE WHO IS INNOCENT AS A LAMB" AND THIS MEANING SHEDS LIGHT ON THE PERSONALITY OF YAKOV.

THE WAY THE STORY IS INTERPRETED AS ESAU EXCHANGING HIS BIRTHRIGHT FOR A BOWL OF LENTILS IS THE LITERAL AND SUPERFICIAL INTERPRETATION. IF ONE THINKS ABOUT IT VERY CAREFULLY, THE WHOLE THING IS ALMOST CHILDISH AND RIDICULOUS. "OH, BECAUSE ESAU PREFERED THE BOWL OF LENTILS THAN THE BLESSING!" OH PLEASE.... IS A BOWL OF LENTILS WORTH CAUSING SUCH FAMILY DYSFUNCTION AS EXPLAINED IN THE STORY? I DOUBT SO.

THERE MUST HAVE BEEN SOMETHING DEEPER AND MORE SERIOUS ABOUT ESAU THAT LED TO HIM LOSING THE BLESSING. AND THAT "SOMETHING" IS IN THE NAME OF "IS-RA-EL" ITSELF. AS IN — IS, "THE RAEL" OR THE INNOCENT AS A LAMB ONE. IF YAKOV WAS THE "INNOCENT AS A LAMB ONE" THAT MUST HAVE MEANT THAT —ESAU PERHAPS WAS NOT THAT INNOCENT AFTER ALL COMPARED TO YAKOV AND MUST HAVE DONE SOME VERY BAD BAAAAD THINGS THAT LED TO HIS DEMISE.

THE NAME ISRAEL"IS A "TITLE OF SUCCESSFUL PASSAGE AND INITIATION PROCESS "JUST AS OTHER TITLES SUCH AS "BUDDHA" AND "CHRIST." SIMILAR TO MANY SPIRITUAL TRADITION'S TITLES PLACED ON INITIATES ALL OVER THE GLOBE AFTER SUCCESSFUL VISION QUESTS AND 40 DAY SPIRITUAL CHALLENGES AND TESTS. IN EACH AND EVERY INITIATION THE INDIVIDUAL HAS TO FACE HIS HER INNERMOST FEARS AND DEMONS AND DYSFUNCTIONS AND OVERCOME THESE SUCCESSFULLY OR BECOME AWARE OF THEM GRANTING HIM HER AT THE CONCLUSION OF THE TRIAL PERIOD THE TITLE OR NEW NAME WHICH REPRESENTS A "SPIRITUAL REBIRTH." THAT IS WHAT THE TITLE "ISRAEL" IS ABOUT TOO. ITS CLEAR TO UNDERSTAND THAT THIS PROCESS DOES NOT MEAN NECESSARILY THAT ALL TESTS ARE PASSED SUCCESSFULLY ON THE FIRST TRY. LIKE THE SAYING SAYS "PRACTICE AND FAILURE LEADS TO …WISER, EVENTUALLY."

BUT THERE IS ANOTHER INTERESTING WORDPLAY WITH THE TITLE "IS-RA-EL." WE ALL KNOW HOW THE STORY OF ISRAEL IS LINKED TO THAT OF EGYPT IN THE EXODUS. AND "ISRAEL" AS A PEOPLE REPRESENTED A COLLECTIVE OR UNION OF PEOPLES WHO SHARED THE SAME VISION AND INTERPRETATION OF REALITY AND THE COSMOS. THEREFORE THE NAME POINTS AT THE CONCEPT OF "UNION." AND IN THE EGYPTIAN PANTHEON THAT COSMIC UNION WAS DEPICTED AS A "TRIAD OF VALUES AND PRINCIPLES DEPICTED AS THE GODDESS ISIS THE BLACK ONE, THE GOD RA THE WHITE ONE AND THE CHILD HORUS OR THE —MIXED ONE." THE CHILD HORUS WHO OCCUPIES THE MIDDLE PILLAR BETWEEN ISIS OR BINAH AND CHOCHMA OR RA REPRESENTS THE "DEITY OR GOD-DESS" OF THIS BIPOLAR WORLD OR REALITY WHOM THE ANCIENTS CALLED "EL." .

SO WHEN YOU ADD "IS + RA + EL" YOU HAVE "ISRAEL" AS THE NAME OF A COMPOSITE DEITY MADE UP OF AN UNION OF 3 PRINCIPLES SUCH AS IN THE YIN AND THE YANG AND THE "YINYANG." YAKOV THROUGH HIS ORDEAL AND BY FACING HIS OWN DEVILISH SHADOW SIDE REACHES CATHARSIS AND UNION WITHIN.

SINCERELY, "ELI-YAHU IS-RA-EL, 2026"

---

### 149. G-ANNE-ESH: THE ARCHETYPAL ENERGY THAT IMPELS NEW BEGINNINGS AND REMOVES OBSTACLES SO THAT A NEW AGE IS BORN

"Although Ganesha has many attributes, he is readily identified by his elephant head and four arms.[8] He is widely revered, more specifically, as the remover of obstacles and thought to bring good luck;[9][10] the patron of arts and sciences; and the deva of intellect and wisdom.[11] As the god of beginnings, he is honored at the start of rites and ceremonies. Ganesha is also invoked as a patron of letters and learning during writing sessions.[2][12] Several texts relate anecdotes associated with his birth and exploits." (WIKIPEDIA)

"G-ANNU-ESH" IS AN ARCHETYPAL ENERGY IN MASCULINE FORM IN THE HINDU TRADITION. HE IS THE REMOVER OF OBSTACLES AND BRINGER OF GOOD FORTUNE. WHEN "OBSTACLES" ARE REMOVED, ARTS AND SCIENCES AND THE NURTURING OF THE INTELLECT AND WISDOM CAN HAPPEN.

THIS ENERGY IS DEPICTED AS AN ELEPHANT WHICH REPRESENTS "STABILITY." DON'T WE GET STABLE SOCIETIES AND COMMUNITIES AND GOVERNANCE WHEN "OBSTACLES" ARE REMOVED SUCH AS EXTREMIST IDEOLOGIES AND FASCISMS AND CORRUPTIONS, ETC. ETC. ETC???/ THE ELEPHANT AND THEREFORE G-ANNU-ESH ENERGY IS LINKED TO THE MULADHARA CHAKRA WHICH CORRESPONDS TO THE ROOT CHAKRA WHICH REPRESENTS EARTH. GANNESHA STANDS FOR THE "ESH" OR "QI" OR SPIRIT THAT IS THE BASES FOR THE WHOLE LIVING MATERIAL CREATION AS IN SPIRIT ENERGY BECOMING MATTER AND MANIFESTING AS SUCH. .

THE ENERGY OF G-ANNU-ESH IS AT THE ROOT OF "THE TREE" OR HUMAN BODY. IT HAS MUCH TO DO WITH THE CLEANSING POWER OF THE CHAKRA SYSTEM AND OBSTACLES FOUND IN THEM SUCH AS THE NEGATIVE MANIFESTATION OF ENERGIES THAT ARE IN A STATE OF IMBALANCE AND DISHARMONY.

G-ANNU-ESH IS THE PATRON OF LETTERS AND LEARNING, THEREFORE HE IS ASSOCIATED TO THE "LIBRARY" CONCEPT IN THE VEDIC TRADITION. GAINING WISDOM AND LEARNING FROM OUR PAST MISTAKES BY LOOKING BACK AT WHAT DOES NOT SERVE US FOR OUR OWN EVOLUTION AND THAT WHICH WE HAVE LEFT BEHIND. THEREFORE, HELPING US MAKE WISER DECISIONS AND PROVIDING US WITH THE ABILITY TO USE OUR INTELLECTUAL FACULTIES FOR THE GOOD OF ALL.

G-ANNU-ESH IS ALSO THE GOD OF BEGINNINGS. THEREFORE, G-ANNU-ESH IS LINKED TO THE GODS AND GODDESSES OF BEGINNINGS IN THE WESTERN TRADITIONS SUCH AS THOSE OF THE THE ROMAN PANTHEON SUCH AS J-ANNU-S. MEANING THAT PEOPLE ARE DESCRIBING THE SAME ARCHETYPAL ENERGY BEHIND GANESHA AS AN ELEPHANT WHILE OTHERS IN THE GRECO ROMAN PANTHEON DESCRIBE IT AS JANUS OR OTHER SIMILAR DEITIES. AS ALL THESE DEITIERS ARE POINTING TO """ THE SAME ENERGY""" BEING DEPICTED DIFFERENTLY BY EACH TRIBE ACCORDING TO THEIR OWN CULTURE AND STORIES AND UNDERSTANDING. THE G-ANNU-ESH IS "THE HOLY QI OR FIRE OF THE ANNU" THAT SUSTAINS ALL

LIFE AND THAT IS THE FOUNDATION OF ALL LIVING THINGS. EVEN THE ROMAN GOD OF BEGINNINGS OR J-ANNU-S SHARES WITH G-ANNU-ESH SIMILAR ROOT WORDS AND LETTERS. J-ANNU, G-ANNU —-S, ESH. .

SINCERELY, "G-ESH-UA FROM THE HOUSE OF ANNU"

---

## 150. THE SERPENT OF THE "TREE OF THE KNOWLEDGE OF GOOD AND EVIL"—-- THE KEY TO HUMANITY'S ASCENSION PROCESS PART I

SO WHO IS THE SO INFAMOUS SERPENT OF THE TREE OF GOOD AND EVIL? OR, WHAT? FOR THE MAJORITY OF PEOPLE, THIS HAS BEEN A MYSTERY FOR A VERY LONG TIME EXCEPT FOR A FEW SOULS IN "ALL TRADITIONS" WHO HAVE KEPT IT A SECRET AND HAVE KNOWN THE —-SCIENTIFIC TRUTHS — ALL ALONG. AT LAST THIS IMPORTANT KNOWLEDGE IN REGARDS TO HUMANITY'S DIVINE INHERITANCE IS COMING TO THE FORE. AT THE RIGHT TIME AND WHEN HUMANKIND IS TRAVERSING A PRECESSION OF THE AGES OF PISCIS TO AQUARIUS.

THE STORY OF EDEN IS NOT —IS NOT — A LITERAL STORY BUT JUST AN INTERPRETATION ABOUT LIFE IN GENERAL AND HOW IT CAME TO BE. IT IS NO DIFFERENT THAN OTHER CREATION STORIES AROUND THE GLOBE. IT IS METAPHYSICAL AND SYMBOLIC. AND ITS IMPORTANCE, RELEVANCE AND TEACHING LIES IN ITS SYMBOLISM.

IN ORDER TO UNDERSTAND "THE TREE OF GOOD AND EVIL" YOU HAVE TO GO BACK TO THE MYSTICAL ASPECT OF THE STORY AND TO THE QABALISTIC "TREE OF LIFE."

AS WE HAVE EXPLAINED BEFORE, THE "TREE OF GOOD AND EVIL" IS THE "TREE OF LIFE!!!" THEY ARE BOTH THE SAME. TO UNDERSTAND THIS BETTER, LOOK AT THE DIAGRAM OF THE QABALISTIC "TREE OF LIFE" AND YOU WILL NOTICE THAT "THE ENERGIES DESCEND FROM TOP TO BOTTOM OR FROM THE UPPER REALMS ALL THE WAY DOWN TO —MALKUT OR EARTH. WHEN THE ENERGIES DESCEND, IT IS EQUIVALENT TO "THE FALL OF MAN" OR ADAM KADMON. MEANING THAT THE "DIVINE FIRE" FALLS INTO THE REALM OF MATTER AND BECOMES —HUMAN!!!

SO WHAT IS THE OPPOSITE OF "FALLING DOWN INTO HUMAN FORM???" THE REVERSE OR INVERSE IS "TO GO BACK UP!!!!"

WHEN THE ENERGIES DESCEND TO MALKUTH, THE TREE BECOMES THE "TREE OF GOOD AND EVIL OR POLARITIES AND DUALITIES." MEANING THAT THE "DIVINE SPIRIT/ SOUL" IS DESCENDING FROM UP THERE TO DOWN HERE BUT TO DO SO IT MUST BECOME "FLESH." BECAUSE WITHOUT

FLESH, MAN WOULD NOT BE ABLE TO REMAIN ON EARTH AND BE UNDER THE LAWS OF GRAVITY. THE WORLD OF DUALITY AND POLARITY AS WE HAVE EXPLAINED BEFORE IS THE WORLD OF MATTER.

AND SO THE REVERSE IS TO GO —UP— AS IN LOOKING AT THE "TREE OF GOOD AND EVIL" FROM MALKUT GOING UPWARDS IN THE OPPOSITE DIRECTION. WHEN THIS HAPPENS, THE DUALITIES AND POLARITIES — UNIFY AND RECONCILE WITH EACH OTHER— AND SO THE TREE BECOMES THE "TREE OF UNION, INTEGRATION AND.....LIFE." MEANING THAT, THE "HUMAN" IS RETURNING BACK TO ITS "ORIGINAL DIVINE SPIRITUAL STATE" AND IS NO LONGER IN THE REALM OF MATTER, DUALITY AND POLARITY. THIS IS EQUIVALENT TO RETURNING HOME OR TO THE INITIAL STATE OF GRACE AND PEACE BEFORE THE FALL AND ITS FRAGMENTATION PROCESSES TOOK PLACE.

MALKUTH REPRESENTS THE "ROOT MULADHARA CHAKRA" IN THE HINDU TRADITION. THE "YESOD" SEPHIRA REPRESENTS THE SACRAL CHAKRA. AND TIFERET REPRESENTS THE SOLAR PLEXUS CHAKRA.

SO AS YOU CAN SEE, THE "TREE OF GOOD AND EVIL" IS A TEMPLATE OF A "HUMAN" AS HUMANITY IS INDEED IN A FALLEN STATE BUT NOT DUE TO ANY ORIGINAL SIN OR TRANSGRESSION BUT BECAUSE — IT IS THE NATURE OF THE REALM OF MATTER TO BE IMPERFECTLY PERFECT AND BE UNDER THE RULES OF CHANGE, TRANSFORMATION, TRANSMUTATION ETC. WHICH ARE FORMS OF DEATH AND DYING. THAT'S THE WAY IT IS — AND NOT BECAUSE SOME LITERAL TALKING SERPENT ATE FROM AN APPLE AND EVERYTHING GOT SCREWED UP AS A RESULT.

EACH SOUL INHABITING EARTH COMES FROM "DIVINE ORIGIN" AND INCARNATES HERE AND —COMES WITH THE FULL KNOWLEDGE — OF THE KIND OF REALM HE OR SHE WILL BE FALLING INTO. BUT FORGETS AT THE TIME OF INCARNATION. AND SO THE AIM IS FOR HUMANITY TO RE-MEMBER AND RECONSTITUTE HIM /HERSELF ONCE AGAIN IN ORDER TO RETURN TO THE "POINT OF ORIGIN" WHICH IS "CONSCIOUS ENERGY OR CONSCIOUS LIGHT OR THE HIGHER SELF."

SINCERELY, "THE SERPENTINE INSTRUCTOR OF MANKIND aka ENNOKI"

---

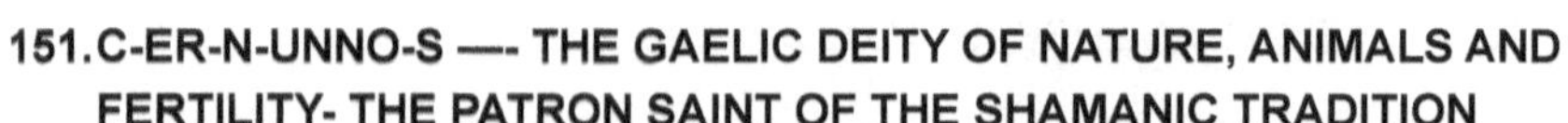

## 151. C-ER-N-UNNO-S —- THE GAELIC DEITY OF NATURE, ANIMALS AND FERTILITY- THE PATRON SAINT OF THE SHAMANIC TRADITION

............ AS WELL AS A DEITY OR SYMBOL AND REPRESENTATION OF LIFE, DEATH AND REBIRTH!

C-ER-N-UNNO-S IS THE ARCHETYPAL ENERGY OR ENERGIES DEPICTED BY THE GAELIC PEOPLE AS A GOD WITH ANTLERS HOLDING A "SERPENT" ON ONE HAND AND A "TORC" ON THE OTHER. IN SOME CASES, RATHER THAN A TORC IS A CORNUCOPIA.

THE C-ER-N-UNNO-S ARCHETYPE IS THE SYMBOL OR DEPICTION OF THE ANCIENT AND HOLY "SHAMAN." HOLY NOT IN THE USUAL RELIGIOUS SENSE BUT IN THE SENSE OF BEING AN INTEGRATED AND UNIFIED PERSON WITHIN. WHO AT THE POINT OF UNDERGOING HIS OR HER SHAMANIC INITIATION AND EVENTUAL TRANSFORMATION, IS GIVEN HIS-HER NEW NAME WHICH REPRESENTS HER/HIS REBIRTH. HAVING UNDERGONE A LIFE-LONG BREAKDOWN OF THE OLD PERSONALITY IN ORDER THAT THE REAL ONE OR DIVINE ESSENCE COMES OUT AT LAST. THE HIGHER SELF.

THE SHAMAN OR C-ER-N-UNNO-S THE PATRON OF SHAMANS HOLDS A SERPENT BECAUSE HE OR SHE HAS BEEN ABLE TO CONTROL AND CHANNEL THE SERPENTINE ENERGY IN HARMONY AND BALANCE TO HEAL AND TEACH AND RESTORE HUMANITY AND PLANET BACK TO A STATE OF RELATIVE BALANCE AND HARMONY THAT AFFIRMS THE SANCTITY OF LIFE ITSELF. THE TORC REPRESENTS THE DUAL NATURE OF THIS REALITY AND BOTH POLARITIES IN THE ENERGY SPECTRUM WHOM THE SHAMAN IS ABLE TO BRING INTO HARMONY AND RECONCILIATION WITH EACH OTHER SUCH AS THE YIN AND YANG PRINCIPLES.

C-ER-N-UNNO-S ANTLER'S POINT TO THE NATURE OF HIS OR HER BEING AS BEING BIPOLAR. S-HE IS IN HARMONY WITH THE DUAL COSMIC AND NATURAL FORCES AND WORLDS. AFTER ALL, THE NATURAL LAWS AND WORLD IS A MIRROR OF THE COSMIC FORCES WHICH SUSTAIN THAT NATURAL WORLD TO WHICH THE SHAMAN IS CONNECTED AND IS AN INTEGRAL PART OF.

HIS SEATING ARRANGEMENT CROSS-LEGGED POINTS TO THE SEATING IN MEDITATIVE AND TRANSCENDENT STATES OF CONSCIOUSNESS AND SPIRITUAL PRACTICES. S-HE IS A "SERPENTINE" AND A CHANNEL OF ENERGIES WHICH INSPIRE HER/HIS TEACHINGS AND AMPLE VIEWS ABOUT LIFE IN ALIGNMENT WITH COSMIC LAW FOR THE BENEFIT OF THE COMMUNITY.

C-ER-N-UNNO-S IS ANOTHER ARCHETYPE OF "DEATH, LIFE AND REBIRTH." SINCE THIS ARCHETYPE IS LINKED TO NATURE, IT REPRESENTS THE NATURAL CYCLES OF — DEATH, DECOMPOSITION AND RECYCLING OF LIFE IN ORDER FOR THOSE SAME ENERGIES AND MATTER TO MANIFEST ENDLESSLY AS EVER MORE NEW LIFE AND REBIRTH.

C-ER-N-UNNO-S IS NOT MUCH DIFFERENT IN REALITY FROM THE TAOIST TRADITIONS IN THE SENSE THAT IT IS THE GAELIC "BODHISATTVA" AND ASCENDED TEACHER WHO HAS BEEN ABLE TO MANAGE WELL AND HARMONIZE HIS HER DIVINE INNER FIRE BECOMING A CHANNEL OF WISDOM. C-ER-N-UNNO" IS ABOUT INTEGRATION OR ONENESS AND IS AN ARCHETYPE OF "DEATH AND REBIRTH" LIKE Y-ESH-UA HIMSELF.

SINCERELY, "IL KORNUTO DE MENDES, CERN-UNNO"

---

## 152. "NAHA - ESH" —THE SERPENT OF FIRE —AS THE CATALYST FOR THE REDEMPTION OF MANKIND FROM A STATE OF UNCONSCIOUSNESS TO A STATE OF CONSCIOUSNESS (THE KEY TO HUMANITY'S ASCENSION)PART II

THE HEBREW WORD FOR "SERPENT" IS "NAHASH." THE WORD "NAHA-ASH" IS RELATED TO THE SANSKRIT WORD "NAGA" AND "ESH" OR FIRE IN HEBREW AND "ASH" IN ENGLISH. IN OTHER WORDS, THE TERM "NAHA-ASH" IS EQUIVALENT TO "NAGA-ESH" OR THE "NAGA OR SERPENT OF FIRE OR —THE ISH or BEING OF FIRE."

THE "NAHA-ESH" OR "NAGA OF FIRE" WAS COILED IN THE TREE OF GOOD AND EVIL'S TRUNK OR MIDDLE PILLAR. THE NAHA-ESH OR "NAGA OF FIRE" IS THE SAME AS THE "SERAPH OF FIRE." SERP-ENT SERAP-H. DO YOU SEE THE SIMILARITIES?

AND SO —

GOING BACK TO THE "TREE OF GOOD AND EVIL," THE TREE IS A "MIRROR" OF HUMANITY. IN OTHER WORDS, IN THE GENESIS STORY WHEN ADAM AND EVE "NOTICE" THE TREE OF DUALITY, THEY ARE SEEING THEMSELVES AS WELL JUST AS SOMEONE DOES WHEN LOOKING AT HIM-OR-HERSELF ON A MIRROR. AND BY NOTICING AT LAST THE TREE OF DUALITY BEFORE THEMSELVES, BOTH ADAM AND EVE ARE SEEING THEIR OWN NATURE BEING REFLECTED BACK TO THEM. IN OTHER WORDS, THEY ARE BOTH...

........AFTER THE "TREE OF DUALITY" WHICH IS THE "TEMPLATE OF ADAM KADMON" THE DIVINE ANDROGYNE.

THE "TREE OF GOOD AND EVIL"IS A —-BI-POLAR —BI-SEXUAL — PRINCIPLE AS DEPICTED BY THE "YIN-YANG" SYMBOL IN THE TAOIST TRADITION, THE ANIMATING ENERGY IN "ADAM" WHO IS "MATTER OR EARTH" IS "QI/ FIRE/ SPIRIT." THIS DIVINE FIRE ANIMATES AND UNITES THE TWIN CONCEPTS OF "GOOD AND EVIL" OR DUALITY. THAT "EVE" WAS TORN FROM THE SIDE OF ADAM, REFERS TO THE "FRAGMENTATION" OF THE WHOLE INTO TWO

EQUAL PARTS. ENERGY DIVIDED AS —MATTER AND MORE SUBTLE FORMS OF ENERGY!

AND SO WHY IS THE SERPENT PRINCIPLE THE KEY TO HUMANITY'S ASCENSION? THE FACT THAT IT IS LINKED TO AND A PART OF THE STORY OF THE "TREE OF GOOD AND EVIL AND OF KNOWLEDGE" POINTS TO ITS ROLE AS AN "ILLUMINATOR AND ENLIGHTENER" OF MANKIND. AND WHEN YOU "EAT" OF THE "TREE OF KNOWLEDGE" WHAT WILL HAPPEN?

"YOU EYES WILL OPEN AT LAST" WHICH — REFERS HERE TO HUMAN REGAINING "HIGHER CONSCIOUSNESS." AND "YOU WILL BE ABLE TO UNDERSTAND THIS REALITY OR MATRIX JUST AS ELOHIM IN GENESIS DO." AGAIN, IT'S ALL METAPHORICAL AND SYMBOLIC OF METAPHYSICAL TRUTHS. SO WE CAN SEE HERE THAT WITHOUT THE SERPENT "TEMPTING" ADAM AND EVE TO EAT OF THE "TREE OF KNOWLEDGE OF DUALITY" THEY WOULD REMAIN IN A STATE OF "UNCONSCIOUSNESS OR SEMI-CONSCIOUSNESS AND UNABLE TO REACH HIGHER STATES OF BEING WHICH IS HUMANITY'S DIVINE INHERITANCE THROUGH THE DIVINE FALL AND SACRIFICE OF ADAM KADMON.

SINCERELY, "ENNOKI aka THOTH REBORN"

---

## 153. TALITHA "COME TO ME!"

You know the story of TALITHA who got very sick to death in the Gospel and whom YESHUA healed from illness. As WE have told you before, languages are related as they share a common origin that later metamorphosed into different languages as the people began to disperse all over the place. Including the continuous migrations of humans who end up adding their particular lexicon to other languages. You have already seen how the Sanskrit and Latin and Hebrew and Arabic and Native American share many "root words."

The Bible story we are speaking of above in this case is the one about TALITA "CUMI:" As Mark 5:41 states:

"And He took the damsel by the hand and said unto her, "Talitha cumi," which is, being interpreted, "Damsel, I say unto thee, arise."

This verse is often translated as "Damsel, I say unto thee, arise." However, have you noticed here that the term TALITHA sounds very similar to English?. TALITHA sounds more like A TERM OF ENDEARMENT such as little TALI or DEAR TALI as in TALITHA such as is the case in many European languages today. But how about the rest of the sentence?

TALITHA… "CUMI!" doesn't it sound like the English word to COME!? As in DEAR TALITHA, COME or COME TO ME.

In the case of this verse, The doctor or healer YESHUA tells TALITHA to come to him to check out if she is alright and can walk and walk with right balance without falling after being diagnosed with fever and disease and after Jesus treated her.

Is it possible that the word COME and CUMI in aramaic are related or mean something similar as in the English language? They definitely sound very close and the meaning too. CU-MI as in COME TO MI (Latin) or ME.

What do you think?

SINCERELY,
"Y-ESH-WA, THE THERAPEUTAE 2026

---

## 154. THE WISE SERPENT OF THE TREE OF WISDOM AND KNOWLEDGE— THE SERPENT COILED AROUND THE TREE OF WISDOM AND UNDERSTANDING IS PART OF THE TREE OF LIFE (THE KEY TO HUMANITY'S ASCENSION PART III)

AND SO AS YOU WILL RECALL, THE STORY OF EDEN IS NOT —WE WANT TO REPEAT AND HIGHLIGHT— IS NOT — LITERAL!!! IT'S SYMBOLIC.

AND SO THE SERPENT HAPPENED TO BE THE WISEST OF ALL CREATURES. IT'S VERY IMPORTANT HERE TO NOTICE THAT THE TEXT STATES THAT THE CREATURE WAS THE—WISEST— IN THE GARDEN. WISEST EVEN THAN ADAM AND EVE WHO BEFORE THE FALL HAD NOT A CLEAR IDEA ABOUT REALITY. "REALITY" REFERRING HERE TO BOTH "YIN AND YANG" OR "GOOD AND EVIL."

IT DOES NOT SAY THE SERPENT WAS STUPID OR SOME OTHER PEJORATIVE TERM. IT WAS "WISE." WISDOM IS LINKED TO THE DIVINE MASCULINE AS CHOKMAH OR "THE ACTUAL SUNNY STATE OF ILLUMINATION" AND TO THE DIVINE FEMININE "FULL MOON STATE" AS "UNDERSTANDING" IN THE TREE OF LIFE. BOTH ARE FOUND IN THE DIVINE ANDROS OR THE SEFIRA OF DA-AT WHO IS A "BISEXUAL AND BIPOLAR UNION" OR STATE IN WHICH BOTH CONCEPTS REPRESENT RESPECTIVELY WISDOM AND UNDERSTANDING. BOTH CONCEPTS OF WISDOM AND UNDERSTANDING TOGETHER REPRESENT — THE STATE OF BEING CONSCIOUS OR AWAKE.

AND SO IF YOU NOTICE IN "THE TREE OF LIFE" THE ARCHETYPE OF Y-ESH-UA IS NAILED TO THE TREE OF DUALITY AND MATTER. "ESH" IS "FIRE" IN HEBREW AND SO THE SERPENT IN THE TREE OF LIFE IS COILED IN

THE MIDDLE PILLAR!!! AND SO THAT MIDDLE PILLAR IS THE SOURCE OF WISDOM WHICH IN THE HINDU TRADITION IS CALLED THE ...

K-UNNE-DE-AL- INNI!!!! (KUNDALINI) —

THE SERPENT OF FIRE COILED AROUND THE TREE OF DUALITY WHICH BECOMES THE TREE OF LIFE WHEN THE SERPENT FIRE ENERGY AWAKENS AND ASCENDS THE MIDDLE PILLAR.

THE MOTHER KUNDALINI OR "WISE SERPENTINE" HAS BEEN AWAKENED BY THE WILL AND GRACE OF THE HIGHER REALMS FOR A VERY LONG TIME, DECADES ALREADY THRU ADAMAS. SINCE THE GODDESS ENERGY MANIFESTS THRU THE MASCULINE AND IMPARTS DIVINE KNOWLEDGE AND GUIDANCE FOR BOTH THE HOST AND THE COMMUNITY. THIS IS CALLED —CHRIST CONSCIOUSNESS AND THE MANIFESTATION OF THE HOLY SHE-KI-INNI WHO IS ALSO LINKED TO THE DIVINE MOTHER BINAH IN THE TREE OF LIFE.

K-UNNE-D-AL- INNI IS LIBERATING BUT DANGEROUS AND CAN LITERALLY BURN A PERSON IF PLAYED AROUND WITHOUT REVERENCE, RESPECT, CONSIDERATION, LOVE AND UNDERSTANDING, AND PERSONAL RESPONSIBILITY. MISTREATING AND MISHANDLING THIS ENERGY WITH LIES AND PERSECUTION AND VIOLENCE, SINCE IT REPRESENTS THE LITERAL EMBODIMENT OF THE GODDESS ENERGY COMMUNING AND CONSORTING WITH THE DIVINE MASCULINE ENERGY REPRESENTING THE GOD ENERGY, CAN LEAD TO UNDESIRABLE AND KARMIC RESULTS AND CONSEQUENCES!!!

THEREFORE, THIS IS THE AGE OF KUNDA-L-INNI. IT IS NOT A COINCIDENCE THAT THE MOTHER OF THE PANDAVAS IN THE VEDAS IS NAMED "KUNTI." KUNTI REPRESENTS THE MOTHER GODDESS IN THE PAN-DAVAS FAMILY AND STORY AND SHE REPRESENTS ALSO THE KUNDALINI ENERGY AND FIRE THAT IS PART OF THE PANDAVAS FAMILY DIVINE HERITAGE AND BY WHOM ARJUNA CAN COMMUNE WITH SPIRIT DIRECTLY. THE PANDAVA'S IN THE VEDIC TRADITION ALSO REPRESENT THE HOUSE OF THE WISE AND UNDERSTANDING IN THE VEDAS.

THEREFORE, "HEED, CONSIDER, PROTECT" THE MOTHER GODDESS MANIFESTING AS KUNTI-AL-INNI :) AND SHOW SOME RESPECT.

SINCERELY, KUNTI OF THE PAN-D-AVA FAMILY 2026

**THE JOURNEY WILL CONTINUE IN BOOK 3....**

www.ingramcontent.com/pod-product-compliance
Lightning Source LLC
Chambersburg PA
CBHW031531150726
47990CB00001B/127